RESTORATION LONDON

Liza Picard

Weidenfeld & Nicolson
LONDON

First published in Great Britain in 1997 by
Weidenfeld & Nicolson

The Orion Publishing Group Ltd
Orion House
5 Upper Saint Martin's Lane
London WC2H 9EA

A catalogue record for this book
is available from the British Library.

ISBN 0 297 81900 3

Filmset by Selwood Systems, Midsomer Norton
Printed in Great Britain by
Butler & Tanner Ltd, Frome and London

CONTENTS

PART ONE: THE URBAN ENVIRONMENT

CONTENTS

ILLUSTRATIONS

FOREWORD

'Indeed many excellent authors there be who have wrote excellent well of some particular subjects herein treated of. But ... there is not one of them hath written upon all of them.'

Hannah Wolley, *Guide to the Female Sex* (1682)

I have a practical mind. I have always been interested in how people lived. The practical details are rarely covered in social history books. Perhaps I lack some secret ability that would enliven such books for me; as it is, I have nearly always found them disappointing. The only answer appeared to be to write a book myself.

I am not a historian. I am a lawyer. I have a liking for primary evidence – not what someone wrote long afterwards, or what someone has concluded from a selection of documents that I have not seen, but what someone said who was there at the time. This has led me down interesting detours, while I reinvented the wheel, and read as many contemporary documents as I could find. It perhaps wasted a lot of time; but it served as an enjoyable apprenticeship.

I had to set myself definite limits, in time and in place, if I were to avoid anodyne generalisations. Samuel Pepys provided my limits: the time (1660–70) and the place (London) covered by his *Diary*. (His *Diary* ends in May 1669; I have finished the decade without him.) I have allowed myself some latitude in time, where slightly later sources appear to relate equally to earlier times, or earlier sources record things which probably continued unchanged; and in place, where things of the right period have survived outside London. On some subjects, the *Diary* provides an incomparable record. I got to know it so well that I fell into the habit of referring to Mr and Mrs Pepys as

Samuel and Elizabeth. I trust the reader will not think this an undue familiarity. References to the *Diary* are to the edition edited by Robert Latham and William Matthews, published in eleven volumes by Bell and Hyman, 1970–83.

Hannah Wolley was a redoubtable woman who published a variety of 'conduct books' in the period; a seventeenth-century Mrs Beeton, dealing not merely with how to cook, but how to run a household. In our day, she would have run anything in sight, with charm and efficiency.

An unexpected mine of information was a man, Randle Holme, who set himself the task of describing everything used in heraldry. His three (part of another exists in manuscript) huge tomes, *The Academy of Armory*, were not published until 1688, but he had been writing them for years, certainly during the period I have chosen. His method was to list, in more or less alphabetical order, every relevant object, linking it to the relevant surname by the formula (taking an example at random): 'He beareth sable a Chamber pot or a bed pot argent – Chamberley or Potts.'

He gives detailed descriptions of men's and women's tailoring, as well as furniture and household equipment, and in case there should be any doubt in his reader's mind as to what each item looked like, there are pages of thumbnail-sized drawings, some of which unfortunately have suffered with time. I was able to read his books in the British Library and the Bodleian Library, except for volume IV, which the Royal Librarian in Windsor Castle kindly allowed me to see.

Nicholas Culpeper was another vivid person in whose writings I immersed myself. He was born in London in 1616, the son of a non-conformist clergyman. He went to Cambridge for a short time when he was eighteen, and was possibly apprenticed to an apothecary. At twenty-four he set himself up as an 'Astrologer and physician', in Spitalfields. He fought on the Parliamentarian side in the Civil War, and was wounded. Perhaps it was while he recovered that he translated the *Pharmacopaeia* used by all physicians, from Latin into English, thereby making it directly available to the average literate man and incurring the wrath of the medical establishment of the time. His style, exemplified in the many books he found time to write, is gentle and paternal. He was concerned to see that the poor, so often ignored in those days, could have some basic kind of medical care, even if it was only self-medication using the herbs that grew wild, instead of costly ingredients recommended by his colleagues. He sound like the kind of family doctor one would like to have.

It was hard to tear myself away from the beautiful flower books of the time, and books of garden advice.

John Evelyn is underrated. He cared passionately about London, and often wrote about it. His *Diary* tends to name-drop, but his description of the Fire, for example, is more evocative than Samuel's, which is more often quoted. In contrast to Evelyn's elegance is splendidly eccentric John Aubrey. Aubrey was born in 1626, the son of an impecunious Wiltshire squire. Like Culpeper his education was interrupted by the Civil War, but unlike Culpeper he never really worked thereafter. His debts overtook him, and an effort to solve his problem in the obvious way by marrying an heiress merely landed him in more trouble. He must have been a delightful man to have in the house, because he spent the rest of his life living with, and on, his friends, and following his antiquarian hobby. He died in 1697. His closest friend described him as 'shiftless ... roving and maggotty-headed', yet was devoted to him. That friend, another of my sources, was Anthony à Wood, as he liked to style himself, scribbling away peevishly in Oxford, where his quiet academic life was disrupted by the periodic incursions of the Court.

A fascinating contemporary source is the *Calendar of State Papers Domestic*. This is a rag-bag of papers about matters which nowadays would fit roughly into the spheres of the Home Office, the Department of Social Security and the Ministry of Defence, with some spice from current scandals. It stretches from a £3 reward offered for some strayed cows in Ashdown Forest, to the several millions voted for the Navy. Much of it, indeed, refers to the Navy: anguished letters from ships' captains to 'Sam. Pepys', asking for supplies of everything from men and masts to beer. The entries are not always clearly dated except by year. The reiteration of 'CSPD' in the notes indicates the many hours I spent reading the *Calendar* in the Bodleian Library, sometimes cross-eyed at the end of the day because the entries are not effectively indexed.

Then I settled down to the statutes passed between 1660 and 1670; and a great deal easier to read they were, than modern statutes. The draftsmen had not discovered the magic device of the schedule, nor had they yet become adept in the double negative qualified by exceptions to be read in conjunction with later inconsistent sections. Of course, the passing of a law has never meant that its provisions were observed from then on. If this happy state of affairs applied, the restrictions on urban development passed in the fourteenth century need never have been, as they were, reiterated by every successive administration. But the very frequency of statutes dealing with the same problem shows, at least, the urgency of the problem. And the 'preambles' or explanations, which tend to be scattered through each Act instead of in one lump at the beginning as now, provide a fascinating picture of the situation which the legislators were trying to cure. To a lawyer, preambles are not part of the Act, and can be ignored. To a historian, I suggest they are worth more than the substantive sections, since they are likely to be true.

Hansard had not yet begun, but volume IV of Cobbett's chatty *Parliamentary History* provided a splendid picture of the Members, once they had decided to recall Charles, frantically scurrying about like a disturbed antheap, each intent on showing how he had really been a Royalist at heart all the time. Luckily someone noticed in time that there was no crown to put on Charles's head, the last one having disappeared in the Troubles, and one was hastily ordered, with a sceptre to match.

Newspapers really got into their stride a little later, but I was able to read most of those in the British Library collection. The Bodleian Library has a rich collection of almanacs, which I found useful as evidence of contemporary thought.

The Register of Patents provided another happy hunting ground. The series began in 1617. None was registered after 1642, until just before Charles's return in May 1660. Thirty-two were registered in the decade 1660–70. The trouble is that not all inventions were patented, and of those that were, not all of them were viable, and there is no indication whether they had any commercial success. One feels that the Marquis of Worcester's invention of 'a watch or clock without string or chain or any kind of winding up [which] if [the owner] ... lay it aside several days or weeks ... it shall go very well and as justly as most watches that were ever made' would have swept the market, long before the Swiss got there; but no. Elizabeth's father Alexander Marchant took out several patents, none of which made him any money, judging by his son-in-law's reluctant handouts to him over the years. Perhaps there was some flaw in his thought processes, which became more evident later when he dedicated to the King a 'proposition' that he could 'draw up all submerged ships even from the deepest waters ... and has discovered King Solomon's mines ... now much fuller than they were in that king's time'. He would have felt at home with an optimist who, in 1687, undertook to teach 'persons to ... remain under water for the space of one, two or even three hours, without any covering over their heads or bodies, the water coming both round and next their naked skin, and so with their perfect senses to work ... in recovering ... merchandise lost under water', a frequent occurrence in those sailing-ship days.

In 1669 a 29-year-old Italian prince was sent off round Europe to 'eradicate from his heart an ill-fated passion'. He was Cosmo, or Cosimo, who became third Grand Duke of Tuscany. His love affair was unusual. He had had the misfortune to fall head over heels in love with his wife, who loathed him and preferred, so it was said in hushed tones, a *perruquier*. Cosmo travelled about Europe *incognito*, which possibly raised more problems than it solved because no one quite knew how seriously to ignore him. Obviously his father expected him to make good – that is, educational – use of his time. Equally obviously, if he were to do all the expected things, he would hardly have time to write about them as well. So one of his entourage took a very full note of all they saw and did, 'under the direction', so he said, of Cosmo. Count Lorenzo Magalotti was the obvious choice, having for ten years been secretary of the Academia del Cimento, an assembly of scientists including several disciples of Galileo.[1]

His account is wordy, and worthy, but it does supply an inimitable picture of London and the English as a well-educated foreigner saw us. He is not always reliable: for instance he thought English gardens dreary compared to the umbrageous terraces of Italy. He could also, from time to time, swallow what looks like a splendid invention for the benefit of tourists. He was shown the crown jewels 'which the kings use at their coronation', but what he saw had been newly made for Charles; and in the Banqueting House he saw the 'drops of blood which fell there' when Charles I was executed outside (perhaps it did splash about rather), 'that they have not been able to obliterate from the spot, though they have frequently washed it in the hope of doing so' (just like Rizzio's blood in the Palace of Holyroodhouse).

The many volumes of Magalotti's account of all Cosmo's travels reposed in an Italian library until 1821, when the English part (and a little about Ireland and the Scilly Islands, since the captain of Cosmo's ship was surprised to find himself in the Irish channel instead of the English one, and so Cosmo was able to see Ireland while the captain recovered his nerve) was translated into English. I refer to it in the notes as Magalotti. (For anyone who is interested, Cosmo reigned from 1670 to 1723, and his wife submitted to him enough to produce two sons before she left him for good. Neither son produced an heir, so to save the family from dying out, Cosmo got his brother Cardinal Francesco to unfrock himself and marry. Even this did not work, and the Medici line died out in 1735.)

There are not many domestic buildings surviving from the 1660s. Ham House in Richmond is a wonderful example of plutocratic living. Chastleton, on the border of Oxfordshire and Gloucestershire, is also now owned by the National Trust. Still under wraps as I write, it beautifully exemplifies a small country house almost untouched since the seventeenth century. There is a terrace of houses in Islington, built in 1658. They are not open to the public, but their graceful front elevations can be enjoyed. Both the Geffrye Museum, in Hackney, and the Victoria and Albert Museum are worth a visit. While you are in Hackney, go and see Sutton House, another seventeenth-century survival in the middle of twentieth-century development.

The difficulty with using original sources is that one never knows whether an event was reported because it was extraordinary and abnormal, or because it was just one more example of modern life. When does an exception become a trend? Equally, propagandists can be misleading, read centuries later. Evelyn wrote a whole book about the merits of eating salad. Was this because people did eat salad, and he wanted to tell them more, or because they did not eat salad, and he wanted to persuade them?

In the last 30 years there has been an immense advance in our knowledge of the early modern period. Where contemporary records are deficient or possibly misleading, I have gratefully relied on scholarly works on specific subjects, which I acknowledge individually in the notes. I hope that the notes are not irritating to the gentle reader, but sufficiently reassure the learned reader, if any.

At this stage, writers normally thank the many people who have helped them, while reserving to themselves the blame for any mistakes. The mistakes are indeed all my own work, but since I rarely venture into original thought I hope they are more a matter of emphasis than accuracy, and that you will at least find the book entertaining, if taken in small doses. I really have few people to thank, except Benjamin Buchan of Weidenfeld and Nicolson, whose friendship has sustained me through the process of paturition and whom I am glad to thank here; my neighbour Peter Stalker, who uncomplainingly accepted the role of my computer guru and many times rescued me from computerised despair; the unknown young man at the next desk in the Public Record Office who saw me struggling to read a horizontally written document in a vertically organised microfiche machine, and silently turned the gizmo round for me; and another kind young man, who has given unfailing moral support to his mother. Even more usefully, he produced a secondhand personal computer, and initiated me into the foothills of its miracles, without which etc.

Liza Picard
Gray's Inn
Hackney
Oxford

PROLOGUE

In the courtyard of the Royal Exchange, the mercantile centre of London, a crowd of men eddies and swirls, their black steeple hats bobbing as they talk.

Have you heard the latest about the King and Lady Castlemaine?
How much is corn fetching?
Has the coal fleet from Newcastle been sighted?
What are you paying for pepper?
Are you interested in a consignment of printed calico from India?
Have you seen Nell Gwynn, showing off her legs in that silly play?
Have you seen the King looking at her?
What do you give for a strong slave nowadays?
What are the trade prospects with Russia?
Have you seen the latest Plague figures?
Did the Consul at Smyrna manage to placate the Greeks?
When is the East Indies fleet expected?
Do you know a good tailor?

To one side stands the Russian Ambassador, with his befurred entourage. The Emperor's English physician had described this scene to him. Things are not done that way in Moscow.

The babble of voices decreases, as men leave for dinner; it is nearly noon. A dapper figure detaches himself from a coterie of naval friends and makes for home, nearby. Unfortunately, Samuel Pepys has forgotten that it is washing day, and the house is in chaos. There is nothing for dinner but cold meat.

PART ONE

THE URBAN
ENVIRONMENT

CHAPTER 1

LONDON

Facts and figures

England in 1660 was prosperous. Few people died of hunger, unlike the peasants on the continent. Waves of enclosures had swept away medieval hovels from English fields, and farming methods were slowly improving as Dutch technology spread. Wool was still the country's mainstay. In medieval times, it had been exported 'unwrought'; it now went through a series of labour-intensive processes, which resulted in lighter-weight, fashion-conscious fabrics ('the new draperies'). Textile finishing was largely concentrated in London. Newcastle sent coal down to London ('sea-coal') in fleets of collier ships, hundreds at a time. Lead was mined in Derbyshire, tin and copper in the West Country, iron in the Forest of Dean. They were all channelled to London.

The population of England was just over 5 million. In villages, solidly built houses clustered round the dual sources of refreshment, Church and Inn. A network of seven or eight hundred market towns provided for the business and social needs of their inhabitants, and of the country dwellers within a comfortable radius. Apart from London, only Norwich (30,000) and Bristol (20,000) exceeded 1,000 inhabitants.[1]

Over 300,000 people, getting on for one in seven of the population, lived in London. In the known world, only Paris and Constantinople were bigger, and they were flagging. London's steady increase had by 1700 outstripped Paris, and by 1750, Constantinople.[2]

'London' comprised: (1) the square mile within the Roman walls, and small areas to the west at Blackfriars, and to the south, across London Bridge, at Southwark. This was the City of London, administered in 26 wards by the Lord Mayor of London and the Common Council of Aldermen. Its population had declined by 20,000 between 1640 and 1660. (2) The 'suburbs'. The rich and fashionable were filling the space between the Roman city of Londinium and the Danish foundation at Westminster. The middle classes were moving west as well, and north towards Hackney. The poor, particularly the thousands dependent on the ship-building and carrying trades, migrated east along the river. The suburbs were booming.

The built-up area extended north to Clerkenwell, with ribbon development along the river and the approach roads. Before the Fire in 1666, the skyline was mainly flat, broken by the bulk of Westminster Abbey, the Banqueting Hall in Whitehall, and St Paul's Cathedral and the Tower in the City. The square medieval church towers did not punctuate the skyline gracefully, as Wren's spires were to do.[3]

The street layout had not changed since the Romans left. The traveller from Kent, or Europe, approached London by 'Kentish Street', through Southwark and across London Bridge. If he was heading north, a straight road led through the city and out by Bishopsgate, towards Hackney. The main east–west axis was Cheapside. From it, Fleet Street and the Strand led towards Westminster. To the east, through Aldgate, lay the open fields. Thames Street, along the river, was constantly blocked with commercial traffic to and from the wharves and warehouses and the Customs House.

There was still only one bridge across the Thames. In 1663 the Lord Mayor petitioned Charles ii for leave to set up two ferries 'on account of the straitness [narrowness] and trouble of passing London Bridge'. The Royal Surveyor of Works supported the petition, 'as being the only expedient to ease the Bridge ... from the multitude of carts drays and drifts of cattle, since His Majesty would not admit of another bridge'. His Majesty promised to think about it; if he did, nothing came of it.[4] In 1664 he was faced with a detailed plan for a bridge between Westminster and Lambeth, to be funded by a toll and a voluntary contribution from 'neighbouring gentry'[5] – with the same result.

London was the principal manufacturing city of England. The development of industrial conurbations in the Midlands was still centuries away. The London needle-makers' monopoly, for instance, covered London and 10 miles round; outside that radius, the trade was shared with Worcester. The manufacture of cutlery was shared

4

with Sheffield. But luxury trades were wholly concentrated in London; and far away the largest national source of income was the new trade of cloth finishing, almost wholly concentrated in London.[6]

Financiers were evolving more sophisticated banking systems; their base was London. Lawyers were well placed in the Inns of Court, including the Temple, which they had taken over when the Order of Knights Templars was dissolved in the fourteenth century; fast boats took them to their commercial clients in the City, or upriver to the law courts at Westminster. The spiritual life of London was supervised from Lambeth, Westminster and St Paul's. The monarchy was established at the Palace of Whitehall, built by Cardinal Wolsey close to the Abbey, and acquired by Henry VIII on Wolsey's downfall. Lastly, London was England's major port, with a safe harbour for sea-going vessels, facilities for building, repairing and supplying ships, and thousands of experienced seamen.

The combination of all these functions in one city goes far to explain London's disproportionate size, compared to other English cities, and to European capitals, where the monarch or the merchants or the shippers might reside in separate places.

It produced a polyglot, colourful crowd. Young people up from the country to serve an apprenticeship or enter domestic service gaped at English grandees in velvet-lined coaches, and fine ladies in sedan chairs escorted by liveried servants and African slave boys. Street sellers and mountebanks rubbed shoulders with sailors and beggars. Foreign languages and Latin vied with the country accents of young gentlemen up from the provinces.

In all this confusion, important announcements needed all the emphasis they could get. The Dutch Ambassador, Van Gogh, described the Proclamation announcing the declaration of war against his country, on 22 February 1664:

On Saturday last, the King's declaration was solemnly proclaimed. Two heralds in their coats of arms with four mace-bearers, nine trumpeters, and two troops of horses assembled at Westminster, where the trumpets sounded, and the declaration was read with great shouting and rejoicing of the people; thence they went to Temple Bar, where the Lord Mayor and Aldermen, in scarlet gowns on horseback, conducted them to Temple Gate where it was read with more acclamation than before, the Horse Guards drawing their swords and clattering them; then again in Cheapside and before the Royal Exchange.[7]

Similar pomp had attended the Proclamation of Charles's return, on 8 May 1660. But then, the new regime's cupboard being so exceedingly bare, the herald had had to borrow a 'rich coat of arms' from Henry VII's chapel in Westminster Abbey, 'to perform the solemnity, which was returned the next day'. His own had been plundered in the recent war.[8]

In 1658, while Oliver Cromwell was still on the throne, Richard Newcourt had published a map of London. Tactfully ignoring recent history, Newcourt invented a mythical history for London, beginning with Uranus and Saturn and ending with Brutus, 'anno mundi 2853' (2,853 years after the world was created). The London in his map was 'the most magnificent and renowned City of Europe, both for the antiquity of her foundation as also for Honour, Wealth and Beauty'. Mr Newcourt wanted to sell his product.[9]

Three years later, John Evelyn presented to Charles II a very different picture, in his *Fumifugium, or the Inconvenience of the Aer and Smoak of London Dissipated*. Evelyn had spent the Interregnum on the continent, where he admired the elegance of modern towns. He deplored that London, 'this glorious and antient city should wrap her stately head in clouds of smoke and sulphur ... that the buildings should be composed of such a congestion of mis-shapen and extravagant houses: that the streets should be so narrow and incommodious in the very centre and busiest places of intercourse'.

The streets

'Narrow and incommodious' the streets certainly were. 'The common Highways leading unto and from the Cities of London and Westminster and the suburbs thereof ... are at present and for some years past have been so miry and foul as is not only very noisome, dangerous and inconvenient to the Inhabitants thereof but to all the King's liege people.'[10] Some streets were paved. The market selling hay for London's thousands of horses and cows was. 'Piquadillo' was paved in 1662, and Holborn two years later. The owners of houses fronting on Pall Mall were obliged to contribute to the cost of paving it.[11] Drury Lane, Hatton Garden, Lord Southampton's development at Bloomsbury, and parts of Bishopsgate were paved. So was the road north from St James's Palace; although it led through the fields, it was used by some eminent people. Streets were not necessarily level, even if they were paved. In 1667 a master paviour petitioned for an Act of Parliament to ensure that the 'accustomed manner' of paving the streets with 'unshapely flint stones, which break like glass, or soft rag stone which quickly moulders, or too small pebbles, and all these laid not on sand or fine gravel but on rough gravel soon carried away by the raker [street-cleaner]' should cease, and 'good stones 10–12 ins square and set 12 ins deep in good sand' – no doubt provided or laid by him – should be used.[12] No such Act was passed.

Otherwise, the City streets were cobbled. The rare side-walks were reserved for pedestrians only by a line of posts. Sometimes the road surface sloped down to a central drain, blocked with rubbish and horse droppings. Sometimes there was no drain at all. When cobbles were clean, they provided a certain amount of drainage. When they were filthy and in poor repair – as all too often – they were lethal. Evelyn again: 'So many of the fair sex and their offspring [have] perished by mischance ... from the ruggedness of the uneven streets.'[13]

Whether paved or cobbled, the pedestrian had a slightly better chance of avoiding the filth thrown from windows, the rain cascading from the roofs, and the litter on the road surface if he could walk along beside the houses, under their projecting upper storeys. But others might have the same idea; 'jostling for the wall' could lead to argument, even to fights and death.[14]

Main streets were prone to traffic bottlenecks. Of all the modern causes of traffic jams, at least no London driver has had to face a drove of up to a thousand turkeys walking to their last home in London storehouses, from their birthplaces in Norfolk and Suffolk.[15] Thames Street, the service road for the wharves and warehouses along the river, was only 11 feet wide in places. There was a major 'conduit' (public water supply) in a building in the middle of Cornhill, and another in Cheapside beside the church of St Michael le Querne, where water vendors and private citizens would congregate to draw water, and inevitably stand and gossip. These buildings were not just shelters for standpipes; they were about the size of, and rather resembled, Victorian gate-lodges. They had originally been sited so as to be handy to as many people as possible, before wheeled traffic came to be the curse that it has remained; they were bound to cause obstructions.

In the Strand, opposite Somerset House near the hackney coach stand, there was a 'most prodigious'[16] maypole. It had been demolished under Cromwell, but was re-erected in April 1661 with great popular excitement, by twelve sailors under the personal command of the King's brother, the Duke of York, in his capacity of Lord High Admiral of England − sailors being the only men who could handle such a tall mast. As it rose, 'little children did much rejoice, and ancient people did clap their hands saying, golden days began to appear'.[17] It was the tallest maypole in London, but far from the only one. 'Maypoles which in the late hypocritical times 'twas forbidden to set up now were set up in every cross-way' (according to John Aubrey), even before Charles's state entry. May-day 1660 was celebrated with maypoles, for the first time since 1654. They gave great pleasure, but they hardly helped the traffic flow.

Side streets were punctuated by narrow alleys barely wide enough for two pedestrians to pass, leading to cramped courts and alleys presided over by an inn or 'tippling house', or to the mansion of some rich citizen; London was surprisingly mixed.

Streets were encumbered by sign boards,[18] hanging from almost every house, nine feet off the ground − in theory − to give room for a man on a horse to pass underneath. They did not always mean that a trade was carried on there, and if it was, they did not always identify it. Sometimes an elaborate code conveyed their meaning. The sign might use part of the arms of the appropriate livery company; so, Cupid and a torch meant a glazier, a cradle meant a basket-maker, an elephant showed where combs of ivory and other materials could be bought, Adam and Eve offered apples and other fruit, and a green man, or Jack-in-the-green, meant a distiller. Over apothecaries' shops hung unicorns' horns and dragons, their fabulous nature extending to some of the remedies sold there. Signs were not always so subtle. A row of coffins meant that a carpenter there could oblige; a bag of nails, an ironmonger. (The nineteenth-century scholarly reading of 'Bag o' Nails' as a corruption of Bacchanals was not, regrettably, correct. Nor did the Goat and Compasses ever mean that God encompasseth us; it was merely a combination of a leather-man's (cordwainer's) goat and a carpenter's compasses). Nursery-men and seedsmen adopted artichokes and pineapples; stationers, a hand holding a Bible, or a pen-knife − a necessary implement for cutting quills into pens. Some private houses had signs, without any particular significance. Residents would direct their friends to the nearest sign, and hope they arrived in time for dinner. An advertisement in the *London Gazette* of 28 May 1668 recommended 'Egbertus Wills, healer of deformed bodies – to be found at Mr White's house at the Cock and Bottle in Aldersgate street.'

After the Fire, this fondness for signboards continued. Signs were not prohibited until 1762. Even then it took another ten years for Londoners to adopt the simple, dull expedient of giving each house a street number.

When the Grand Duke of Tuscany came to London in 1667, his secretary Magalotti was impressed by the fact that 'streets are lighted till a certain hour in the morning by large lanterns', and when they had gone out 'you may find boys at every step, who run before you with lighted torches'. He must have been lucky. Householders had a duty to hang out a candle or a lantern from dusk until nine o'clock, during the winter, but from the frequency with which this duty had been repeated in regulations since the fourteenth century, one can only suppose that it was not generally observed. Mostly, the City streets were ill-lit or dark.

In the suburbs between London and Westminster, developers were beginning to lay out wide paved streets 'elevated in the middle with channels for water at the sides',[19] and elegant squares. Covent Garden Piazza had been built in 1631, on the site of Westminster Abbey's convent garden. Lincoln's Inn Fields were laid out between 1640 and 1660. The Earl of St Alban's (the contemporary spelling) was developing the area round St James's Square. In 1659 Abraham Arlidge, 'carpenter', had begun a comprehensive scheme in Hatton Garden, designed for merchants and others who wished to move out of the City, but not too far. The last of his 372 houses was completed in 1694.[20]

Water supply

A network of elm pipes was laid under the main streets.[21] They were tolerably water-tight, except at the joints, and where small boys had created fountains from judiciously bored holes. Regulations provided that, in time of fire, pumps should be carefully inserted at pre-determined points – the early fire hydrants. In the conflagration of 1666 this was forgotten and people tore up the streets and punctured the water pipes here, there and everywhere, reducing the pressure to nil.

In 1609 Hugh Middleton had completed the construction of his New River, bringing pure spring water 38 miles from rural Hertfordshire to a reservoir at Islington, and thence to 30,000 houses in the city. (The reservoir, called the Ducking Pond, attracted wild-fowl. It was a pleasant country resort for shooting ducks, and fishing – not for ducking witches or scolds.) For a quarterly subscription of between 5s and 6s 8d, a householder could be connected to the mains by a lead 'quill' or pipe. By the 1660s the supply to him ran only two or three days a week, so he needed a storage tank in his cellar. Stagnant water run through elm and lead pipes must have had a certain bouquet. No wonder it was not usually drunk, the more so considering the offences that were – again – prohibited in 1669: not only 'the opening of pipes from the said river without permission', but also 'the defiling of it by drains, watering cattle, keeping geese, casting carrion'.[22]

As long ago as 1581 a Dutchman, Peter Morritz, had installed a water wheel under the northernmost arch of London Bridge. (The Dutch excelled in dealing with water, even then.) The disadvantage of his wheel was that it worked when the tide was right, but not otherwise. A better idea was to pump the river water up to the top of a 15-foot tower, which gave enough pressure to serve the houses roundabout. But this too ran into trouble, when the Queen Mother objected that it spoilt the view from Somerset House. It was, she said, 'inconvenient'. The alarmed 'undertakers' petitioned the King to allow them to build elsewhere, or they would be 'ruined and clamoured against by hundreds of people who have laid pipes and taken leases for water'. They got their licence, on condition that the new 'waterwork' was not more than 15 feet high.[23]

By 1667 the New River company was competing with Sir Robert Viner and the other owners of the 'Thames Waterwork in Durham Yard'; Sir Robert's company protested at being 'excluded from St Clement Danes [north and west of Somerset House] and other parishes, where their pipes have been laid twenty years, nor from Covent Garden, which they were just preparing to serve, having spent £8,000 in preparation to supply the western parts of London, and for which the small proportion allotted to them in Bloomsbury will be no compensation', while the New River company wanted to 'continue their pipes where they now are ... and to lay, remove or amend pipes in counties Hertford and Middlesex, and in London and Westminster'.[24] One can begin to see why the cobbles were in such poor repair.

Luckily for the developers of Piccadilly and Pall Mall, useful springs were discovered nearby. Supplying water was a paying proposition. An annual rent paid to the Crown for the Piccadilly springs, of 6s 8d for 60 years, must have left a considerable profit, even after the expense of laying the pipes.[25]

Where piped water was not available, or too expensive, there was usually a well in the garden, often cosily juxtaposed to the cess-pit. Those who had no supply at all would fetch water from the nearest conduit, or buy it from itinerant 'water tankard bearers', who might for a small tip even carry it upstairs for them.

Pollution

Householders were forbidden to pave the floors of their stables and pigeon-houses. Animal and avian dung was a valuable source of saltpetre (nitre, the main ingredient of gunpowder) and a useful supplement to the supply imported from India by the East India Company. 'Saltpetre men' would periodically scrape off the top layer of dung-soaked earth. An Act of 1656 obliged them to give the householder reasonable notice before they came in. There must have been a fair degree of evasion; pigeon dung was much sought after by market gardeners, being particularly good for asparagus. The smell of a clean, paved stable may be acceptable. When the saltpetre men were late, and the weather was hot, it was a different kettle of fish.

The Victualling Office for the armed forces had a slaughterhouse on Tower Hill. How did its raw material arrive? Clattering down from the shires on its own feet (specially shod for the journey),[26] through Hackney by Mare Street, along Bishopsgate, turning left with shouts and moos at Leadenhall Street? Or up from Kent, straggling across the Bridge? Or did it come by boat, to be unloaded at Tower wharf and driven protesting up the hill? There were other, private slaughterhouses in alleys and yards all over London. There was one in Newgate Street, convenient for the market there. Magalotti saw 'vast hordes' of cattle in the fields outside London, waiting to be driven in, 'the English eating more meat than anything else, on this account there are slaughtered there, *every day*, besides other

11

animals, 3,000 oxen': even allowing for Italian ebullience with figures, a great many animals. Butchers kept their forward stock in their back yards, and slaughtered as needed: for instance in 1662 Eleanor Davies, of the Maypole, Strand, was licensed 'to kill and sell all manner of fresh meat except beef during the ensuing Lent',[27] after which, presumably, she slaughtered her stock, including beef cattle, as needed. In the reign of James I a Londoner had kept 200 pigs in his yard, and this was only a side-line; he was a starch maker by trade. The habit had not died out by Victorian times, although after the eighteenth century abattoirs needed licences.[28]

City and royal authorities had tried for centuries, with only partial success, to discourage 'noxious' trades from operating in their main market, London. When animals have been turned into meat, their skins become available to the tanners, their fat to the soap-boilers, and their bones to the glue-makers: all markedly smelly trades. The tanners treated raw hides with dog turds and urine. There were 80 tanneries south of the river.[29] The soap-makers made do with urine only. Another use for urine was in the processing of alum, essential to London's textile-finishing trade. (How was all this urine collected? Under some Roman emperors, convenient receptacles could be found at every street corner. I can find no comparable system in 1660s London; but it was a saleable commodity, called 'old lant', then and for a hundred years and more. The Victorian housewife relied on Scrubb's Ammonia, put up in bottles.)

As early as 1634 a hopeful inventor had patented a heating process for dyers, soap-boilers and other trades that heated liquids in vats, to prevent 'the great annoyance of smoke' from them. A slightly later patent added 'foulness' to the smoke. Evelyn's list of pollutors included brewers, bakers, salt-makers, sugar-boilers, chandlers (candle-makers), hat-makers and 'some sort of fish-mongers', as well as slaughterhouses, soap-boilers and glue-makers. There were kilns of some kind in Scotland Yard, beside the royal palace of Whitehall. It is just possible that they were part of the royal Office of Works, which was in Scotland Yard. Mr Newcourt discreetly omitted them from his map, but they can be seen as large as, or larger than, life in an earlier map of 1582, belching out the smoke that Evelyn complained of in 1661, when 'a presumptuous smoke issuing from one or two tunnels [kilns?] ... not far from Scotland Yard did so invade the Court that all the rooms, galleries and places about it were filled and infested with it, and that to such a degree, as men could hardly discern one another for the cloud'.

Even when 'noisome trades' obeyed the rules and stayed away from London, air-borne pollution was blown into the city from the lime kilns at Limehouse or across the river at Bankside. By 1680 the dyers long established at Southwark, who relied on drying their finished cloth in the open air, were moving away down-river to the clean air of Crayford.[30]

Evelyn focused his main attack on industrial polluters. But a huge proportion of the smog afflicting London came from ordinary domestic fires. Sea-coal was more acrid and sulphurous than coal produced by modern methods; 'oleaginous', according to Magalotti.[31] London is only recently free of foul-smelling, lung-wretching, filthy smogs, when asthmatics sealed their windows and stayed indoors, and still died. As Evelyn put it, 'Almost one half of them [who have] perished in London die of phthisical and pulmonary distempers. The inhabitants are never free from coughs and importunate rheumatisms, spitting of impostumated and corrupt matter.'

Before the Fire, there were more than 100 parish churches within the walls. It was the custom to bury notable parishioners in the church itself. Evelyn deplored 'that superstitious custom of burying in churches or having their dormitories in the very heart of cities, where frequently churches are built, I neither think it decent nor sufferable'.[32] The vaults became more and more overcrowded. When the Plague struck, the churchyards became full of rotting flesh. Coffins were not always used. On 30 January 1666, Samuel Pepys was frightened 'to see so many graves lie so high upon the churchyard' in his local church, St Olave's, 'where so many have been buried of the plague'. In all, 194 parishioners had died, of whom 146 had been buried in the churchyard and the rest in The New Churchyard near Bishopsgate, established in 1569 for the burial of the poor. How space was found for 146 corpses in St Olave's tiny churchyard defeats the imagination. Certainly bodies and coffins were piled on top of each other.[33] The next day Samuel noted that 'many about the city that live near churchyards are solicitous to have them covered with lime'; he hoped St Olave's would be done. The City magistrates did indeed order that all churchyards used for plague deaths should be covered with lime, but the Earl of Craven, one of the very few City dignitaries who stayed in London throughout the Plague, reported that 'the churchyards have not been so generally covered with lime, in respect of the dearness and scarcity thereof but much fresh earth and lime has been laid in many churchyards'.[34] The stench in churchyards was still 'offensive and unwholesome' in

November 1666.[35] Many hundreds of corpses were summarily tipped into pits, hastily dug in any available open space, and as summarily covered; they cannot have smelt any sweeter.

Public executions were usually followed by the gruesome process of eviscerating and dividing the corpse. The four quarters were nailed up here and there through the City, especially over the city gates, and stayed there rotting until the birds picked the bones clean.

There were few public lavatories. Richard Whittington, that admirable man whose charities have been so overshadowed by his fictitious cat, built a 128-seater, equally divided between men and women. He died in 1423, and his 'longhouse' was not maintained. In 1660 the usual practice was to nip into an inn, or a friend's house. But there was always a convenient corner or accepted 'pissing place'. Anthony Wood bitterly, and understandably, resented the casual excretory habits of the courtiers, when Charles II moved to Oxford: 'Though they were neat and gay in their apparel, yet they were very nasty and beastly, leaving at their departure their excrements in every corner, in chimneys, studies, coal-houses, cellars.'

Waste disposal

Household waste comprised food, paper, sweepings, ashes and excrement. Some food scraps could be disposed of by sale; one of the cries of London was 'Any kitchen stuff have you, maids?' The rest could be put out for the birds. Paper could be used to kindle innumerable fires. The flimsy paper on which the mass-circulation ballads and chap-books were printed could easily find another use. Sweepings could probably be swept finally out into the street, against the rules.

But (leaving excrement on one side for the moment, as people did all too often) there remained a heap of rubbish that the householder had to dispose of, somehow. In 1654 John Lanyon had tendered for a central contract to replace the parochial system, which was not working. His 'Proposals' deserve citing, for the picture they give – although biased, and six years before our period – of London's streets:

> It is too apparent that notwithstanding many persons and considerable
> sums of money are employed for cleansing the streets yet they grow

daily more offensive with dust and unwholesome stenches in summer and in wet weather with dirt, which occasions a swarm of Coaches [because people refused to walk], to the disturbance of the City and the increase of noisome soil that ... being washed into the common sewers [drains] and passages and thence into the Thames, the sewers are much obstructed ... and the River itself, especially above Bridge, made daily less navigable. Besides the Avenues [main roads] to the city are almost all day pestered with those Carts which only carry away some small part of the soil [dirt] out of the streets and are made exceeding noisome and almost impassable with dirt carelessly spilt by the way to the common Laystalls [tips], which being so many and so near the City yield a great and contagious stench, offensive to passengers [passers-by] but especially to the [out]skirts of the town, which else would be the most delightful places, and what wind so ever blows brings those noisome vapours into the city itself ... The rakers being insufficiently paid employ their carts from time to time on more profitable jobs and are not under any general superintendence.[36]

John Lanyon's proposals were not accepted. An Act of 1662 tightened up the parochial organisation. 'Whereas great quantities of sea-coal ashes, dust, dirt and other filth ... are daily thrown into the streets lanes and alleys of the Cities of London and Westminster', citizens were to sweep their frontages daily, and on Wednesdays and Saturdays[37] put their rubbish out in 'baskets tubs or other vessels ready for the Raker or Scavenger'. The rakers and scavengers were allowed to 'lodge their Ashes dust dirt or other filth in such vacant public places in or near the streets or highways as shall be thought convenient ... for the accommodation of country-carts returning empty', which does not seem a very efficient system.

Excrement was collected by the night-soil men. Regular, tidy emptying of private cess-pits was the ideal, but in 1660 Samuel was not pleased to find that his neighbour's cess-pit was full 'and comes into my cellar'. Five nights later − a considerable interval, in the circumstances − the night-soil men arrived, and slopped their way through Samuel's house. Three years later Samuel got his own back, when the night-soil men emptied his cess-pit through that same neighbour's house. Two other neighbours, senior to Samuel in rank, agreed between themselves to have their cess-pits emptied through Samuel's office. Many houses did not have cess-pits, some even have no privies. Chamber pots were emptied from upper windows, without so much as a 'Gardez l'eau'. By the 1662 Act, the scavengers and rakers 'shall every day except Sundays bring carts, dung-pots or other fitting carriages where such carriages can pass and shall at their approach make distinct and loud noise by a bell horn clapper or otherwise and make the like noise in every . . . alley . . . into which the said carts cannot pass and abide there a convenient time'. In hot weather, one doubts if such audible notice was needed.

Noise

Street noise was excruciating. Two drays (the heavy goods vehicles of the time) could pass, just, in a street 14 feet wide. Any narrower – and Thames Street was 11 feet wide in parts – and it came to a shouting match, there being no Highway Code. Iron-shod wheels crashed and screeched over the uneven cobbles. Animals protested as they were driven to market, or the slaughterhouse. Samuel was woken one night by a 'damned noise between a sow gelder and a cow and a dog' in the street below;[38] and when the sow-gelder had duly advertised his trade by blowing on his horn, and got down to work, a further discord arose.

Horses neighed and stamped. The drivers of wagons and hackney carriages, notoriously foul-mouthed, expressed their views of other drivers. Overhead signs creaked and squeaked. Street vendors yelled their advertising slogans and apprentices bellowed from their masters' open-fronted shops. From the windows came the sound of music, and otherwise, as enthusiastic amateurs strummed and sang. Dogs barked at the traffic, cats howled in the alleys, singing birds added their trills, flocks of pigeons cooed on the roofs. Leather-soled shoes clattered on the cobbles, joined on a rainy day by iron pattens. The 'distinct and loud noise' of the dung-carts was heard daily. No wonder that those who could afford to, lived away from the streets, and those who could not, lived upstairs. What an unspeakable relief when the traffic died down and the shops shut and only the watchman was left, calling out the time and a weather report.

CHAPTER 2

THE HOUSES

Newcourt's map-view

Richard Newcourt's 1658 map is a 'map-view' or picture-map: a formalised bird's-eye view, assuming a high-flying bird making north, and surveying the scene below, from Westminster to Limehouse. In an elegant flourish, Newcourt assures the purchaser that his map is drawn to scale. The built-up area is filled with a conventional design of zig-zag roofs, the west side of each roof catching the sun and the other side in black shade. A few notable buildings are distinguished, a few streets are named, and a numbered index gives 130 churches 'by which the eye may be guided to the eminent streets on which they stand'. Major green spaces are shown, such as Lincoln's Inn Fields and the gardens of the mansions along the Strand and in the new developments near St James's Palace, and the Drapers' Company's garden in the City. The general effect, however, is of a uniform mass of tightly packed houses.

But London never has been uniform. Since masons' labour was expensive, successive builders made use of their predecessors' work where possible, reusing old foundations and incorporating walls and arches and even single stones into new buildings. So, delete Newcourt's houses and fill in his street layout with a higgledy-piggledy mixture of large and small, rich and poor, old and new, industrial and domestic, brick and stone and timber. Add thousands of smoking chimneys – there are none in the map-view – and scatter green spaces here and there. Now, if the bird could see anything at all through the smog, it would have a more accurate view.

Tresswell's surveys

Between 1585 and 1614 a surveyor named Ralph Tresswell was employed by several large London landowners to produce accurate, measured plans of their properties. These plans,[1] which have survived, show who lived where, in how many rooms, how big the rooms were, even whether they had fireplaces or privies. Widow Kinrich lived in a little house in Billiter Street, of just two rooms, one above the other, each about 14 feet square. She had a garret, but no yard, or garden, or back door, or privy. Widow Smith a few doors up the street had a cellar, as well as a privy. Both houses backed on to a rambling property with two vast gardens, occupied by Sir Edward Darcy.

The editor of Tresswell's surveys grouped the properties into four categories:

one-room plan houses
two-room plan houses
medium-sized houses with up to six rooms on each floor
larger houses.

There is no reason to suppose that London houses changed markedly in the next 70 years. Some of them became empty and derelict, as people deserted the City for the suburbs. The predecessors of the unimpressive buildings along the Strand in front of Somerset House, which were already there when Inigo Jones designed his Palladian entrance early in the century, were probably the 24 houses that had formed part of the Queen Mother's dowry in 1625, but had somehow got into such disrepair that special measures had to be taken to get them repaired before they fell down.[2] Another change was that most of the Tudor long galleries had been subdivided by the mid-seventeenth century. But in general, Tresswell's plans typified many houses in the City, before the Fire of 1666.

The one-room plan houses included authorised houses like Widow Kinrich's. They could also be the kind of accretion that grows up everywhere, like weeds. A temporary stall acquired a roof, then the walls were strengthened and another storey appeared – and another and another. John Stow, writing in 1598,[3] described the process. What began as greengrocers' stalls turned into houses three, four or even five storeys high, still on the sites of the original stalls. A fishmonger's stall transformed itself into a 'tall house'. The south side of old St Paul's was 'defaced' and hidden by the houses that had sprouted from the stalls selling knick-knacks to tourists.

Two-room plan houses in City side streets were mostly the trading premises of small craftsmen. The shop/workroom gave on to the street to catch passing trade, while the stockroom ('warehouse') lay behind it. The family lived above. In 1664 a two-room plan house in New Street, Fetter Lane, not far from the City boundary, containing 'a cellar, now made a kitchen, a shop, two chambers, and a garret' was let for £14 a year, with a £10 premium.[4]

Houses outside the constricted City could be more spacious. There is a terrace of four two-room plan houses still surviving in Islington, which was a country district when they were built in 1658. They have three storeys, garrets and cellars. Access to the middle two houses is by a narrow arched brick passage, straight out of Vermeer. The two rooms on each floor are about 15 by 18 feet.

Pictures of London events such as funerals and processions before the Fire show streets lined with timber-framed houses, apparently two-room plan – certainly with single gables, facing the street. This can be misleading, since a group of two or three single-gabled houses, each with its own flourish of individuality, might be internally linked to form one substantial dwelling. That was one advantage of timber-frame construction. As long as the frame was not disturbed, internal partitions could easily be constructed, moved or demolished. Such views are also misleading because they show only the street frontage. Many houses, like Sir Edward Darcy's, were hidden from sight.

The 'misshapen' appearance that John Evelyn deplored was exacerbated by the practice of (unlawfully) encroaching on the airspace of the street by throwing forward (French *jeter*; hence 'jetties' or 'jutties') each successive storey, by as much as 18 inches. If two jettied four-storey houses faced each other across a street 11 feet wide, a pedestrian would not see much sky when he looked up. Someone in the top storey would have a splendid view of the room over the way, but not much else.[5]

As to 'medium-sized' and larger houses, Tresswell's surveys show how a considerable mansion and its grounds might be screened from pollution and noise by a fringe of small houses, such as Widow Kinrich's. City Aldermen who were obliged to live within the City, rich merchants who did not want to be too far from their trading premises, and magnates with no family seat outside London could enjoy the pleasures of gardens and even an orchard or two, and a spacious mansion looking over them, secluded from traffic and passers-by. These mansions might be brick or stone or timber framed, romanesque or Renaissance; magnificent or crumbling; centuries old or spanking new.

Many were converted monastic buildings. London had been well provided with religious foundations. Holy Trinity Priory was founded in 1108, just within the City walls at Aldgate. Its church was huge, its cloisters extensive, its rent-roll plutocratic. But by 1532 it was debt-ridden, and its Prior was glad to surrender all the buildings to Henry VIII.[6] Henry sold them to a property developer called Thomas Audley, who unroofed the chancel and the nave of the church and built two imposing houses, one for himself and one for sale. Audley's house (later known as Duke's Place, after Audley's son-in-law, the Duke of Norfolk) survived until at least 1676. Smaller houses were contrived out of the chapels round the choir: one-room plan houses, with secular jettied rooms sprouting incongruously over monastic arched windows.

Audley died in his great house, in 1544, before the main wave of monastic property redevelopment began. In 1547 Henry VIII decided that the wealth of monastic foundations could more usefully fund such necessary expenditure as wars, palaces and international conferences. Hence the Dissolution of the Monasteries: not, as one might be forgiven for thinking, melting them away like sugar-lumps in a cup of tea, but putting them into compulsory winding-up, leaving their buildings intact and available.

So the White Friars left their house on the river beside the Temple, and the Black Friars theirs, just outside the City walls. The Carthusians of the Charterhouse and the nuns out at Clerkenwell, the monks of St Bartholomew's Priory and the Grey Friars at Newgate, the Augustinian ('Austin') Friars by All Hallows and the cross-bearing ('Crutched') Friars south of Aldgate, and St Helen's nuns near Bishopsgate – away they all went, some to the secular life and some to sister houses, some with pensions and some destitute, leaving their buildings silent and empty. But not for long.

Whitefriars yielded 'many fair houses', according to John Stow. The newly formed Society of Apothecaries took over part of Blackfriars. Charterhouse was transformed into a magnificent mansion in which Lord North entertained Henry's daughter, Queen Elizabeth. The nunnery at Clerkenwell had been transformed into rows of desirable residences by 1658. The site of St Bartholomew's had been laid out as streets of two-room plan houses by 1581, except for the part always occupied by the annual Fair; one end of the church (which still survives); and part rededicated as a hospital. The Grey Friars' buildings were used as an orphanage. Sir William Powlett built himself a 'great house' in the Austin Friars' buildings. He divided their church in two, the west end going to the Protestant refugees from Holland, 'to be their preaching place', and the altar end meeting the ignominious fate of 'household uses as for storage of corn, coal and other things'. Later 'the monuments of noblemen there buried in great number [and] the paving stone ... which cost many thousands' were sold for £100 and the sad wreck was used for stabling horses. The buildings of the Crutched Friars were made over into a carpenter's yard, a tennis court and a glass factory. The nuns' church at Bishopsgate became the parish church.[7]

Many Londoners must have lived in stone houses with arched windows and graceful pillars, and perhaps even the occasional angel.

It was not only religious buildings that survived from the distant past. In 1466 Sir John Crosby, a grocer and wool merchant, had built himself a house in Bishopsgate. He incorporated in it parts of the house already on site, which had belonged to an Italian merchant. According to Stow, Sir John's house was of 'stone and timber, very large and beautiful'. Large it certainly was. The 'hall' (principal room) was over 60 feet long, the 'parlour' almost as big. The house survived intact for more than four centuries. Samuel must often have passed it. (In 1907 the hall was moved to Chelsea Embankment, lock, stock and barrel. It is still there.)

Here is the story of another plot, in Seething Lane. In 1303 a goldsmith, Roger de Frowick, lived there,[8] conveniently near the Mint, which was in the Tower. Perhaps his architect was inspired by the stone ornaments of the Abbey up-river at Westminster, in the French gothic style. Or he may have preferred the gentle brick of Lambeth Palace, parts of which date from 1297. By 1461 the site belonged to a wool merchant, John Warre, a contemporary – perhaps a friend – of Sir John Crosby. Did the new owner decide to demolish de Frowick's outmoded building and start from scratch? And if so, did he follow Sir John into stone, or the Archbishop of Canterbury into brick?

Another 100 years went by, and the site was bought by Sir John Alleyn, a rich silk merchant, who had twice served as Lord Mayor of London. About this time, a magnificent house was going up, just round the corner in Crutched Friars. Its jettied frame glittered with double-height windows, separated by friezes embellished with armorial shields and grotesques. The door-cases were elaborated with herms and scrolls and strap-work. There was not a square inch without some decoration.[9]

Sir John was a 'man of great wisdom and charity'. Perhaps he deplored such conspicuous consumption, and built in a less flamboyant style. Or did he decide to outdo the Crutched Friars mansion?

In 1553, eight years after Sir John's death, the Muscovy Company was founded.[10] Its object was to find a sea passage to China by sailing round the north of Russia. It was the first English 'joint stock' company. Its other claim to fame is that Sebastian Cabot was its Governor. Its full title was 'the Mystery and Company of the Merchant Adventurers for the Discovery of Regions Islands and Places Unknown', but it settled down to the mundane trade of importing flax, wax, tallow, fish and whale ('train') oil and furs from Russia. When it outgrew its original quarters, and trade seemed to justify the purchase, the company bought Sir John Alleyn's old house, in 1564. Did the shareholders emulate their European competitors, and the East India Company,[11] and adorn their new headquarters with whales and tritons and ships and mermaids, and whatever else they thought appropriate to advertise their trade? Perhaps they overextended their resources. Sixteen years later they sold the building to Queen Elizabeth's counsellor and spy-master Sir Francis Walsingham. He died there in 1590.[12]

In 1603, the year of James I's accession, the Earl of Northumberland bought the place for £2,000, no doubt anticipating a property boom when James and his courtiers and hangers-on eventually reached London. But the Earl was unlucky. He sold it three years later for only £1,800, with a public house thrown in. The purchasers, John Wolstenhulme and Nicholas Salter, split the property between them. Wolstenhulme took the northern part. When he put it on the market in 1654, the Navy Office snapped it up for £1,400. They were understandably keen to move from the premises on Tower Hill that they had been sharing with the Victualling Board, 'by reason of ... being annoyed by the slaughter house of the Victuallers'.[13] Wolstenhulme's part of the original house, alone, was big enough to provide substantial lodgings for the senior officers of the Navy Board and their clerk, as well as office accommodation and a garden. And here, on a fine July day in 1660, Samuel Pepys and his wife moved in, 'mightily pleased with our new house'.

There is no means of knowing what that building looked like. Although it escaped the Great Fire of 1666, it was burnt down in

1673. All that we can safely deduce is that the original dwelling-house, before partition, must have been very substantial, with its own gardens.

Similar stories could be told of many buildings within the City, as successive owners built, and rebuilt, and adapted, and modified and divided their houses, and prospered, and declined.

One group of buildings deserves a paragraph of its own: the houses on the Bridge. The first sight that greeted the traveller from Europe was an arch crowned with stakes on which were impaled, until they rotted and fell off, the heads of traitors. John Aubrey has a story of how Sir Thomas More's head fell into the lap of his favourite daughter, who took it away and buried it. After that welcome, the traveller pushed his way through arches under the tall houses built over the Bridge, the ground storeys of which were used as shops. Getting through the traffic could take so long that it could be quicker to dismount before it and take a boat.[14] The exteriors of the houses were astonishingly elaborate; a cross between Queen Elizabeth's Palace of Nonsuch out at Greenwich, and an early twentieth-century mansion block. Residents with windows over the river enjoyed, as a modern estate agent would say, freedom from drainage problems – on a windless day.

As to building materials, Sir John Crosby had gone against the trend, in using stone rather than brick. In 1425 the Drapers' Company used brick for its new hall. Lambeth Palace's gatehouse (1490) was of brick. In 1518 the Benchers of Lincoln's Inn chose brick for their gatehouse on Chancery Lane, and the buildings behind it. Henry VII built his palace at St James of diapered brick. His son, with all that religious stone at his disposal, chose brick for his new palace at Bridewell, where the Fleet river joined the Thames.

Anything built in the City after 1605 should, in theory, have been built of brick or stone, not timber. James I, Britain's first king, determined to emulate Rome's first emperor, Augustus, who 'found the City of Rome of brick and left it of marble'. James wanted to go down in history as one who 'found our City and suburbs of London of sticks [timber] and left them of brick'.[15] Timber buildings were still allowed in side streets, where they would not show, and, by special dispensation, in the marshy areas of the eastern suburbs, where the piles necessary to support a brick building would have been prohibitively expensive.

There was a brief vogue for stepped brick pediments such as the merchants of Antwerp and Amsterdam favoured. The East India

Company's headquarters had an elaborate stepped façade topped by an armed man and flanked with whales. The vogue faded when James I appointed Inigo Jones[16] as Surveyor-General of the King's Works, in 1614.

Jones had come back from Italy fired by Palladio's neo-classical ideas. His first royal commissions, both in stone, were the Queen's House in Greenwich, for James's queen, and the Banqueting House in Whitehall.[17] The Crown was well placed for the best stone, since it was Lord of the Manor of Portland. For non-royal clients, Jones used brick. His Italianate piazza in Covent Garden was an innovatory experiment in persuading Englishmen to live cheek by jowl, behind elegant, uniform façades, instead of in fiercely idiosyncratic and 'misshapen' houses. The pilasters and frieze of the 1658 terrace in Islington derive, remotely, from Jones's Palladian designs. No doubt many other London houses made similar gestures in his direction.

He was the most famous architect to borrow classical ideas, but not by any means the first. Many Elizabethans had preferred the flat roofs of a classical design, to steeply pitched gables, for the opportunity they gave of surveying their gardens and the distant hills of Hampstead, and enjoying the comparatively quiet, clean air. There are many references in the *Diary* to musical parties on the roof. One may infer that part, at least, of Sir John Wolstenhulme's house was flat roofed.

But the most influential building of all was designed not by Jones but by a comparatively unknown follower, Roger Pratt. Evelyn called it 'the best contrived, the most useful, gracefull, and magnificent house in England'. Samuel found it 'the most elegant place for prospect that ever was in the world, it even ravishing me'.[18] Magalotti admired it. It was built for the Earl of Clarendon, Charles II's Chancellor, on an 8-acre site looking across Piccadilly to St James's Palace and backing on to open country. It was the elegant epitome of all that we think of, mistakenly, as 'Wren' – an elaborate gateway on Piccadilly, leading to a wide courtyard as in any proper country house, with two wings, a central block with a pediment and a cupola, and a balustrade linking the skyline. It was copied all over England; yet it lasted only sixteen years.

The unfortunate Clarendon and his house had become identified, in the popular mind, with the sale of England's last continental possession, Dunkirk. As if that were not enough, he was blamed for Charles's marriage to a barren queen; and, in the way small irritants have of being more intolerable than major grievances, he was said to have used the stone earmarked for rebuilding St Paul's, for his own house.[19] Mobs broke down the trees in front of the house, and daubed graffiti on the walls. An anonymous letter was sent to the King: 'All think [the Chancellor] treacherous in counsel, blame him for the selling Dunkirk and the present war, mortally hate him, and wish to see his Dunkirk house level with the ground.'[20]

In December 1667 Parliament passed an Act banishing and 'disenabling' the Earl of Clarendon. He had little choice but to leave his beautiful house, and retire to France. His house reverted to the Crown,[21] and Charles sold it to the Duke of Albemarle in 1675, who demolished it in 1683, to make room for redevelopment.[22]

Near Clarendon House was a square of ten or twelve houses, each costing 'not less than £1,000', developed by Sir John Denham and Sir William Poulteney.[23] The Earl of St Alban's was building '13 or 14 good houses' – extraordinary that they never seemed to be sure how many – 'in St James's Fields, fit for the dwelling of persons of quality, and needed for the beauty of the town and convenience of the Court. The King had ordered such houses to be erected there ...'.[24] Two other great houses on Piccadilly survived Clarendon House, built by Lord Berkeley and Lord Burlington. The elegant West End of London was taking shape.

The Fire

The summer of 1666 had been dry. On a sweltering Saturday, Thomas Fariner worked all day in his bakery in Pudding Lane, near London Bridge. Perhaps he slaked his thirst unwisely, perhaps he was just tired. When he shut down the ovens and went to bed, he missed one red ember. In the small hours of Sunday, 2 September, he was awoken by the smell of smoke. A fresh easterly wind had sprung up, and fanned the ember into flame...

The fire burned fiercely for four days and nights. By Thursday it had burnt itself out. The wind had changed, and was blowing the flames back to the ashes.[25] The valiant efforts of the fire-fighters, including the King and his brother, and sailors brought in at the last moment to demolish houses and make fire-breaks, had all been pointless.

Wenceslaus Hollar, Charles's 'Scenographer, or designer of prospects', produced two views of London: 'A true and exact prospect of the famous city of London, from St Mary Overy's steeple in Southwark, in its flourishing condition before the Fire' and 'Another prospect of the sayd citty taken from the same place, as it appeareth now after the sad calamitie and destruction by fire'.[26] Looked at quickly, they seem to be little different. In the second, St Paul's still rears its bulk in the west, church towers and spires still stand. A closer look shows that St Paul's is roofless; the lead had melted, run down into the crypt, and destroyed the stock of paper and books stored there for safety. The stone walls of the huge building still stand, kept up only by force of habit, the mortar having been destroyed in the heat as the internal beams burned. What at first sight looks like a careless rendering of the original plate, on the south side of St Paul's, is a chaos of rubble, where houses had once stood. Churches formerly half-hidden behind houses are shown down to ground level; but they no longer have their full complement of turrets and towers. The medieval Guildhall stood 'for several hours together, after the fire had taken it, without flames ... in a bright shining coal as if it had been a palace of gold or a great building of burnished brass'.[27] Now it was a charred wreck.

Almost the whole of the City, 436 acres, 'lay buried in its own ruins'.[28] A small area survived to the north-east, including the Navy Office, but to the west the flames had leaped the walls and burned a corresponding area, like a hideous shadow. Some 13,200 houses had gone, including shops and inns and tippling houses. So had all the public buildings from which the City was administered. The General Post Office had gone, and the gaol at Newgate, and nearly all the food markets.

'In three days the most flourishing city in the world is a ruinous heap, the streets only to be known by the maimed remainder of the churches.'[29] A Kensington resident, writing to a friend in the country on 8 September, described how 'my gardens were covered with the ashes of papers, linens, plaster-work etc. blown hither by the tempest'.[30] Sixty miles away in Oxford, Antony Wood wrote in his diary: 'the wind being eastward blew clouds of smoke over Oxon the next day ... the sunshine was much darkened ... the moon was darkened by clouds of smoke and looked reddish'.

London had always been subject to the risk of fire, but it had never suffered such a cataclysm. Many people attributed it to divine wrath at the goings-on of Charles and his frivolous Court. Others blamed foreigners, who had to lie low until xenophobia, never far from an English crowd, was appeased by the death of an unfortunate, blameless Frenchman. Charles himself, taking no personal responsibility, attributed it to 'the hand of God'.[31] The real causes were the dry summer, the wind, the narrow streets and wooden houses, and the ill chances that many merchants and prosperous men who might have taken quick action were away in their country houses, enjoying a weekend respite from city heat, and that, near the fire's source, the warehouses on the river were full of oils and flammable goods. When they exploded into flames, the fire was unstoppable.

The aftermath

Temporary rehousing was fast and efficient. The Exchequer moved to Nonsuch out at Greenwich, commandeering 'as many lighters and carriages as needful'. Other government departments found themselves temporary offices. The Heralds' Office was burned, but they managed to save all their records, a notable achievement that enabled them to fight off a takeover bid for the pedigree market by the Company of Painter-Stainers.[32] The shopkeepers in the Royal Exchange moved to Gresham College, and reopened their doors for trade in December.[33] Private individuals with enough clout were rehoused promptly; Alderman Backwell's 'business being of great importance', he too moved into Gresham College, evicting someone further down the ladder. Sir Robert Viner, having managed to get his stock of money and jewels stored in Windsor Castle,[34] moved his affairs to Broad Street, with other Lombard Street merchants, 'having by the good providence of God been entirely preserved by a timely and safe removal of all his concerns, almost 24 hours before the furious fire entered Lombard Street'.[35] God seems to have played an ambiguous role.

Lesser 'burnt Londoners' – 200,000 of them – had escaped to the open fields of Islington and Highgate. It took them only four days to find themselves permanent shelter. Others camped out on Moorfields, and in every open space they could find, with their pathetic bundles beside them. Some went to other cities, where the Christian welcome they received was no doubt tempered by a royal Proclamation exempting them from the closed-shop rules of the local guilds. Some emigrated to the colonies in America and the Caribbean; even St Helena had an influx.[36] Some sheltered with friends or family in the suburbs, and found conditions there so much more to their liking than the old, constricted ways of the City that they were glad to settle there, despite the steep rise in rents. Houses that had been available for £40 per annum rose to £150 overnight.

Others picked their way back over the smoking rubble and defiantly set up shacks of fallen bricks and charred wood, in the ruins of their houses. They were not alone in that desolate landscape. 'Foot-pads' (muggers) found the ruins a useful no-go area. 'There are many people found murdered and carried into the vaults among the ruins...'.[37]

The difficulties and dangers of clearing the ruined buildings, with the aid, only, of manpower and horsepower, must have been prodigious. The site of St Paul's had to be completely cleared, somehow. The west end still stood, with its massive Corinthian pillars, and 'the principal walls ... together with the remains of the roof of the larger nave and of the pilasters which support it ... [Otherwise] one sees only a huge heap of stones cemented together by the lead with which the church was covered',[38] which made the task of demolition no easier. In August 1668 the King issued directions to the Lord Mayor:

> [Since a] great part of St Paul's church has to be re-edified and other parts taken down, so that there will be an extraordinary quantity of stony rubbish ... we wish you to order the said rubbish to be carried to the low parts of Fleet Street [which would have to bear unusual loads of rebuilding materials until the wharves on the river were reopened] and other places, till raised to the designed level, and no other to be used whilst there is sufficient from St Paul's. This will not only ease the vast charge of repairing the said Church, but provide for raising the said places with sure and lasting material.[39]

Somewhere under Fleet Street is the rubble from old St Paul's. The timbers of the Guildhall had to be dismantled carefully, since some of them could be used again. The present Guildhall contains wood salvaged in 1666, and again in 1940. London Bridge was blocked by fallen debris. Only the houses at the north end caught fire. Residents in the others had a grandstand view. Workmen were set to clear the bridge, by the light of torches. They got 4s each.

The fire had stopped just short of the main market building at Leadenhall. Other temporary food markets were opened, by Proclamations of 5 and 6 September. Bread and other food were distributed. (This relief effort misfired; the bread was navy biscuit. 'The people being unaccustomed to that kind of bread, declined it, and so it was returned in great part to His Majesty's stores again, without any use made of it', since the markets 'were already so well supplied'.)[40]

The Court was besieged by petitioners: for instance, 'Sarah, widow of Francis Crafts ... for grant of aid towards rebuilding houses worth £5,000 burnt ... whereby she and her children are reduced from a plentiful condition to turn servants'. But Parliament declined to vote any public money, and Charles had none of his own to give; indeed he 'declared to his City of London upon the occasion of the late calamity by the lamentable fire that no man's loss was comparable to his'. On 10 October there was a nation-wide voluntary collection in parish churches. Devon contributed £1,480 6s. Merioneth managed £1 16s.

An information office was set up in Bloomsbury[41] so that mail for previous city-dwellers could be forwarded to their new addresses in the suburbs, to 'remedy the interruption of trade through the Fire'. An optimistic proclamation ordered 'all persons who have taken plate, goods, building materials etc. from the ruins of the houses demolished by the late Fire either wilfully ignorantly or of purpose, [in order] to return the same to the owners, to bring them to the armoury in Finsbury Fields, there to be kept and inventoried for restoration to the rightful owners'.[42] History does not, so far as I can tell, relate its success.

The rebuilding

In an ideal world, London would at last have received the thorough replanning that John Evelyn and others had long advocated. Evelyn produced an elegant City plan, within days. (He was rash; a less well-known citizen, one Valentine Knight, published 'rebuilding propositions ... with considerable advantages to his Majesty's revenue ... as if His Majesty would draw a benefit to himself from so public a calamity to his people'.[43] For this disgusting behaviour, he was arrested.)

But the real world demanded that, because there was no viable substitute for the complex of functions fulfilled by the City of London, it must resume normal operation as soon as humanly possible. The kind of redevelopment the idealists wanted would have necessitated a clean sweep of all the complicated land titles that had accrued over centuries, which would have been unacceptable. So everyone who claimed any interest in burned premises had to submit not only 'a perfect survey' of his plot, but also details of his legal title – not so easy, if all the documents had burned with the house.[44]

The pragmatic solution that was adopted worked remarkably well. A week after the flames had died down, Charles issued a Proclamation promising 'a much more beautiful city than that consumed ... but the inconvenience of hasty and unskilful buildings must be avoided, and lest any should obstinately erect such buildings, on pretence [on the pretext] that the ground is their own, the Lord Mayor and others are authorised to pull down the same'.

By the end of November, the huge task of demolition was nearly over. The winter rains quenched most of the sullen embers, and helped to lay the black, pervasive dust, although Samuel noted that the ruins were still smoking as late as February 1667.

In that month, and with uncharacteristic speed, Parliament passed two Acts. One set up Fire Courts, to determine disputes between landlords seeking to enforce their tenants' obligations to rebuild, and tenants who were ruined. (No such thing as fire insurance existed; it came into being as a result of the Fire – too late for many – in an 'Insurance Office at the Backside of the Royal Exchange', under the aegis of Dr Nicholas Barbon, the son of Praise-God Barebones, who had given his son the baptismal name of If-Jesus-Had-Not-Died-For-Thee-Thou-Hadst-Been-Damned.) Normal litigation on such promising matters could have kept lawyers in comfort for generations, while London's rebuilding waited. Despite such expedition there was a backlog of business after a year. The court decided to sit at 8 a.m. and 'order the speedy hearing of the cases in arear'.[45] In general, its judgments were so clear and fair that many potential litigants, seeing the trend, settled out of court anyway.

The other Act was the Rebuilding Act, which dealt, as efficiently, with the physical effects of the Fire. At a single stroke it abolished a client's right to niggle with his architect interminably, about dimensions and construction methods. It imposed a set of clear, inflexible Building Rules to be incorporated in every building contract. It specified the height of each storey and the height of each kind of house. No house, even 'mansion houses of the greatest bigness' for 'citizens and other persons of extraordinary quality' could exceed the uniform height regulations, no matter how secluded the mansion. For the rest, there were three sorts of houses: the 'least sort' fronting 'by-lanes', which could have two storeys only, with cellar and garret;

the second sort fronting 'streets and lanes of note', which could have three storeys, cellar and garret; and the third sort, fronting 'high and principal streets', which could have four storeys. Down-pipes and gutters were obligatory, and 'no jetties, windows or anything of the like sort shall be made to extend beyond the ancient [former] foundation line'. Once again, but this time with more chance of conformity, 'all the outsides of buildings [are to] be henceforth of brick or stone'.

The price of building materials was controlled, and building labour was encouraged to come to London by the relaxation of closed-shop rules, and high guaranteed wages. Written tenders were invited, from 'all persons who are willing to serve and furnish this City with timber, brick, lime, stone, glass, tiles, slates and other materials for building'.[46] A new building won a seven-year tax (hearth money) holiday.[47] If a plot remained empty for three years, it could be compulsorily acquired and sold.

The only respect in which the Rebuilding Act fell short of Charles's promise in October was in segregating industrial areas. His promise that those 'whose trades are carried on by smoke are to live together in some quarter to be assigned to them' was watered down to excluding 'trades and occupations judged noisome or perilous in respect of fire' from 'high and principal streets'. (Can one infer some degree of pressure from the City?)

By March, the Common Council had decided which streets fell into which category. There were only six 'high and principal streets', and 214 'streets of note'; the rest were 'by-lanes'.[48]

By April 1667 the street lines – slightly amended from the old lines, but not enough to cause serious grievance – had been staked out, and those who had the funds to rebuild could apply for a licence, which was granted on site. There must have been some curious scenes, as official surveyors hurried over the rubble, jumping cellars and dodging carts and trying to keep track of suspiciously mobile stakes. Only one new street, King Street, was laid out, connecting the Guildhall and Cheapside. The rest of the streets still followed the medieval layout.

For the first time there was a brisk market in City properties. Commercially minded property owners banking on a property boom collected portfolios of titles, and invested in large-scale development. In March 1669 Samuel noted that a Mr Jaggard, who had made his pile out of salt, was building 'many brave houses' near Billingsgate. That April, Alderman Backwell showed Samuel 'the model of his houses that he is going to build in Cornhill and Lumbard [*sic*] Street; but he hath purchased so much there, that it looks like a little town, and must have cost him a great deal of money'.

As well as large-scale redevelopments, there must have been thousands of individual deals to help family members, in those days of limited investment opportunities and extended families. Samuel lent a cousin £350 on 4 January 1668, 'to enable him to give to build his house again'. £300 would have paid for a house in a side street, £400 a house in a principal street, so it looks as if the cousin was aiming at a three-storey house on a 'street or lane of note', with £50 over for restocking or refurnishing.

Building materials

Bricks for the rebuilding lay ready to hand.[49] 'The Earth about London, rightly managed, will yield as good Brick as were the Roman bricks ... and will endure, in our Air, beyond any stone our Island affords' – thus Christopher Wren, the leading Commissioner appointed to oversee the rebuilding. Suburban residents were encouraged to 'digg and cast up the ... ground for the making of brick'. There was an unavoidable delay before locally made bricks were ready. Meanwhile, brickmakers in Kent and the Thames valley surveyed their yards, rubbed their hands, and loaded barges for London. The brick clay 'dugg and cast up' immediately after the Fire weathered over the winter, to be moulded into bricks from April onwards. Given good drying weather, the earliest that London-made bricks could be ready was May 1667. From that summer they began to pour into the City, by dray and cart and packmule, from St Giles in the Fields and Moorfields, and as far away as Islington and Hackney.

Native timber for building had long been in short supply. The expanding Navy had an option on any worthwhile trees. (For decades, applicants for patents had stressed how their inventions would save fuel and so benefit the Navy. It took between 500 and 700 trees to build a ship.) There was a surge in the import of softwood from Norway, Russia and Scotland; so urgent was the demand that the stringent protective measures of the Navigation Acts, which required imports to be carried in British-owned ships, were relaxed.

By the end of 1667, 150 new houses stood scattered on the desolate site. Each house had to provide 'toothing' for the next to be built. For a while the new streets must have looked like an orthodontist's nightmare. The pace of rebuilding soon quickened. By the end of 1671 nearly 7,000 houses had been completed. Then the impetus slackened. In all, about 8,000 new houses were built to replace the motley collection of 13,200 destroyed.

By 1669 two essential landing stages (confusingly called 'stairs' or even 'bridges') at Billingsgate and Puddle Dock were open for business. The Royal Exchange, essential to mercantile London, functioned for a while in Gresham College; by the time Magalotti saw it, in June 1669, the merchants could again 'assemble every day to transact business' on the ground floor, and 'over this, four spacious galleries in which are many shops, surpassing those of the New Exchange' in the Strand.[50]

Three new markets were begun in 1670. The new Guildhall was finished in time for the Lord Mayor's banquet in November 1671. The Customs House was completed in the same year, on a site recommended by a commission set up under an Act of Elizabeth, whereby 'no goods are permitted to be landed in any port in England or Wales except on quays or wharfs appointed by the Queen's Commissioners ... [The Commission was] rendered needful by the mutation of quays, cranes, wharfs etc. since the late fire of London.'[51]

London's prisoners had to wait for rehousing − where? and had anyone remembered to let them out, as the Fire roared nearer? − until 1672, when four new gaols were able to accommodate criminals and debtors, the latter sadly increased by those whom the Fire had ruined. Two more landing stages were completed, and a start was made on the projected New Quay along the river bank. The Fleet river was, briefly, made navigable. Of the 52 livery companies' halls which had been destroyed, 22 were built by 1673. But at last, energy flagged. The New Quay never attained its planned glory, and the old dirty habits of Londoners soon blocked the current of the Fleet.

The City had worshipped in 109 churches. This was generally agreed to be excessive, considering the drop in population. Many of the 87 burned churches were never rebuilt. Of those that were, it was sometimes possible to reuse parts of their walls or foundations, but many had to be totally demolished. From 1670 onwards, Christopher Wren's spires gave the City skyline a graceful charm it had never possessed before. The foundation stone of St Paul's

Cathedral was laid on 25 June 1675. It was not completed until 1711, by when Charles II was dead, his brother had come and gone, and their cousin William III had died. But to build such a masterpiece, with the existing technology, in 36 years, was an awe-inspiring achievement.

The Monument to celebrate the rebuilding was itself completed in 1677. It was understandably grandiloquent, but not altogether accurate. The inscription blaming the Fire on 'the treachery and malice of the popish faction' disappeared during the reign of (Catholic) James II. The details of the Fire inscribed on the Monument − for instance, the number (13,200) of houses destroyed − have always been accepted as at least a realistic estimate. But it is surely impossible to believe the assertion that, although 'to the estates and fortunes of the citizens [the Fire] was merciless ... to their lives [it was] very favourable'. Three thousand people died in the earlier 'Great Fire' of 1212, when London was less densely built. From contemporary accounts of the terror and confusion in the narrow streets, the inference is inescapable that many died in 1666. They do, whenever crowds panic in confined spaces. The Bills of Mortality, which were supposed to show the cause of every death in the City, were, exceptionally, not published for the critical week. Perhaps the rich were able to escape in time, as they had escaped the Plague, and the poor were incinerated, uncounted and unmissed; their calcined bones, mingled with ashes and burned bricks, helped to level the site for rebuilding.

Another cavil could be levelled at the Monument by the ungenerous. 'The work was carried on with diligence, and London is restored ... at three years' end, the world saw that finished, which was supposed to be the business of an age.' Diligence was undoubted, but three years was a blatant understatement. Seven years would have been nearer the truth, and still have compelled astounded admiration. Even in 1673, and despite the terms of the Rebuilding Acts, 1,000 building plots were still empty. More seriously, the property boom had not happened. Nearly 3,555 new houses were still unoccupied − getting on for half of all those rebuilt. Many people preferred the suburbs.

The really intransigent caviller has two further points to make. Was the reborn London a mellow red-brick colour, or a nasty yellow? And, whatever colour it was, was it really so transformed?

London stock bricks, which were largely used in the rebuilding, are a mixture of yellow and khaki, weathering to an overall dinge.

The Victorians used them too, and they still flash past train windows approaching London termini. Perhaps red was used for the parts that showed, yellow for the parts that did not. It is hard to tell, since representations of post-Fire London tend to be monochrome prints. There is the occasional red vista. Canaletto included some in his paintings of London a few years later. The front elevation of the terrace in Islington, built pre-Fire, is in red brick, so are Gray's Inn Square (1680) and Bedford Row (1680). There are no coherent survivals in the City from which to imagine its overall colour after the Fire.

And the second cavil? In 1676 the first proper map of London hit the market: 'A Large [it certainly was: 8 feet long, 5 feet high] and Accurate Map of the City of London Ichnographically Describing all the Streets, Lanes, Alleys, Courts, Yards, Churches, Halls and Houses etc. Actually surveyed and delineated, by John Ogilby Esq., his Majesty's Cosmographer'.[52] For the first time, we can notionally perambulate the streets, marvelling at the promised accuracy. We can compare, with admiring curiosity, a newly built area with its unregenerate neighbour – and we find it just as congested as ever. There is no difference between the density of the pre-Fire buildings at the north end of Mark Lane, for instance, and those at the south end, which were burned and rebuilt. And enough of the old unregenerate London survived to appal foreign visitors. A French visitor, 30 years later, described the old wooden houses as 'the scurviest Things in the world as appears very plainly from whole streets still remaining, nothing but Wood and Plaister and nasty little windows, with but one Casement to open, the Stories were low and widened one over another, all awry and in appearance ready to fall'.[53]

Enough cavilling. There must have been a hundred pessimistic traditionalists wringing their hands and lamenting, for every Christopher Wren imbued with positive energy. In less than ten years the financiers, planners, architects, merchants, timber-importers, brick-makers, builders, stone-masons, plumbers, carpenters and brickies created a new city.

And apart from the churches and St Paul's Cathedral, which we enjoy looking at, but rarely use, it has practically all disappeared.

CHAPTER 3

INTERIORS

The rooms

Elizabeth took dancing lessons in a room with a bed; which so disquieted Samuel that he had to go and check that the bed-covers were still unruffled, after each lesson. He was pathologically jealous of the dancing master. Why could she not have danced in 'our dancing room', or the dining room, or the parlour, or the 'upper best chamber – a rare room for music'?[1] Perhaps Samuel was not so unreasonable. A 'chamber' was a bedroom if there was a bed in it. It would have a 'closet' leading off it, where clothes could be hung, and another where the 'close-stool' was kept. (Later, when water was laid on to upper floors, a flushing lavatory changed this closet into a water-closet or WC; initials thankfully recognised all over the globe.)

The division of rooms by function was still fairly new. Samuel refers to so many rooms by their function or colour-scheme that it is almost irresistible to try to plan them out; but it is a hopeless task, aggravated by his sometimes using different names for the same room. In his official lodgings, he seems to have had (in the order in which they appear in the *Diary*):

a study for himself
a parlour
a 'little room' taken over from his neighbour
a room they called the nursery, in 1661 (but they remained childless)
a 'little green chamber where the maids lie'
Elizabeth's bed chamber
a dining room

'our matted chamber'
a new dining room in the roof extension
Elizabeth's closet
a study for Samuel's secretary
Samuel's room
'the red chamber'
'the green chamber'
a new closet for Elizabeth in the roof extension
the upper best chamber, or music room
'our dancing room'
Samuel's new closet
his 'old closet, now my little dining room'
'the great chamber'
a 'long chamber where the girl lies'
'the blue chamber'
a dressing room
a room for Elizabeth's woman

as well as a kitchen and the normal collection of pantries, larders, store cupboards and cellars. However you look at it, this seems a fair allowance of rooms for one middle-class, childless couple. But I suspect that many of the rooms were not very big.

Each spouse had a 'closet' (sometimes also, confusingly, called a 'cabinet'). This was *de rigueur* in a fashionable household. Its essence was that it was small, so that it could house whatever treasures its owner most prized, to be shown off to an audience of, at most, two at a time. The Duchess of Lauderdale, who certainly was not short of cash, organised for herself a delightful doll's-house-sized closet in Ham House in Richmond, which would be overcrowded if more than two ladies joined her for a cup of chocolate.

It was by now usual to have a room set aside for a dining room. There was no particular reason for it to be near the kitchen. Indeed, one did not wish to have cooking smells in the upper part of the house, and water, more necessary to the cook than to the owner, was laid on only as far as the ground floor, where the kitchen was.

Next to the dining room, it was handy to have a room to go to while the table was cleared. This was sometimes done at an earlier stage than we would do. The company would adjourn during the process of 'dessert' (from the French *desservir*, to clear the table), and settle down to a 'banquet' (pronounced 'banket' and approximating to our 'dessert') of light refreshments such as fruit, nuts and sweetmeats,[2] in less formal surroundings, perhaps in the 'withdrawing room' next door, or in a separate 'banqueting house'.

Grand houses had several banqueting houses in the gardens and on the roof. The Duchess of Marlborough still observed this convention by installing them on the roof of Blenheim Palace, where they look like tables with their legs in the air. There was one in the Walks of Gray's Inn. They are often misnamed summer-houses, which conveys their size, if not their function. They were not the grand edifices that 'banqueting house' conveys to us, except in royal circles, where they had replaced the medieval Great Hall.

James I had gone in for grandeur in his Banqueting House. It had been given priority, as part of a new palace which was to replace Wolsey's rambling Whitehall, but the rest of the palace was never built. The function of that Banqueting House was not to shelter a few nut-eaters, but to impress fellow-monarchs and ambassadors. Inigo Jones's design replaced a temporary building of canvas and wood, which had been in use for years, and can hardly have been impressive by then. (How relieved ambassadors must have been.) Charles I walked through one of its first-floor windows on to a platform where the headsman's axe awaited him. Eleven years later, his son, 'glutted [exhausted] with the ceremonies of the day'[3] of his triumphant return must have taken profound satisfaction in making the Commons wait for him there, and swear allegiance to him.[4] It is pleasant to relate that on the Queen's birthday, 16 November 1664, there were 'divertisements' (*sic*) in the Banqueting House, during which 'a chariot ran several times round the room, forced [pulled] only by one or two men',[5] which sounds very like High Jinks in the Mess.

A word on kitchens. Staple foods and cleaning materials needed more space in the shape of cupboards and storage rooms than nowadays, with deep-freezers and conveniently packaged detergents. Sand, for instance, in constant use for cleaning, came in barrels or sacks. Close-stool pans and chamber pots were usually stored downstairs during the day, near the kitchen, having been emptied in the cess-pit; surely, even in the seventeenth century, they had a shelf, or even a room, to themselves? Perhaps they shared it with the candlesticks, which needed cleaning before dusk fell.

In the kitchen itself, those horrid fly-papers that predated aerosols had not yet been invented. Flies were deterred, to some extent, by the much more charming means of 'flower-pots' (not empty containers, but pots of aromatic or fragrant flowers and plants), standing on each window-sill. The colour blue was thought to be unpopular with flies, so cupboards and shelves might be lined with blue paper, and confectioners used it to wrap purchases. (Readers with long memories may recall packets of sugar in heavy blue paper, in pre-war grocers' shops.) With its white walls and brightly burning fire reflected in polished pewter, brass and copper, and with nosegays at every window, the kitchen must have been the most cheerful room in the house.

Samuel referred to his 'great chamber'. How big was 'great'? There must have been some very big rooms in the original building before it was subdivided, but Samuel, the most junior tenant, was unlikely to have been allotted any of them. It may be justifiable to look at a description of a house fairly near, in Aldersgate, built in 1452 and rebuilt sometime before 1558.[6] It had a 'great hall' 28 by 17 feet – not all that big by our standards, and modest by those of Sir John Crosby (see page 21) – and a 'fair large chamber' over it, slightly smaller. There was a 'large chamber' 24 by 16 feet, 'also a little study adjoining to the said chamber'. The business premises on the ground floor comprised a 'fair large chamber' 23 by 16 feet, 'also one counting house and one house of office [lavatory] to the same belonging'. Perhaps Samuel's 'great chamber' was, say, 24 by 16 feet.

The Aldersgate house had a 'long gallery', 69 by 8 feet. These galleries, which had been such a feature of Tudor houses, had mostly been subdivided by the mid-seventeenth century.[7] They had provided exercise space, in bad weather, as well as a display area for family treasures, particularly portraits. Tresswell's plans show how such galleries had been peculiarly suited to London's long narrow plots, stretching down one side of the plot, and often providing a covered area underneath, in the yard or garden. As to exercise, perhaps the climate had improved. Display now tended to be concentrated in cabinets or closets. So refurbished houses were left with an awkward space, to be chopped into small rooms rarely wider than 8 feet, or 10 feet at most. A double bed would go in, just, with its head against the partition across the former gallery. Perhaps Samuel acquired some of these truncated rooms.

He does not seem to have had any garrets. If there had been any, the maids would have slept up there, but a house such as the Navy Office, with extensive space on the 'leads' – the flat, lead-covered roof which could be used for musical parties or closed in, as it was later, making new rooms – would not have the triangular, timbered roof-space available for servants that gabled houses had, and that the terrace of houses in Islington still has.

There was, of course, no room reserved as a bathroom. At Ham House there was a room devoted to ablutions, but it may have been a 'sweat' or steam-bath, rather than our kind of bathroom. There were latrines over the cess-pit, for the servants, and 'houses of office' anywhere they could be conveniently sited, from the cellar to the leads. One of Samuel's neighbours sited his there, which spoiled Samuel's music parties on the roof because the neighbour would leave the door open; these conveniences were not, remember, flushed.

A demonstration of the flexible use of rooms was given by the unfortunate Lady Sandwich one day in 1664, when she was taken short and called on her friends, the Pepys. Samuel's diary entry reads like a nightmare. He was minding his own business – that is, gossiping – at the Royal Exchange nearby, when

> news comes that my Lady Sandwich was come to see us; so I went out, and running up (her friend however before me) I perceive by my dear lady's blushing that in my dining room she was doing something upon the pott; which I also was ashamed of and so fell to some discourse, but without much pleasure, through very pity to my Lady.

Poor Lady Sandwich. Why had the servants not ushered her into a bed chamber with a comfortable close-stool – or even a 'pott' – which she could have used in private? Why the dining room? And how does one conduct a conversation with a young man, even a remotely connected family friend, in such circumstances?

Drawing a veil over Lady Sandwich's predicament, let us contemplate the ceiling. Pre-Fire ceilings must have varied as much as pre-Fire houses. We know the maximum permitted ceiling height in houses in the City, rebuilt after the Fire; and these heights must in fact have been observed, to comply with the mandatory external roof levels. Rooms in two-storey houses could be 9 feet high, the 'second sort of building' could have rooms 10 feet high on the ground and first floor, 9 feet on the second, and the 'third sort of building', on 'high or principal streets', had spacious rooms 10 feet 6 inch high on its *piano nobile*. The 'mansion houses of the greatest bigness' could have rooms as high as the owner pleased, 'as long as he exceed not four storeys'. (Did a roof-top banqueting house count as a 'storey'?)

Interior decorating

Interior decorators ('upholsterers') must have been delighted to see Charles back from the continent, where the French Court was bubbling with elaborate – and expensive – decorating ideas.

The first necessity in any house was to hide, or at least disguise, naked plaster. 'Hanging a room is to fix about it either cloth, damask, gilt leather, arras or tapestry, or any other thing that will cover or hide bare walls.'[8] The only room where walls were left bare, and limewashed annually, was the kitchen. As well as maximising natural light, limewash had a slightly antiseptic effect, and discouraged insects.

The cheapest way to 'cover or hide bare walls' was paint. Bold curlicues and flowers glowed on dark backgrounds. Biblical scenes uplifted the soul, coats of arms boosted the self-respect, allegorical figures taxed the memory.[9] The effect could be rich, while the bill for materials was low. Naturally occurring earths were the mainstay, in warm colours of umber and ochre. It has to be said that a fashionable upholsterer would be horrified by a commission to use such an outmoded technique, but many splendid painted walls survived in quiet corners.

Next in order of cost were similar designs on painted cloth. This, too, was beginning to fall out of fashion, but no doubt survived in old-fashioned houses. As late as 1684 one Mary Marshal patented her late husband's invention for 'makeing stayning and colouring of stuff to such a degree that it hath been and is taken for tapestry hangings'.

Wallpaper shops arrived in London in 1660. The paper came in thick sheets, stuck or nailed to the wall, or to a canvas foundation on battens. It took another 70 years for someone to work out how to join the sheets together into a roll. The designs were printed monochrome motifs, or hand-coloured elaborate scenes. Flock printing had, regrettably, been invented nearly 50 years before.

The range of upholstery textiles spanned the extremes of cost and elaboration.[10] At the bottom of the range there was a strong, cheap, linen-based fabric with a woven pattern, called dornix, very like a 1930s folk-weave. Wool cloth such as serge or baize was also cheap, but sadly liable to moth damage. Cold draughty passages could be transformed by the red West Country cloth used for riding cloaks, with or without a small stamped pattern. Wool could be used to 'counterfeit' costly imported silks and velvets. After all, the light level was fairly low, no one would notice. But the truly luxurious went in for silk satins and velvets, damasks and brocades, to give the most sumptuous effect. In 1665 the Queen spent £3,580 10s 7d on 'rich velvets, gold stuffs etc. for furnishing [her] bedchamber';[11] and that was just one room.

Silk fabric was usually less than a yard wide. Every width was 'paned' (made into a panel) by a colour-contrasting border which added gaiety and hid the seams (occasionally uneven; imagine hand-sewing a great chamber's-worth of velvet). Damask could be used on satin, velvet on damask, gilt leather on everything, patterned with 'painted fruitages and flowerages'.[12] Then the edges of the borders could be finished with elaborate silk tassels and fringe, in yet another colour.

Colours were, to put it mildly, unrestrained. The perennial problem in imagining the contemporary effect of colours, whether on walls or on people, is the effect of ageing. Occasionally a scrap has survived behind a shelf or in a cupboard, from which the whole scheme can be reconstructed. This has been done, with appropriately startling effect, in the Queen's House in Greenwich. The Duchess of Lauderdale juxtaposed purple and yellow, red and orange. Samuel used purple for his cabinet, belatedly finding it rather dark.

Printed calico from India appeared on the English market early in the century.[13] At first the East India Company had sent bullion to India, to buy piece-goods there for bartering in the Spice Islands even further east; gradually, Indian cottons infiltrated the English market, for use in both clothing and upholstery. They were admirably colour-fast, a skill which evaded English printers until the late 1660s, when at last they understood the use of alum as a mordant. From 1669 English production of printed calicoes threatened the East India Company's monopoly. The company warned its agent in Surat that 'now of late they are here in England come to a good practice of printing large branches for hangings of rooms'. The 'branches' were vertically organised flowering trees rooted in a brown *rocaille* base. Favourite colours were a deep vibrant raspberry red and indigo blues from pale to almost black.

In 1663 Samuel 'bought my wife a Chinke: that is, a painted Indian Callico for to line her new study, which is very pretty'. The usual word was 'chint', derived from a Sanskrit word meaning multicoloured. It did not acquire its plural form, chintz, for another century.[14] Samuel seems to have been the only person to use 'chinke'; can his shorthand, for once, have let him down?

There was a small output of *toile de Jouy* type patterns. In 1665 John Evelyn admired Lady Mordaunt's painted calico hangings, 'full of figures great and small, prettily representing sundry trades and occupations of the Indians with their habits'.

Tapestries retained their long-established market. For centuries they had produced some degree of insulation in freezing stone castles with no damp-proof courses. They were hung well out from the wall, hence the gap in which poor old Polonius died. James I had set up a factory at Mortlake, in 1619, to supersede foreign imports, but customers preferred the continental to the home-produced article, despite heavy duties. (Neither the French nor the Dutch attempted 'Scotch pladd', for which there was a mercifully brief vogue, met from Kidderminster.) 'Histories' featured the bloodier bits of the classics and the Old Testament. 'Imageries' were peopled with gods and goddesses. A favourite design was 'playing boys' (putti) in vineyards. A whole tapestry could be devoted to 'forest work', 'verdure' or 'buskedge'. Here again, the colours have faded and changed. Verdure in particular is now often a dreary blur of sedge and khaki. Add rose and carmine to the flesh tints, clarify the yellows, add a good dollop of blue to the skies, scatter the trees with emerald, and you would come somewhere near their initial impact.

The great advantage of tapestry was its adaptability. It came with a separate border which could be juggled about to fit the tapestry to the wall-space. It could extend round corners and over doors – cut a flap for the door, it could always be sewn up again later.

In 1659, £49 bought a set of seven pieces 12 feet high and over 91 feet long:[15] an extraordinarily good buy. It would have covered the walls of a palatially high room say 30 feet square, allowing for the windows. Samuel, after much agonising, spent £83 on a second-hand set of The Apostles, for his 'great room'.

Embroidery was usually confined to bed hangings, a sufficiently engrossing task for the amateur embroiderer, with or without professional help. But there is a whole wall, in a dark ante-room in Chastleton House, the seventeenth-century survival in Oxfordshire, covered with an embroidery in flame-stitch. When I saw it last, the colours were variants on shades of beige. I believe it has been miraculously restored, as only the National Trust knows how, to its original colours of amber, coral, ochre and vermilion. The creator must have been happy with the result of all those hours of work, in lightening a gloomy corner.

Textile hangings could be taken down for cleaning or moving. Samuel's house was stripped to the bare walls as the Fire roared nearer. Hooks on the fabric slotted into eyelets in the plaster, or in battens on the walls. Precious fabrics would be mounted on batten frames, which had the merit of keeping them taut and flat. The 'Necessaries to be provided for the King's Household' on his restoration included 'tenter hooks, hammers, tacks and such like necessaries'.[16]

Textiles have a nasty habit of retaining smells, as anyone knows who has smelt the curtains in a smoker's room. Gilt leather or wood panelling were favoured for dining rooms, since smells did not cling to them.

Gilt leather probably originated in Moorish Spain; fine leather was embossed with florid patterns blocked or shaded with gold. It still gleams on the walls of rich merchants' houses in Antwerp, long a Spanish possession. But a seventeenth-century London upholsterer did not use such a lavish application of gold leaf. Panels of calf skin were embossed with an intaglio pattern of geometric motifs or exuberantly naturalistic flowers, and painted in some cheerful scheme, the flowers in their natural colours, even down to the stripes and spots of a 'flamed' tulip. The background was covered with silver foil which was varnished, giving a sumptuous golden glow. Unfortunately the silver has blackened with the passage of time to a dull blackish grey. Something of the original impact can be imagined from samples surviving in Ham House in Richmond and in Broughton Castle in Oxfordshire, where the background was not foiled but painted, in both cases a lovely cerulean blue. It is hard to imagine why the Duchess of Albemarle replaced this colourful extravaganza with a dull geometric pattern, until one remembers that the present wall-covering has acquired its shades of mud and greige only since she hung it; when new it was not only fashionable, but glitteringly colourful. Charles had the cabins of his new yacht hung with gilt leather, which, although unpredictable in wet weather, at least enabled him to cut the total cost to only £1,850; less than his brother's, who had not thought of sea-going leather.[17]

Wood panelling ('wainscoating') was often arranged above and below a dado rail. Medieval linen-fold pattern had given way to large, plain panels framed with a simple – for a change – moulding. Newly sawn oak is a warm amber. It darkens naturally with age (and unnaturally when antique dealers think it looks more authentic that way). The walls of the Stuart room in the Geffrye Museum are a pleasant mid-brown. But oak was becoming scarce, and deal or pine was cheaper. The Victorians were not the first to use paint treatment to upgrade them to look like more expensive wood or even marble. Seventeenth-century craftsmen were adept at graining. Although it is hardly domestic, I recommend Christopher Wren's Sheldonian Theatre in Oxford as a splendid example of marbling and graining, the latter unfortunately resembling mulligatawny soup. I suspect it has been restored.

If woodwork was painted, there was no Brilliant White vibrating with fluorescent whiteners and ageing to a dingy yellow. The colours were likely to be shades of various woods, whether grained or not; white; or pale tints of ivory/cream/blue/grey/green. The unfortunate, but authentic, strident blue incorporating crushed glass coloured with cobalt ('smalt'), which can be seen in the redecorated Queen's House in Greenwich, had gone out of fashion by 1660, but no doubt survived here and there. Sometimes the painter added a *trompe l'oeil* effect, of panels or perspectives. In the Islington houses, there is a palimpsest of panelling, from 1658 to Victoria. The oldest panels are painted with − a pattern of panels.

Mirror glass was expensive. On that day in May 1660 when Charles was waiting for the wind to change and allow him to set sail for England, he must, if he had eyes for anything but the weather, have been impressed by the 'large room all lined with glass' where the Dutch States General entertained him.[18] Such prodigal use of glass was not to be met in England, but tile-sized pieces could be butted together. Having hung his study in purple, Samuel considered using mirror glass above the fireplace to lighten the effect. (Could anything redeem purple walls in a small room?)

Seventeenth-century upholsterers saw no reason to give the eye a rest at the top of those busy walls. Friezes in painted wood or plaster told their own stories, undeterred by the action going on in the boskedge below.

Ceilings were, predictably, ornate. There is a replica of a 1669 ceiling in the Geffrye Museum. Its ponderous baroque swags must have been the despair of housemaids, in those coal-burning days. Apart from grand ceilings by Verrio and his school, ceilings were usually left white, and re-whitewashed periodically.

If, despite panes and borders and fringes and friezes, the effect was still a little dull, touches of gold here and there could work marvels. Samuel had his wainscoted parlour 'gilt' in 1660 – probably out of naval funds; there was a lot of gilding in seventeenth-century ships.

The use of rush matting on floors had gone out of fashion, which anyone who remembered its delicious country smell *when new* must have regretted; but it did harbour fleas and other livestock, and was impossible to clean. Runners or squares of thin woven matting from North Africa, Spain and Portugal could be lifted so that the floor could be swept. Woolly rugs comforted bare feet getting out of bed. Prosperous households had moved their oriental carpets from table to floor. Still richer households might follow the French fashion of intricately patterned parquet, introduced by the Queen Mother. But in general, as long as the walls were covered, there was nothing wrong with gleaming wood floors. (We forget the noise that leather-soled shoes make on wood. It was bad luck on Samuel that Elizabeth's feet gave him no audible warning of her approach, while he was engrossed in seducing the maid.)

Heating

In small rooms such as cabinets, the fireplace was set across one corner. Where architecture and space allowed, it was likely to be in the centre of the wall facing the windows. The fireplace surrounds might be faced with 'Delft' tiles – not necessarily imported, a factory in Southwark had begun production early in the century; and not necessarily patterned with motifs and figures, a plain ivory-cream was common. If there was no fireplace, or the fire smoked badly, a brazier of hot coals or charcoal could be brought in from the kitchen.

Smoking chimneys seem to have been a common problem. They had been built for burning wood, which needs different management from coal. In 1662 Elizabeth's father, with another man, patented 'a way to prevent and cure the smoaking of chimneys either by stopping the tunnel towards the top and altering the former course of the smoak, or by setting tunnels with checks within the chimneys', which sounds exactly what a modern engineer would advise; but judging by Samuel's continued, reluctant handouts to his father-in-law, it was not commercially successful.

The fireplace and overmantel were as ornate as possible. The overmantel in a cabinet provided the perfect display space for collections of curios and china. In larger rooms, space in the overmantel was left empty to receive a suitable picture.

Coal-burning fireplaces needed different equipment from the old-fashioned wood-burning hearths. Fire-irons of polished brass rested on tall brass firedogs with bulbous finials which reflected the firelight. In ultra-fashionable houses the 'chimney furniture [was] of plate/ For iron's now quite out of date';[19] which does seem to push conspicuous consumption too far.

Lighting

The fire was a source of light as well as heat. Firelight was supplemented by candle light, in polite circles, or by the feeble light of a taper (a poor relation of a candle, thin and limp) where show was not important. A really good party was signalled by an extravagant glitter of candles. In general, the level of illumination was far lower than we are accustomed to – in both senses. A candle is of little use if it is too far away. A single candle in a candlestick would be placed on a small table beside the user. Candles in 'branches' fixed to the walls or hung from the ceiling had to be at a convenient height for snuffing and replacing. These had an advantage over candles standing on tables: the rats could not get at them. An Emblem Book of 1638 depicts a candlestick with no fewer than four rats climbing about on it:

> Loe how the rats catching me all alone
> With envious teeth my body cease upon.[20]

Candles needed constant attention; from the same source, the verse beside a picture of candle snuffers and an 'extinguisher', shaped like a dunce's hat:

> Th' extinguisher and snuffers that are by
> Tels thee O man that sometime thou must die
> And lest thou should in darkness still remain
> The tinder box will light thee once again
> But snufft from all corruption shalt thou be
> And shine with God and saints eternally.

The invention marketed by the 'King's French Church' (more

exactly, the Roman Catholic church in the Savoy, under the protection of the Queen Mother) in 1661 is the more amazing – 'a device ... for all clocks and pocket-engines to awaken at any hour and light a candle at the same time ... which will cost but 20s'; or you could go further, and for the same price have an 'Engine called the Bright Watch warmer for ringing a bell, lighting a faggot and a candle at any hour appointed', or, once you were awake and hard at work, a similar device which would light successive candles 'every hour or halfe'.[21]

A vivid warning of the dangers of living with candles had been printed by order of the Lord Mayor, twenty years before the Fire, as 'Seasonable Advice for preventing the mischief of fire that may come by negligence, treason or otherwise'.[22] It lists almost every cause of fire that modern fire brigades still encounter, except replacing electric fuses with hairpins and looking for gas leaks with matches. It deserves to be quoted almost in full:

Some hath been burnt by bad Harths, Chimnies, Ovens or by pans of fire set upon boards: some by Cloaths hanged against the fire: some by leaving great fires in chimnies, where the sparks ... fell and fired the boards, painted cloths, Wainscots, Rushes, Matts ... some by ... shooting off pieces [firing shot-guns up the chimney, a brisk way of cleaning it]; ... some by setting Candles under shelves; some by leaving candles neere their beds; some by snuffes or candles, Tobacco-snuffles [pipe dottle]; and some by drunkards, some by warming beds; some by looking under beds with Candles; Some by sleeping at work, leaving their Candles by them ... or by foule chimnies ... some by Candles falling out of their Candlesticks; some by sticking their Candles upon posts ... And some have been fired a purpose by villany or Treason.

Orders to be observed that fire may not happen:-
Is that every housekeeper ... to see to the fire and Candle, and to shut the Sellar-windows, dores, casements, garret windows, and to stop holes ... that fire may not come in by Treason or otherwise ... Seeke to prevent fire at the beginning, and by the sight of smoake, to look for it ... If you will use Candle all night, let your Candlestick be a pot of water brim full, and set it where it shall stand, and then light a Candle and sticke a great pin in the bottom of the Candle, and let it slowly into the water, and it will burn all night without danger ...

48

Orders that if fire should happen ... to prevent the miseries thereof:-
Then the Bells going backward, doth give notice of fire ... all those
of higher or level ground should throw downe water, to run to the
place where the fire is, and there stop it ... If water-pipes run through
the streets, you may open it against the house that is a-fire ... Where
mild fire is, milke, sand, urine, earth or dirt will quench it...

I can only add that a comparatively safe lantern was available, made
of pierced iron, with a pierced shutter that could be closed but still
show some light. Its design had not changed since Guy Fawkes used
one to see his traitorous way to the gunpowder in the basement of
the House of Commons.

Furniture

It may seem curious to begin this section with doors and windows.
Modern lawyers have developed a comprehensive code of landlord's/
tenant's fixtures, which certainly relieves us from doubt about who
owns the front door. Seventeenth-century lawyers were not so sure,
or perhaps successive occupants put the doors and windows in the
moving van without pausing to check. Lawyers sometimes annexed
to title deeds lists of doors, windows, locks, shelves and other
'carpenter's work' which were to be treated as part of the building,
by physically linking the list into the seal on the document, by a silk
thread. (Inevitably most of these wax seals have disintegrated now,
and the lists have fallen out and got lost, but there were still a few
in the deeds I read in the Guildhall library. It is a curious experience
to open the stiff, folded vellum, making a most unscholarly noise.
Each deed was dark brown and dusty on the outside, but the inside
was pure white, and the ink still as black as when it was first
penned.)[23]

John Evelyn nostalgically described his forefathers' furniture,
before Charles came back with his continental ideas. Cupboards
and chests and the 'sturdy oaken bedstead and furniture of the house
lasted one whole century; the shovel-board[24] and other long tables
both in Hall and Parlour were as fixed as the freehold; nothing was
moveable save joint-stools'. And very uncomfortable they were.
Suddenly, a transformation. Furniture became movable, purpose-
designed, elegant and comfortable.

Take beds, for example. They were such important status symbols that the Commons, in the middle of arranging to invite Charles to return, and drafting interminable speeches of welcome, and appointing emissaries, found time to include in the list of 'Necessaries to be provided for the King's Household', 'a rich bed to be of velvet, either embroidered with gold or laced [trimmed with gold braid], lined with cloth of silver or sattin ... Two beds more for the King's Majesty, to be removing beds ... and all necessaries to each bed....'[25] One cannot resist wondering how soon His Majesty put his loyal Commons' practical benevolence to thorough use.

The functional framework began with a four-sided box, the floor of which was a network of rope, which gave some flexibility, or boards, which gave none. There was room under it for a folding ('trundle' or 'truckle') bed for a servant. Into that box went a thick undermattress stuffed with straw or wool, and then a thinner top mattress filled with feathers or wool. The sheets were tucked under this mattress, but the blankets ('ruggs') and coverlets just lay on top. To discourage their inveterate habit of slipping off in the cold small hours, 'bed-staves' like huge toothpicks could be pushed down between mattress and framework.[26] Above the sleeper towered a superstructure ('tester') supported on four posts. All surfaces – the inside and outside of the tester, the bedhead, the sides of the framework and even the posts – were covered with fabric. No wood showed, unlike Tudor four-posters. The tester was finished with floor-length curtains, often embroidered by the housewife, which could be drawn round the bed and fastened to exclude any dangerous fresh air.

To prevent any risk that the ensemble of draped, gathered, lined, embroidered, colour-contrasted hangings might be too plain, each corner of the tester was crowned with a large fabric-covered or gilt cup, holding white or dyed, dust-trapping, ostrich feathers. The enclosed space made a small room on its own, giving at least visual privacy to the occupants, while a servant slept in the same room on the truckle bed.

Beside the bed, a chair. Chairs in general metamorphosed from four-legged square-set stools with added backs ('back-stools') to the elegant walnut chairs, with tall carved backs and cane seats, that stayed in fashion for decades. But I suspect that even where these lovely pieces had taken up residence, the chair beside the bed was often a humble back-stool, because on it reposed, at night, the 'pott'.

The use of chamber-pots seems to have continued, even when

there was a close-stool within easy reach. Charles' magnificent 'rich bed' came with a matching chair of state, two high stools, one foot-stool and two cushions, and 'one close-stool suitable to [matching] the bed'. Close-stools were usually built on the lines of a thunder-box, and padded, which must have been comfortable, if insani-tary.

Although no one had yet invented a pot-cupboard, someone had thought of a way to avoid the inconvenience of chests, where the vital skirt or doublet was always at the bottom. Instead of lifting the lid and taking everything out, you could pull or draw out sections of the chest, in layers. Putting it more simply, the chest of drawers had arrived.

No elegant bedroom was complete without two small matching tables to hold candlesticks ('candlestands'), and a dressing table supporting a mirror, or a dressing box with a mirror in the lid. Candlestands in the form of blackamoor boys, called *guéridons* after a popular black vaudeville artist of the time, were beginning to cross the Channel from Paris.[27] The dressing table was covered down to the floor with oriental carpet or home-produced 'turkey-work' or a length of some sumptuous fabric. This was protected from cosmetics by a fine but washable linen cloth ('toilet' or 'toilette' from the French for a little cloth: a splendid example of words changing their meaning).

Another essential for the fashionable home was an elaborately decorated set of small drawers behind doors (a 'cabinet'). Here the new trade of cabinet-making displayed its virtuosity, in veneering and marquetry and lacquering, to brilliant effects. Cabinets were often constructed with a secret drawer or cupboard. Samuel acquired a 'pretty Cabinet' which he gave to Elizabeth,[28] 'and very con-veniently it comes for her closet. Stayed up late finding out the private boxes, but could not do some of them.' One longs to know whether Elizabeth succeeded where Samuel had failed. Perhaps she too kept a diary...

As furniture increasingly adapted itself to human nature, the pleasure of a post-prandial nap produced 'couches' or day-beds, and light meals could be set out on small movable tables, such as – surely – Samuel used for his suppers at Elizabeth's bedside when she was indisposed.

Samuel possessed various musical instruments, which were beauti-ful decorative objects. Virginals[29] were widely owned; Samuel observed, in the frantic evacuation of September 1666, how 'hardly one lighter or boat in three that had the goods of a house in, but there was a pair of virginals in it'.

The stock of household linens needed a linen cupboard: a tall, shelved 'press'. Another press might contain cloaks and coats, hanging from pegs, sometimes on hangers. The fashion was to crown presses with at least a pair of matching vases, reconciling the passion for dust-trapping decoration with some slight regard for running children and pets on floor level.

Books for show in a lady's cabinet were displayed on an elegant hanging shelf. More robust libraries were housed in shelved book-cases, sometimes protected by curtains. Samuel designed innovative glass-fronted book-cases, for his own library.

Pictures were often hung in spaces left for them in the panelling or overmantel. Otherwise, they hung from large visible nails banged into the walls through tapestry, panes or wainscot. Maps, topo-graphical views and portraits of the owner and his wife were popular. Samuel had himself and his wife painted twice. He had, unknowingly, an indirect contact with the most prominent woman artist of the time, when he was frantically trying to get the paperwork in order for his appointment as Clerk of the Acts. He had to pay £9 to a Mr Beale,[30] whose wife Mary became the family breadwinner in 1670, charging £10 for a three-quarter portrait in oils, £5 for head and shoulders.[31]

Mirrors were elaborately framed. To see one's hemline, let alone one's face, in a wall-hung looking glass was possible only if the glass was sharply canted forward.

Curtains were usual, but not yet elaborate. They hung on horn or metal rings, from metal rods – imagine the noise of drawing them.

The pulley mechanism of sliding sashes was yet to come from Holland, with William III. The lower third of a window could be slid upwards and latched on a ratchet. In bitter weather, a thick rush mat or painted screen of oiled silk could be fitted into the lower part of the window embrasure as a draught-excluder.

Another comforting anti-draught measure was the square foot-warmer, just the right height for the feet, containing hot coals or charcoal. Shown in so many Dutch interiors, it was surely used in England too. And everywhere, spittoons. John Evelyn complained that people spat, constantly and profusely.

Fashionable impedimenta included terrestrial and celestial globes (Samuel bought a pair for £3 10s), barometers ('weather glasses') and exotica such as silver-mounted coconut shells and ostrich eggs, and tropical shells. Elizabeth's brother gave her some shells, to decorate her closet. The beauty of shells is lovingly depicted in a portrait of John Tradescant, the seventeenth-century gardener, with a friend. He and his friend together take up half the canvas, the shells take the rest.[32]

Lastly, a puzzle: Samuel, who was prone to colds which he attributed to such traumas as washing his feet, 'put up a spitting-sheet, which I find very convenient'.[33] Even Randle Holme is silent as to its nature.

CHAPTER 4

GARDENS, PARKS
AND OPEN SPACES

Gardens

The first gardening book to be printed in England was Thomas Hill's *Most briefe and pleasaunte Treatyse, teachynge howe to Dress, Sowe and set a Garden*, in 1563. Encouraged by its success, Hill expanded it into *The Gardener's Labyrinth*, in 1577, which was still selling in the 1660s. The first gardening book aimed at a female readership was William Lawson's *The Country Housewife's Garden*, which by 1669 was still being reprinted, under the title *A Way to get Wealth*. Like Hill, Lawson was a practical man, with a pleasantly avuncular style. (It was he who suggested that flowers and vegetables should each have a separate area of the garden, since they needed different methods of cultivation – although some might stray from one to the other. Yet he recommended 'Bankes and seats of camomile, penny royal, daisies and violets, [which] are seemly and comfortable'. They were certainly fashionable, despite the disadvantages of damp in the bones and stains on the clothes.[1]) Readers of the ubiquitous almanacs could rely on gardening advice, usually tied to the movements of the planets.

We assume that every aspect of life has improved since the seventeenth century. A keen gardener, reading Parkinson's *Paradisi in Sole* (1656) or John Evelyn's *Almanac* (1666) will begin to wonder. Parkinson listed 100 different daffodils, 50 different hyacinths, 154 different tulips. Evelyn's annual planting plan could produce several flowers in bloom throughout the winter, with a variety of winter 'salletings' and fruit. Like any Sunday gardening correspondent, he told his readers what to do in the garden, month by month, from manuring the asparagus beds in January, to 'continuing your hostility against vermin' in December.

Gardens were expected to provide space for walking exercise. Grass 'carpet-walks' were scythed, which never produced the motor-mown felt of today, no matter how skilfully done. Paths were more often paved or gravelled, for dry-shod walking. Both grass and gravel were rolled with stone rollers.[2] Evelyn gives a recipe for weed-killer, using 'tobacco waste'. Beds were laid out formally in rectilinear shapes, edged with box, thrift, cotton lavender ('rare and novel', according to Parkinson), tiles, pebbles, lead cut into patterns, or even 'sheeps' shank bones, head upwards'. In the beds, 'knots' still survived, although one school of thought described them as 'Dancing Masters' niceties'.[3] Elaborate swirls of coloured sands and gravels were outlined in slow-growing evergreen or silver-leaved plants. More modern gardeners filled in the edgings with flowers and coloured foliage. In the centre of each bed, a tall shrub or a statue added height, the statue painted in realistic colours.

'Alleys' of trees trained to meet overhead or clipped and inter-woven ('pleached') into walls provided shady walks in summer, and shelter from winter winds. An alternative retreat for meditation could be found in a 'wilderness' – the misleading name for a tight quincunx of small trees.[4] Pots and urns were spaced along low walls. On the other side of the wall, an orchard of fruit or nut trees. Set against the wall, one of those fashionable, rheumatics-inducing, plant-covered seats. In a corner, an arbour covered with fragrant honeysuckle and jasmine. And, if at all possible, a mound with a winding path to its summit, and a two-storeyed banqueting house, from which one could survey the garden while toying with a glass of wine and a sweetmeat.

The hedges round the garden could be of sweet-smelling briar roses, or pyracantha, which 'made a glorious show in the winter'.[5]

In the middle of Whitehall Palace there was a 'beautiful meadow laid out like a garden [sic: Magalotti again] planted with trees and beautiful roses, and having four rows of statues in the middle'. Two of Charles's mistresses, the Duchess of Richmond and the Countess of Castlemaine, had apartments looking over it – and presumably giving on to it, for it must be where Samuel saw Lady Castlemaine's underwear hanging out to dry, presumably on the rose bushes.[6]

There are many pictures of seventeenth-century gardens. The owners of grand estates had their houses and gardens, as well as their wives, painted for posterity. There are charming and scholarly reconstructions of seventeenth-century gardens at Hatfield, Kew, Lambeth and Pitmedden. But the most evocative representation I know is a piece of furniture: a seventeenth-century dressing case in the Victoria and Albert Museum. Its lid opens to reveal a model garden. There, in miniature, are the paths and statues and knots and hedges, just as the enchanted recipient may have seen them from her window.

A list of all the plants available in the 1660s would be tedious to any gentle reader who is not also a bigoted gardener. I will confine myself here to noting a few which I had mistakenly associated with the Victorians. Many had arrived from the developing English colonies across the Atlantic, and the Dutch possessions in the Far East and South Africa. There was a well-established convention among gardeners that discoveries should be shared, across international boundaries and despite wars. African marigolds were known to seventeenth-century gardeners, so were datura, and hollyhocks (which even crop up in Pharaonic Karnac), snapdragons, tuberoses, day lilies, thalictrum and that dull flower called Marvel of Peru, which has as much to do with Peru as Flos Jovis has to do with Jove. M. de l'Obel had begun work in Hackney, on the classication of plants, as early as 1570. We owe lobelia to him. Laurus tinus, beloved of the Victorians, flowered in January, and clematis in February. Auriculas had come over with the Huguenot refugees, and already provoked keen competition. White and red rhododendrons gladdened the hearts of those with acid soil.

Few flowers had been bred into double forms. On the other hand, their natural perfume had not been bred out of them. Their flowering season may have been shorter than modern forms, although some of Parkinson's tulips could, he said, 'endure above three months'. To those modern gardeners prepared to dispense with fuchsia and dahlias, perhaps the main gaps would be chrysanthemums, repeat-flowering roses, for which they would have to wait another two centuries, and yellow roses. Roses were white, red or striped white/red. Dutch growers could persuade a yellow rose (*Rosa hemispherica* or *sulphurea*) to bloom for their painters, but only in heated greenhouses.[7] *Rosa foetida*, a single yellow, had reached Europe before 1600, but does not seem to have caught on in England.[8]

Parkinson quoted, with understandable reserve, the advice of 'some' that a white rose grafted on a broom (*genista*) would produce a yellow rose just as surely as a rose grafted on a holly would be evergreen. From a less erudite source, an almanac, comes this advice on 'how to make vines have the taste of cherries': pull a vine shoot through a hole in a cherry tree. And if you have a 'sour-fruiting' tree, manure it with pig's dung 'to make it bring forth sweet fruit', and pour honey into a hole in the trunk. They certainly believed in trying.

The seventeenth-century Londoner was well off for garden centres. By mid-century, nurserymen were specialising in the supply of plants and seeds to the retail market, while market gardeners grew vegetables ('herbs'). Several seedsmen/nurserymen operated in or near the City.[9] Leonard Gurle ran an extensive nursery between Spitalfields and Whitechapel, identifiable on Ogilby's 1676 map. He specialised in fruit trees, but also supplied shrubs and seeds. William Harman at Shoreditch also supplied fruit trees, exporting them as far as Ireland. Robert Hill's shop at the Three Angels in Lombard Street had supplied seeds to John Winthrop, for the new settlement in Massachusetts. Seeds and plants could be bought from Edward Fuller in the Strand and Theophilus Stacey outside Bishopsgate, Charles Blackwell at the Holborn end of Fetter Lane and George Ricketts in Hoxton, where the unusually fertile soil supported several nurseries. Rickett's 1688 catalogue includes 15 tender plants, 34 flowering trees, 18 winter-flowering plants and shrubs, and 39 other 'flowers and choice plants', counting as one entry such descriptions as 'iris, bulbous, great varieties' and 'primroses, many colours and sorts'.

But, just as now, friends could be relied on for cuttings and roots from their own gardens. Lady Hobart in Chancery Lane to Sir Ralph Verney in Claydon, Buckinghamshire: 'Pray send me som grens to set against my new wall and some Jeseney and hun-icuckells.'[10]

The labour of gardening does not change much over the centuries. Spades and rakes have been modified only slightly since the Middle Ages. Scythes have been supplanted by mowers, and plastic hose has to some extent replaced watering cans, which by the 1660s were replacing those 'water-pots' of clay with holes all over them, from which the water was prevented from pouring until the right moment by an ingenious use of water/air pressure. Thomas Hill explained it beautifully:

The common watering pot for the garden beds with us, hath a narrow neck, big belly, somewhat large bottom, and full of little holes, with a proper hole formed on the head to take in the water, which filled full, and the thumb laid on the hole to keep in the air, may on such wise be carryed in a handsome manner ... the beds at one instant shal not fully be watered, but as the earth and plants drink in, so gently sprinkle forth the water, in feeding the plants with moisture, as by a brest or nourishing Pap, which like handled, shall greatly prosper the tender plants comming up, where they otherwise by the hasty drowning with water, are much annoyed, and put in hazard of perishing.

All you needed, and he did not explain, was a tank deep enough to immerse the pot in.

A page of Evelyn's *Almanac* is filled with drawings of mostly familiar tools. Only a cloche in the shape of a four-poster bed complete with tester and curtains would cause raised eyebrows on the allotment. All the same it is such an excellent idea that I might try it.

Samuel visited two gardens in Hackney (another fertile district), in the summer of 1666.[11] At Brooke House, owned by the Earl of Bath, 'the gardens are excellent; and here I first saw oranges grow ... Here were also great variety of other exoticque plants, and several Labarinths [mazes] and a pretty Aviary.' The orange trees and the tender green 'exoticques' will have been grown in pots, which spent the winter in an orangery or a specially designed 'green-house' (not yet a glass-house made of glass, but a house for tender evergreens). Evelyn gives a design for a green-house, 12–13 feet deep, 10–11 feet high, preferably built against a wall which had a heat-generating dungheap on the other side of it, for winter warmth, or a stove (hence, 'stove-house').

Lord Bath's town house was in Holborn. It had a garden of urban dimensions. He probably brought his tender 'greens' and orange trees into town to enjoy them, when he could not escape to Hackney. Even after the Fire there were still mansions scattered about in London, inhabited by City aldermen who were obliged to live within the City, and by old-fashioned nobility and gentry who resisted the drift to the smart western suburbs. Lord Aylesbury had four extensive gardens round his house at Clerkenwell Green. Lord Berkeley nearby had two. The Marquess of Dorchester and Lord Gray were neighbours, each with gardens, near Charterhouse.[12]

The surveyors compiling the post-Fire maps carefully drew in countless gardens isolated in the middle of a block, not attributed by them to any owner; neatly divided into beds and knots, each curlicue shown. There is a space off Chancery Lane, divided into long straight beds; can it be the remains of Gerard's garden? (His garden was thereabouts. He died in 1612.) We do not know the extent to which the gardens in Tresswell's plans had been built over by 1660; but if the houses were basically unchanged, as I have suggested, there must still have been countless small gardens tucked away at the back of the long narrow plots.

As well as private gardens, each City livery company had its garden, for the refreshment of its members and – sometimes – fortunate neighbours. The Drapers' Company had a garden of nearly one and a half acres. In 1636 the gardener, who was expected to keep order in it, was admonished for letting in a 'multitude of ... mean quality and rude behaviour, some of them being apprentices, servants and children, running leaping and disordering themselves'. There were even 'some young men and maids in wanton and uncivil manner dallying and disporting themselves to the offence of good people'. Schoolboys 'scorned to be spoken to by the Gardener', and young men refused to give way to members, at the bowling alley. From now on, he was told, only 'such as shall be of the better sort of this Company, and the neighbours and inhabitants near this place, and also such citizens of the better rank and condition as shall be thought fit' were to be allowed in; an enterprising woman who was charging an unauthorised entrance fee of a farthing – and if someone had not got a farthing, she told him to go home and get one – was sacked.

During the Interregnum, the garden perforce became more sober, and the bowling alley was put down. But as soon as Charles came back, the garden was redesigned. There were to be 'summer-houses', and a new 'plot with a [sun]dial in it ... and a Maze ... and the rest in grass-work', with five statues (as long as they did not cost more than £100). The Fire destroyed the company's hall, and much of its income-producing property, but there were funds enough after building a new hall on part of the garden, to clean and *repaint* the statues, relay the bowling alley and install a sundial again, and purbeck marble paving.

When all these glories were complete, the 'idle and lewd people and rude boys' came flocking back,[13] but Magalotti found it in 1669 'a beautiful garden for walking in'. Ogilby's 1676 map shows the maze, and the bowling alley, with an unidentified building which must be the Drapers' new hall, about midway between the garden

59

and the 'Dutch Church'. Tracing the site back through Stow and the dissolution of the monasteries (see page 20), it is possible to imagine that the Draper's garden soil had been continuously cultivated since the Augustinian Friars had first dug it, perhaps 400 years earlier.

The Inns of Court, too, maintained their Walks, primarily for their members, who could discuss knotty problems while perambulating, but open to anyone who cared to stroll decorously through them. Samuel was fond of Gray's Inn, where he could see 'many beauties', including the greatly admired Frances Butler, and 'great store of gallants'. It was a good place to gather the latest court gossip and fashion news. Even in the winter, the Walks were 'very pleasant' in the snow and frost. Perhaps the advantage of Gray's Inn lay in its very remoteness. Beyond its gardens the fields stretched to the hills of Hampstead, and a fresh country breeze blew, instead of the stink that invaded the Temple from the tanneries across the river when the wind was from the south.

The royal parks

Hyde Park and St James's Park had been part of the medieval royal domain fenced in for hunting ('emparked'), which stretched from the gates of Whitehall to Hampstead Heath.[14] Henry VIII would have found London life intolerable without hunting.

Hyde Park was opened to the public by James I, a privilege confirmed by Charles II on his restoration. Even before he landed from Holland, 'Londoners in their finery' flocked to the park to celebrate his return.[15] The improved design of coaches encouraged the *bon ton* to display themselves and their equipages in the 'Ring' or 'Tour'. The season began surprisingly early, in March. In the spring of 1663, Samuel watched Charles in one coach and his mistress Lady Castlemaine in another, driving elegantly round the park. A month later the show was different: the King's Riders with their 'managed' horses, doing tricks. Samuel was there again on 22 April 1664, 'where great plenty of gallants, pleasant only [but] for the dust'. A week later, the Ranger was ordered to 'water the passage from the gate to where the coaches resort in the Park, to avoid the annoyance of dust, much complained of, the expense to be borne by a charge of 6d on each coach, and to prevent all horses coming into the park except such as have gentlemen or livery servants on them, as they cause much dust'.[16]

In 1664 the Ranger was given a lease of 55 acres in the north-west corner of the park, so that he could fence it off for an apple orchard, delivering half the produce to the King's Household – after all, it was the King's park – and 'reserving a way therethrough from Westminster to Kensington'.[17]

St James's Park had been marshy in Henry VIII's time; so much so that James I thought it appropriate to try crocodiles there, for a novelty. Newcourt's 1658 map followed the Commonwealth habit of dropping the Saint from its name, but the title, at least, was resanctified by Charles. The great French architect Le Nôtre, who was working for Charles's mother, recommended that the rural charm of St James's Park should be preserved, but Henrietta Maria, who was allotted St James's Palace on her return, pined for all things French, and employed Le Nôtre's rival André Mollet to impose a formal layout of *patte d'oie*. The long axis was a 'canal' (here meaning a straight, ornamental sheet of water; it was 2,800 feet long and 100 feet wide) with two short lines of trees at an angle, all radiating from an elipse of 'sweet limes'. Exotic water birds were installed on an island in the middle of the canal. They still enliven the park, but the parrots and cassowaries in gilded cages[18] have long ago left Birdcage Walk.

Charles liked this park. He could exercise his notorious habit of outwalking his advisers and courtiers along Constitution Hill (so named after Charles's constitution, nothing to do with jurisprudence), and play the new game of Pell Mell there. He poured money into the park. He spent £400 on a lodge, and £1,700 on bringing water (for the canal?) to it from Hyde Park.[19] He launched on the canal the two 'gundalos'[20] given him by the Doge of Venice. The gondolieri brought their families over from Venice, not knowing the habits of the English King, who avoided paying wages for as long as possible; in the end they managed to get home, sadder and wiser.[21] Charles bought plants for the physic garden and the flower garden. The Surveyor of the Royal Gardens observed sourly that some anemones and ranunculus planted there were worth only between £14 and £18, not the £118 claimed.[22] With all these treasures within, it was necessary to build a wall round the park, which cost £2,400, funded from a windfall of prize money in the Dutch wars.[23]

Samuel, too, approved of St James's Park. By March 1661 it was 'now a very fine place', and by July 1662 'more and more pleasant, by the new works'. In December 1662 he saw for the first time people 'sliding with their Skeates' on the canal, which must have been an ideal skating rink. But neither Charles nor Samuel frequented it at night, when

> Nightly now beneath [the trees'] shade
> Are buggeries, rapes and incests made,
> Unto this all-sin-sheltering Grove
> Whores of the Bulk and the Alcove
> Great Ladies, chamber maydes and Drudges,
> The Ragg Picker, and Heiress Trudges,
> Carrmen, Divines, Great Lords, and Taylors,
> Prentices, Poets, Pimps and Gaolers,
> Footmen, Fine Fopps, do here arrive
> And here promiscuously they swive.

– according to Lord Rochester, who could be expected to know.[24]

During the Plague the park was shut, a melancholy index of London's misery.

Pleasure gardens

Next to St James's Park was a privately owned pleasure resort occupying part of the mulberry garden that James 1 had planted for his silk-worms (see page 107). Charles 1 had finally abandoned the production of silk as a commercial project, but the mulberry trees still survived. In 50 years they had grown into substantial trees, planted in the 'wilderness' or quincunx pattern that must have provided admirable opportunities for hidden 'dallying'. Samuel described them as 'only a wilderness, that is somewhat pretty, but rude'[25] (did he mean unpruned?). On his first visit he found it 'a very silly place, worse than Spring-garden [another similar resort nearby, but without mulberry trees] and but little company and those a rascally roguing whoring sort of people' – which did not stop him from going twice more.

Anyone who has lived near a mulberry tree will be all too aware of a disadvantage that Samuel did not mention: birds are fond of ripe mulberries, which have an almost immediate laxative effect on them; it is impossible to get the dark red stains out. I have not seen any remedy suggested in any of the household recipe books I have read.

Open spaces

Londoners could always walk in the Artillery Grounds – subject, of course, to the Trained Bands' musketry practice – or on Bunhill Fields, or the fields of Finsbury Manor, which the City leased from St Paul's in return for lead for the cathedral roof: the very lead that ran down into the crypt in the Fire, and destroyed the booksellers' stocks. In Finsbury Fields the windmills shown on a map of 1562 were still creaking round grinding corn, but the washerwomen who had dried their customers' shirts and shifts on the grass there had rolled up their bundles and gone elsewhere by the 1660s, no doubt discouraged by the pollution.

The claustrophobic pressure of a metropolis did not afflict seventeenth-century Londoners. Evelyn had suggested that London should be surrounded by a Green Belt planted with sweet-smelling herbs and fragrant shrubs, the prunings of which could be burnt in the City streets, making an aromatic change from the pervasive stink. This glorious dream was beyond the imagination of less gifted men; but at least green fields were never far away. It is pleasant to think of Charles in August 1668, when he went with his brother and his bastard son, the Duke of Monmouth, 'in their barges to Vauxhall, whence they intend to take their recreation in fowling along the river and toward New Park, returning to Whitehall for dinner'.[26] Lesser mortals too could take a boat upstream and picnic on the river bank at Barn Elms,[27] or walk across the Bridge and over the fields to Lambeth,[28] or out to the 'ducking-pond fields' at Islington,[29] or the fields beyond St Pancras;[30] or make an expedition to Vauxhall Pleasure Gardens, where the service might be slow but 'the wenches' – Elizabeth and her maids – gathered pinks, and 'the boy' crept through the hedge and gathered 'abundance of roses',[31] and nightingales sang.

CHAPTER 5

COMMUNICATIONS

By river

The site of England's capital was not a matter of chance. It had
been dictated by two factors.[1] The first – invisible but fundamental –
was the nature of its subsoil. If Britain were commercially and
militarily to be incorporated in the Roman Empire, the invaders
had to ensure access to the rich hinterland, and to the strongholds
of opposing British tribes. An army moving north from a south-east
bridgehead had to cross the Thames. The banks on either side of
the river, before it widened and became unbridgeable, were marshy
and prone to flooding. There were three exceptions to this soggy
picture. There was a narrow spit of gravel at Southwark; too small
to accommodate a settlement, but sufficient to support one end of
a bridge or causeway. There was another, on the opposite bank, to
take the other end of the crossing. Here, the Romans built their
city. It spread north; east as far as the defensive fort beside the
crossing; and west as far as they needed. They enclosed the whole
area with a wall, and built themselves a home from home, as far as
possible, considering England's appalling climate and its remoteness
from the civilised pleasures of Rome.

The third exception to the predominant marsh was further west,
upriver: a small island (Thorney Island) of gravel on which Edward
the Confessor built his great Minster, which was finished just in
time to accommodate the coronation of his successor, William the
Conqueror, and has been used for royal occasions ever since.

The other factor which determined the site of London was the
tide. The Thames was tidal for 30 miles above London.[2] At high
tide, sea-going merchant ships could rely on sufficient depth to

unload in the City, as long as the channel was kept dredged. The Romans built massive wharves, the remains of which still survive. By the seventeenth century there was a sophisticated series of quays and wharves on the north bank of the river.

High tides brought their problems. In December 1663 there was an exceptionally high tide, and 'all Whitewall [was] drowned'.[3] No doubt the Romans had suffered too. But setting the risk of flooding against the advantages of a site giving access by river to inland England, and able to service sea-going ships, it was inevitable that London should grow up where it did.

The Romans' first bridge, of pontoons lashed together, soon gave way to a wooden bridge. Every now and then it fell down; once it was pulled down by an invading Norseman. The first stone bridge, which lasted 600 years, was built in 1209. In the seventeenth century its nineteen stone arches still stood on their piers, with their bases protected by 'starlings' of wood and rubble. When the tide was ebbing or flowing, the water boiled through between them with such frightening force that people usually landed before the bridge and walked round to the next landing place to rejoin their boat. Samuel once had to stand on one of the starlings while the watermen dragged the boat through the 'lock' (waterway).[4] On another occasion, he had '*la belle* Pierce' and Elizabeth with him when 'the tide being against us when we were almost through, we were carried back again with much danger, and Mrs Pierce was much afeared and frighted' – he did not say how Elizabeth felt.[5] Another time, he walked 'over the piles through the bridge (while two others were aground against the bridge and could not get through)'.[6]

Apart from its turbulent passage under the bridge, the Thames flowed slowly, between its marshy banks. Since it was both sluggish and shallow, it froze more easily than nowadays. Samuel noted, in the winter of 1665, how 'the river beginning to be very full of ice', it became 'troublesome getting over'. Two days later the river was frozen.[7] Five days later the ice began to thaw, and Samuel's boat went through 'with crackling and noise', which not surprisingly made him 'fearful'. He should have been fairly used to it; the river froze over in 1660, 1663, 1665 and 1667. (The famous Ice Fair, when the ice lasted for several weeks and chestnut vendors sold hot chestnuts from burning braiziers on it, was not until the winter of 1683/84.) The thick November fogs combining river mist and polluting smoke must have made any journey hazardous, not only river travel; nor can the frequent hailstorms and thunderstorms of the time been comfortable for passengers in small boats.[8]

Another hazard, pollution, was more unpleasant. Samuel 'was much troubled today to see a dead man lie floating upon the waters; and had done (they say) these four days and nobody takes him up to bury him, which is very barbarous'.[9] The ships that crowded the river threw dead rats and plague-stricken corpses and the detritus of the crew into the water, to join the industrial waste of the bankside tanneries and other noisome trades using the river water.

Nevertheless, the Thames provided an incomparable setting for pageants. Charles II went by state barge to the Tower, the day before his coronation. Two days later there was a firework display on the river, 'before the King'. A year later Charles's bride was greeted by a magnificent water pageant, the whole of the river being covered with richly caparisoned boats. Civic events such as the annual Lord Mayor's parade used the river. Apart from such highspots, royal barges, the Lord Mayor's barge and the ornate barges of grandees often made their colourful way up and down the river, the King meanwhile enjoying the 'choice noise of trumpets' voted to him by the Commons on his arrival,[10] or other gentler music. This delightful habit of music-making on the water was shared by Samuel, who was often moved to song; but he was not the only one. On 7 July 1667 'a boat full of Spaniards' were singing, too.

Watermen were strictly controlled, in theory at least. They were not allowed to ply for hire on Sundays, when the river must have been uncharacteristically quiet. Samuel made use of the Navy Office barge or galley. He felt slightly awkward when the Duke of York noticed him in it and called across, from his own barge; he was perfectly properly going down to Woolwich on naval business, but he had an uneasy feeling that he had been 'too profuse' in using official transport.[11]

Wherries were the omnibuses of seventeenth-century London; solidly built craft that ran regular passenger services between Gravesend and the City, and down-river from the shires. The most frequently used form of river transport was a shallow-draught skiff, with a 'tilt' or hood, similar to the canopy of a gondola, to keep the passengers dry[12] (although I doubt if it did, in the kind of driving rain that London specialises in). Newcourt's map shows the river speckled with these small craft, like so many water-beetles; one or two men rowing, one or two passengers sitting at the other end. Magalotti estimated that in the 20 miles between Gravesend and

London Bridge there were more than 1,400 ships, 'not counting the other smaller ships and boats, almost without number, which are passing and repassing incessantly, and with which the river is covered'; and upstream there were '10,000 small boats' between Windsor and the Bridge.

Consider these smaller boats for a moment. Imagine yourself in a long, full skirt, and stays that prevent you from bending. It is low tide. The water has receded, leaving an expanse of stinking black mud. 'Stairs' or jetties (in the modern sense) take care of that: you advance down one until you can step into the boat. But has anyone washed the mud off the jetty? I doubt it; watermen are a surly lot. Trying not to slip, and holding up your skirts as best you can, you step into the boat. Perhaps, shall we say, you are no light weight. The boat rocks alarmingly. Accustomed to this – as you must be – you walk carefully to the passenger bench. There are only about 4 to 6 inches of freeboard. You sit down. Here, my admiration for seventeenth-century ladies knows no bounds. How do you sit down, with no rail to hold on to, in a long skirt which you are trying to keep out of the filthy bilge, wearing a rigid corset down to your navel, and perhaps troubled with a touch of what we now call arthritis? Worse still, how do you stand up again?

More dignified terms, from John Evelyn: 'What fractions and confusions our ugly stairs bridges and causeways make and how dirty and nasty it is at every ebb [tide] ... so as next to the hellish smoke of the town there is nothing doubtless which does more impair the health of [London's] citizens.'[13] River noises and river smells must have been a constant background to life in London.

By land

The choice was between braving the cobbles on foot or on horseback, or taking a chair, a hackney coach or, for the favoured few, a private carriage. Samuel thought nothing of walking from Seething Lane to Marylebone and back, or to Gray's Inn and on to Islington, as a summer treat, or from Greenwich down to Woolwich, 'staying several times to listen to the nightingales'. At night, with or without street lighting, boys carrying 'links' (long sticks with wax-impregnated wadding at one end) could be hired, to light the way and perhaps serve as a bodyguard. But there was always a fear that they might be in league with criminals,[14] so some people preferred to buy a link to carry themselves.[15]

Horses could be hired from livery stables. Samuel did not own a horse himself. He borrowed a 'stone-horse' (stallion) one day, and rode it to Hyde Park; which was all very well until it 'began to fight with other horses, to the endangering him and myself'.[16] If there were many stallions in the throng of London traffic, equine battles must have been terrifying. Women rode side-saddle, or pillion – that is, behind the rider with both legs together on one side of the horse, like sitting on an ambulant armchair, steadied by one arm round the rider, which must have been extraordinarily uncomfortable after a while. When Samuel and Elizabeth decided to go for a country outing one day, he hired a mare and a side-saddle for her.[17]

Sedan chairs had the great merit, for invalids and finely dressed women, of conveying their passengers from their own rooms to that of their physician or host, without exposing them to the outside air.[18] As Randle Holme put it, 'this is a thing in which sick or crazy persons are carried abroad, which is born up by the staves by two lusty men'. They could be booked in advance or hired from a rank.

Hackney coaches (or carriages – the terms seem to have been interchangeable) had been available since 1625, when Captain Busby set himself up with four coaches, at the Maypole in the Strand. They were licensed to ply for trade from fixed stands. An Act of 1662 provided that only 400 licences could be in issue at any one time.[19] It also laid down the rates – and the penalty for 'exacting more'. The coachman could charge 18d for the first hour and 12d thereafter, with a daily maximum of 10s. To go from the Inns of Court west to St James or Westminster, or east as far as the Royal Exchange, cost 12d; further east as far as the Tower was another 6d.[20] A licence cost £5 and was a valuable commodity, since it was granted for life, and sometimes even for the life of a surviving widow.[21]

A hackney could hold up to six people, and Samuel seems to have used them as frequently as a modern businessman uses a taxi. But they had their disadvantages. The only way of shutting out bad weather was a blind made of leather or pierced metal, which made the interior dark (Samuel on occasion found this convenient); and after the Plague there was a perceived, and real, danger of infection from sufferers who had been carried in them. Hackney coachmen were notoriously unmannerly; so much so that in 1662 the Lord Mayor ordered the City constables 'to be always personally ready

... to suppress disorders in the City arising from hackney coachmen ... who by their rudeness and insolent behaviour to persons of quality riding or walking through the City, compel them to trade in the suburbs' – to the loss of the City within the walls.[22] John Evelyn described London as 'pestered with hackney-coaches and insolent carremen'.[23]

The most elegant, ostentatious, extravagant way of getting about London was by private coach. Here was a splendid opportunity for conspicuous consumption. There were many niceties only to be appreciated by the *cognoscenti*. For instance, the coachman of a countess was obliged to drive bare-headed, come rain or shine: to make his mistress's rank unmistakable to *hoi polloi*, a bald-headed man was preferred, his scalp gleaming wetly in the rain.[24] London roads were so pot-holed that the leather straps that secured the body of the coach on to its chassis were loosely slung, to give some primitive shock-absorbing – and produce *mal de mer* in the sensitive. The ironshod wheels might also be padded. Nevertheless coaches were hardly comfortable, or even safe: 'The King going to a play ... this afternoone, had his coach overturned ... but blessed be God had no hurt. The leathers whereby the coach hung, broake, and so the coach fell from the wheels.'[25] The windows of up-to-date models were made of glass – hence they were called 'glass coaches'. Coaches could be hired for about 5s a day.[26]

Almost at the end of the *Diary* period, Samuel achieved his ambition to own a coach of his own, instead of borrowing from his friends or being ashamed to be seen in a hackney. It cost him £53 – £13 more than it has been estimated was needed to maintain a middle-class lifestyle for a year.[27] If there exists a stony-hearted reader of his *Diary* who for any reason disapproves of Samuel, even his heart must be melted by Samuel's pride when he and Elizabeth, in their best clothes, set out in their new yellow-varnished coach,

> with our new liveries of serge [for the coachman and boy] and the horses' manes and tails tied with red ribbon and the standards thus gilt with varnish and all clean, and green raynes, that people did mightily look upon us; and the truth is, that I did not see any coach more pretty or more gay than ours all the day.[28]

But even private coaches were not exempt from the curse of modern cities – traffic jams. In 1661, while parliament was sitting and London was unusually full, Samuel was held up in a hackney coach for an hour and a half.[29] Five years later, he gave up after half an hour and did some shopping instead.[30] We are comparatively free of another nuisance: in poor districts, gangs of children whacked horses, 'by reason of which they sometimes cast their riders, to the hazard or loss of their lives or limbs: or else they shall be throwing of dirt or stones into the coaches, or at the [window] glasses'[31] – and the glass was not safety glass.

Travel out of London could be by the regular carrier's cart, or by public coach, or by hired or privately owned horses, or by post-horses and post-coaches. Planning a journey was more complicated than now: for instance, how far away was the destination? The almanac writers gave the distances from London to Edinburgh, Oxford and York as 328, 47 and 150 miles; nowadays they are usually reckoned to be 378, 57 and 193 miles, measuring from city centre to city centre. Only in 1674 was a 'description of England ... undertaken by the express command of King Charles II' and published by that indefatigable map-maker, Ogilby, 'in a large volume in folio'. The pocket edition followed in 1699. York turned out, with most admirable accuracy, to be 192 miles from London.

Mr Ogilby gave the prospective traveller a running description of the way. For instance, for Huntingdon you would take the 'Barwick' (Berwick) road; points to watch for were 'an easy ascent of 4 furlongs called Sandford Hill [now Stamford Hill] often frequented by high-way men' and a gibbet on the right, from which you would do well to avert your eyes, and nose, and turn the other way, to catch a glimpse of 'Theobalds, the King's house, pleasantly seated on the left'. You would miss Amwell, the source of the New River, by 20 furlongs, but you might be inclined to pause at Ware, 'much talked of for its great bed'.

Without Mr Ogilby's maps, the traveller could rely either on Providence, as Parson Josselin did – 'two mercies god afforded us, safety and protection on the road, conveniences and quiet at our inns' – or take a guide; who, as so often happens to intrepid voyagers in places unknown, might or might not know the way. Samuel wanted to avoid going through the Forest of Bere on his way to Portsmouth, but the countryman he hired to take him by the Havant road 'carried us much out of the way'.[32] Even for nearby places such as Chatham and Dartford, Samuel took a guide.[33] After all, there was no map, and without local knowledge the rare signposts would be of little use.

The system of post-horses and post-coaches was set up as part of the centralised postal system. The local postmaster had to have ready horses and 'furniture' (saddles and harness) to hire to anyone 'riding in post by commission, or without'. The charge was 3d per horse per mile, and 4d for the (obligatory) guide, who brought the horses back at the end of the stage. If the postmaster could not provide horses 'within the space of one half hour after demand', the impatient traveller was allowed – indeed compelled – to find them himself, if he could. He was let off the penalty that he otherwise risked, for setting up in competition with His Majesty's mail.[34]

Samuel gives some times for various trips:

Deal to London, two days; including Gravesend to the Temple by water.

London to Dartford, 2 hours.

Cambridge to London, a long day's ride.

London to Rochester, 3 a.m. to 10 a.m.

London to Epsom by coach, 5 a.m. to 8 a.m.

The usual distance a coach travelled in an eight-hour day was about 30 miles. 'Flying coaches' to Chester, Oxford and Cambridge went no faster, but delivered their exhausted passengers the same day, after twelve to fourteen hours of being jolted and shaken.[35] Samuel survived a *seventeen-hour* journey to Cambridge. As a safety measure, glass windows in a private coach were taken out and replaced by canvas screens before a country journey.[36]

The state of the road might vary from choking dust in summer to glutinous mud in winter. Despite Mr Ogilby's explicit directions, few highways were more than open spaces over which there was a legal right to pass and repass. Anyone who has tried to enjoy a country walk where the footpath is also a bridleway may be able to imagine winter conditions. On a trip to Wisbech, in the middle of the Fens, Samuel's horse sank 'to the belly'.

The joys of travel were summed up in Samuel's laconic entry: 'Up finding our beds good but we lousy'.

Londoners did not view the countryside with much favour. Those who had inherited or acquired a country property escaped to it in the malodorous London summers, or banished their wives there to do them good, while themselves enjoying a bachelor life in London. After Samuel inherited a modest family property in Brampton, near Huntington, he despatched Elizabeth there every summer. Predictably, she, who had never lived in the country in her life, hated it, and managed to upset everyone within sight. Not for her, Hannah Wolley's advice to 'those who are too remote in the country' to 'let them acquaint themselves (if they can) with some prudent person who is frequently at Court which is the source and foundation of fashions'.[37] Elizabeth would have endorsed a later poem:

> Then melancholy crows the cock
> And dull is the sound of the village clock.
> The leaden hours pass slow away;
> Thus yawning mortals spend the day.
> If these are comforts for a wife,
> Defend, defend me from a country life.[38]

By letter

The 'Royal Mail' meant what it said: from 1662, carrying letters was a monopoly reserved to the King. His Postmaster-General tried – sometimes unsuccessfully, as in the case of the (mostly) retired highwayman/postmaster at Harwich[39] – to employ only honest persons who were loyal to the regime. They regularly opened and reported on suspect correspondence, 'therefore the disaffected send their letters other ways',[40] such as by 'private foot-posts, stage-coaches, carriers, etcetera'.

The Society of Friends must have had a well-organised private postal system, since 'the posts were so laid for the searching of letters that none could pass unsearched',[41] and yet their meetings, which were forbidden by law, were always known to the Friends in advance. This was not strictly unlawful. The Act had exempted from the King's monopoly 'such letters as shall be sent by coaches, common carriers, carts, waggons and packhorses', and letters 'to be sent to any private friend ... in their ways of journey, ... or by any messenger sent on purpose, concerning the private affairs of any person' – which does not seem to leave a lot.

The days of departure from the chief continental cities and of their arrival in London 'in periods of from 3 to 25 days' were published. Inland mail left the central General Post Office at 2 a.m., for the principal cities in Scotland, England and Wales.[42] Letters could be left with authorised agents, for delivery to the Central Office. The postmen were supposed to travel at 7 m.p.h. between March and September, 5 m.p.h. in the winter.[43] It was found that they could make better time than horses, which could go faster but only for short distances; and the post 'may better be performed by men exercised in it, by reason footmen can go where horses cannot'.[44] On arrival at the post town, letters were dispatched locally, if not collected by the addressees. There is a whiff of insider dealing in a complaint that a certain merchant 'has had most singular advantages, having had his letters many hours before a general dispatch could be made to all the merchants'.[45]

A merchant in Edinburgh could expect to receive London news within four days, and had ample time to draft his reply to catch the return mail leaving Edinburgh three days later. The Bristol service was slicker: the mail arrived at 7 a.m. on the day after leaving London and the return mail the next day reached London 26 hours later,[46] a turn-round of three days, which compares well with present-day times. The York turn-round was five days. Samuel had news of his mother's last illness by a letter written by his brother in Brampton, Huntingdonshire, the day before.[47] Perhaps his brother just caught the mail, or perhaps the letter was sent 'by a messenger sent on purpose'; not unnaturally, Samuel does not say.

Official mail was carried by the postboy in a separate bag called the 'Packet', which took priority over mere 'bye' letters. Official letters were marked 'Haste, Post, haste for thy life'; and in case the postboy could not read, this stark message was supplemented by a sketch of a gallows with a hanging corpse.[48]

The charge was paid on delivery. It depended, for inland mail, on the number of sheets and the distance: one sheet cost 2d for up to 80 miles, 3d for more than 80 miles. Heavy items such as legal documents were charged by weight. Letters for the continent or the 'dominions beyond the seas' were charged either 'by the letter' (sheet), or by weight. The system covered Italy, France, Switzerland (via Geneva), Germany (via Hamburg, Cologne and Frankfurt), Flanders, Holland and even 'Constantinople, Aleppo, and all parts of Turkey', to which a single sheet could be sent for a shilling, or a packet weighing an ounce for 3s 9d; which does not seem excessive, if it got there. Letters for the dominions overseas had to travel in English-owned and English-manned ships.

Incoming overseas mail had to be posted by the captain, on arrival, to the main Letter Office in London, for onward transmission, even if its destination was just round the corner from the port of arrival.

The exemptions allowed by the 1662 Act were unfortunate, and led to constant complaints. On the one hand, although 'the collection of letters and packets, and the horsing of men, by persons not authorised by the Post Master General are strictly limited [by the Act], yet several carriers, stage coaches and others take upon themselves to collect letters ... in some stages double to what the post brings, by which means the just profits and dues are much impaired'.[49] On the other, the post was so 'uncertain and irregular' that even Crown servants such as naval officers who needed to get a message safely from Chatham to London used an independent contractor, whom the local postmaster roughed up 'with menaces of violence if he made any resistance'. While they were all arguing, the tide was lost.[50] To be fair to the Postmaster-General, the 'uncertainty' of his service may have been exacerbated by another branch of His Majesty's service, the press gangs. 'Most of the postboys on the Kentish road are pressed, so that unless some course be taken, expresses and envoys cannot come or go.'[51]

A pendant to the story of the Post Office. Charles used its profits to fund a handsome pension for his mistress, Lady Castlemaine.[52] Two months after arranging the pension, Charles in his official capacity was 'requesting' from the East India Company a loan of £20,000 for the use of the Navy, because of the 'exigency of his affairs and the difficulty of raising money on credit'.[53] Lady Castlemaine had had remarkably little difficulty in assuring her financial future, but the Navy was a different matter.

PART TWO

THE HUMAN
CONDITION

CHAPTER 6

MEDICINE AND DENTISTRY

Expectation of life

The life expectancy of a baby born in England in the decade 1660–70 was 35 years.[1] But this did not mean that everyone born in 1660 could expect to die in 1695. Of all those babies, about a quarter would die before their tenth birthday, particularly in their first year. Accidents, diseases and epidemics thinned out the survivors. A woman who had married at the usual age of 26, and had come safely through two confinements, would celebrate her thirtieth birthday in 1690. With so many risks behind her, she could look forward to another 30 years: she was exactly middle-aged, although she did not know it. Six years later, the most dangerous decade of her life was behind her; women were four times more likely to die in the first decade of marriage than men.[2] If she lived to see her fortieth birthday, she had 24 years ahead. She had long passed the milestone of 35. If she was the one in ten of her coevals who hung on for another 20 years, she could reasonably expect to see 72. By then the age differential that still applies was in place. There were more old women than old men.

In other words, the length of the course was shorter than ours, but the finishing post had the same habit of receding as the runners approached. As I write, the most recent figures of life expectancy for women (men in brackets) are for the two years 1989–91: at birth, 78.7 (73.2); aged one year, 78.2 (72.9); aged 15, 64.4 (59.1); aged 45, 35.2 (30.5); and aged 65, 17.9 (14.2).

The trouble with the 1660s figures is that they are, perforce, estimates and averages, no matter how brilliant and diligent the scholarship that has calculated them. The figure of 35 is an average, applying to the population as a whole. Comparing the lives of countrymen and Londoners, we may suppose that men and women lived longer in the country than their contemporaries in crowded, dirty London.

The logical reader will by now have spotted that, just as the ranks of 1660 babies thinned over the years, the knees they sat on belonged to survivors of past decades, so that the whole equation should be repeated, to see how many survivors there were in 1660, and how old they were likely to be. Quite right; but I will only add to this already complicated picture that the expectation of life at birth during the whole of the previous century had been slightly higher, and leave logical readers to play with the figures as they like.

Medical treatments

What do you do when you hurt yourself, or feel ill? Do you leave well alone? Or touch wood and cross your fingers? Or consult your mother, or someone else in whose advice you have faith? Or go to a doctor?

Leaving well alone has a lot to be said for it. It can even be said in Latin: *vis mediatrix naturae*, the healing strength of nature.

Sir Kenelm Digby's weapon salve, or sympathetic powder, belongs here, although he would have regarded this as an outrageous misclassification. In 1658 he gave a lecture at the University of Montpellier (England not being comfortable for Royalists at the time), describing an infallible remedy for wounds: take the sword that inflicted the wound, and treat it with an elaborately compounded salve. The ingredients included moss from the skull of an unburied man – 'there is great quantity of it in Ireland'. Meanwhile, just keep the wound covered with a clean linen cloth, and it would soon heal. It may well have done. The ministrations to the sword at a distance deflected attention, and bacteria, from the wound, leaving the healing strength of nature to operate undisturbed.[3] Sir Kenelm's 'sympathetical powder, prepared by Promethian fire' was later advertised as not only curing 'all green wounds that come within the compass of a remedy' – a careful limitation of liability – but

78

'also the tooth-ache infallibly',[4] which does somewhat erode one's faith in its power.

Magic and superstition

Samuel, the bastion of the Royal Navy and organiser of the Civil Service, wore a hare's foot round his neck to ward off colic – not that it did. Elias Ashmole put his faith in three spiders, to avoid the plague.[5] 'We commonly see the toothache, gout, falling sickness, biting of a mad dog and many such maladies cured by spells, words, characters and charms', wrote Robert Burton in his *Anatomy of Melancholy* in 1628. Spells, words, characters (especially 'Egyptian' ones, i.e. hieroglyphs, news of which had been filtering through to Europe since the early sixteenth century) and charms did not lose what power they had in the next 40 years.

One example of magic healing was bound up with Restoration politics: Charles II's divine gift of healing the King's Evil by 'touching'. Robert Herrick probably spoke for many, in his poem 'to the King, to cure the Evil', although it is just possible that some of his fervour may have been induced by a desire to stand well with the authorities, so excessive seems his sentiment to our unbelieving eyes:

> ... O! lay that hand on me,
> Adored Ceasar! and my faith is such,
> I shall be heal'd, if that my KING but touch.
> The Evill is not yours: my sorrow sings,
> Mine is the Evill, but the cure, the KINGS.

All Charles's predecessors had Touched, right back to holy Edward the Confessor. It had been the sole function of royalty that Charles had been able to exercise during the long and impoverished years of waiting. No sooner was he at last settled on the throne than the queue for Touching began.[6] By the end of July 1660 – a mere two months after his return – *Mercurius Publicus* reported the system: 'His Majesty since his return having touch'd for the Evil near 1700 persons, and there being at present above 1000 more in London come from several parts attending for the same, His Majesty is graciously pleased to dispatch all that are already come, and ... to defer the rest to a more reasonable opportunity.' Patients were to go to 'Mr Knight His Majesty's chirurgeon who lives in Bridges

Street at the sign of the Hare in Covent Garden on Tuesday and Thursday next ... when they will receive tickets for the Wednesday and Friday, which two days His Majesty is pleased to set apart for this so pious and charitable work.' When the system was running smoothly Charles achieved the staggering throughput of 4,000 a year. In March 1667 the *London Gazette* announced that 'by reason of the great heats that are growing on, there will be no more Touching for the EVIL till Michaelmas next; and accordingly all persons concerned are to forbear their Addresses until that time'.

Most of the patients suffered from scrofula (tuberculosis of the lymph nodes in the neck, often attributable to milk from cows infected with bovine tuberculosis) but many hopefuls in the queue displayed other miscellaneous symptoms.[7] The process was regarded as a normal part of medical resources: 'as the Doctor says that [my son] will not be better until he has the King's touch again, I want to know when I shall bring him for that purpose'.[8] This hopeful parent may have been unlucky. Application through the usual channels had to be accompanied by a certificate (not yet in triplicate) from the sufferer's minister and churchwardens that this was his first time round. 'Certain persons (too many one would think) who having the Kings-Evil and have been touched by His Sacred Majesty, have yet the Forhead [cheek? brass neck?] to come twice or thrice.'[9] In London, the Banqueting Hall was used. If Charles was out of London on a Wednesday or Friday – for instance for the racing – he still gave up his time. Here is Magalotti's account of a session he watched in Newmarket:

> As soon as [Charles] appeared the two assistant ministers [i.e. officiating parsons] dressed in their surplices began the prayers [in the Book of Common Prayer: omitted from modern editions] with a great appearance of devotion ... [Charles having taken his seat and the invocations having been read,] His Majesty began the ceremony of touching the patients in the part affected. These were conducted into the King's presence, one at a time and as they knelt before him he touched them with both his hands ... [After more prayers, during which the King remained seated, and was probably given a chance to wash his hands,] the diseased came again in the same order as before, to His Majesty, who put round their necks a ribbon of an azure colour, from which was suspended a medallion of gold, stamped in his own image.

In 1662–3 one of the Crown's expenses totted up by the Commons was £5,000 'angel-gold (for the King's Evil)'; which was more than Prince Rupert got, or the 'Secretaries of State and Intelligence', both together.[10]

There were some successes, and Charles perhaps showed a side of his nature which was not much publicised. In 1662 he was reported as displaying his 'heavenly and meek disposition' – it has to be admitted that this sounds more like his father than Old Rowley[11] – and touched 'a child of 7 years old ... having been long blind by the King's Evil ... and immediately after by the mercies of God had her eyes opened for as she there plainly beheld His Majesty washing his hands in the bason'.[12]

Another remarkable cure was recorded by Elias Ashmole. He had refused to arrange for a Welshman called Arise Evans to have a place in the queue, so Arise, who had something very wrong with his nose, made his own plans. He stationed himself in St James's Park, on Charles's probable route. It paid off. 'The King coming at him', recounts Ashmole,

> he kneels down and cries God Bless Your Majesty. The good King gives him his hand to kiss, and he rubbing his ulcerated and scabby Nose therewith, which was plentifully stockt with purulent and fetid matter: within 2 days after his reception of his sacred Majesty's favour, I saw this Evans cured, and his ulcerated nose dryed up and healed.[13]

Ashmole did not record Charles's reaction. As *Mercurius Publicus* put it, 'by the Grace of God he hath in an extraordinary measure had good success'.

The French kings Touched too. Five days before Charles's triumphant return, Louis 'stroked about 1,200 sick folks' in a French monastery garden.[14] But patriotic Englishmen should ignore this pretension. As a contemporary almanac writer put it:

> All lawful monarchs, God's viceregents are
> And by his Princely Patent govern here;
> But all have not an equal grant from Heaven.
> The Cure o' th' Evil to Britain's Monarch's given!
> Whose royal touch hath healed our leprous land,
> 'Tis therefore TREASON not t'obey's command.[15]

– the general idea being that our monarch could do things that other mere continental monarchs could not.

The trouble with Touching as evidence of Charles's divine authority to occupy the throne was that he was not unique. Other people could do it too, and commoners at that, in particular an Irishman called Valentine Greatrex or Greatrakes.[16] He Touched hundreds, including Flamsteed, the Royal Astronomer, and notched up several successes, possibly due to his insistence that only a clean linen cloth (again) should be applied to the infected site. Charles was so intrigued by Greatrex that he invited him to Court in 1666 to demonstrate his powers. Greatrex did not do well under his rival's cynical gaze, so he went home to Ireland.

Non-qualified advisers

A quick reference to an almanac might be instructive. Remedies for the most usual ills were given, sometimes with a helpful address at which to buy, for example, 'LOCKIER's Universal PILL curing any disease curable by physick ... sold by H Brougis a printer next to the Red Lyon Inn'.

There were all too many quacks and 'wise women' about. There was 'scarce a pissing-place about the City' where their services were not advertised.[17] Failing that, hand bills could be consulted on street corners and door posts and even – a favourite place – the Smithfield gate of St Bartholomew's Hospital. Quacks could be genuinely useful. They would attempt the repair of a hare-lip, which surgeons would not usually touch. They could also diagnose an illness in the patient's absence, solely from his urine, a practice condemned by the College of Physicians as 'piss-pot science', forgetting that they had done exactly the same only a few decades earlier.[18]

'Wise women' had their own herbal remedies, applied with incantations and spells. The latter at least rarely did the patient harm, and the herbal remedies had probably stood the test of time, the more toxic ingredients having been discarded in the light of experience. A wise woman was the first port of call for many pregnant women reluctant to engage the professional and expensive services of a midwife.

Most households had their own store of medicines, and housewives were expected to know how to use them. Family 'receipt' (recipe) books recorded useful tips collected from friends and forebears. Here is one 'to gett away warts: take black snayles and gash and cutt them with your Knife then take the liquor which comes from them and anoynt your warts with this liquor 3 or 4 times every day till

PROFESSIONALS

all bee gon'.[19] Most remedies were based on plants, but snails quite
often made their way in, as did woodlice and worms.[20]

'Conduct books', the Mrs Beetons of their day, enjoyed an
enormous vogue in the seventeenth century. They always included
a section on home nursing and household remedies. Hannah Wolley
largely cornered the market with a series of publications, such as
her *Observations in Physic and Chirurgery*. ('For corns, pare your corns
well and then take a black snail and bruise it...')

The earliest book on first aid, 'by which those who live farre from
Physician or Chirurgeon may happily preserve the life of a poor
friend or neighbour until such a man may be had to perfect the
cure', had come out in 1633.[21] It possibly lacked that immediate
practicality so needed in first aid. For instance, a person bitten by a
mad dog should be thrown into the nearest water (with a rope round
him? – surely essential, but not mentioned). When he had swallowed
'a good quantity' he could come out. If he could swim (note:
remember to ask him before throwing him), he should even be held
under, until he had swallowed 'enough' (how much was that?). If he
could not – or even if he could – death by drowning seems more
likely than a cure for hydrophobia.

But if none of these sources of help sufficed, professional help had
to be sought.

Professionals

Physicians

London was well provided with qualified physicians. Their status
was unquestioned. There was even an English physician, Dr Collins,
in residence at the Russian court, as physician to the Emperor.[22]
They had mostly studied in Europe; the medical sciences as taught
in Oxbridge would not pass muster in a twentieth-century medical
faculty. Qualification could be obtained without arduous study:
Caen, for instance, had no medical faculty, but it would provide a
medical degree if the price was right.[23]

The 'art' of a physician was 'noble ... since we know our blessed
Saviour to have cured the sick', wrote Henry Peacham, anxiously
differentiating the men who could pretend to nobility, from plebs
such as 'common chirurgeons, mountebanks, unlettered empirics,

and women doctors (of whom for the most part there is more danger than of the worst disease itself)'.[24]

Medical skill is one of the most difficult areas of seventeenth-century life to assess. We nowadays take for granted that there will be a cure – a drug, an operation, a course of treatment – that will remedy whatever has induced us to go to the doctor. We know at the back of our minds that some maladies are incurable even now, but we close our eyes to the possibility of our illness being one of them until we must believe it. We forget that the huge advances which enable the privileged western world to expect health and long life began only a century ago, accelerating in the last 50 years. Before then, all that could be done in most cases was to help the patient to defend himself against the attacking disease.

The work of 'natural philosophers' (we would use the word 'scientists'), such as Harvey on the circulation of the blood and Vesalius on the brain, must have interested physicians and others who liked to be aware of current scientific thought, but it had no immediate relevance to medical practice. So the blood was pumped round the body by the heart instead of being drawn round it by the moon: how was that knowledge to help a seventeenth-century physician examining someone with swollen ankles and shortness of breath? The advances in theoretical knowledge had not yet filtered down to the practical physician.

The habit of close, careful, direct observation was by no means unique to Harvey. Many clinical descriptions by seventeeth-century physicians could hardly be bettered now; but modern pathology, with its panoply of laboratories and equipment, was not available to them. All they could do was to apply the old, well-tried wisdom passed down to them from the ancient Greeks, via a detour through the Arab world during the Christian Dark Ages.

So, after this portentous but necessary introduction, let us look at medical practice in London in the decade 1660–70.

The theory of 'humours', entrenched in medical thought, derived from the Greek idea of balance. There were four vital forces in the body: blood, phlegm, black bile and yellow bile. If one of them got out of kilter, it had to be rebalanced, like a central heating system being rebalanced by a plumber.

The best way to do this was to draw off some of the unwanted element (bleeding a radiator) by bleeding the patient, or draining his system in other ways, such as by making him vomit or sneeze or spit, or giving him a 'purge' (laxative) or 'clyster' (enema). Matter could be made to exude from purpose-made cuts or ulcers kept open by 'tents' or 'setons'. Anthony Wood had a seton on his leg for several years, to treat his attacks of ague. It got rather messy in the end; 'too much of the humour issued out'.[25]

Another way of producing this desirable result was to apply irritant ointment such as cantharides, to produce blisters. Anthony Wood's mother, who had gone to her doctor with a pain in her hip, died in agony from the huge cantharides plaster he slapped on to the painful place.[26] Another way of producing blisters was to heat small cups and upend them quickly on to the patient's back or scalp ('cupping'). Either way, the blisters were pierced and kept open to let the noxious matter out.

All these expedients had the merits of visible, fee-earning action by the physician, and impressive reaction by the patient. If, nevertheless, the sufferer recovered, his return to health was attributed to the physician's 'cure' (then having its primary meaning of 'care'). Poor Charles II, dying of a stroke and kidney failure, had to suffer bleeding and enemas, cantharides on his scalp and red-hot irons on his feet, as well as a total of 58 drugs, all in his last five days.[27] The energy of his physicians was much admired in professional circles.

The simple herbal remedies of the Greeks had long ago acquired accretions of weird and wonderful ingredients. The current fashion was polypharmacy. Something in the mixture was almost bound to work. (The logical possibility that something else was almost bound to be toxic was dismissed.)

The official London *Pharmacopoeia* (list of drugs) first came out, in Latin of course, in 1618. It included moss from the skull of a man who had died a violent death; the saliva of a fasting man; and the blood, fat, bile, viscera, bones, claws, sexual organs and excreta of miscellaneous animals, birds and insects.[28] To facilitate the passage of the huge resultant bolus down the patient's throat, and the passage of his fee from the patient to the physician, the pill could be coated in gold; this was thought to make it work better.

Some ingredients were indicated by the 'doctrine of signatures'.[29] When God created the world, he knew exactly what he was doing and wasted no time. Since, axiomatically, man was his most important creature, everything below man in the 'great chain of being' was designed specifically for man's good. Some creatures were obviously good for man, such as his best friends, dogs. The utility of some other things was not so self-evident, but God had kindly left a sign ('signature') on some of them, for man to read. The leaf of *Euphrasia officinalis* (eye-bright) is eye-shaped; therefore it must be good for eyes. Boil it up and slap it on.

As if all this were not enough, astrology played an essential role. If the eye-bright failed to work, it was not, ever, the fault of the physician. Someone had blundered in their astrology.

Every human being is born under a certain conjunction of stars and planets. So far, so good. But it was generally believed that the subsequent movements of those stars and planets influenced that human being throughout his life. And that was only the beginning. Every part of the body, every disease and symptom, and every plant had its own zodiacal sign.[30] Before prescribing, all these permutations had to be worked out.

In 1640 Nicholas Culpeper had set up in practice in Spitalfields, as 'Astrologer and Physician' (note the order). He wrote many books, some published after his death in 1653, and most in circulation up to the nineteenth century. He was determined that people should not be ill needlessly, just because they could not read Latin, or were poor. First he translated the *Pharmacopoeia* into English, to the annoyance of his professional colleagues; then he published his own *Complete Herbal And English* [i.e. written in English] *Physician*, using herbs that could be gathered from the fields, costing nothing. In his shorter *Physick for the Poor* he set out various 'simple' purges, clysters, suppositories (including an ingenious one: a fig turned inside out and anointed with salt and oil), and other medicines to make the patient sweat and urinate and defecate and sneeze and spit – all means of rebalancing the humours. He threw in a few other recommendations. May dew was a good beauty lotion; so was 'the urin of a boy that is sound'. A bull's pizzle would increase seed. Horses' testicles, smoked, and those unfortunate snails, helped in childbirth. Culpeper deplored the cost and impurity of imported opium, and explained how to extract it from 'our own country poppy'. 'Nerves' could be strengthened by lizards, boiled alive.

And so on. Culpeper's recipes are so charming, and the glimpses of him in his writings so charismatic, that we almost swallow everything he says. But he was an astrologer before he was a physician. In his *Herbal* he gave astrology its full weight. For instance, the usual practice was to treat the disease with its 'sympathetic' herb. He recommended standing this already complicated idea on its head, and in some cases – which he did not specify – treating the disease with its opposing herb, astrologically speaking. Not content with that, he changed the rules of affinities. You might well have thought, blindly accepting the traditional authorities, that henbane was a herb of Jupiter. Not so. It grew in 'saturnine' places such as 'where they empty the common Jakes' (latrines), '*ergo* tis a plant of Saturn'. And equally *ergo*, it was good for tinnitus, headaches and swollen scrotum. Similarly, wormwood was under Mars, because it grew in 'martial' places such as forges; therefore (the argument was no doubt clear to him, if not to us) it will 'make a moath scorn to meddle with the cloth' (it keeps moths out of wool) and is a 'powerful agent against the gout and gravel'.

Gout and gravel have a common cause, the precipitation of uric acid. A 'powerful agent' against one would help a case of the other. It may well be that wormwood contains some relevant drug. But, reading Culpeper's *Herbal*, one sometimes has an irreverent feeling that anything that happened to be growing nearby could be boiled up, slapped on or slurped down, and might well do you some good, if the stars were right.

Apothecaries

Apothecaries were under the control of the Royal College of Physicians. They were shopkeepers, not gentlemen as physicians were, but they were sometimes more useful than physicians, if they could produce a remedy that might work without involving the physician's fee. For many people, they fulfilled the function nowadays performed by the general practitioner. As well as diagnosing, they prescribed their own nostrums, or suggested a ready-made medication. The seventeenth century saw a plethora of proprietary medicines that could be bought over the counter. Anderson's Scots Pills, invented in 1635, were still being sold in 1876 as an aid to general well-being and virility. Daffy's Elixir was still going strong in 1929 as a panacea for most ailments and a source of longevity. Simpson's Golden Eye ointment is the oldest 'private' remedy, and (I think) can still be bought today.[31]

The apothecaries provided the ships' surgeons with their chests of medicines and drugs. It is hardly surprising that they asked to be paid in advance for this nationally important service.[32]

Surgeons

Chirurgeons (pronounced 'surgeons') were not, in seventeenth-century terms, gentlemen either (although some of them confused

87

the issue by qualifying as physicians as well). They served a practical seven-year apprenticeship, without attending university. They earned their living by wielding sharp instruments, like their brethren the barbers, with whom they shared a livery company. Not for them the dignity of a royally recognised College.

Yet despite their lack of academic qualification, surgeons could be highly respected. Charles II's surgeon George Moretto successfully petitioned to be allowed to 'erect a stage in both Universities, and in any other place in the kingdom', where he could practise his medical and surgical skills and sell his medicines. (He seems to have combined all three branches of the healing profession.) He annexed testimonials by nine London residents, to 'the wonderful cures of wens [tumours], hare-lips, cancers, blindness etc. performed by George Moretto on his stage at Tower Hill, those for the poor being done for charity'. This public display is not quite what one expects of surgeons, especially royal ones. The mystery is further confused by the endorsement on the petition: 'mountebank'.[33]

The stage presentation seems to have been an accepted way of seeing your medical adviser at work, and assessing his professional skills. In 1667 John Russell, a 'mountebank' and, like Moretto, a practitioner in both physic and surgery, was granted a licence 'to erect a stage in London or elsewhere, to vend his medicines', and two months later Toussaint le Jond, 'operator in physic *and* surgery', was licensed to 'erect a stage or theatre in any town of England or Wales and to vend his balsams and remedies'.[34]

The presence of a surgeon was so vital on board ship that crews would refuse to sail without one. In one battle, the ship's surgeon had already died when the captain suffered such a wound to his arm that he had to be 'dismembered' by an able seaman, whose skill unfortunately did not extend to stopping the bleeding. The captain died anyway.[35] John Woodall, who was appointed surgeon-general to the East India Company in 1612, wrote a famous manual called *The Surgeon's Mate*, published in 1617, covering not only the surgical emergencies that a ship's surgeon was likely to meet, but also the scurvy that bedevilled long voyages. He recommended its treatment with citrus fruit, as had Sir John Hawkins as long ago as 1590.[36] This was, tragically, forgotten for centuries, while humours and blood-letting flourished.

'Cutting for the stone' (lithotomy) was the main curative operation undertaken. Diet may have played a part in the stones and gravel in kidney and bladder, apparently so common in both sexes in the seventeenth century. Current thinking is that the generally high intake of protein, and the adulteration of flour with chalk to whiten it, may have been contributory factors.[37] St Bartholomew's Hospital had appointed a specialist lithotomist as long ago as 1612.

The pain that Samuel suffered from the stone in his bladder must have been totally disabling, to make him decide, at the age of 25, to undergo surgery. The odds were heavily against him, as he must have known. In 1662 another patient 'who is throwing himself on god to be cut of the stone'[38] probably attributed the successful outcome to the day of prayer held for him. Samuel's survival was due to the chance that he was first in that day's list, so the surgeon's instruments, and his hands, were fairly clean, and the kind cousin in whose room the operation was done had undoubtedly scrubbed her table, as any good housewife would. Lithotomists developed a high degree of dexterity. Samuel's stone is thought to have been about the size of a tennis ball, but it was identified, grasped and removed through a 3-inch incision, in 50 seconds at most. Before the invention of anaesthesia, surgeons did not have time for a careful investigation. It was a matter of in and out as fast as possible; but most patients died, from a combination of shock and sepsis.

An operation ('couching') to ameliorate the effect of a cataract where the lens of the eye (the 'apple') has become opaque has been carried out for many centuries, but it was limited to displacing the lens downwards, still within the eyeball. The patient could see, after a fashion, and certainly better than before the operation, and he would be prescribed pebble spectacles.

Trepanning was also done. It involved taking a disc one or two inches in diameter out of the skull, to release cranial pressure caused by advanced syphilis, accidental trauma or a brain tumour. Prince Rupert had it done twice, in 1667,[39] which 'gave him present [immediate] ease by letting out a great deal of corrupt matter'; he lived another fifteen years. The operation sounds fearsome to a layperson, yet it was done by the ancient Egyptians and the aboriginals of North America. (Skulls in the Museum of Science dating from Neanderthal times show successive holes in the same skull; its owner must have survived the earliest.)

A visible breast cancer could be excised, but the patient usually died. A baby might be delivered by Caesarian section if the mother was likely to die anyway. Internal growths and malfunctions had to be endured, with or without opium and other painkillers, until death supervened.

The absence of modern anaesthesia did not necessarily mean that Samuel was fully conscious as the surgeon made the incision from anus to scrotum. Alcohol could dull the senses. Opium could produce a loss of consciousness. It could also produce death, if the surgeon had a heavy hand or the patient had an idiosyncratic reaction.

Or the patient may have simply gritted his teeth, as in the following description of a lithotomy (translated from the French), which Marin Marais (1656–1737) set to appropriate music:

> The appearance of the apparatus –
> Shuddering at the sight of it –
> Resolving to climb on to it –
> Climbing on to it –
> Descending again.
> Solemn thoughts...
> Securing of the arms and legs with silken cords.
> Now the incision is made –
> The pincers are inserted,
> Now the stone is pulled out,
> Now the voice dies away to a croak.
> Flowing blood...
> Now the cords are removed.
> Now one is carried to bed.[40]

Hospitals[41]

Imagine a city institution caring for the sick. It has far more administrators than medical staff. It is chronically underfunded. It is a teaching hospital, with a waiting list for admissions, and outpatients' clinics where patients wait to see specialist or general consultants, and a system of paperwork. The nursing staff are distinguishable by their blue uniforms. There is an effective outreach department.

This is not a description of a modern hospital, but St Bartholomew's Hospital in the decade 1660–70. The only element I have omitted, misleadingly, is that St Bart's patients then had to produce proof that as well as being sick they were poor.

'The House of the Poor, commonly known as St Bartholomew's hospital in the City of London, of the Foundation of King Henry VIII', to give it its full title, was a survivor of Henry's dissolution of the monasteries (see page 21). He had handed it over to the City in 1547, with most of its medieval endowments: rent-producing properties in London and elsewhere. The two documents by which he did this served as the hospital's constitution until the inception of the National Health Service in 1946. At first the City Aldermen effectively ran the hospital. Gradually they were superseded by 'Governors', who tended to be non-medical benefactors given this title in gratitude. Fortunately, perhaps, for the hospital they became too numerous to be a useful governing body – by 1683 there were 278 of them – so the running of the hospital was done by a small committee, which met regularly and dealt with the appointment of medical and nursing staff, as well as matters of finance.

There was a staff of two or three general physicians, two or three surgeons, one or two specialists in 'cutting for the stone' (an appointment first made in 1623 and held by various surgeons until 1687 when Lithotomy joined general surgery), and a woman to treat the prevalent 'scald heads' (infantile eczema) and other skin diseases. St Bart's had no obstetric department. Pregnant women were sent to St Thomas's hospital, the other London hospital, which had a lying-in ward.

Venereal cases were sent to one of the outstations, at Kingsland in Hackney or the Lock at Southwark. These had been used as isolation wards for leprosy, along with others at Knightsbridge, Highgate, Hammersmith and Mile End, but leprosy had practically died out by the seventeenth century, so two were retained for the new disease, the Great Pox, and the others were closed. The Kingsland 'foul ward' was in a former chapel, hardly bigger than the average village hall. The Lock (so called from the French loques, or rags used to bind leprous sores, nothing to do with forcibly restraining patients) had the added amenity of a 'hott house for the use and benefitt of the patients there'.[42]

St Barts had fifteen nursing sisters, who wore blue cloth dresses. Since the dissolution they were, of course, laywomen. Their knowledge was gained by experience rather than through any formal teaching, and there seems to have been no age limit for the post. Their duties included fetching the patients' food from the Buttery (distribution point): 'Sisters ... shall personally and not by any patient or deputy fetch the bread and other meal ... [but when] in case of some violent sickness or *infirmity of age* they cannot, [it could be fetched by] such honest patients as the Matron shall appoint.'[43]

The sisters were assisted by 'helpers', sometimes called nurses. This was just as well, because in addition to fetching the patients' food – and, presumably, drink – and feeding those who could not feed themselves, they were responsible for washing the sheets and the patients' linen; and if this were not enough, in their spare time they spun the flax issued by the Matron, to be woven by an outside contractor into linen and returned for making up into sheets for the wards by the sisters and any able-bodied women patients.

The patients' diet would horrify a modern dietician, but was at least sustaining for those poor people. They were entitled, daily, to 12 ounces of bread, 8 ounces of beef or mutton, or butter and cheese, 1 pint of meat broth or porridge, 3 pints of hospital-brewed beer, and an unspecified amount of ale. The lack of fresh vegetables was countered to some extent by the 'scurvy drink' brewed by the nursing staff. In the state of medical knowledge then existing rest, good food and 'tender loving care' probably produced as many cures as could be hoped for. Tlc they certainly got: an applicant for a certain medical post was rigorously questioned as to whether he was prepared to live in, and

> constantly attend the poore in his owne person ... there being an absolute necessity for the same, not only for the due preparing and administration of Phisick to the poore and to assist and help them in their extreammes of sickness which frequently happened to end distempers and cures, but also to provide meat, drink, fireing, lodging, and other necessaryes about the poore, and carefully see distributed att every meale to each patient his quantity and proportion, and to keep alwaies in good order and government the said poore, which cannot be effected without personall attendance, without the daily hazard of the welfare, if not the lives, of the poore patients, hee being the only person ... on whom [the Governors] can rely.

This was too much for the applicant. He promised a deputy if he could not attend, but this was not good enough, and his application was refused, even though he had taken the trouble to get a letter of recommendation from the King.

There were about twelve wards, and a total of 200–300 beds. (This would be consistent with a note in the Calendar of State Papers Domestic in 1667, that 1,383 people had been 'relieved' by St Bartholomew's, 114 buried from the hospital, with 196 at the date of the report 'remaining under care'. Figures for St Thomas's were 1,241, 144 and 255.) Ward rounds, so much a part of life in a teaching hospital nowadays, were conducted by both surgeons and physicians. 'At least three days a week the master surgeons themselves shall come to dress their patients or to stand by and direct' for the benefit of their apprentices. Surgeons were not allowed to operate until their patient had been seen, and the proposed operation approved, by their professional seniors, the physicians.

During the Plague, the Matron, Margaret Blague (whose name deserves commemoration) stayed at her post, unlike the two phys-icians on the staff, who retired to the country. The Governors rewarded her 'for her attendance and constant great paynes about the poore in making them Broths, Caudles and other the like Comfortable things for their accomodacon in theis late Contagious Tymes, wherein she hath adventured herselfe to the great perell of her life'.

The next cataclysm was the Fire. The hospital itself was untouched, just, but much of the City property on which it depended for its income was destroyed leaving it short by £2,000 a year. In an attempt to recoup this, and to help some of its homeless shopkeeper tenants whose liveliehoods had gone, the hospital Gov-ernors built nineteen little (10 feet square) shops, scattered through the hospital grounds. Half the wards were shut, and five sisters dismissed. The temporary planning permission for the shops expired in 1668.[44]

It is hard to assess the seventeenth-century version of that constant of modern hospitals, waiting lists. On one hand, a sick poor person could not hope for admission unless he or she could produce written proof of poverty (like the GP's certificate that may open the door to many welfare benefits). And yet the Governors employed a posse of between six and eight beadles, to scour the streets and bring in any sick they found. Perhaps it worked in the same way as 'elective surgery' and accident and emergency cases work now – the urgent cases are dealt with somehow while the others have to wait.

I have concentrated on the sick poor. The 'middling sort' would be cared for at home, or possibly in the home of a woman who would charge for her services; the equivalent of a private nursing home or hospital today.

Medical risks

Birth and infancy

Many women trusted in the experience and moral support of their female friends and to the local 'wise woman'. To call a midwife took courage. Midwives believed in intervention. They liked to be seen doing something. They also liked to press on, to their next fee-paying patient. If the membrane bag of fluid in which the baby had developed had not broken by the time the midwife arrived, she would put her hand up the mother's vagina and break the membrane with a specially sharpened fingernail, or a sharp-ended thimble, or a thin coin. (At that time, the edges of small coins were not milled, and a used groat was sharp.) Then the baby ought to have begun its journey down the vagina. If it delayed, it was assisted, or impeded, by the midwife, shoving and tugging and meanwhile exhorting the mother to push.

The Chamberlen family (a father and two sons, all physicians) had invented obstetrical forceps in 1647, but they kept their knowledge to themselves. They also evolved a neat metal 'crotchet' about 12 inches long, to help in the removal of a dead foetus from the mother's womb. Both these instruments decreased the occasion for the midwife to use her hands, and may have been more efficient. The Chamberlens' unprofessional selfishness with their forceps (it was found many years later, hidden under the floor of their house) has assured them a place in medical annals, unjustified statistically by the number of women who benefited from their services.

It was not surprising that premature or delicate babies rarely lived. If only the fittest survived the ordeal of birth, this may go some way towards explaining the stamina that carried most of them through their next few years. Two years after he had published his discovery of the circulation of the blood in 1649, Harvey published *De Generatione Animalium*, in which he blamed high infant mortality on midwives' unnecessary manipulations. In 1687 a midwife estimated that two-thirds of miscarriages, stillbirths and maternal deaths in childbed were due to her colleagues.[45] Nothing, it seemed, would stop them.

Babies were swaddled as soon as they were born. Sometimes the resultant bundle was stiffened with wooden supports.[46] Swaddling has commended itself to many cultures, over many centuries, and the human race has continued; it cannot have been all bad. The

94

bundle was opened up several times a day, and baby and wrappings were washed. That, at least, was the theory. If it was followed, was a swaddled baby much more uncomfortable than today's baby, surrounded by hard, sodden cellulose and clammy synthetics? The baby's movements were restricted; but, again, good practice was to release the wrappings gradually, as the baby grew. Many babies had rickets, and support was often thought to be necessary for that reason alone.

Babies acquired some immunity to surrounding germs through the placenta, and would have acquired more from the colostrum that preceded their mothers' milk. But colostrum was rejected as 'witch's milk',[47] and in any case many babies were given to another woman to breast-feed. Since she was already lactating, her nursling never got this purpose-made immunisation.

Any immunity that a baby did inherit from its mother was directed to the germs in her environment. Here, again, good intentions went astray, like colostrum. Fond parents who could afford it sent their babies off to wet-nurses in the country, away from dirty, smoky London. But the babies' immunity did not avail them against the germs waiting for them in raw country winters, and they sickened and died.[48] Teething was a major cause of infant death. A well-meaning adult would take pity on a crying baby and lance its sore gums with her fingernail, or the ubiquitous coin, and wonder why it caught fever.[49]

Childhood

For those who survived babyhood, a host of childhood illnesses lay in wait: measles, mumps, whooping-cough, scarlet fever, German measles, diphtheria, meningitis, erysipelas and miscellaneous 'fevers', including typhus.

Rickets, sadly recurring nowadays, had emerged, or been identified, in the previous century. It rarely killed, but it caused misshapen spines and legs, and narrow pelvises that would later bring trouble in pregnancy. Culpeper, for all his astrological crankiness, wrote a treatise on rickets that was a curious mixture of acute clinical observation and − rubbish. He correctly described its outwardly visible signs, but attributed its cause to the 'stupefaction of the spirit' of the parents, who may have further contributed to their offspring's fate by masturbating. He noticed that 'parents that are more strong and lusty and accustomed to labour' seldom have 'rachitic' (rickety) children. He suggested that this might be due to the 'coarse cloths and woolly integuments' that poor babies were wrapped in, which made them scratch and bring the blood to the skin, whereas rich babies lay quietly in 'soft linen cloths'. He had observed accurately, but misinterpreted his observation. The children of poor parents such as farm labourers probably spent more of their time in the open air than pampered rich children, and so suffered less from that combination of lack of sunshine and of Vitamin D which conduces to rickets.

Culpeper prescribed the usual depressing list of vomits and purges, but at least he advised that they should be 'gentle' and 'lenitive'. He did not positively discourage the standard treatment, which was 'scarification of the veins in the hollow of the ear', two or three times a week. He merely doubted its effectiveness. He recommended that it should be done if at all, with an 'instrument or sharp pen-knife', rather than the 'ordinary blunt knife' used by his fellow-practitioners, who took 'no notice of the pain and crying of the child'.

Women

Girls began to menstruate (menarche) between fifteen and seventeen.[50] Adolescent anaemia ('green sickness') had to wait until they married, when the regular injections of semen to which they would then be entitled would cure them. Unfortunately the 1660s were a peak period for young men to leave England for the colonies; as many as 25 per cent of women never married.

It was important that menstruation should be regular, otherwise the humours would get out of balance. Men could sweat to expel impurities, but since women's humours were cold and watery, they could not sweat, so they menstruated instead.[51] If menstruation stopped, for any reason except pregnancy, the body would become a putrifying sink of humours, and the blocked-up blood would go to the head and cause melancholy. (It is interesting that one of the methods of treating this unnerving state of affairs was by a pessary soaked in the appropriate medicament. One more step and they would have had tampons. Perhaps some brave, unrecorded women did.) A menstruating woman was wise to stay at home; otherwise she ran the risk of turning wine sour and sugar black, and making pickled meat go rancid.[52]

There was no effective contraception available to women. Men might use prophylactic sheaths made of sheep's intestines, or leather, or even linen tied on with ribbon, but only to protect themselves against disease, not to protect their partner against conceiving. As Mme de Sévigné put it, sheaths were 'an armour against enjoyment and a cobweb against danger'. An inference can be drawn, from the small number of children in the average family, that some means of family limitation was used, presumably *coitus interruptus*,[53] or that almost forgotten means, abstinence.[54] A woman would be most fertile from 16 to 26, but the average woman passed those years unmarried and probably virgin. By the time she was 26, and married, her fertility was reduced not only by her age, but also by constant subclinical and more serious infections and, perhaps, by the infusion of lead from pewter dishes and water-pipes.[55]

Abortion might be procured by the skill of a 'wise woman', or self-medication, using the herbs which Culpeper and others advised pregnant women *not* to take, or those recommended to 'bring down the courses'. Randle Holme listed several 'whores physics' used to procure abortions. (Recently an Italian woman died of an overdose of parsley, which she had taken as an abortifacient.)[56]

Childbirth was a dangerous time for mothers, as well as babies. We left the midwife at the mother's bed, just after the baby had been born. Now she can get on to her next patient, but there is one more thing to be seen to: the afterbirth (placenta) must not stay inside the mother. Normally it is expelled as part of the natural process, but that could involve a short wait. So once again, the midwife intervened, reaching into the weary mother's vagina and pulling. Acute inversion of the uterus is fatal.

Puerperal fever was studied, understood and, largely, prevented only in the nineteenth century. In its heyday, it wiped out a quarter of the mothers giving birth in the world's biggest maternity hospital, in Vienna. Keen medical students dashed from post-mortem examinations in the morgue, across the corridor, and into the maternity ward, for their next lecture. The occupant of the first bed they stopped at, by the door, usually caught the fever and died.[57] Figures of maternal mortality from this or other causes are not available for the seventeenth century; but there is no reason to doubt that the midwife's dirty hands, grubbing about inside the mother's body, produced the same fatal result as the Viennese students before they paused to wash thoroughly between morgue and ward.

The menopause, at about 50,[58] was thought of as the beginning of old age. The few women who survived so long no doubt suffered from that post-menopausal growth of facial hair, and skin blemishes, well known to be part of the normal appearance of witches. They were also prone to thinning of the bones (osteoporosis). If they fell and broke their hips, there was no miraculous hip replacement operation. They probably died.

Men

Male exterior plumbing and other arrangements have always been envied by girls, resentfully contemplating the inconvenience of menstruation from menarche to menopause. But if the number of remedies in *Herbals* is any indication of the frequency of the complaint, 'pain in the cods' and swelling of the scrotum were common male afflictions. Serious prostate troubles tend to occur after the age of 60, not before. Not many men lived to that age. Few seventeenth-century medical textbooks mention prostatitis.

The female hormone oestrogen endows pre-menopausal women with some degree of protection from hardening of the arteries and associated problems. No preventive or palliative medicine was available to men.

'The great pox' (syphilis: the name came later) was thought of as primarily a male problem. Although an alternative view attributes it, like so many things, to the Crusaders' experience of the Near East, it had probably arrived in the western hemisphere towards the end of the fifteenth century from Haiti, where Columbus's men had gone down with it like ninepins: a *quid pro quo* for the smallpox and measles they distributed. By 1494 the pox had reached Naples. So, too, had the French King's multinational army, encamped round the city. When the siege was lifted, the soldiers laid the Neapolitan whores and then limped home through Europe, scattering spirochetes as they went. Each nation on their route blamed another. For the French, it was the Neapolitan Disease, for the English, the French Pox; for the Turks, the Christian Disease; and for the Chinese, the Ulcers of Canton, where the Portuguese had a settlement – an interesting example of world-wide xenophobia.

The treatment was daunting. The first symptom was a small ulcer or chancre on the penis. Three to six weeks later, when the unwise copulation was forgotten, the secondary stage announced itself with rashes and open sores. This all-too-evident stage was treated, with some success, with mercury, which had been the standard treatment for skin diseases for centuries before syphilis arrived.

Randle Holme described immersion in a 'doctor's tub ... in this, pockifyed and such diseased persons are for a certain time put into, to stew, not to boyl up to a height but to par-boyl; from which Diseases of *morbus gallicus* [French Pox: at this stage Randle Holme loses his composure], *noli me tangere, miserere mei* etc., and from such a Purgatory, *Libera nos Domine.*' In contrast, Samuel speaks quite casually of a newly married acquaintance who 'is come to use the Tubb; that is, to bathe and sweat himself, and ... his lady is come to use the Tubb too; which [Samuel's informant] takes to be that he hath and hath given her the pox'.

The full treatment involved isolation, semi-starvation, steam baths ('sweats') in mercury vapour, enemas, ointments and pills – all containing mercury. If a little medicine did a little good, how much more good a lot of medicine would do. While the mercury debilitated and deranged the patient, the disease attacked the soft tissues of his nose and palate, and loosened his teeth and hair. At least this encouraged silversmiths to develop their skills, in making false silver noses to cover the gaping holes of the nostrils. In Italy, Tagliacozzi had succeeded in transplanting a flap of skin from the patient's arm to his head, to create a new nose,[59] but that level of skill had not reached England.

If the secondary stage was treated with apparent success, the patient would marry with a good conscience, and beget children. If the disease had not been eradicated, it could still infect his wife, and the children she bore him. And syphilis was not easily beaten. It could lie dormant for decades. As long as 30 years after the unlucky encounter, the tertiary stage might emerge. The sufferer could become paralysed, or mad, or both, for which there was no cure. It has been suggested that 'many of the older and better-class families died out as a result of the indiscretions of boys sowing their wild oats' – and harvesting syphilis.[60]

Gonorrhoea ('clap') had been known in England since the Norman occupation, at least. The Normans called it 'chaudepisse'. It had always been regarded as a passing inconvenience, until up-to-date physicians heard about syphilis, confused the clinical picture, and prescribed for their appalled patients a course of mercury.

Other infectious diseases

Men, women and children – but especially children – encountered three serious risks: smallpox, bubonic plague and tuberculosis ('consumption').

The effects of smallpox ranged from a slight indisposition to death. Queen Elizabeth caught it and survived unscathed – if her portraits are to be believed. Dorothy Osborne, who had rejected so many suitors because she loved William Temple, caught it just before her wedding and went to the altar with a sadly scarred face.[61] Charles caught it during the long wait on the continent, and recovered. His youngest brother, who had ridden into cheering London by his side in 1660, caught it and died. Children were particularly susceptible to smallpox. A little girl who caught it in September 1666

> was in great danger of losing her sight. She was all over her face in one scurf, they running into each other ... About November she went abroad in the house; only lost by the sickness her fair hair on her head and that beautiful complexion God had given her. The Lord supply her soul with the comeliness of his grace ... making her lovely in his sight.[62]

Inevitably, the 'cure' was energetic, including copious bleeding. A contemporary physician, Dr Sydenham, recommended open windows, light bed-clothes and rest, but he was a lone voice crying in the wilderness. The unmistakable scars were common. Perhaps every other passer-by in the street displayed them. They were even, in some circumstances, an advantage; a maid with pockmarks would not inconvenience her employer by catching smallpox again.

Bubonic plague is the most famous of the seventeenth century's tribulations. It was endemic in London. The weekly Bills of Mortality[63] were eagerly read, to see 'in the Plague time how the sickness increased or decreased, so that the rich might judge of the necessity of their removal, and Tradesmen might conjecture what doings they were likely to have',[64] and stock up with plague remedies (all 'infallible' and quite useless), while the poor anticipated a probable, awful, death. There had been four outbreaks in the previous century, the last only 40 years ago. Some people still alive remembered it. Younger people read the ubiquitous almanacs, which listed memorable events including the last two plague epidemics. Almanac readers will have had the advantage of an unusual explanation for the periodic outbreaks: a cosmic fart. 'The pestilence generally derives its natural origin from a Crisis of the Earth whereby it purges itself by expiring those Arsenical Fumes that have been retained so long in her bowels ...'.[65]

Most people attributed the Plague to the wrath of God. Infection began with a flea bite. Common enough, but this flea lived on an infected black rat. The result, after ten days' incubation, could take either of two forms: bubonic, where the lymph glands blew up into 'buboes', often in the groin because the flea had landed on the sufferer's leg; or pneumonic, where the bacillus went directly to the lungs. In the bubonic type, which was prevalent in the 1665 outbreak, death usually occurred within five days after the incubation period, but the sufferer had a 30 per cent chance of recovering, to die of some other germ instead – there were plenty about. In the pneumonic type, he had no chance. He died in three days or less.

The terror of the 1665 outbreak was unforgettably described by Defoe, writing 60 years later, from contemporary records (and infinitely more readably than he wrote about dreary Robinson Crusoe). Samuel described its melancholy advance, week by week. On 16 June he took a hackney coach. It went more and more slowly and finally stopped. The coachman got down and said that he was 'suddenly stroke very sick and almost blind'. 'God have mercy on us all', said Samuel, as he left him to it and got into another coach. Defoe estimated the total mortality in London at 100,000. A contemporary doctor estimated it at twice this. The Bills of Mortality recorded 68,596 deaths from plague, but the notorious unreliability of the Searchers' figures was aggravated in those awful months, by desperate survivors trying to persuade them that the indisposition from which their beloved spouses had just died did not necessitate their own incarceration.

After the 1665 outbreak, black rats, which were not immune to the plague bacillus, were displaced by brown rats, which were; so host rats did not die, scattering their population of infected fleas abroad. The risk of a human contracting plague from an infected rat became minimal. In addition, the Fire burnt out many rats from the City. They never found brick and stone houses so comfortable as the old timber ones, with runs and passages through the plaster.

But the most industrious, steadiest destroyer was tuberculosis. If you think of it as a nineteenth-century illness, generally suffered by operatic sopranos and cured in sanatoria, you are wrong. In most years in our period, it was the principal cause of death. Its relentless, debilitating decline was often attributed to witchcraft ('fascination'). It took a brave physician to suggest, in 1664, that it might have other causes, even though he was wide of the mark in identifying those causes as 'touching unhealthy bodies' or 'vapours from sick women'.[66] Culpeper, who had included so many remedies for it in his books, died of it.

Graunt, the founding father of statistics, made some *Observations on the Bills of Mortality*. In the twenty years to 1661, he found the main cause of death to have been consumption (44,500), then 'infants' (32,000), ague and fever (nearly 24,000), plague (over 16,000), 'old age' (nearly 16,000), teething and worms (14,000) and smallpox (10,500). Plague easily headed the league table in 1665, but this was a temporary distortion. After 1665, plague could be forgotten. The proportions, if not the precise figures, of Graunt's other observations remained valid.

Mental illness

It is difficult to assess the incidence of this affliction; it did not receive much publicity. 'Melancholy' had had a whole *Anatomy* written about it 40 years earlier. Burton divided its causes between witchcraft and diet. Peacock flesh and parsnips, for instance, should both be avoided; also celibacy. Who shall say he was wrong?

Women were thought to be prone to a most distressing ailment: a wandering womb, which upset their mental balance – not surprisingly. Even Harvey, the brilliant scientist who discovered the circulation of the blood, believed this. The theory was that the womb actually rose up to the sufferer's head; quite how, through all the intervening structures, was not clearly explained. It is one thing to say, metaphorically, that 'your heart is in your mouth', but quite another to have your fainting fits seriously diagnosed as your womb in your head, or a 'fit of the mother'. That observant clinician Dr Sydenham found that what appeared to be fits of the mother were also experienced by some of his male patients. It was a significant advance in medical thinking when a whole group of mental/psychological illnesses was attributed to hysteria, to which both sexes were prone, instead of blaming an errant female womb. (The word 'hysteria' derives from the Greek word for womb or uterus; the idea of a wandering womb was slow to relax its grip.)

Treatment of mental illness was either by isolation in the bosom of the family (not always a comfortable resort), or a private nursing home,[67] or by incarceration in England's only mental hospital, 'Bedlam' (a contraction of St Mary of Bethlehem), where the inmates furnished an entertaining spectacle to Londoners. In 1667, 22 'lunatics' had been brought in during the preceding year, and 25 had been cured and discharged, leaving 59 still there.[68] ('Lunatic' comes from the Latin word *luna* for the moon, which was thought to influence, or cause, madness.)

Minor ailments

Let us turn to a less sombre topic: Samuel's well-documented constipation. The diet of a prosperous seventeenth-century Londoner was heavy on protein, light on roughage. Result – constipation; treatment – purges and clysters. 'I have taken a purge' was an acceptable excuse for non-attendance at the office. Gout was all too familiar. Circulation-of-the-blood Harvey had practised an unusual cure for his gout: 'he would sit with his legs bare, if it were frost, on the leads of [his brother's] house, put them into a pail of water, till he was almost dead with cold, and betake himself to his stove, and so 'twas gone'.[69] Coughs and colds played their usual obligato, amplified, according to John Evelyn, by the foul smoky atmosphere.

Accidents and industrial diseases

When the only means of assisted locomotion was a four-footed beast of uncertain temper, falling off your horse must have been a common occurrence. Pedestrians suffered from road traffic accidents too. John Evelyn lamented that 'so many of the fair sex and their offspring perished by mischance ... from the ruggedness of the streets'. I cannot believe that men, who were more often out and about than women, went unscathed.

Accidents to women at home, such as scalds and burns, were frequent. Cooking at open fires, in long skirts and trailing sleeves, was second only to childbirth as a cause of death in women.[70]

The risks to people involved in the manufacture of white lead used in paints and glazes were far graver than the risks of absorbing it through the skin as a cosmetic ('ceruse', considered in the next chapter). The Royal Society knew of the risks, but saw no reason to worry.

Lead was an element in pewter. In 1651 Noah Biggs had published *The Vanity of the Craft of Physic*, deploring the use of lead for even the very laboratory equipment used to prepare medicines, let alone the water supply. 'Every kitchen wench' knew that vinegar on pewter produced a white substance 'like ceruse', which caused stomach upsets. But his plea fell on deaf ears,[71] and pewterers continued to die of 'plombism'.

Mercury was used in the manufacture of beaver felt for hats. Despite its role in the treatment of syphilis, it was known to cause insanity – hence the saying 'mad as a hatter'.

There was no climate of opinion compelling employers to look after their workforce. Even if there had been, the normal producer was a family concern which accepted the risks as part of life.

Spas

The health-giving properties of Epsom and its salts had been marketed since 1639, and Epsom was only three hours away by coach. The celebrated wells at Sydenham had been known since 1648. The waters of Streatham spa, discovered in 1650, were known to cure worms and melancholy.[72] A lady who left London for Knaresborough to escape the Plague regretted her flight: 'the first instant we arrived at the nasty Spaw [we] have now began to drinke the horid sulfer water which [is] as bad as is posisable to be imajaned'.[73] The heyday of English spas came later, when Bath blossomed into balls and crescents, but already in July 1669 Sir George Talbot 'arrived at Bath on Monday and [found] the town exceedingly empty and no person of note there ... I use the bath daily, and shall stay until Friday.'[74]

Dentistry

It is just possible that dental health was better in the seventeenth century than in ours. Recommended daily care included scraping away plaque. Sugar was known to cause caries. Sugary snacks had not been invented. If a child's teeth grew in crooked, there was no orthodontist to fit a brace, but at least the enamel was not constantly assaulted by sweet foods and drinks. When caries did occur, it was thought to be due to a worm in the tooth, and an 'operator for the teeth' in the local market or fair would remove the worm and hold it up for inspection by his admiring audience. Meanwhile, oil of cloves was used to deaden the pain; with – of course – bleeding, purges, cupping on the spine and blisters behind the ears. Once extraction became unavoidable – and operators seem to have had a curious reluctance to get in there and pull, unlike midwives – a large pair of pliers should do the trick. But it might still be possible to kill the nerve by cautery, and apply strong acid to make the tooth fall apart on its own.[75]

False teeth could be made of elephant ivory, hippo tusk or ox bone. Hippo tusk had the merit of staying whiter than ivory, which tended to yellow. Implanting teeth from a donor (there was a glut of human teeth on the market after the Plague), or from a less visible site in the patient's own mouth, was practised, with what permanent success is unknown. Instead of implantation, the tooth might be anchored to its neighbours by silver wire, or silk thread. The French were better at false teeth than the English. Even in the previous century their king's morning ritual, conducted in full view of visitors, had included his valet's fastening in 'some things of bone with fine wire to the adjoining teeth on either side'.[76]

Robert Herrick (1591–1674) wrote a short poem on false teeth:

> Glasco had none, but now some teeth has got;
> Which though they furre, will neither ake nor rot.
> Six teeth he has, whereof twice two are known
> Made of a haft, that was a mutton-bone.
> Which not for use, but meerly for the sight,
> He wears all day, and draws those teeth at night.

So Glasco's dental prosthesis was just for show. He could never go out to dinner. Could one eat, in wired teeth? Did the French king manage his formal banquets edentulous? The only possible answer is, it all depended.

Modern Americans bare two magnificent rows of teeth when they smile. Queen Victoria showed one row of small, dingy teeth when, rarely, she was amused. Mona Lisa showed none. Could it be that, when caries and accident caught up with our seventeenth-century ancestors, they kept their mouths shut about it?

CHAPTER 7

CLOTHES, JEWELLERY, COSMETICS, HAIRDRESSING, WASHING AND SO ON

Clothes

You may well think, no difficulty here. Lots of portraits, and a few garments in museums. Why search further?

But: portraits are an admirable guide to the clothes people wore to be painted in, but untrustworthy as to what people actually wore. Samuel hired an Indian gown, for his portrait. Elizabeth got herself up as St Katherine, for hers. Some of Lely's beauties, languishing in loose satin, would have been naked from the waist up, if they had moved.

And: the garments that have survived in museums are usually the ones that were kept for best, such as the lovely silver tissue dress in the Museum of Costume at Bath. It escaped the fate of most expensive clothes, of being handed down to successive wearers, and altered according to fashion and fit. (This goes some way to account for the small size of most museum garments; it is easier to take in than let out. When finally no one could get into great-grandmother's ball dress, it took to mothballs and, with luck, a museum.) Workaday garments, too, were handed down. It is a recent and welcome change that poverty no longer means a wardrobe of old cast-offs, obviously, contemptibly, out of date. No museum houses working clothes; they finally wore out, as rags.

Before opening the wardrobe door, or lifting the lid of the chest, a reminder. The only textile fibres available until recently were wool, flax, silk, cotton and hemp. With the exception of hemp, they could be, and were, mixed in a bewildering variety of blends, with names that are impossible to remember (except for linsey-wolsey, which was a blend of linen and wool). One example of the confusion that easily overwhelms the student of textile history: a particular kind of fluffy-surfaced woollen cloth made in the West Riding of Yorkshire was called 'cottons'.[1] Another reminder: there were no dry-cleaners.

Wool was grown, spun, woven into woollen 'cloth' (the soft kind) or 'stuff' (worsted; the smoother hard-wearing kind) or knitted; dyed, finished and made up; all in England, the later stages mostly in London.

There was an English linen industry, but its product was fairly run-of-the-mill. Fine linen was imported from Holland, France and Germany. Linen could be gossamer-thin, such as cambric (from Cambrai), or stout enough for canvas. Linen thread could be knitted.

Silk was mostly imported from France and Italy, as filament ('thrown' on to bobbins) or fabric. Thrown silk needed a further process ('twisting') before it could be woven or knitted. James I had tried to encourage a home industry, by importing silkworms and making mulberry trees available at the subsidised price of three farthings each. Some of these trees survive, but the silkworms were not happy, and his son Charles I had to give up the idea.

Cotton was increasingly percolating the London market from both India and the new colonies on the east coast of America. From the middle of the seventeenth century there was a thriving import of printed Indian cottons for women's dresses and soft furnishings, and fine Indian muslins were competing with linen cambrics.

Hemp was used to make ropes and sails, and hard-wearing clothes for labourers, such as the 'hempen homespuns' who celebrated Duke Theseus' wedding during *A Midsummer Night's Dream*.

Women's clothes

Magolotti found the style of English women's dress 'very elegant, entirely after the French fashion', and was impressed by their 'extreme' neatness.

The general line was unchanged throughout the decade: a low-necked, full-sleeved, pointed bodice and a full skirt open down the front to show an underskirt. (The unique silver tissue dress in Bath is not open down the front, which demonstrates how unwise it is ever to make a general statement.)

But before we make a more detailed examination, pause for a moment in a bedroom in the early morning. The garments put ready for wear, I suggest, were a comfortable front-fastening loose jacket and a plain, full skirt, or a one-piece dress that could be put on without help – a 'habit or garment generally worn by the middle or lower sort of woman, having gored skirts, and some wear them with stomachers',[2] i.e. they fastened in front.

No one in England would have dreamed of being painted in such comfortable clothes. But in Holland, where it was not done to appear aristocratically leisured, and painters preferred real life, jackets often crop up in pictures, trimmed with fur for the winter, light-weight for the summer. Vermeer's *Woman Reading a Letter* is wearing one as a maternity dress. Elizabeth had an 'old morning gown' that Samuel 'used to call ... her Kingdom, from the ease and content she used to have in the wearing of it'.[3] She could put it on when she got up, without needing help with stays or boned bodice, both of which fastened behind.

The 'body' or 'pair of bodies' for normal wear had a low, round neckline and narrow, sloping shoulders. The fullness of the sleeves was set into the sides of the armholes, thus avoiding the leg-of-mutton look of the Victorians. The waistline was at or slightly above the natural waist. The bodice ended in tabs round the sides and back, and a point in front. It was either slightly stiffened and lined, and worn over a stiff corset, or lined, interlined with canvas and stiffly boned; the effect to wearer and onlooker was the same. The boning was ferocious. The best description comes improbably, from a man, Randle Holme. Down the middle of the bodice front was a busk: that is,

> a strong piece of wood or whalebone thrust down the middle of the stomacher [the front panel] to keep it straight and in compass, that the breast or belly shall not swell out too much. These busks are usually made in length according to the necessity of the person wearing it: if to keep in the fulness of the breasts, then it extends to the navel, if to keep the belly down then it extends to the honour.

Imagine sitting down, with a piece of wood digging into your honour.

The skirt was set on to a band, in small pleats, except for a few flat inches at the front. The skirt waistband went over the bodice tabs at the back and sides, and under the bodice point at the front.

(Surely this must have been apt to come unstuck? It always, of course, looks immaculate in pictures. Perhaps this was one of the uses for the pins that so often feature in literature. 'My life is not worth a row of pins', etc. Safety pins had not yet been invented.) Skirts for informal wear were shorter than floor length. In an enchanting panel of bobbin lace in the Victoria and Albert Museum of 1675, the lady's skirt is nearer her knees than her ankles. Granted, she is escaping from a leopard. Also, she, or at least the lace, is Italian.

The front edges of the skirt could be temporarily pinned back out of the way, to save it from mud, or for housework or cooking; or permanently fastened back into a bustle effect. The underside of the skirt would then be lined or faced. In October 1666 there was a brief fashion for a train to the skirt: a most disastrous fashion, surely, in a wet season when London was, if possible, even dirtier than usual from the aftermath of the Fire. Samuel thought it 'mighty graceful'.

The underskirt ('petticoat') was meant to be seen and admired, especially the front panel and hem, which were often decorated and stiffened with metal braid ('lace') incorporating so much gold or silver that the silversmith who sold it would take old lace in part exchange, knowing he could burn the silk or parchment backing and recover the bullion. (The trimming we call 'lace' was usually known as 'point [de Venise, etc.]' – but not always.) So much bullion went into lace that in 1661 it was seriously proposed to restrict its use because of the adverse effect on national finances.[4] The Queen Mother had a profitable monopoly imposing quality control 'because of the corruption of gold and silver laces and fringes by mixing the thread with copper, tin, etc.';[5] she perhaps was able to exert pressure to preserve its extensive use. Usually a reference to 'lacing' a garment meant applying this braid to it, which could be done at home, producing a costly effect for only about £6.[6] Rather surprisingly, the production of this precious commodity, under the aegis of the Company of Gold Wire Drawers, was sometimes farmed out to parish workhouses; there were '85 sheds for the spinning gilt and silver thread' in the parish of St Giles Cripplegate, which employed 'poor Parish Boys and Girls to the number of 1,275', the total labour force being 6,208.[7] Petticoats for cold weather and cold unheated draughty houses, could be lined and quilted. Skirt and bodice and, perhaps, petticoat made a 'suit'.

Under the skirt, or under both petticoat and skirt, a woman tied her 'pocket'. Hence the nursery rhyme about Lucy Locket losing her pocket and Kitty Fisher finding it. The wearer got at her pocket through an opening ('placket') in the skirt, and, probably, the petticoat as well. A much-respected and pompous seventeenth-century author, Henry Peacham, surprisingly ends his book *The Art of Living in London* with an anecdote about a tradesman's wife who went to the play, without her husband, and lost her purse. Husband – 'Where did you put it?' 'Under my petticoat, between that and my smock.' 'What' quoth her husband, 'did you feel nobody's hand there?' 'Yes' quoth she 'I felt one's hand there, but I did not think he had come for that.' This makes sense of the advice to 'keep thy foot out of brothels, thy hand out of plackets' in *King Lear*, Act III, scene 4.

Kitty Fisher may have been in luck: pockets could be elaborate embroidered confections, such as the

> needlework wallet in tent stitch and some moss work in coloured silks and gold and silver thread, with a full length portrait of Admiral Sir William Penn [Samuel's neighbour and colleague], father of the founder of Pennsylvania [and of the rather hoydenish girl who probably created the 'wallet'] ... unwrapping to reveal two pockets, one embroidered with his coat-of-arms, the other with a leopard, lined with burgundy-coloured satin and tied with a plaited tie of orange and silver thread

which was sold by Christie's in 1987.[8]

Elizabeth's best clothes, as noted by her husband, were made of silk fabrics that were perilously easy to spoil. She had a 'lutestring' suit in the wet February days of 1661. Lutestring was a fine silk stiffened with gum.[9] One shower and it would have been ruined. In December 1662 she was wearing taffeta (a plain weave usually given a lustre finish equally susceptible to rain-spotting) of which Samuel, let alone Elizabeth, was 'almost ashamed' because 'all the world wears *moiré* (another finish, with the effect of water-marks, which, again, would be ruined by real water). By January the next year Elizabeth duly got her *moiré* suit, and that autumn, a velvet coat. The *moiré* suit only lasted eighteen months, when it had to be replaced by another.

In 1638 one Peter Ladore had patented 'a perfect way ... to gloss plain and figured sattins ... and likewise to gloss and refresh such as have taken wet in the way ... at the instance of the Mercers he hath at his great costs and charges erected a fabricke [factory] neer unto [the] Cittie', but nothing more was heard, so far as I know, of him or his fabricke.

Silk has always been prized for its ability to take dyes. The Huguenot silk-workers[10] gradually infiltrating the London trade brought with them a sophisticated range of weaves, dyes and finishes. Colour printing on silk or cotton, as opposed to woven patterns, lagged behind until the use of alum as a mordant to fix the dye was thoroughly understood, in the mid-1670s.[11] Elizabeth's 'flowered grey silk' and her 'flowered tabby suit' (tabby is not, here, a cat, but the name of yet another weave) will have been brocaded (the flowers were woven in), not printed.

Ladies with no pretensions to fashion (and those with such pretensions, when they were not on show) wore wool. Women did not often make wills because most property was owned by men; but when they did, they carefully disposed of their clothes, as valuable bequests with years of wear in them. A lady who died in 1660 worth £150 in cash disposed by will of her household linen, tidily, then started on her wardrobe. Her sister got her 'plain stuff gowns and black petticoat', and a cousin her 'best stuff gown and best petticoat'. Another cousin got her 'best wide cloth petticoat' and her 'riding suits'. But enter yet another cousin, who was to have 'my cloth gowns, my petticoats and bodices'.[12] Fortunately, perhaps, it was the custom to make one's will only when Death was staring one in the face; otherwise an already confused picture might have been further complicated, if the 'best stuff gown' had had to be demoted, after further years of wear.

Elizabeth's new flowered tabby stayed unworn for more than a year. She went into unrelieved black, on the death of her mother-in-law (whom she detested). After three months Elizabeth went into 'second mourning', sporting a black *moiré* bodice and a 'short petticoat laced with silver lace'. But it did not do. Samuel disapproved. It was too soon for such levity.

Mourning had inflexible rules.[13] It was a status symbol. Wealth could be gauged by the width of the black ripples spreading outwards from a death in the family; social rank, by the extent to which a household shared with the Court any occasion for royal mourning. The aristocracy made the supreme sacrifice of wearing wool, instead of silk, in bereavement. The wardrobes of great ladies contained black wool gowns for just such an emergency. The Duchess of Somerset made her will in 1686.[14] Having disposed of her 'rich crimson bed' and its ermine coverlets, and a 'rich carved gilt new

111

coach lined with crimson', and a sedan chair, she finally arrived at 'one new fine black cloth gown (not laced)' and 'one fine new black cloth long gown and petticoat'. These must have been the mourning clothes, unworn, held in reserve for contingencies; not part of the Duchess's regular wardrobe, but very welcome to persons of lower status as additions to their wardrobes, as well as for mourning the Duchess in.

Elizabeth's lutestring suit was bought ready-made from a silk merchant ('mercer'). She was probably a standard size, but in any case the rigidity of the bodice meant that the wearer adjusted herself to fit it, rather than vice versa. The fastening could expand or contract, within reason.[15] Cloaks and riding clothes too were sold ready-made.[16] But in general, clothes were made to order, by 'taylors' (for women as well as men). The extent to which this applied to mourning is difficult to gauge. There were only three clear days between Elizabeth's order and the delivery of her mourning. Surely tailors held a stock of black ready-mades, for adjustment as necessary? There was an immense amount of hand-sewing in a suit of lined, interlined and boned bodice, voluminous skirt and petticoat, the sheer bulk of which would daunt a modern dressmaker accustomed to machine sewing and clear artificial light.

One hopes that Elizabeth's new flowered tabby suit was still in fashion when she could at last wear it. Fashions changed once a year, at Easter, and at the direction of Paris – even then, and even when England was at war with France. In 1662 Elizabeth and Samuel went to Gray's Inn 'to observe the fashions of the ladies' before ordering Elizabeth's new spring ensemble. The pre-eminence of Gray's Inn, as a fashion forum, over the other Inns of Court is puzzling. I have suggested that it had advantages over the other Inns, of country views and fresh air; but those were advantages to walkers and strollers, not devotees of fashion.

By the late 1660s more reliable advice was available to Elizabeth, at least, in the shape of garments directly imported from France by an enterprising acquaintance, M. Batelier.[17] The earliest publication that could be called a fashion magazine came out in Paris in 1672.[18] *Le Tailleur Sincère* was a technical journal for the trade. From 1673 *Le Mercure Galant* began publication, also, of course, in Paris. (A later development was the import of fashionably dressed dolls or mannequins, outside our period.)

Working women wore comfortable front-fastening bodices and skirts (see Vermeer's *Kitchenmaid*), made at home or bought from markets or street vendors, or their mistresses' cast-offs if they wished to be more fashionable.

Underwear was usually made at home. In comparison to the outer layer, it was simple in the extreme: a voluminous T-shaped shift of white linen, with ribbons or tape ('inkle') at neck and wrist to produce the characteristic frill emerging at the neck and sleeves of the bodice. The neck frill could be pulled up to fall over the top of the bodice, taking the place of a separate collar. There was no equivalent of a brassière. Bodices and stays pushed the breasts upwards, sometimes to danger point if portraits are to be believed. Elizabeth was probably unusual in wearing knickers ('drawers'). I have no information as to their cut. Even Randle Holme is silent. I can only say, remember that there was no elastic. Sanitary towels were made of linen that had reached the end of the line; they were washed and reused, as they were until well into the twentieth century.

In bed, women wore shifts and embroidered night-caps, very becoming over curl-papers.

Outside the house, the head would always be covered, either by a high-crowned hat or, more fashionably, by a gathered hood ('whisk') anchored to the top-knot by a pin; or even both at once. Masks ('vizards') began as the mark of a prostitute, but (inverting the usual order of things) became fashionable, indeed normal, outdoor wear for a lady. They were either held to the face on a short stick, like a glorified lorgnette, or clamped on to the face by a button held between the teeth, which must have considerably inhibited conversation.

Mr Mackintosh's rainproof coats were far in the future. Among the inventions patented between 1617 and 1692 (the first volume of the Patents Register), two were for waterproofing fabrics; 'a commodity which ... is very likely to be of very good use and benefit to the common wealth' and 'saving much leather that is now wasted in covering of coaches and wagons'. But neither seems to have had any commercial success. A heavy wool 'surtout' or 'mantle', sometimes with attached hood, or a caped cloak, were the best available means of keeping out the rain. For finer ladies, there were 'wadded' (padded: probably quilted as well) cloaks, and mantles of silk.[19] Riding cloaks were traditionally made of red West Country cloth (hence, Little Red Riding Hood). On horseback, a 'safeguard' could be wrapped round the rider's skirts, to avoid at least some of the dirt.

In the summer, parasols protected the complexion. In the winter, fur tippets and muffs were comforting. Gloves were always worn outdoors, often elaborately embroidered, laced and scented. Stockings were of knitted silk, fine wool or linen thread, in descending order of cost and fashion. They were kept up above the knee by knitted garters. In the 1660s stockings tended towards bright colours and patterns, even embroidered with metal thread, but from 1670 they quietened down to match the petticoat or skirt. Collars and cuffs of fine linen or muslin were edged with point for best. Although the import of foreign point was forbidden in 1667, to protect the native industry, fashionable ladies still wore smuggled French or Italian point.

Shoes were 'straight' – that is, the same for left and right foot – which accounts for the peculiarly lop-sided appearance of shoes that have survived in museums; but not many have and, again, they tend to be the kept-for-best kind – delicate confections of embroidered satin or kid, not designed for walking in the filthy streets of London. The answer lay in 'galloshios':[20] backless shoes with high heels and platform soles, into which the wearer could slip her elegantly shod feet; or pattens: 'irons to be tied under shoes ... a thing of wood like a shoe sole, with straps over it to tye over the shoe, having an iron at the bottom to raise the wearer from the dirt'.[21] Elizabeth was 'exceedingly troubled' by some new pattens.[22] New or old, they sound a most perilous invention. The shoe sole might be raised above the ground 4 inches or more. Imagine tottering along in pattens, on wet, slippery, uneven cobbles. Chopins, a continental form of galloshes, were even higher, but do not seem to have caught on in England.

Young women could flutter delicately painted, half-circular folding fans, with all their potential for flirtation. Randle Holme also depicts a 'matron's fan': a formidable bunch of ostrich feathers set in a heavy handle, ' being more comely and civil for old persons than the former, which is stuft with nothing but vanity'.

Jewellery

Pearls, 'of which they wear necklaces of very great price',[23] were still the most covetable jewellery. A Frenchman, M. Jacquin, had invented artificial pearls in about 1660, but they do not seem to have spread to England.[24] In 1660 Samuel spent £4 10s on a string of pearls for Elizabeth. They may have been native river pearls. English merchants were importing 'false pearl necklaces' from Venetian glass manufacturers from at least 1667.[25] They came in three sizes, 'good', 'middle' and 'small seed pearls'. Presumably they were glass beads, pearlised with some kind of varnish; yet, thinking of the shallow Venetian lagoon, one is tempted to wonder whether 'cultured' pearls were already in the seventeenth century being grown in Venetian oysters. Five years later, when Samuel had come up in the world, he rashly promised Elizabeth another pearl necklace, which she chose herself, perhaps not trusting his ability to tell a 'false pearl necklace' from a real one. It cost £80, an enormous amount for those days; but it was a 'very good one', of three rows.

The diamond ring he gave her in 1665 cost £10. Elizabeth chose Samuel's Valentine present to her, in 1668: a 'turkey' (turquoise) stone in a ring, set with 'little sparks of diamonds', which cost him nearly £5.

At the other end of the scale, Charles spent the colossal sum of £9,750 for a 'great pair of diamond pendants' (earrings), and £1,200 for a pair of pearl pendants, in 1668;[26] only a year later, he spent £2,800 on a 'jewel' for the Queen, and £6,000 on 'two large diamonds' (recipient unknown).[27]

Elizabeth acquired a watch, for £12, which may have looked pretty – there are some enchanting examples in the Ashmolean Museum in Oxford, shaped like walnuts and pomegranates – but alas did not keep time.[28] The spring balance movement which was to revolutionise watches was not invented until 1675. Rewards for lost watches were often advertised. It must surely have been a lawyer who lost a 'gold watch in a shagreen case studded with small brass pins with a seal and a key of a cabinet tyed to it in a satin ribbon between Lincoln's Inn Fields and Westminster Hall (if not in the Hall)', for which £5 reward was offered in February 1661,[29] 'with hearty thanks'; and perhaps a sea captain who 'lost at the Fleet Tavern door in Cornhill about noon 21 January 1661 a round high Watch of a reasonable size, showing the day of the month, age of the Moon, and Tides'.[30] 'Alarum' watches could be had[31] from France, though whether they were reliable I doubt.[32] Other trinkets were seals and toothpick holders; 'There was lately lost a gold toothpick case, with two tooth-picks in it, one silver, the other gold. At one end of the case was a seal with 3 Huntsmen's horns; at the other end a seal with a stag.'[33]

Men's clothes

Parliament knew, when it invited this 30-year-old man to come back to his father's throne, that Charles was penniless. Money was voted to provide him with a bed to sleep in, and a crown to be crowned with, and a sceptre, 'the estimate of which amounted to about £900'[34] – for which Alderman Viner was still waiting years later.[35] By the time Charles crossed Tower Bridge, he was magnificently dressed in a doublet of cloth of silver and a cloak heavy with gold lace.[36] (Did he think, as he clattered over the Bridge, of the days in Brussels, when he was trying to borrow £200 and even asked the potential lender 'if you can dispose your friends to assist you with the loan of such money as they can spare, we will take it very kindly from them'?)[37] The procession that conducted him to his Palace of Whitehall was almost equally splendid. It was led by a troop of 300 gentlemen,

> all in cloth of silver doublets, then 1200 in velvet coats ... purple liveries ... sleeves of cloth of silver and very rich green scarves ... blue liveries laced with silver lace ... seagreen and silver ... grey and silver ... red cloaks with silver lace ... black velvet coats with gold chains ... His Majesty's life guard of horse ... Aldermen in their scarlet gowns and rich trappings ... the Lord Mayor, next to him the Duke of Buckingham and the General [Clarendon], and then [at last] the King's Majesty between the Dukes of York and Gloucester [his younger brothers].

After that, the five regiments of horse and two troops of noblemen and gentlemen must have fallen a bit flat.[38] At his coronation, he wore garments ordered and begun in Paris – where else? – and finished in London. They cost £2,271 19s 10d, which was not paid for years.[39] 'His Majesty's life guard of horse' were adorned with 206 'plumes of feathers'[40] specially imported from France, duty-free.

But Charles was in some ways not as profligate as he has been painted. He was profligate of his time, resenting the necessity to spend it on business, but exuding charm when he could postpone the dreary duties no longer. He told Bishop Burnet that 'he was no atheist, but he could not think God would make a man miserable only for taking a little pleasure out of the way'.[41] He could be profligate of money, channelling state funds in the direction of his mistresses or his gardens or his palaces, and ignoring worthy causes such as the hundreds of petitioners hoping for their just desserts. But from time to time he made an honest effort to reduce his personal expenses.

In 1668 he instituted, or at least agreed to, a review of the cost of his household, which must have caused alarm and despondency in various offices which had gone their peaceful way since the Middle Ages. The master of the royal otter hounds objected that 'for some years past [he was] commanded upon duty by the King himself, for near 6 months in the summer time'; but from 1668 he was allowed only £700 a year.[42] The royal hawks, which lived in the royal mews opposite Charing Cross, cost rather more; their establishment was reduced to £1,594 17s 6d. The royal buckhounds had to make do on less, only £1,500 a year. Meanwhile, the Navy 'in times of peace' was expected to function on £20,000, and the Office of Works had to keep the royal palaces and parks in good repair for £8,000 a year.

The euphoria of the Restoration had been reflected in an outburst of frivolity in men's clothes, the most startling example being 'petticoat breeches'. Randle Holme described them as 'all open, like a short petticoat, having no sewing up between the legs', and perhaps producing a *frisson* of cross-dressing as well as foppishness. Sometimes the legs were divided, but they were so wide that Samuel knew a man who 'put both his legs through one of the knees of his breeches and went so all day'.[43] I rather doubt this, because petticoat breeches were heavily trimmed with yards and yards of ribbon, and also they were worn at half-mast, hanging precariously from the wearer's hips, no longer attached to the doublet, so the extra weight of two legs on one side would have pulled the whole garment down; but it made a good story.

With petticoat breeches, the serious follower of fashion wore a short doublet ending well above the waist. The gap was filled by an expanse of billowing linen shirt trimmed with point. A true martyr to fashion would show even more shirt, by leaving his fly undone.[44] A further delicate touch was added by 'linings' in a contrasting colour, flapping below the hem of the breeches.

No wonder that in May 1662 (still owing his tailor) Charles told the surprised Commons that he 'could not but observe that the whole nation seemed to him a little corrupted in their excess of living. All men spend much more in their clothes, in their diet, in all their expenses, than they had used to do'.

The moderate fullness of normal breeches was pleated into a

band at about knee level ('closed'), or left loose at the knee ('open'), which could show a reasonable glimpse of contrasting linings. Pockets were let into the side seams. The grotesque penis-covers of the Tudors had detumesced into buttoned flies, but the name ('codpiece') lingered on. Normal doublets buttoned to the neck; the waist was at about its natural level, with a skirt-like extension, varying in length with changing fashion, enabling the waist band of the breeches to be fastened to the waist of the doublet, under its skirt, by hooks and eyes – or leather tabs, which could be let down in the case of growing boys.

This general line had been unchanged, in essence, for many years. But change was creeping in. First, the doublet was unbuttoned to show another garment between it and the shirt, referred to in the *Diary* by that indefinite term 'waistcoat'. Samuel had a 'false tabby' waistcoat laced with gold under his doublet, in 1661, and a 'black baize waistcoat faced with silk' in 1663. Baize was a soft woollen cloth; the back of his waistcoat was warm and not meant to be seen, the front was visible and decorative. Taking this theme further, in the winter of 1664–5 he had a 'waistcoat cut open at the back', a kind of decorative dickey.

In January 1662, the Russian Ambassador had appeared at Court, to startling effect. His favourite accessory was a hawk on his wrist, which cannot always have been convenient, but the rest of his costume inspired Charles to desert the French fashion camp and go Russian. He took time to consider. It was not until 15 October 1666 that Charles strode into view wearing a black silk three-piece suit remotely derived from the Russian Ambassador's national costume. His coat and 'vest' both came to knee level, leaving little to be seen of the closed breeches. Even then, his vest was 'pinked'[45] with white, the knees of his breeches were 'ruffled' with black ribbon, and rows of non-functional buttons and buttonholes replaced lace trimming. But it was an advance towards rational dress for men – the progenitor of the boring suits imposed on them now.[46]

Charles had given notice of his intention, as early as 11 October.[47] Most of his cronies had had time to order their own ensembles. It took Samuel all of three weeks to get his, which was not bad going, considering the lack of cutting instructions. At first he found the New Look rather draughty, 'my vest being new and thin, and the Coate cut not to meet before on my breast', but he liked himself 'mightily' in it, 'and so doth my wife'.[48] He cannot have been the only man to be discussing with his tailor, a few months later, how to convert a wardrobe-full of doublets and breeches into these new-fangled garments.[49] Randle Holme described them as 'a stret bodied [tight-fitting] coat close to the body and arms, without a doublet, under it a waistcoat with side or deep skirts almost to the knees [called] chates [= cheats] because they are rich and gaudy before, when all the back part is no such thing'.

The rules of mourning applied even more strictly to men than to women, men being more in the public eye. All surfaces had to be not only black but dull. When his mother died, in 1666, Anthony Wood paid 2s for 'black buckles to my vest' and 6d for 'blacking my russet shoes', and he borrowed a 'mourning-gown'. When Samuel went into mourning for his brother, he even had the soles of his black shoes blackened, in case they should shock the congregation as he knelt at the front of the church.[50] Others met this difficulty by wearing special cloth shoes.[51] Samuel's mourning wardrobe included a mourning belt, presumably of dull leather. After coats and vests came in, the rules of mourning required the diagonal sash worn over the coat to be of dull silk, black to mourn a man and white for a woman or a child. Hat bands too must show grief, in the form of 'weepers', lengths of thin mat black or white silk falling down the back. The aristocracy reluctantly put aside its silks and went into wool, in the first extremity of sorrow.

Charles's three-piece suit included an embryonic tie, modern man's sole badge of individuality. The neckband of the shirt would normally be covered by a wide starched collar ('scallop') or a long narrow strip of linen ('cravat'), both trimmed with point. Samuel showed uncharacteristic restraint in the plain neckerchief he wore for his portrait.

Charles was asked by the London wool trade if he would demonstrate his support of native products, by wearing wool. He got as far, occasionally, as a wool/silk mixture. Samuel 'put on my new silk suit, the first that ever I wore' on 10 July 1660, but had cloth suits for normal wear. Even after he had decided that 'I must go handsomely', in October 1664, coloured cloth was adequate. By the next summer, a 'plain ordinary suit' for the summer was of silk; but then, Samuel was rapidly going up in the world.

The shirt was slightly more structured than a woman's shift. Moderate fullness at the neck was pleated into a band, which might be slightly frilled. Since it fitted round the neck, unlike a shift, it had to have an opening down the front, which provided an occasion for cascades of point. The neckband fastened with strings, ending in elaborate tassels or pom-poms. The sleeves were full, ending in frilled wristbands. Shirts, like shifts, were invariably made of white linen, of widely varying weights.

Every schoolchild used to know that Charles I went to his death wearing two shirts, to prevent cold shivers that might be mistaken for fear. One of these shirts is in Windsor Castle. It is made of heavy linen, with small neck and wrist frills. (The ghoulish may like to know that the neck shows no signs of undue wear.) The other is in the Museum of London. 'Shirt', in the modern sense, it is not. It is a thigh-length knitted garment of heavy silk, elegantly patterned in blue and white stripes, and no doubt invincibly warm.

What did the average man, without Charles I's wardrobe, wear to keep himself warm? Samuel, too, refers to wearing two shirts, in the autumn of 1666. Usually he wore a linen 'waistcoat', but there was also a garment called a 'half-shirt' which he 'left off' in October 1661, to put on a 'waistcoat' as well as the 'false tabby waistcoat' we have seen. Dr Jaeger's faith in wool next to the skin was not current in the seventeenth century; these undergarments were linen. It would have been much more comfortable to wear a knitted linen undervest than two layers of woven fabric; yet the latter seems to have been the case, judging from the waist-length, woven undershirt in which Charles II's funeral effigy was dressed.[52]

Underpants ('drawers') were not so equivocal. They were ankle-length, knee-length or shorter fly-fronted garments of woven or knitted linen, with a draw-string at the waist. If they were long, they had stirrups under the foot. Samuel sensibly supplemented his with a rabbit skin, before a long ride.[53] Charles II's funeral effigy wore short, full-cut silk drawers.

In bed, men wore long night-shirts, and elegant embroidered night-caps – to judge from the survivors in museums – to keep their heads warm, especially if they had shaved their scalps so as to wear wigs comfortably.

Men, too, had their 'morning gowns', also known as 'night-gowns', 'dressing gowns' or just 'gowns'. These were descendants of the long, warm medieval robes whose wearers were so shocked when naughty young men displayed themselves in buttock-hugging hose, which eventually turned into breeches. To call these robes 'dressing gowns' in the modern sense would be misleading.

Samuel had a purple 'shag' (plush) gown trimmed with gold buttons, which was acceptable wear in his office on a cold day. He had another for working at DIY at home, and still another that he grabbed to wear as he rode through the Fire on top of a cartful of furniture. When it came to having his portrait painted, none of these would do, so he hired an 'Indian' gown, which looks as if it was made of heavy plain silk. ('Indian' could mean Turkish, or anywhere east of Suez, such as China; imports from both were coming on to the market in the 1660s.) Seven years later, the plutocrat Sir Robert Viner was painted also wearing a loose silk gown, in his case a sumptuous brocade. There is an evocative description of a sea captain, during the Dutch wars, who brought his ship back to its home port safely, 'walking the deck in his silk morning gown'.[54]

Shoes were straight. There was a vogue for red heels, and for red linings to the tongues, which were folded back to show the lining, fetchingly shaped in a cupid's bow. Shoes were fastened with ribbons or, later, buckles, which provided yet another focus for conspicuous consumption. Men wore pattens and galloshios too. Another of Anthony Wood's jaundiced descriptions of Charles's court in Oxford: having dealt with their petticoat breeches and other garments 'highly scented bedecked with ribbons of all colours', he goes on: 'And this apparel was not only used by gentlemen and others of inferior quality, but by soldiers, especially those of the Life Guard to the King, who would have spanners hanging on one side and a muff on the other, and when [it was] dirty weather some of them would relieve their guards in pattens.' According to Randle Holme, a spanner was 'a thing made of iron ... by which the springs of wheel locks are wound up', wheel locks being contemporary small arms. One feels for these elegant young men, having to ruin their ensembles with a nasty brutal piece of iron.

Boots were worn not only for riding and walking in those muddy streets, but also for dancing and parties. They had loose baggy tops, which surely impeded graceful movement. Further inappropriate decoration was provided by boot hose, the tops of which cascaded over the boots in a flurry of point. For hard wear, boot hose were still made in the old-fashioned way, of woven linen laced up the back, footed with a separate woollen sole.

Workaday stockings were of wool or linen thread, fashionable ones of silk. Knitted stockings illustrated an economic quandary of the time. It was received wisdom that deserving people on poor relief, such as children, the elderly and agricultural workers in the long winter between harvest and ploughing, should be put to work. What better employment for them than hand-knitting, and hand-knitting stockings, in particular? It was a skill that children could learn easily, and it could be exercised by several people gathered round one fire and working by its light, or by one person doing another job at the same time, such as guarding sheep.

The authorities had no particular interest in any mechanical contrivance that would make this labour redundant. When William Lee was, therefore, refused a charter by Queen Elizabeth for his knitting frame, he took his invention to France instead. After his death there, his workmen brought it back to Nottingham, and the Nottingham knitting industry was born. By 1658 a standard 15-inch, 24-gauge, 360-needle frame contained 2,066 separate pieces of iron and wood: an astounding example of pre-Industrial Revolution machinery.[55]

But it was not appreciated. An experienced hand-knitter, working at times by firelight or candle light, could turn out a pair of stockings in a day, to the customer's requirements, where a frame-knitter, who needed good daylight to work by, would not generally exceed that rate by much, over a six-day week, and he needed start-up capital and a long run before he could make a profit. The London market preferred hand-knitted hose. Most of the frame-knitters' production was exported to the American colonies.

Christopher Wren thought of a modification to the knitting frame which would have enormously increased production. The frame-knitters refused to pay him the £400 he asked, for this apparently good idea. They had to explain to him that such a surge in production would swamp their market. According to Aubrey, 'Sir Christopher was so noble ... that he breaks the model of the engine all to pieces.' Nothing, especially economic practice, is as easy as it looks at first sight.

Cloaks varied from the circular waist-length ones that made the wearer look, to our eyes, like an up-ended ice-cream cone, to a more practical calf length. Samuel was scathing about a servant who insisted on flinging his cloak over his shoulder 'like a ruffian'.

Keeping one's head covered is almost unknown today, which leaves modern man with no gesture to make when passing the Cenotaph or attending a funeral. Even as recently as the 1920s, the Jarrow Marchers' gaunt faces stare, in old photographs, from under shabby hats and miserable caps. In the seventeenth century, covering your head, and taking your hat off to show respect, were taken for granted. George Fox, the founder of the Society of Friends, upset everyone by insisting on keeping his hat on, even in court when

122

facing the full panoply of the legal system. When William Penn, one of his followers, insisted on keeping his hat on in the presence of the King, Charles took his own hat off. 'Friend Charles,' said Penn, 'why dost thou not keep on thy hat?' 'It is the custom of this place', said that affable monarch, 'that only one man should remain covered at a time.' Aubrey described the classic absent-minded professor of his time as so forgetful that he would even 'sometimes be going out without his hat on'. A workman wore a round cap shaped like a beehive, with a button on the top, 'used now by all labourers and handicraftsmen who cannot conveniently work (especially in the summer time) with their hats on their heads'.[56]

The best hats were made from beaver fur. Beavers, and Canada, had recently been discovered. Hats changed from the steeple-crowned shape associated with Guy Fawkes, to a shallow, wide-brimmed shape that cannot have been particularly stable. Samuel's hat fell off into a puddle one day, when he was riding, and was ruined. A new one cost him £4 10s.[57] He should have been wearing his velvet riding hat. Hat brims were trimmed with ostrich feathers. Robert Crofts, the King's Featherman ('Plumarius Regis'), did well out of supplying ostrich feathers for hats, beds and carriages.[58] (Where did all these ostrich plumes come from?) Sometimes a more than usually dashing young man fixed part of his hat brim to the crown of his hat: the precursor of the next century's cocked hat.

Indoors, it was pleasant to remove one's wig and slip on a turban or a soft brimless cap. Samuel had a 'velvet studying cap', presumably for studying in.

He also had a collection of sticks or canes, including a 'knotted cane' (bamboo, or rattan?), a cane 'to walk with' which cost him 4s 6d, a 'varnished staff, very fine and light to walk with', a 'Japan [lacquered] cane with a silver head' and a 'stick-rapier or 'rapier-stick' – he used both terms, but either way dropped and broke it. He also had a 'little sword with gilt handle', and another silver-hilted sword and belt to wear with his new coat and vest. This was the sword he kept ready, drawn, on his knees, as he rode nervously through the ruins, after the Fire.

A *mouchoir* – it was not done to call it a handkerchief, or to blow one's nose on it – was a large sheet of filmy, scented linen which could be elegantly wafted about. It was not till the advent of snuff-taking that handkerchiefs retired to pockets. Muffs, often made of or lined with fur, were worn by both sexes, including the young officers who so irritated Antony Wood (see page 121).

The new-fashioned suit was completed by a coloured 'shash' worn over one shoulder and across the chest, and a wide leather belt round the waist. Gloves for normal wear were plain leather but it did not take much − a birthday, a Valentine present − to soak them in perfume and load them with lace and embroidery.

There remains the ultimate ensemble: the shroud. Here, from 1666, the wool trade had the last say. Shrouds, the usual post-mortem wear, had to be wool. Even trimmings, and the linings of coffins, had to be wool. In 1678 Amy Potter, widow, patented her invention of woollen lace 'to be used in ... the making up of dresses and other things for the decent burial of the dead'. (*Le dernier cri?*) Parish registers had to record that the deceased had been duly 'buried in wool'. But, as usual, there was a loophole for the rich. If they could not bear the thought of wool next their cold dead skin, they could buy their way out with a fine, and enter the next world in a silken shroud.

Cosmetics

A pink-and-white complexion was not always conferred by Nature, which often dealt a further blow in the shape of disfiguring smallpox scars, resembling very bad cases of acne. Help was at hand. Pockmarks could be disguised, or even filled, and colour corrected, by ceruse. This pernicious compound of white lead had been around for years. Venetian ceruse was more prized than the English product, since it contained a higher lead content. By 1661 the *virtuosi* of the Royal Society noted that persons involved in its manufacture tended to suffer from cramps and blindness, but they did not communicate their misgivings to their wives. The first woman known to have died of ceruse poisoning was Lady Coventry, in 1760, but many before then must have dwindled to an early grave. Ceruse was bought as a white paste, to be diluted with water or white of egg, and applied with a damp cloth. One disadvantage was immediately apparent, as soon as the wearer smiled: the white of egg cracked. A few hours later, the lead could darken to a menacing grey. It is hardly surprising that some ladies relied on starch or ground alabaster, powdered over an oily foundation.

A rosy flush on the cheeks was produced by cochineal. 'Spanish paper' was conveniently impregnated with it. Eye make-up was limited to colouring the upper eyelid with henna or blue crayon, which could also be used to touch in delicate veins on the bosom. A red crayon could deepen lip colour. The snag of these crayons was that they tended to blur and fade, for lack of a fixative. Eyelashes were not tinted. Carroty Lady Lauderdale left her eyelashes white. But eyes could be made to shine – and unfocus – by belladonna drops.

Ceruse had a depilatory effect on eyebrows and hairline, but even non-users sometimes plucked their eyebrows, and gummed on, above the natural brow-line, false eyebrows of mouse skin, which – especially when combined with ceruse – gave the wearer an expression of pained surprise.

If facial hair was still a problem, depilatories such as cat dung mixed with vinegar were recommended. The famously eccentric Lady Newcastle preferred to retain her beard.

Recipes for beauty washes and lotions abounded. Most London ladies would rely on the local apothecary's shop for their orange flower water and apricot cream, and other skin foods, imported from France and Italy – or so the label said. But since May dew was known to be an infallible beauty lotion, Elizabeth cannot have been the only Londoner out in the countryside early on the first day of May, squeezing the dew from linen clothes spread under – preferably – oak trees. Puppydog water made of wine and roast puppy was said to be good, too.[59] Freckles were a constant worry, judging from the plethora of remedies prescribed for them in herbals and family receipt books. Cowslip washes which eliminated freckles could as certainly, it was said, banish wrinkles.

Complexion dazzling, lips and eyelids coloured – time for the final touch: patches. 'The Exchanges (for now we have three great Arsenals of choice vanities) are furnished with a daily supply and variety of beauty-spots ... cut out into little moons suns stars castles birds beasts and fishes of all sorts.'[60] Lady Castlemaine was firmly of the opinion that all ladies should wear them all the time, except when in mourning.[61] And not just one at a time. A coach and six galloping horses in black taffeta still left room for several crescents and diamonds and circles in black or red leather. The fashion, which had lasted for at least twenty years, must have been both uncomfortable and worrying. How fast was the gum? Were the six horses still galloping, or had they fallen? Only the distracted gaze of one's *vis à vis* would tell.

125

Hairdressing

The fashionable hair colour was dark. (When Samuel referred to a 'black' woman, he meant a brunette.) Unfortunates with red hair could either brazen it out – neither Nell Gwyn nor the Duchess of Lauderdale was exactly unsuccessful in her chosen *métier* – or try the effect of a lead comb, as recommended by Randle Holme for use 'by such as have red hair to make it of another colour', clearly a desirable object. Red hair is particularly difficult to disguise by colour rinses. There were plenty on the market. One, involving lime, ceruse and an ounce of 'powder of gold', had to be left on all night, during which it set hard. By morning, when it was chipped off, the insomniac user was a lovely brunette – or bald. The typical English mouse who was not prepared to deal regularly with pale roots could take the easier option, and go for a good yellow, with a barberry or saffron wash.

Not for seventeenth-century ladies, the cosy hair-brushing sessions of the Victorians. Combs were the thing, aided by tongs and curl-papers. They were made of boxwood, blackthorn, ivory, bone, horn or tortoiseshell. Anyone whose memory goes back beyond the invention of plastic will know that such combs could not be washed, since water opened minute cracks which agonisingly trapped stray hairs. Combs were cleaned with small brushes like modern stencil brushes (easily mistaken for anachronistic shaving brushes, but identifiable by their embroidered handle-covers). A set of combs, with a comb-brush, in an elaborate dressing case with a mirrored lid, made a handsome present.

Women's coiffure had varied only slightly since the days of Charles I. The bun ('top-knot') had moved from above the nape, to the crown of the head. The side hair was still curled into tendrils. Side ringlets clustered at the temples or fell carelessly to the bosom. All this took a lot of hair. Extra locks and ringlets could be bought, and periwigs covering part of the head allowed the natural hair to be maximised. Curling tongs were heated on small charcoal braziers; the smell of singed hair must have been familiar. Curl-papers worn all night were a safer expedient. Unfortunates with naturally straight hair risked looking like drowned rats on wet days. (Even Dutch painters did not immortalise this degree of naturalness.) I cannot believe that women, practical as ever, did not evolve some way of keeping their hair in curl. Sugar and water would work, to some extent, so would a weak solution of glue. The curious absence of recipes may, of course, mean that the answer to the problem was too obvious to need recording.

There was a brief fashion for arranging side curls to dangle from a wire frame standing out at right angles to the head, above the ears ('wired locks'). Another fashion was for 'white' or 'fair' locks, to which Samuel violently objected.[62]

Baldness is primarily a male problem. Julius Cesar veiled his bald pate in a laurel wreath. (How did he get it to stay on? It must have been unbearably tickly, as well as precarious.) Men have been bald before and after him, but are rarely shown in portraits with shiny occiputs. There have always been wigs, of varying degrees of authenticity. When Charles II came to his long-delayed throne, he had a mane of curly black hair. In only three years he turned 'mighty grey,'[63] which he could not bear, so he had his head shaved and took to black wigs; an immense relief to those with thinning or non-existent locks, who could decently take to wigs, too. But wigs had their snags: principally, livestock. Samuel had been wearing wigs for some years when he laconically recorded that his periwig maker had brought him a wig 'full of nits – his old fault'.[64] Wigs do get dirty, as any barrister knows. But nits ... The acceptance of fleas and lice and nits as a normal part of life has, thankfully, changed.

Charles's wigs grew more ponderous as his age grew weightier. Wigs, added to natural hair, become intolerably hot. The norm was to have the hair cut very short, or shaved.

Shaving was usually done by barbers. Beards were rare (although Randle Holme records a 'beard brush', like a comb-brush, made of bristles and hogshair). Charles wore a thin moustache for most of his adult life, but most men wore no facial hair. They were, however, hardly clean-shaven, according to our standards. Here, I can cite an example of an English painter committing to canvas a true, but less than ideal, picture of his sitter. The artist, John Riley, prided himself on realism at the cost of flattery. When Charles saw Riley's portrait of him, he is reported to have said, 'Is this like me? Then odds fish I am an ugly fellow.' There is, in Gray's Inn, a portrait by Riley of a seventeenth-century barrister, with very perceptible swarthiness round his jaw; an instance, I suggest, of the imperfectly shaved state of most seventeenth-century men, for most of the time.

Holbein's superbly detailed portrait of Sir Thomas More in an earlier age shows individual hairs on his chin and cheeks, at least half an inch long. Technique had not improved much since then: it was still a matter of a cut-throat razor and warm water, or, for the strong-minded, rubbing the stubble off with a pumice, which sounds both painful and ineffective.[65] Safety razors and beard-softening creams had yet to be invented. Not all men elected to endure the ordeal of shaving, or more probably being shaved, every day. Barbers' shops displayed the well-known red and white striped poles. Barbers could be summoned, to dash through the streets to their clients carrying a small pot of hot water and a 'washball'. If the daylight had gone, they would use a nerve-racking form of illumination: a candlestick with an extra candle in a cross-piece attached halfway up. 'This' – the main upright – 'he sticketh in his Apron strings on his left side or breast when he useth to trim by candle-light',[66] leaving the client's nose and hair to take their chance.

Washing and so on

It is quite possible, with careful attention to detail, to keep clean and smell sweet without a daily immersion. Hands and face – ceruse permitting – were washed several times a day in a small bowl balanced on a tripod-legged table (the ancestor of the 'wash-hand basins' in our bathrooms). This was probably the extent of Samuel's normal morning ablutions; one day he was late for the office, and 'run down, without eating or drinking or washing'.[67] Toilet soap was imported from Spain ('Castile' or 'castle' soap) and Italy. The rest of the body could be rubbed down from time to time, with a linen cloth wrung out in water perfumed with herbs or essences. Samuel 'rubbed himself clean' after a long hard morning, before an important meeting.[68] Hannah Wolley gave recipes for bath essence 'in which bathe the body two hours before meat ... to cleanse the body and make it comely'; obviously a tiring experience.[69]

Elizabeth went off to a public bath-house at least once, sneered at by her husband. She may have gone to the St Agnes-le-Clair baths in Tabernacle Square, Finsbury, or Queen Elizabeth's bath at Charing Cross, or the bath named after Queen Anne because she used it, but long antedating her, in Longacre.[70] According to Samuel, she went to a 'hothouse',[71] where she will have taken a 'sweat', resembling a sauna. This gave Elizabeth such moral, not to say physical, superiority that Samuel was banned from the matrimonial bed until he too had at least 'cleaned himself with warm water',[72] an event deserving a diary entry.

One hopes that Elizabeth checked with an almanac before she went off to her ablutions:

> baths are commonly used for pleasure than for profit, especially where hot houses are over much haunted ... Be wary and circumspect in resorting to them without cause and immediately after or with such persons as be unclean ... If any will enter the bath for cleanness sake [apparently a curious idea], let the moon be in Libra or Pisces ... Before you enter into any bath your body must be prepared and purged ... The time of tarrying in the Bath is commonly one hour ...[73]

As early as 1629 a 'Doctor of Physicke' had taken out a patent for 'bathing waterworks ... which are likely to prove very profitable to all [the King's] subjects as well in the time of health as in sickness'. I do not know the extent to which he persuaded his fellow-subjects to use them.

Samuel did occasionally wash his feet. Such rash exposure could, and in his view did, lead to undesirable consequences, such as colds.

Did people smell? The answer must be, yes: unless they were so leisured as to be able to indulge in lengthy complicated ablutions. Sometimes they smelt of scent and body odours, sometimes only of body odours. But if everyone smells, it is hardly noticeable, or offensive. After all, the streets must have stank on a hot day, and the houses too if the night-soil men were late (see Chapter 1, page 15).

Remember, if you can bear to, that there were no dry-cleaners, and the wool and silk outer layers of clothes could not be washed. There were, however, non-perspirants. Mary Evelyn's poem 'A voyage to Maryland or the lady's dressing room' refers obscurely to 'scent of gousset ... though powdered alum be as good/Well strewed on and well understood'. *Gousset* is an old French word for the armpit, or the smell thereof. Alum has a dessicant effect on the skin. Hannah Wolley was more down to earth: 'for stench under the armholes, first pluck away the hairs of the armhole and wash them well with white wine and rosewater wherein you have boiled Cassia lignum'. Culpeper favoured a systemic approach: the seed of wild rocket, 'taken in drink, carries away the ill scent of the armpits'. Clearly it was recognised as a problem.

It has to be said that our habit of wearing few underclothes, so that part of our outer clothes – jerseys, jeans, T-shirts – comes in contact with our skins but may not be as frequently washed as our underwear, would scandalise a fastidious person in the seventeenth century, who was meticulous in protecting the outer, visible layer by wearing between it and the skin a shirt or shift, which could be often washed.

The teeth

If English women had a defect in Italian eyes, it was that their teeth were not very white.[74] It could easily have been worse.

Just as there were no hair brushes, there were no tooth brushes, either. In 1649 Mary Verney wrote to her brother, who was in exile in Paris, asking him to get her one of 'the little brushes for making clean of the teeth' that she had heard that the French used. In the catalogue of Tradescant's Curiosities which eventually formed the basis of the Ashmolean Museum in Oxford, the list of 'utensils' includes 'a Turkish tooth-brush'.[75]

The English way was to rub the teeth with salt, on a finger, or a little vitriol (sulphuric acid) on a piece of wood, which certainly whitened them nicely, but destroyed the enamel. 'Toothpowder' or 'dentifrice' could be bought from apothecaries. A fashionable French one was made of powdered cuttle-fish, coral, cream of tartar, Armenian bole (a kind of clay) and powdered roses. You might, if you had plenty of time, prefer to make your own, using, for instance, the recipe of 'Mr Ferene of the New Exchange, Perfumer to the Queen [Henrietta Maria] so much approved of at Court':

> First take eight ounces of Iris roots [usually called orris-root] also eight ounces of Pumistone, and eight ounces of Cutle-bone, also eight ounces of coral, and a pound of Brick if you desire to make them red, but he did oftener make them white, and then instead of the Brick did take a pound of fine alabaster; all this being thoroughly beaten, and sifted through a fine searce [sieve], the powder is then ready prepared to make up in a paste, which may be done as follows.
>
> Take a little gum Dragant [tragacanth], and lay it in steep twelve hours, in Orange flower water, or damask rose water, and when it is dissolved, take the sweet gum, and grind it on a Marble stone with the aforesaid powder, and mixing some crumbs of white bread, it will

come into a Paste, the which you make Dentifrices of what shape or fashion you please, but rolls is the most commodious for your use.[76]

Hannah Woolley reminded her readers that 'it is uncivil to ... pick [your teeth] at or after meals, with your knife or otherwise',[77] but pick them they did. They were admirably conscious of plaque,[78] described by an early operator for the teeth as a 'stone-like substance commonly called the scales or scurf of the teeth'. He recommended regular professional scaling, and the frequent use of toothpicks. Sets of neat little scrapers could be bought, in shagreen cases like modern manicure sets. Magalotti reported that 'at the conclusion of dinner [not, of course, in Court circles], they dip the end of the napkin into the beaker which is set before each of the guests, filled with water, and with this they clean their teeth and wash their hands'. Hannah did not approve of that either.

CHAPTER 8

HOUSEWORK, LAUNDRY AND SHOPPING

Housework

Ever since fossil fuel replaced wood on London hearths, London housewives have battled with its grimy side effects. John Evelyn, who lived in the comparatively clean air of Deptford, blamed 'that hellish and dismal cloud of sea-coal' for

> spoiling the moveables, tarnishing the plate, gildings and furnitures and corroding the very iron bars and hardest stones ... [It] scatters and strews about those black and smutty atoms upon all things ... insinuating itself into our very secret Cabinets and most precious repositories ... [and] spreads a yellowness upon our choicest pictures and hangings ... Though a chamber be never so closely locked up, men find at their return all things that are in it even[ly] covered with a black thin soot.[1]

Let battle commence; but how?

The principal weapons were brooms. Randle Holme illustrates a 'Beazom; some [housewives] for washed and rubbed [polished] rooms have beazoms made of swines bristles set in round pieces of wood like brushes with long handles', the handle set upright in the centre of the 'round piece of wood', which could be heavy enough to function almost like a modern floor-polisher. A royal servant, Bridget Holmes, lovingly painted by John Riley in 1686, when she was 96,[2] is still carrying her beazom. They could be bought from itinerant street vendors, who also sold 'mapps' (mops, made of coarse woollen yarn),[3] with handles about a yard long. Another cry of

London was, more curiously, 'Old shoes for some brooms'; here, the 'broom' is the kind we now call besoms, used by gardeners and witches.

The street vendors also sold sand, for scouring the stone floor of the kitchen, and for cleaning pots and pans. Polish for wooden floors and furniture was made at home out of candle-ends and turpentine, with perhaps a little oil of lavender added to perfume it. The thin imported rush mats were easy to lift and shake, unlike old-fashioned rush matting.[4]

Moths were a constant worry. Hannah Wolley advised that 'the furniture [be] often beaten in the sun and well brushed'; a counsel of perfection in the English climate. Meanwhile, it was worth trying the deterrent effect of oil of spikenard, drawn round the turkey-work cushion on a chair with a 'pencil' (here, a small paint brush; graphite rods enclosed in wood had not yet been invented). Textiles such as wool-embroidered bed hangings and tapestries should be shaken and beaten, regularly. Beds should be 'often turned' – a formidable task, with those mattresses.

Pewter shone with a watery lustre[5] from burnishing with the plant called horsetail, or marestail, that we think of as an ineradicable weed. It was so useful that, if there were a temporary shortage, supplies of it were imported from Holland ('Dutch rush'). The present-day habit of leaving pewter a dull grey would have horrified a seventeenth-century housewife. Brass was cleaned with horsetail, too, or with charcoal and 'rotten stone', a kind of soft limestone.[6] Silver was cleaned, after washing it in soapy water, by rubbing any spots with salt and vinegar and then coating it with a paste of chalk and vinegar, drying it by the fire or in the sun, and polishing with a warm linen cloth.[7]

The small, irregularly surfaced, greyish and greenish panes in seventeenth-century windows would not repay – indeed might not withstand – much polishing. The inner surfaces were cleaned from time to time, but I have seen no reference to window cleaners for the outside. The casement windows of pre-Fire houses were within the reach of indoor servants. The sash windows of houses built after the Fire, but before the adoption of the Dutch contraption of pulleys and counter-weights, must have presented problems.

Laundry

In most households this was not a weekly occurrence, despite the old song about 'dashing away with a smoothing iron', which allots a laundering task to every day of the week except Sunday. Indeed, a certain status was implied by the infrequency of washing days: you had such a stock that you could defer washing day for weeks. Some great houses washed only twice a year.

Samuel quite often recorded washing day because it was traumatic for him; he disliked dining on cold meat.[8] In 1663 Elizabeth and her maids did the washing on 2 March and again on 25 March; in 1664, washing days blighted Samuel's life on 1 and 22 February and 21 March. We do not, of course, know whether there were intervening washing days, but these intervals would be unsurprising. Probably the weather was the deciding factor, once an adequate pile had accumulated.

Washing

The technique was different from anything we use. The pile of shirts, shifts and drawers, bed linen and table linen waiting to be dealt with were all white, and as their name − which still survives, but is now inaccurate − implies, made of linen. (Towels were not the 'Turkish' looped-pile cotton kind we use, but linen honeycomb weave, which is surprisingly absorbent.) They filled the kind of capacious 'buck basket' that Falstaff had been able to hide in.[9] The 'buck tub' was of similar capacity, but barrel-shaped. The linen was loosely arranged on 'buck sticks' jammed across the tub, the cleanest things at the top and the dirtiest things at the bottom. Then the 'ley' (lye) was poured in, and the linen was left to soak.

The normal household ley was made from wood ashes and urine. Beech or fir ash was best; burnt ferns were good too. Very greasy things needed a ley of strong soda. After some time the ley was run off by a spigot at the foot of the tub, into another shallower tub (the 'underbuck'), and poured in again at the top of the buck tub; or, depending on progress, a stronger ley, or a hot one, might be used.

Once the linen reached a reasonable state of cleanliness, it was rinsed with clean cold water. This was not the moment for the

134

supply to be cut off by the water company, or for the domestic storage tank to run dry. Rinsing could at least begin in the bucking tub. It involved energetic stirrings and shakings, and rearrangement of the buck sticks, to avoid pockets of washed-out dirt soaking into folds; and anyone who has handled just one wet bath towel may be able to imagine the weight of all this wet linen. Any remaining dirty patches were dealt with by beating and scrubbing.

If Elizabeth had decided to wash the chintz she had hung her room with, she would have used a slightly different technique, spreading the fabric in the shallow underbuck and using a ley of bran water.

Then everything had to be dried. Linen has the useful quality of being stronger wet than dry, so it could be twisted and wrung out as hard as the available muscle-power allowed. Thomas Tusser, in the preceding century, had helpfully observed:

> Go wash well, saith Sommer, with sunne I shall drie,
> Go wring well, saith Winter, with winde so shall I.

A garden provided bushes on which to lay the damp clothes in summer. Aromatic bushes such as rosemary were big enough for shifts, and might impart some fragrance. Clothes lines could be bought from street vendors. (Pegs were a surprisingly late invention.) Lady Castlemaine was not too grand to hang out her washing in the royal garden in Whitehall,[10] where her 'finest smocks and linen petticoats' did Samuel 'good to look upon'.

But in the winter? The kitchen was warm, but clean linen would run the risk of smuts from the cooking fire. Occasionally the structure of the old-fashioned long gallery, stretching down the length of the plot, survived at first-floor level, giving a covered area below, which must have been useful on washing days. Dutch and Swiss houses of the period had drying-lofts. In English houses, the top storey was usually the servants' quarters. If the attics were also used for drying laundry, which seems the only possible place except in hot summers, all the damp sheets and shirts had to be carried through those tall houses and up the stairs. No wonder there was no cooking done on washing days.[11]

In 1667, when even Samuel could hardly grudge a slight increase in household expenditure, Elizabeth and her maids took the washing to professional 'whitsters' (launderers) over the river. Even then, she spent the whole of the next day at the whitsters; but she seems to have been satisfied with the results, since two weeks later she took her friend Mrs Turner to them, presumably with Mrs Turner's washing.

Only the everyday stuff was bucked. There was a huge repertoire of skills needed to deal with gossamer-fine linen trimmed with point, and textiles other than linen. Hannah Wolley listed many such skills, for the benefit of 'all maidens who desire to be chambermaids to persons of quality', since 'I find so many gentlewomen forced to serve, whose parents and friends have been impoverished by the late Calamities, viz the Late wars, Plague and Fire, and to see [sic] what mean places they are forced to be in because they want [lack] accomplishment for better'.[12] Silk stockings, for instance, should be washed by rubbing them with sailcloth (coarse linen) wetted in soapsuds, and when nearly dry 'pluck them out with your hands' and iron them on the wrong side. To get ink out of linen, soak it overnight in two or three lots of fresh urine. To get grease spots out of silk or wool, steam the fabric with a 'live ember' of coal or wood, wrapped in a wet linen cloth. Considering the use of candles and tapers, there must have been many such spots, especially on the shoulders of someone standing under a guttering candle branch.

White starch was imported,[13] until the Corporation of White Starch Makers was re-established in 1661,[14] with a monopoly of making and selling starch. It was used for collars and cuffs, and perhaps small items of table linen. The starch had to be made up for each wash, a fiddly job involving boiling water and cold water and vigilance to avoid lumps. Some enterprising housewives added a touch of indigo, to give a good white.

Furs could be taken care of by the furrier.[15]

Ironing

The shape of the iron illustrated by Randle Holme is much the same as a present-day one – narrow at one end to deal with gathers, broad at the other to cover as much surface as possible, with a handle placed so that the user can vary the pressure exerted. The difference is in the source of heat. Holme's picture, which unfortunately is not very clear, seems to allow for a piece of iron, heated at the fire, to be inserted in a box between the handle and the ironing surface, a system that was still going strong in East Africa in the 1950s, turning out miles of immaculate tropical wear. But the seventeenth-century iron may have been heated directly at the fire, and anxiously kept clean with that useful sand.

The 'poking-sticks' (steel rods of about 8 inches long that could be heated), which had produced the complicated folds of the previous century's ruffs, gave their name, it is said, to Piccadilly, via a series of variants. They did not entirely disappear with ruffs. Holme shows headgear such as 'hooded nightrails' and 'quoifs' which seem to have depended on the use of poking sticks to produce regular indentations in their frills.

Large surfaces, mercifully, were not smoothed with a smoothing iron, but carefully folded and set to dry in a press (like a very large flower press), with a wooden screw on top to regulate the pressure. The pattern of the squares thus produced on bed linens and table cloths can often be seen in paintings, from Italian primitives onwards. The really enthusiastic Dutch housewife could enrich this effect by including in the press a board embossed with a pattern, producing an effect like damask. I have seen nothing similar in England, nor any reference to this laborious system. That may be because the idea never caught on here, or because no such board has survived. It is tempting to suppose that in that age of counterfeit textiles and grained woodwork, the up-marketing potential of an embossing board was grasped in both hands by a few progressive housewives.

Shopping

The cries of London: street vendors

Street vendors[16] each had their accustomed rounds. Perishables were sold by women, often from containers carried on their heads, such as baskets of strawberries, cherries, asparagus and fish, and cans of milk. One hopes that the vendors managed to avoid rubbish, and worse, thrown out of upper windows as they passed. Fruit had improved immeasurably as Dutch cultivating methods spread to England. Cherries, for instance, turned into juicy spheres sold on thin sticks, irresistible in those dusty streets. Asses' milk was thought to be safer for babies than cows' milk; milch-asses were led from door to door and milked to order.

Men dealt in heavier, longer-lasting commodities such as coal and sand in sacks, water in wooden pails or long hods, and second-hand clothes.

Some goods were frivolous: hobbyhorses and 'fine singing birds' such as canaries, or larks and thrushes from the wilds of Hampstead. Others were more serious. The ink-seller (7d a pint) also provided ready-trimmed quill pens. The man collecting for the 'poor prisoners' rattled a slotted box, the shape of which has not changed from that day to this; he would gratefully receive contributions of food for them too, to keep them from starving.

Services as well as goods were offered: knives were sharpened, chairs mended and chimneys swept. The chimney sweep carried a bundle of rods and a long broom. A small boy walked beside him with smaller brooms. The use of climbing boys began after the Fire. The boys aged between five and eight, often climbed naked; the foul soot of sea-coal fires were carcinogenic. Other children carried trays of 'long thread laces, long and strong'.[17]*

The constant repetition of each trader's raucous cry had to be audible whole streets away, to alert potential customers. It was recognisable by its cadence and rhythm, rather than by articulated words. (The curious yodel of the milkman and the long-drawn howl of the rag-and-bone man were heard in London streets as late as the 1950s; in neither case were any words distinguishable.) The charming familiar image of a demure lavender-seller in a pretty hat and dainty shoes would have been laughed at by those tough, loud-voiced traders.

Shops

According to Magalotti, 'London abounds in provision of all kinds ... every delicacy or expensive luxury'. The New Exchange in the Strand had 'two long and double galleries ... in which are distributed in several rows great numbers of very rich shops of drapers and mercers filled with goods of every kind and with manufactures of the most beautiful description. These are for the most part under the care of well-dressed women ... many are served by young men called apprentices.'[18] The New Exchange had been getting rather old-fashioned by the 1660s, but when the Fire destroyed its rival in the City, it enjoyed a boom time.

The Royal Exchange in Cornhill was quickly rebuilt after the Fire. Shopping there was a leisurely and enjoyable experience. One

* The great variety of street cryers' trades is set out below in this note, on pages 298–9.

Bun hill

Moore

129

Esplanade

10

62

74

1

74

Guild

Hall

44

Cheap Side

London *the glory of Great Britaines Ile*
Behold her Landschip here, and tru pourfile.

THAMESIS   FLVVIVS   South warke

(above) View of London from Southwark before the Fire. In our terms, London was still small. The built-up area stops far short of the hills of Highgate and Hackney on the horizon.

(previous page) Part of Newcourt's 1658 map of London (see page 17). Aldersgate Street curves up the left side. The open area with trees halfway down on the right is part of Moorfields. The next open space, inside the old City wall, is part of the Drapers' Company's garden. Cheapside runs along the foot. The 'suburbs' outside the wall are less densely built-up than the City within the wall.

Meliora Retinete

(left) John Evelyn (1620–1706) wrote memoirs covering the whole of his life, also books on gardening and aboriculture. He advocated 'green' city planning.

(right) John Aubrey (1625–1697) wrote entertainingly about people and oddities he knew or knew of.

(right) Samuel Pepys (1633–1703) in 1666. Pepys kept a detailed diary between January 1660 and May 1669, when he had to give it up because his eyesight was troubling him. He is holding the manuscript of a song he had composed that he was very proud of and is now almost totally unheard, whereas his *Diary* is unforgettable.

(below) Elizabeth Pepys (1640–1669) in 1666. She is dressed, as the fashion was, as someone else, for her portrait. In her case she was painted as St Katherine, hence the palm branch.

(below) Nicholas Culpeper (1616–1653), astrologer and physician, wrote many medical books aimed at helping his poorer patients (see page 86). Note the signs of the zodiac in the frame.

Clarkenwell greene

Hatton garden

Long lane

Smith field

S. Barth Clos

Grayes Inn

Holborn hill

Holborne

Holborn bridge

Theuer gun lane

Shooe hill

St. Martens lane

S. Martens

Warwick lane

Bushell streete

Pater noster row

Paules Church yard

Old Change

Cheape side

Watling stre

Shooe Lane

Potter la ne

Harp alley

Fleet lane

Old Baylye

Fetter lane

Fleet River

Gold Smet Cort

White Fryars

Black Fryars

Luckgate hill

S. Ann

Carter lane

Carter lane

knightr

Part of Lin colnes Inn fields

Lincolne Inn fields

Thames Streete

THE RIVER

A GENERALL MA
of the whole Citty of Lon
with Westminster & all
Suburbs, by which may
computed, the proportion
that which is burnt, wit
the other parts standing

a. Tuttle Fielde,
b. S. James Fields,
c. Market Fields,
d. S. Giles Fielde,
e. Lincolns Inn
f. Grayes Inn Fields
g. Hatton garden,
h. Moore fields,
i. Spittle Fields,
k. East Smithfield,

l. Tower h
m. Artilerye
n. Charterha
o. East Smith
p. Clarkenw
q. Southampt
    garden,
r. Prata in
s. Charing C

Westminster

St. James Parke

S. Georges fields

South warke

Lambeth

W. Hollar fecit 1666

(previous pages) Map of London by Wenceslaus Hollar in 1666 after the Fire. Most of the area inside the City wall was burned to the ground. The Fire leaped the wall in the west and almost reached the Temple. The houses on the north end of London Bridge were burned.

(above) Sedan chairs and hackney carriages waiting for fares outside the Banqueting Hall. On the right is the entrance to the Palace of Whitehall.

(below) Another view of Inigo Jones's Banqueting Hall contrasting with the earlier Palace of Whitehall. St James's Park is in the foreground, with the 'canal' where Samuel Pepys first saw people skating.

A pre-Fire, timber-framed
house with jettied storeys
next door to a post-Fire, brick
house with the regulation
flat front.

This sixteenth-century mansion
in Crutched Friars survived until
at least 1792, when this drawing
was made (see page 21).

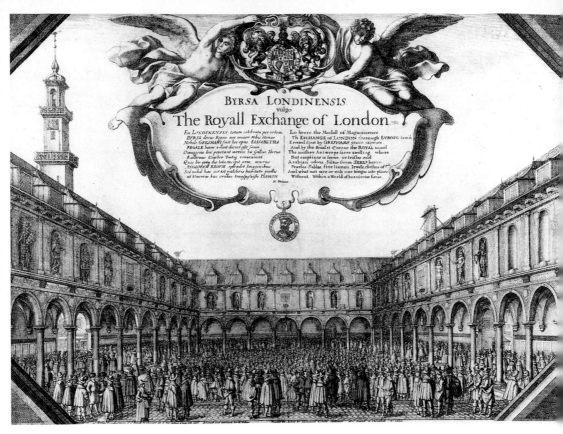

The Royal Exchange was the centre of commerce and gossip.

This terrace of houses built in 1658 on Newington Green in Islington still survives. (The ground floors have been boarded up.) The brick pilasters and arches echo Inigo Jones's neo-classical designs.

might take 'a most delicate dish of curds and cream' with the manageress/owner, or a passing friend.[19] Wenceslaus Hollar published a print of the Royal Exchange including a poem, the last four lines of which read:

> Arabian odours, silks from Seres [China] here,
> Peerless sables, jewels, clothes of gold
> And what not rare and rich our Kings take places,
> Without. Within, a world of beauteous faces.

Copy-writer's syntax, but the sense is clear. Perhaps the Latin version beside it is better grammar.

Improbable as it may seem, Westminster Hall was another shopping centre, the shops sharing the space with the country's principal law courts.[20] (How many shoppers looked up to the ghastly exhumed heads of Cromwell and his generals, Ireton and Bradshaw, which rotted there from February 1661 until the 1680s, when there can have been little left of them?)[21] Samuel often dropped in to buy himself some item of clothing – a shirt, silk stocking, gloves – and to survey the pretty women. He was not, apparently, deterred by one Solomon Eccles, who chose Westminster Hall as the most effective place to show himself (to the lawyers or the shoppers?), 'naked except for decency', with a chafing dish of fire and brimstone on his head, crying 'Repent, repent'.[22]

Shops opened at 6 a.m., or 8 a.m. in winter, and stayed open until 8 or 9 at night, or nightfall in the winter. (We are so accustomed to the availability of artificial light that we constantly forget how dependent people were on the natural pattern of daylight and darkness.) Some of them seem to have acted as social centres. Elizabeth spent hours at her tailor's, whose premises seem to have acted as a club where women could foregather without necessarily buying anything.

Most shops had shutters hinged at the foot, which were folded down and propped, to form the counter, during trading hours, and bolted up at night. In the narrow streets of the pre-Fire City, those protruding counters were yet another hazard to pedestrians. They were not supposed to project more than 30 inches. If the upper part of the shutter was made to form a roof over the open front, it had to clear 9 feet from the pavement,[23] to enable riders on horseback to pass under it safely. The Rebuilding Act provided that 'no jetties, windows or anything of the like sort shall be made to extend beyond the ancient foundation line of any house, save for the stall boards [of shopkeepers] when their shop windows are set open'. The opportunity of forcing shopkeepers to keep within their boundaries was not taken.

Samuel was impressed by the shops in the rebuilt Exchange, which had fixed windows, shutters that were taken down and stored during the day, and counters inside, and were much more comfortable. Fixed windows could create a market by displaying the goods for sale inside, a practice which spread to the let-down-shutter kind of shop, where the apprentice might compose a tempting display of goods day by day on the open counter,[24] standing nearby all day to see that it remained in place.

The medieval tendency for shops selling one commodity to congregate in one district still applied to some extent. Although the main place to buy food was the markets, a few shops were branching out into specialities such as cheese, which did not 'go off' too quickly.[25] Most small shops on side streets sold the produce of their owners – pewter plates and dishes, belts, boots and shoes – and all the other things a household needs. The principal streets were occupied by grander traders,[26] such as John Burroughs, cabinet maker to Charles II, in his premises at 'the Looking Glass', on Cornhill; two opticians, both in Ludgate Street, one at the Archimedes and Two Golden Spectacles, the other at the Archimedes and *Three* Golden Spectacles; and Moxon, the scientific instrument maker, at the Atlas in Warwick Lane, where Samuel bought 'a payre of globes, cost me £3 10s – with which I am well pleased, I buying them principally for my wife, who hath a mind to understand them ... But here I saw his great Window in his dining-room, where there is the two Terrestrial Hemispheres, so painted as I never saw in my life ... done by his own hand.'[27]

Only freemen of the City of London had the right to run a shop in the City, or within a certain distance of the City boundaries. This was a jealously guarded privilege. It was sometimes inherited by widows, who could add to their assets in the remarriage market the prospect of continuing their late husbands' trade.

The Fire brought another change: the beginning of serious advertising. An 'office' opened, 'at the Peacock in the Strand, for advertisements of all sorts, except State affairs; viz, robberies, publications, residence of physicians and artists, medicines, prices of goods, etc.'[28]

Markets

The City

Markets existed primarily to enable country people to provide London's growing population with perishable food, such as meat, poultry, vegetables, fruit and dairy produce. They were owned by the City authorities,[29] which frowned on itinerant hawkers and petty chapmen trying to sell such things as linens and confectionery, which should be sold in proper shops, owned by proper City freemen. Correspondingly, City freemen were not generally allowed to trade in markets.

They had existed since medieval times. The Fire brought rationalisation, but the markets did not stray far from their ancient sites. Produce was segregated into categories. A 'herb market' sold garden produce, from cottage gardens and the numerous market gardens surrounding London. A 'flesh market' sold beef only, while a 'white market' sold poultry and other kinds of meat.

Before the Fire

Leadenhall was the most easterly of the City markets. (It is still there, mercifully enabling city commuters to take the evening's dinner home in their briefcases.) It can be traced back to 1296 and probably got its name from the lead roof of a medieval manor house. Since the fourteenth century it had provided a market site, as well as housing the retail premises of the nail-makers, lead merchants and tanners, with space left over for a City granary and a repository for materials used in the pageants which the citizenry enjoyed. It must have been a huge complex of buildings. It was ideally suited for a market, being tucked away behind two important streets, Cornhill and Gracechurch Street.

By 1660 most of the buildings round the main courtyard were used to store and sell woollen cloth. The East India Company used some of them. The central courtyard was used as a flesh market, on those days of the week when the tanners were not using it. On the site of the original garden of the manor house was the Greenyard, which was shared between 'foreign' (non-Londoner) ironmongers and cutlers, a fish market and a white market.

Between 1657 and 1663 the market days for Leadenhall and the Greenyard were four a week, and the trading hours from 7 a.m. in the summer, 8 a.m. in the winter, until 7 p.m. (summer) and 5 p.m. (winter). But the Butchers' Company was not happy with these hours – they were constantly being renegotiated – and the markets reverted to the 1646 rules: Wednesdays and Saturdays only, opening at 5 a.m. and closing at 5 p.m. (8 a.m. and 3 p.m. in winter). The first two hours were reserved for housewives; after that, the street traders could buy the perishables they hoped to sell that day.

The Stocks market lay west of Leadenhall, at the junction of Cornhill and Cheapside, about where the Mansion House is now. It can be traced even further back than Leadenhall, to 1282. Its name refers to the 'stokkes' (stalls) of the butchers and fishmongers who used it; who in this case, exceptionally, were City freemen.

A herb market and a white market were scattered along Cheapside and up and down the neighbouring side streets, creating major obstacles to traffic there. The Cheapside merchants objected to the mess in front of their shops, so in 1657 the herb market was moved to a site near St Paul's. Just as everyone had got used to this, it was moved again, to Aldersgate Street, causing the Gardeners' Company (market gardeners) to complain that their members found it too far from the river. Another white market sprawled over the streets further west, in and around Newgate Street, just north of St Paul's.

After the Fire

Leadenhall market was providentially untouched. City and country butchers, fishmongers and a white market could all be accommodated there. Temporary herb and white markets were set up further west, and the decried herb market in Aldersgate Street was able to continue; so a breathing space was created for that favourite English occupation, a committee.

The committee had an unusual advantage over its predecessors, who had been thinking about reorganising the markets for decades. For the first time since the Romans, there was money and land available.

Leadenhall courtyard settled down as a flesh market for four days a week, the other two trading days being allocated to the sellers of tanned and raw hides. The fishmongers and the ironmongers stayed on, as did the adjacent white market. The City bought some ground nearby for a herb market. The housewife could do all her marketing there, if she lived within easy walking distance.

The old site of the Stocks market had been a traffic hindrance. It was shifted out of the main thoroughfare, by using the site of a burned church that was not to be rebuilt.[30]

Two more burned churches provided the nucleus of a site on which to house the herb and white markets that had grown up in and round Cheapside. This was called Honey Lane market, after one of the churches.

In 1633 the Bishop of Bangor, who had been a vicar of Hackney, had given £30, with his love, for repairing the causeway from Hackney to Shoreditch used by 'the inhabitants of the parish of Hackney, but especially the poorest sort of people, that maintain their liveliehood by carriage of burthens to the City of London'.[31] Part of Honey Lane market was called the Dorcery, from the 'dorsers' (large baskets carried on the back) used for the transport and sale of vegetables. Here, surely, are the kind Bishop's beneficiaries, still bent under their burthens of garden produce 30 years on. One is glad to see, in the 1677 plan of Honey Lane market, a good big 'resting stone' at the entrance, on which they could set down their loads.

The suburbs

As the population spread out from the walls, they needed new markets; but the City authorities were not enthusiastic about competition for their own profitable enterprises. In 1664 the inhabitants of Stepney and Hackney petitioned the King for a market. 'There are 40,000 families in the manors, 12,000 of whom are seamen, ropemakers or manufacturers [here used in the original sense of making something by hand] having small stocks, who lose much by going to London markets.'

The petition was referred to the Attorney-General, who reported that 'the citizens of London have a promise that no market should be granted within 7 miles of London, but that lately several such markets have been granted and this one is found ... not prejudicial to neighbouring markets [i.e. in the City]'.[32] A few months later a weekly Saturday market at Stepney was granted to the Earl of Cleveland.[33] It did so well that the Earl was granted a second market day in the week, in 1667.

Further west, the Earl of Clare was granted a three-day weekly market in Clement's Inn Fields (now the site of the London School of Economics), since 'the neighbourhood, having lately grown populous, was inconvenienced for want of a market',[34] and the Earl of St

Alban's, who was developing the area round Pall Mall, was granted a three-day weekly market in Pall Mall fields, and a twice-weekly cattle market in the Haymarket.[35] The Earl of Southampton 'and his heirs for ever' were granted a market beside their new square in Bloomsbury, four times a week – it must have been a very up-and-coming district – in 1667, with a market for live cattle and 'hey' every Friday.[36]

Payment

An acute currency crisis bedevilled the early years of the Restoration. It was all very well to paint out Cromwellian inn signs, and restore His Gracious Majesty's head to them, with or without his oak tree; but it was not so easy to restore his face to the coinage of his realm. Clearly the Commonwealth coinage had to continue in use for a while. More than a year after Charles's return, 'the calling in of the money inscribed "the Commonwealth" must be suspended awhile: there are great quantities of it, and the Mint is not yet supplied'.[37]

When the new currency did come, in 1662, it was handsome – what there was of it. There were gold 'guineas' (so called because some of the gold was imported from Guinea by the Africa Company) and half-guineas, crowns and half-crowns, silver crowns and half-crowns, shillings, sixpences and smaller coins, so small that they tended to get lost. The edges of the principal coins were, for the first time, milled, which made coins – and pockets – last much longer.

But there was a dire shortage of coins of small denominations, such as a housewife needed for everyday shopping. This had been an increasing problem since James I's day. It had reached such proportions that something was about to be done about it when the Civil War broke out. Shopkeepers evolved a pragmatic solution: trade tokens. In the 1660s, there were 3,543 'tokeners' in the City, the suburbs and Westminster.[38]

Tokens were usually made of lead, tin or copper, sometimes leather. They were mostly worth a halfpenny or a farthing; only the coffee-houses found it worth their while to issue 1d tokens. They were usually round, sometimes heart-shaped, square or hexagonal. They were about the size of a modern 1p or 5p piece. Shopkeepers kept boxes with compartments for each issuer. (They would need to cater only for those tokeners in the same shopping area – not all 3,543.) When they had enough, they returned them to the issuer, who changed them for silver or notes.

In the short length of Chancery Lane, 28 shopkeepers issued tokens. In Seething Lane, where Elizabeth lived, we know that Ralph Bonnick at the Black Dog and Edward Radcliffe at the Pied Dog issued tokens for halfpennies, Thomas Rivers at the Grocer's Arms and William Vaston, chandler, issued tokens for a farthing; there may have been more whose tokens have not survived.

Nemesis struck, for City shopkeepers, in 1666. Tokens, cash, records, stock and premises all went up in smoke. The Drapers' Company went so far as to hire a silversmith to refine the debris of its office, where the Clerk's desk had contained rent paid just before the Fire, all, of course, in coin.[39] In March 1668, Prince Rupert and the Duke of Norfolk suggested to the King that they should make 'current farthings' to prevent 'the loss and inconvenience by private tokens in case of removals etc., as appeared in the late Fire of London',[40] but it took another four years for the Mint to begin turning out copper farthings. Meanwhile Lord Lucas delivered a passionate speech in the House of Commons, in February 1670, complaining of all that was going wrong: for instance,

> there is a scarcity of money: for all that money called 'breeches' (as fit for the coin of the old Rump) [i.e. the Commonwealth currency, which had been called in by then] is wholly vanished ... and of his now Majesty's coin there appears but very little; so that in effect we have none left for common use but a little old lean coined money of the three former princes [Charles I, James I and Elizabeth, who died in 1603] and what supply is preparing [being prepared] for it? I hear of none, unless it be of Copper farthings.[41]

In 1666 there was 'a slanderous and false report ... spread abroad that there is an intention to raise the value of the coin of the realm ... which may ... much prejudice the public affairs ... His Majesty being much displeased [or so his economic advisers said] has ordered [anyone spreading such rumours] to be proceeded against according to the nature ... of so great an offence';[42] quite how was not stated.

Prices

It has been calculated[43] that consumer goods such as cloth, leather, tallow candles and wheat were more or less stable during our period – 1662, 1666 and 1667 being mildly inflationary years, and the prices in all years being lower than at the end of that century. As an alternative to this impersonal statement, a few examples, from the *Diary* and other sources, will flesh out the picture.

Clothes[44]

5s bought a pair of worsted stockings.

15s bought a pair of silk stockings.

19s bought just over 4 ounces of silver lace.

20–30s bought a man's hat, unless it was beaver, which cost £4 5s.

£1–3 bought a man's periwig.

30s bought a pair of boots.

40s bought seven pairs of women's white gloves, six plain, one embroidered.

45s bought a 'fine scallop'.

£4 bought a woman's country suit.

£8 10s bought a velvet cloak.

£12 a yard was the value of fine Flanders lace (point), 9 inches wide.

£17 bought a man's plain suit and cloak.

£20 bought Elizabeth an Easter outfit.

£24 bought Samuel a silk suit.

Food[45]

1d bought 1 lb of the cheapest cheese, or three red or white herrings. It would also buy a loaf, but the size of the loaf varied. It was controlled by the City authorities: for instance, 1d bought a loaf weighing 10 ounces in January 1665, 13 ounces in May and 14 from July onwards.[46]

2d bought a flounder (a kind of flat fish).

4d bought a pound of the cheapest butter, or a pint of cream, or a quart of whey.

5d bought a pound of brown sugar.

6d bought a leg of beef, or a cauliflower, or a lemon, or two oranges (only one in a theatre).

8d bought a pound of sausages.

9d bought a pound of bacon.

1s bought a chicken in a market; or a chop, bread and cheese and beer, in an inn; or a pint of oysters.

1s 3d was the controlled price of 12 lb of cod.

1s 6d bought an ox tongue.

2s bought 1 lb – a vast amount – of pepper.

2s 6d bought a pound of coffee (but it could cost up to 6s 8d) or a pound of chocolate (but the 'perfumed' kind cost up to 10s).[47]

3s 4d bought a 4 lb loaf of sugar.

5s bought a dinner of roast beef for four, in an inn, or 100 eggs, or 100 asparagus at top price.

10–16s bought a whole lamb, but it was usually sold by the quarter or side.

20s bought the ingredients for an elaborate twelfth-night cake.

£5 bought the ingredients for an elaborate dinner, and supper, for eight.

£7 a month covered Samuel's housekeeping bills.

Fuel

The price of coal varied, depending on the arrival of the collier fleet from Newcastle. During the Dutch wars, the fleet was often delayed by the need to wait for a convoying warship. In December 1666 the price was £3 3s per chaldron (about 1.75 tons; but scales to weigh such amounts would have been expensive even if they were available, hence it was sold by volume. The small quantities sold to the poor were particularly easy to falsify.) By the next summer, when the price usually fell, and people stocked up for the winter, it had risen to £5 10s per chaldron. Three months later it had fallen to 28–29s. After the Fire a tax of 12d per chaldron was charged in London to pay for the rebuilding.

Transport

To hire a hackney cost a minimum of 1s, plus a negotiated charge.

£50 bought two carriage horses, or a coach.

CHAPTER 9

COOKING, MEALS, FOOD AND DRINK

Cooking methods

The easiest way of making raw materials edible was, as it had been since man invented hard pots, to boil them in water over the fire. A large iron or brass cauldron was hung over the fire from a 'pothook' which gradually became more elaborate, enabling the cauldron to be moved up and down, and slung at the back of the fire or brought forward. Vegetables were kept together in nets; meat and puddings were wrapped in cloths. Although different foods could thus be kept physically separate, it is difficult to see how their flavours did not merge. The surface of the boiling liquid had constantly to be skimmed with a 'scummer', 10 or 12 inches in diameter, according to Randle Holme, 'set orderly with holes'. There would be wooden or metal ladles within easy reach.

Delicate dishes and sauces could be cooked in small 'chafing-dishes' or saucepans, over a charcoal brazier, or on a separate charcoal-fired stove, often placed to one side of the main fire. The sites of these subsidiary stoves can often be identified, in restored Victorian kitchens in old houses; the holes for the pans have gone, but the long window giving a good light, and the convenient height of the work surface, still remain. Randle Holme describes the seventeenth-century palette knife: 'an iron made thin and flat at the straight side'. There were smaller scummers 'to turn things in a frying pan or stewed in a stew pan, as [for example] eggs fish flesh or fritters'.

Joints of meat and large fishes could be roasted on spits in front of the fire, made to revolve by an ingenious use of the current of heat going up the chimney. The mechanism involved is sometimes mistaken for the innards of a large clock, which indeed it resembles. Failing such a 'jack', a dog was put into a treadmill wheel hung on the wall (Edmund Verney used his beagle hounds, when they were free), or a servant was detailed to turn a handle. She may not have spent very long at this tedious chore; a small chicken takes about twenty minutes to cook on a spit.

The spits were of various shapes and sizes. A fish would need a basket shape. Small birds could be threaded on to several thin rods, with a clasp to keep them in place. Elizabeth had a spit big enough to accommodate a whole turkey – just.[1] It must have been difficult to prevent it from singeing as it turned. (It will not have been as monstrously huge as those now produced by modern methods.)

Constant basting was needed, with a long-handled spoon. Often a small dish was built into the spit assembly, at one end, to contain a spiced and seasoned sauce. This dripped off the turning joint, with its fat, into a dish on the hearth, and could be reused – as long as the kitchen maid resisted the temptation of the itinerant buyers of 'kitchen stuff'. Small joints could be roasted in a Dutch oven in front of the fire. Frying could be done over the main fire, in a long-handled skillet, or at the charcoal stove.

Elizabeth's kitchen had an oven; she made 'pies and tarts to try her oven with', soon after she moved into the Navy Office.[2] It may have been a separate structure, instead of being built into the chimney of the kitchen fire. It was heated by burning logs which were taken out when the oven was hot enough.

Many households relied on the baker to bake their pies, especially large and elaborate ones. Even when they had an oven, housewives sometimes preferred the lasting, even heat of the nearby baker's oven. Elizabeth sent out for baking a venison pasty she had prepared at home.[3] This was in July; perhaps she did not want to heat the kitchen by using her own oven. In London it was usual to buy bread, rather than bake it at home.

The recipes I have quoted below often use 'a spoon' as a measure. There was only one size of spoon then in use, roughly equivalent to our dessert spoon. It was fairly easy to measure liquids, in standard pint jugs or mugs. As to weights, some authors were more specific than others; but when the ingredients themselves were unlikely to be standard – how dry was the flour? – it would be a waste of time to do other than rely on the cook's experience.

Meals

The cosy family breakfast beloved of modern cornflake manufacturers did not happen. Samuel records various 'morning drafts' and breakfasts, from cold turkey pie and a goose, and 'red herrings' (kippers?), and 'a great deal of wine, a barrel of good oysters, and anchovies' with two cronies, in various pubs, to 'bread and butter and sweetmeats and strong drink' at a friend's house, and 'chocolatte' or whey at home. Those whose stomachs could not face wine and anchovies in the morning probably drank whey or weak beer, and ate a piece of bread.

Samuel sometimes had a 'mid-morning draft', on the same lines as his breakfasts; probably a social occasion with friends, like our morning coffee.

The high spot of the culinary day was midday dinner. We are so accustomed to a linear organisation, in which course follows course and five courses would be excessive, that the horizontal organisation of previous ages seems most curious. We drink our soup; the plates disappear and – at an elaborate dinner – we toy with a morsel of fish. Then we wait for the meat course to appear. That dealt with, we may consider a sweet, cheese, a savoury, fruit. Few of us want to eat all of them. Mrs Beeton called this 'Service *à la Russe*', 'scarcely suitable for small establishments, a large number of servants being required to carve, and to help the guests ... where practicable, there is no mode of serving a dinner so enjoyable as this'.[4] Samuel called it 'the French manner'[5] and mentioned it twice; it does not seem to have caught on.

Even in Mrs Beeton's day the more usual way was to put several dishes of one course on the table at once: 'thick grouse soup, removed by crimped cod and oyster sauce', for instance, with another soup 'removed by' fillets of turbot, and two other fish dishes. There were only three such courses, and entreés, followed, of course, by dessert and ices. I turned to Mrs Beeton for help in understanding how 1660s Londoners dined, but I am not sure the picture is any clearer, save that both eras enjoyed tables laden with dishes, from which the happy eater chose sweet and savoury, meat and fish, as he went along, while everything got cold, and there was a shocking amount of wasted food at the end.

When England was Catholic, fish-eating fast days were strictly enforced. It comes as a surprise to find Protestant Charles issuing a

Proclamation complaining that the law prohibiting the eating of meat in Lent was not being observed;[6] but he had in mind the encouragement of fishermen, whose seafaring skills he might need in any war. All 'innholders, keepers of ordinary tables, Cooks, Butchers, Victuallers, ale-housekeepers and taverners' had to give £60 surety that they would not cook or serve 'flesh' during Lent, or even 'on Fryday nights, either in or out of Lent', and butchers were forbidden to kill 'flesh' during Lent. In return, fishmongers were bound to 'sell their fish ... at moderate and usual rates and prices'. People 'whose condition really requires other dyet, such as are aged or infants, women with child, sick persons and such whose health and constitution is known to be prejudiced by continually eating fish', could get a Dispensation to eat Flesh from the Faculty Office near St Paul's, no doubt on payment of a fee.

A patent registered in 1668 was for 'preserving and bringing of salmon alive and well conditioned to the City of London'. Lampreys (a kind of eel) were also transported live, according to a warrant licensing their export 'alive out of the Thames to the United Provinces [the Netherlands]' in 1663.[7]

Samuel, for one, does not appear to have taken too seriously the prohibition of meat during Lent. Every March, he gave a dinner party to celebrate his having survived his operation for kidney-stone. In 1662 the date certainly fell within Lent. (Easter Sunday, a movable feast, fell that year on 30 March.) He regaled his guests with two stewed carp and some salmon – so far, so good – and six roast chicken – one each! – and two ox tongues and cheese. By 1663 twelve people put away 'a fricasee of rabbits and chicken, a leg of mutton boiled, three carps in a dish, a great dish of a side of lamb, a dish of roasted pigeons, a dish of four lobsters, three tarts, a most rare lamprey pie, and a dish of anchovies', not forgetting 'good wine of several sorts'. They are bound to have had the usual 'banquet' of sweetmeats, as well.

Apart from the gargantuan quantity, this meal contains a staggering amount of protein and little roughage. Was it typical of the diet of a prosperous seventeenth-century family? Evelyn wrote a whole book about salads; but he was an enthusiast for many good but lost causes. Samuel, whose *Diary* was certainly not designed to further any good cause, records few vegetables; perhaps they were on the table but he did not like them. Was Evelyn a voice crying in the wilderness, or preaching to the converted?

While these questions reverberate, let me cite a 1664 recipe for 'a grand sallet', which confuses the whole issue:

> Take in the spring time the buds of all kinds of sweet herbs and of violets and a handful of capers 7–8 dates cut in slices one handful raisins of the sun stoned one handful blanched almonds handful currons 5–6 figgs sliced preserved oranges in slices, mingle ... set a standard of paste [pastry] in the middle of the dish put [the mixture] about the standard add 4 half lemons stick in bits of rosemary with preserved cherries 4 hard boiled eggs quarters of hard boiled eggs and slices of lemons garnish with slices of preserved oranges, between each slice a little heap of capers[8]

– and never a bit of lettuce.

I incline to the view that there were plenty of vegetables on a seventeenth-century table, certainly by our period, and that the reason for their absence from Samuel's *Diary* was that he took them for granted, and concentrated on the more expensive meat. For centuries, vegetables had been the diet of the poor, with an occasional bit of bacon from someone's pig if they were lucky, or a rabbit if they were brave. To admit to eating vegetables was thought unfashionable by some. But what did the gardeners do with the produce of their kitchen gardens,[9] and the stall-holders in the herb markets, with their goods? As a final argument I rely on an Order made in January 1664, 'that the keepers of the King's gardens and orchards at Whitehall, Hampton Court and Greenwich supply a daily proportion of the best sorts of fruits suitable for the season and herbs for salads etcetera meet [fit] for the tables of the King and Queen'.[10]

In the references to food in Samuel's *Diary*, oysters crop up often; they were then plentiful and cheap. At the other end of the social scale, swan was served on special occasions, and venison was a prestigious gift, its receipt proudly noted by Samuel. His idolised Lady Sandwich was kind enough to give him half a buck, when it arrived from the Montagus' country estate; but, 'it smelling a little strong', Samuel got rid of it to his mother,[11] still savouring, no doubt, the honour of having received it. Venison often 'smelled a little strong', having come to London by coach or carrier and not on its own feet like beef. There were many recipes to alleviate this – whether they succeeded or not is hard to tell. There were ways, too, of making beef masquerade as venison, but they did not fool Samuel at other people's tables, if the venison pasty was 'palpable beef'.[12]

Some parts of animals and fishes not usually eaten by us were approved by Samuel, such as a sheep's head, sheep's trotters, a calf's head, calf's trotters, a 'fin of ling [a kind of fish] and some sounds [entrails]', 'umble pie' made from the umbles (entrails) of venison, an ox's cheek and an udder. Palates, noses and lips of any beast were edible. ('Boil till tender.')[13]

Perhaps the most memorable of Samuel's dinners was the pickled sturgeon he was given on 11 May 1662, which unfortunately he kept until an honoured guest happened to arrive, on 26 June, by when 'my stomach was turned when my sturgeon came to table, upon which I saw very many little worms creeping, which I suppose was through the staleness of the pickle'.

When such a disaster struck, the better course would have been to send for a take-away. 'Victualling houses' and cookshops – 'places to buy meat and drink ready for the belly', as Holme elegantly puts it – would deliver; the only thing to watch out for was that the cook's dishes were, naturally enough, marked with his name. To send in the dinner still in those dishes, as Samuel's servants once managed to do,[14] gave the game away, but they should have been forgiven; it was, after all, washing day.

At least Samuel did not subject his guests to one of those joke pies in which one compartment was baked blind (filled with flour or beans, which were emptied out after the pie was cooked). Then a snake, or some blackbirds, could be inserted into the empty compartment, so that when the pie was opened, and the birds began to sing, and flutter about scattering flour and droppings everywhere, or the snake wriggled up the table frightening guests into fits, the host's wit could be commended. But 'this is only for a wedding to pass away time',[15] which can drag at such gatherings.

Pastry was often used as we would use foil nowadays, to enclose meat and stop it from drying up in the oven. Such a pastry case was called a 'coffin', and was not meant to be eaten. Nor were the fortunate revellers expected to masticate the blackbirds' temporary home.

In the evening, supper was prepared and served by the light of candles and tapers; one good reason why it was simple, and often cold – the other being the lasting effects of the midday meal.

It is often said that, up to the advent of winter feeding for stock, or even up to the invention of refrigeration, meat had to be highly seasoned to disguise its rank taste. I have never been altogether convinced of this. For one thing, it can only apply to the winter; in the summer, stock was killed practically on the customer's doorstep, and although the meat may have been unhygienic, it was certainly fresh. Did people change their preferences for highly seasoned food, depending on the calendar? And if meat was so far past its sell-by date in the winter, surely there would have been severe outbreaks of food poisoning? Although 'surfeit', covering a multitude of digestive troubles, was a recognised cause of death, people ate high venison, as people today eat high game, without disaster. I suggest that medieval and early modern people put a lot of salt and pepper on their food simply because they liked it.

Salt for cooking came from the brine springs in Cheshire and Worcester, and from Tyneside. England was nearly self-sufficient, needing to import only small amounts from France, which had the unfair advantage of being able to use solar power to evaporate sea water. 1660s Londoners certainly had a passion for pepper; its import shot up, from £48,000 as an average of 1634 and 1640 figures, to £80,000 as an average of 1663 and 1669 figures.[16] Londoners also had a sweet tooth. The increase in the import of sugar from the West Indian colonies was even more marked: for the same dates, consumption rose from £106,000 to £292,000.[17]

Recipes

A list of recipes would be as tedious as a list of plants. I shall try to give you the flavour of them. Their language is bracing.

To rost a Pike:
Open yr. Pike at ye gills cuttinge all out, then cutt and slit towards his Belly out of which take his Gutts & keeping his Liver wch you are to shred very small with Marjoram, Time & a little winter savory, to this putt some pickled oysters & Anchovies both of them whole for ye Anchoves will melt & ye oysters should not be shred. you must add butter according to ye bigness of ye Pike/if ye pike bee yard longe, then put to ye hearbes a pound of butter & if lesse then lesse butter all these things being well mixed togeather then put a blade of Mace into ye Pikes belly then his belly bee soed up, but take not of his scales then lay him to ye fier and let him rost very leisurely ofen basting him with Clarett wine & Anchoves & butter mixed together & allso wth what moisture falls from ye Pike & when hee is rosted

154

enough adde to ye sawce that wch was in him & all that is in ye pann too & a fitt quantitie of butter too, after squeeze out ye juice of 2 or 3 oranges & if you please into ye dish.[18]

But who wants to eat a yard-long pike? As to 'taking not of[f] his scales', another recipe starts: 'Take a male Pike, rub his skin off whilst he lives ...'. Pike can be ferocious. Nevertheless they seem to have had a reputation justifying the risks of cooking them. Another cookery writer of the time stood no nonsense: 'Take a male pike alive, [and] splat him in halves ...'.[19]

This 'Ryce pudding' suddenly turns into sausages:

Steepe it in fair water all night; then boil it in new milk and drain out the milk through a Cullinder; mince Beef-suet handsomely, but not too small, and put it in the rice, and parboiled Currans, yolkes of new laid Egges, Nutmeg, Cinamon, Sugar and Barberries: mingle all together: wash your scoured guts, and stuffe them with the aforesaid pulp; parboil them and let them coole.[20]

And lastly, to make sugar cakes or Jumbals:

Take two pound of Flower, dry it and season it very fine, then take a pound of Loaf-sugar, and beat it very fine, and searce [sieve] it, mingle your Flour and Sugar very well, then take a pound and a half of sweet butter, and wash out the salt, and break it into bits with your flour and sugar, then take four new-laid Eggs, and four or five spoonfuls of Sack, and four spoonfuls of Cream; beat all these together, then put them into your Flour, and knead them to a paste, and make them into what fashion you please, and lay them upon paper or plates, and put them into the Oven, and be careful of them, for a very little thing bakes them.[21]

That recipe shows how laborious cooking was. Newly milled flour had to be dried before it could be used. There were several grades of sugar, from the cones or 'loaves' which had to be broken up, pounded in a mortar and 'searced', to the 'double refined' sugar, of the consistency of coarse salt, which would still have to be pounded and searced before use.[22] Salt was added to butter to preserve it, and had to be washed out before use. The oven had to be just right ... How delightful did the cries of the girl selling 'Dutch biskets', and the Colly Molly Puffe man, sound from the next street.

155

Cookery books

Any gentle reader who has honoured me by looking at the endnotes will have seen that I have drawn on various contemporary sources. Archdale Palmer's book is a splendid example of the collection of household hints collected and written down, and kept for handy reference in a kitchen drawer, that we have all made, or at least meant to make. He notes the source of every recipe, and the date when he got it. Many relate to those all-important horses, and to such male concerns as how to clean riding boots; but he gives equal care to his daughter's way of 'washing Ribbands cleane' (in castle [castile] soap and fuller's earth) and his sister's 'cure for ye stone' (based on woodlice). Scattered through these invaluable notes are cooking recipes. Obviously Palmer saw his book as a family treasure, to be passed down to future generations in his family. Many families must have possessed such books. Perhaps some of them survive, in dusty cupboards, still.

The seventeenth-century housewife did not have to rely solely on family records. This was the golden age of 'conduct books', which included chapters on home-made 'simples' (medicines), cosmetics, sweetmeats and beverages, alcoholic and otherwise, as well as everyday cooking. Hannah Wolley was not alone in the field, but she was perhaps the first to identify an insatiable market for such 'how to do it' books. The level of skill she expected was high. For instance, few modern housewives would be familiar with the use of an alembic, for distilling, let alone have basic diagnostic knowledge. The format remained unchanged for 200 years; Isabella Beeton's book followed just the same lines, even to the seasonal menus and the lists of duties for servants. Nowadays we may have cookery books in the kitchen, and medical advice books in the bathroom; enthusiasts may have books on making wine and beer, somewhere. Hannah Wolley crammed all this into each of a series of books – *Guide to the Female Sex, The Ladies Delight, The Accomplished Ladies Delight, The Cook's Guide* and *The Queen-like Closet* – all going into many reprints.

Drink

Water was hardly palatable and rarely safe, even the New River water, once it had been through elm pipes and lead quills (see page 10) and lain in domestic cisterns for some days. Ale was the normal drink, or beer. Ale was the old English drink, made of malted grain and water. In the sixteenth century, the Dutch habit of adding hops and making beer had spread to England. Even the sick poor in St Bartholomew's hospital were entitled to three pints of beer a day, as well as an unspecified amount of ale.[23] Boys at Eton had their daily allowance of beer, and were punished if they did not get through it.

Magalotti was astonished by the English workman's habit of going to what his translator called 'public-houses' but the seventeenth-century customer called alehouses:

> It is a common custom with the lower order of people, after dinner or at public-houses, when they are transacting business of any kind, to smoke, so that there does not pass a day in which the artisans do not indulge themselves by going to the public-houses, which are exceedingly numerous, neglecting their work, however urgent it may be.

This sounds more like a complaint by an employer of labour than a direct observation, but clearly 'going round to the pub' has a long history; and once there it is unlikely that the seventeenth-century working man sat and smoked, without a glass of ale or beer at hand.

For home consumption, beer and ale were bought by the barrel by those who could afford it, and by the jug by those whose capital would not stretch so far. A penny-halfpenny bought a gallon of small (weak) beer, threepence a gallon of strong beer. Magalotti found English beer 'far better than ... any other country', and bottled beer, which was just coming on to the market, 'delicious and exquisite'.

Wine was also bought by the barrel. Prices were controlled: in 1661, Canary and Spanish sweet wines could be sold at up to 18d the quart, French wine at 8d a quart, and Rhenish (what we would call Rhine or German wine) 12d a quart. The most popular wine was still the white dry (*secco*, i.e. sack) wine imported from Spain and the Canaries. Sherry and Malaga were not yet fortified. Wine was not sold by the bottle; for one thing, cork stoppers had not yet been developed. The host would decant an *ad hoc* quantity before the meal at which it was to be served.

It was chic to have your own bottles for use at table, with your crest embossed on them. Samuel rose to this on 23 October 1663: 'my new bottles – 5 or 6 dozen – with my crest on them'. The present-day marketing of *le Beaujolais Nouveau* finds an echo in the *Diary*: in November 1666 Samuel approved the 'new French wine of this year, very good'. There were some English wines. Samuel mentions some 'very good red wine made by Lady Batten' at Walthamstow; but the English climate has never been ideal for viticulture. Perhaps Lady Batten was looking to save the duty on foreign wines.

Cow's milk was also thought – probably rightly – unsafe. Milch asses were led round the streets and milked there and then, for those with delicate stomachs, or children for whom a wet-nurse had not been found. Buttermilk was used, and the modern passion for yoghurt was presaged by Miss Muffet and others eating 'curds and whey', produced when milk sours and separates.

Tea, coffee and chocolate were still luxury drinks. A recipe for coffee makes one wonder why anyone drank it, it sounds so revolting:

Take a gallon of faire water & boyle it until halfe be wasted, and then take of that water one pint, and make it boile, & then put in one spoonfull of the Powder of Coffee and let it boyle one quarter of an hour, stiring of it two or three times, for fear of it running over, and drink it as hot as you can, every morning, and fast an houre or two after it.[24]

CHAPTER 10

SEX

A seventeenth-century traveller in time who was able to put the clock back by, say, 5,610 years or so[1] to watch the untutored coupling of Adam and Eve[2] would conclude that not much had changed. Indeed the basic mechanics of the exercise remain constant. But our own attitudes to sex have changed so radically since the discovery of reliable contraception, the pandemic of AIDS and the clamorous proliferation of pornography, that if we are to look back to seventeenth-century sexual life with any understanding, we have to identify our own assumptions before we can examine the attitudes of that age. Since sexual relationships mostly take place in domestic surroundings, a chapter on them properly belongs in this book. Whether it properly appears after 'cooking, meals, food and drink' may be debatable.

Intercourse before and during marriage

Sexual intercourse between couples before marriage is quickly disposed of: there was, practically speaking, none. Illegitimate births and pre-nuptial pregnancies have been calculated for the three centuries 1541–1841. They were at their lowest during the Puritan interregnum, 1650–60. This might be expected, in view of the sanctions that punished any transgression. But they rose only fractionally in the Restoration period, perceived by us as so licentious.[3]

Did couples engage in sexual activity not resulting in pregnancy? I have to say, I do not know. Either the taboo prohibited full intercourse, but allowed caresses short of intercourse; or it affected

159

the whole territory of sexual excitement. I incline to the second view. The average age of marriage, 26, came more than ten years after sexual maturity. If full sexual intercourse had to be, and was, deferred so long, sexual arousal must surely also have waited, instead of being constantly stimulated, as now,[4] but without any prospect of satisfaction.

And yet, consider women's clothes of the time, which enabled men like Samuel all too easily to get their hands down bodices and up skirts. On the general assumption that human nature does not change, and that most men would take such easy opportunities for titillation, perhaps women lived in a constant state of alert to avoid unwanted approaches. One wonders why women tolerated those draughty and inconvenient clothes so long. Samuel met one woman who was not prepared to put up with his advances, during church service one day; she took out a formidable pin and made it clear that she would use it if Samuel persisted. Samuel moved away.

The female orgasm was known to exist, but was not accurately understood. Ever since the ancient Greeks it had been known for a fact – by men – that pregnancy could not occur unless each party reached orgasm: a convenient theory not wholly extinct now. If a rapist could point to the resulting pregnancy of his victim, she must have enjoyed his onslaught – hence, it was not rape. That admirably practical midwife Jane Sharp was not so definite: 'Extream hatred is the reason why women *seldom* or never conceive when they are ravished.'[5]

Samuel had an uneasy moment after a particularly satisfying (to him) extra-marital bout: 'there, after some caresses, *je l'ay fouteé sous [sic] de la chaise deux* times, and the last to my great pleasure; mais *j'ai grand peur qe je l'ai fait faire aussi elle même. Mais* after I had done, *elle commençait parler* as before and I did perceive that *je n'avais fait rien de danger à elle*.'[6] The all-importance – to a man – of avoiding orgasm in the woman, unless she was his wife *and* he was prepared to risk her conceiving, would seem to us unacceptably selfish.

With this limited scope for female enjoyment of the sexual act, it is the more surprising that women were thought – by men – to be dangerously highly sexed animals lying in wait to devour them, poor things. 'Of women's unnatural, insatiable lust what country, what village does not complain?' asked Burton in 1621; I doubt if male illusions changed much in the next 40 years,[7] although I have not come across any such complaints. In 1662 a pornographic pamphlet went so far as to identify a disease afflicting many women – *furor uterinus* or womb frenzy, to be placated only by copulation.[8] Eve was generally blamed for The Fall, and for the end of Adam's happy gardening life in Eden. Sexual intercourse was her fault (although the relevant passages in Genesis do not, to my mind, spell out exactly how). Since the vagina was such a potent mantrap, far better not linger there; erection, penetration, ejaculation, withdrawal – get them all over, safely and fast.

For a woman, sexual intercourse was still indissolubly linked to the hideous dangers and pains of childbirth: a link which has been severed only in our day by easily available and effective contraceptives. Nor did she claim, as a modern feminist might, that women are *entitled* to orgasm.[9] Semen was recognised to be good for women, but ejaculation need not necessarily be accompanied by mutually satisfying love-making. A wife's marital duties included being available to her husband whenever the fancy took him. She must have known, from anecdotal evidence, that conception can result from unwilling intercourse, whatever the ancient Greeks said.

All in all, the marital bed cannot have promised much pleasure. A woman must sometimes have welcomed menstruation, during which intercourse was taboo (in case it harmed the man, menstrual blood being full of evil humours). Her medieval sisters had been able to rely on the church's disapproval of sexual activity, as well as weddings, during about seventeen weeks centred on religious fasts. Although almanacs continued to give the 'Times prohibited from marriage', the taboo against sexual intercourse during those times no longer operated, with the possible exception of Lent.[10]

The infrequency of Samuel's love-making with Elizabeth may surprise the modern reader, aware that Samuel obviously loved his wife dearly and certainly did not suffer from frigidity or impotence. For example, on 2 August 1667 he noted that had not lain with his wife for six months. To those readers of the *Diary* who object that Samuel no doubt enjoyed other women during this time, I can say that he 'did *hazer* whatever I *voudrais avec*' one, with his wife sitting beside him, in a coach, on 2 February; enjoyed various encounters on ten other occasions; and had intercourse, probably, three times; not a priapic record, surely?

Other sexual practices

Lesbianism was known, but not regarded as criminal.

As to buggery, Samuel sanctimoniously recorded that 'blessed be God, I do not to this day know what is the meaning of it, nor which is the agent nor which the patient'; but his friends assured him that 'buggery is now almost grown as common among our gallants as in Italy, and the very pages of the town begin to complain of their masters for it' (that is, it was not in their contracts of employment).[11]

In that context, what is meant is anal penetration of another person, also known as sodomy. The Navy Articles passed by Parliament in 1661 provided that 'buggery or sodomy' in the Navy should be punished by 'death without mercy'. The term 'buggery' was also used, confusingly, to include what a modern lawyer would call bestiality – intercourse between a human and an animal. The exceptions to the Act of Free and General Pardon, Indemnity and Oblivion passed on Charles's return included 'the detestable and abominable vice of buggery committed with mankind or beast', which remained a capital offence.

The existence of an offence on the statute book does not, of course, provide any index of the frequency with which it is committed in real life. The rackety young men who frequented the Court made sure their propensities were known; Sir Charles Sedley's exhibition on the balcony of a well-known restaurant in Covent Garden, 'acting all the postures of lust and buggery that can be imagined',[12] attracted a crowd of a thousand onlookers – and a fine of £500 for riot. Whether the man in the street, watching, emulated him is unknown.

Culpeper thought that masturbation by adults led to rickets in their subsequent children. Rochester described it more tolerantly as a 'kindly easement of Nature'.[13] There was something to be said for it by the Humorists (believers in the theory of humours) too: in moderation, it relieved the danger of build-up of semen, which might have unbalanced the humours.[14]

So far as a liking for flagellation may be a consequence of boyhood beatings, there must have been a lot of it about. Rochester in his poem 'Farewell' refers to it: 'as aged Lechers whip't, their lust renew'.

Oral sex was described in a periodical called *The Wandering Whore* (see below), but in Latin. Non-Latinists had to rely on other sources.

Other deviant practices devised by human kind to procure sexual satisfaction probably existed in holes and corners as they do now, the difference being that now we cannot avoid knowing of them.

Pornography

A modern user of dirty books would reasonably expect them to be illustrated, and written in English. He would have been frustrated by the works available in the 1660s. Few pornographic works were illustrated. An exception was Aretino's *Postures*, which contained pornographic illustrations to his sonnets. The illustrations have unfortunately gone the way of all flesh; at least, there are none left in the British Library's copy.

Worse still, most were in French. There was a surge in the production of pornography in France in the 1660s.[15] Samuel solemnly recorded how he called at his bookseller, 'where I saw the French book which I did think to have had for my wife to translate, called *L'escholle de Filles*'. It was so 'bawdy and lewd' that he was rooted to the spot, but of course was ashamed of reading it, as many a browser in dirty bookshops probably is. Three weeks later he had another hour's free read – and bought it, in a plain cover. The next day, a *Sunday*, he read it: 'a lewd book, but what doth me no wrong to read for information sake'. Having been both instructed and excited by it, he burnt it, thereby depriving his wife of the chance of being either.[16] Samuel must have had the 1655 edition. In 1688, after it had been printed in England, the printer and a bookseller were prosecuted, and fined £2 and £1 respectively, a trifling trade expense for a book in steady demand.

L'Ecole des Filles leaves no stone unturned, although modern theory may not always agree with some of the information it purveys; such as that there is no risk of pregnancy as long as the woman keeps moving during orgasm, or the partners' orgasms are not simultaneous. But it was relatively earthy, compared to another widely circulating book purporting to be a *Dialogue Between Tullia and Octavia*, initiating the reader into flagellation, group sex, *voyeurism* and other deviant practices. The *Dialogue* is remarkable in suggesting that literate women – the only ones who could enjoy its delights – were rarely virtuous, but then no virtuous woman would be reading it.

Another book in circulation since 1658, *Rare Verities*, described

163

bestiality and lesbianism, and retailed as established facts folk tales some of which are still with us, such as that bald men and red-haired women are lecherous.

Everything printed in England was subject to censorship, but the censors were more concerned to prevent the dissemination of seditious matter than to clean up pornography. The sellers of dirty books and pamphlets could thumb their noses at the censors in any case, since their market was largely supplied by anonymous manuscript copies run off by the hundred in back-street scriptoria or copying shops.

Equally ephemeral were dirty pictures – but lacking whatever sanctity print or manuscript confers on written material, they have not survived, so far as I know, even in learned libraries. Which is a pity; I would like to have seen the series of drawings in Madam Cresswell's famous brothel, which one way up depicted religious subjects, but when reversed were erotic.

Prostitution

1660 saw the first number of a short-lived publication *The Wandering Whore*, written as a conversation between four characters in the course of which the names and addresses of 26 'Crafty Bawds' (in the context, brothel-keepers such as Mrs Cresswell)[17] and 44 'common whores' are given. Subsequent numbers contained amplified lists. Of Mrs Cresswell, 'I hear you admit of very few but Citizens, and Citizens wives, whose pictures you keep in readiness for your best customers to chuse upon': the 1660s call-girl.

In 1668 the 'poor whores, bawds, pimps and panders' of London petitioned the most eminent of their number, the Countess of Castlemaine, 'for protection against the company of London apprentices, through whom they have sustained the loss of habitations, trades and employments'.[18] The petition was signed by two notorious brothel-keepers, Cresswell and Damaris Page, on behalf of their sisters 'in Dog and Bitch Lane, Lukener's Lane, Saffron Hill, Moorfields, Chiswell Street, Rosemary Lane, Nightingale Lane, Ratcliffe Highway, Well Close, Church Lane, East Smithfield'. That covered a wide swathe of east London.

The complaint was against the traditional Shrove Tuesday riots by the apprentices, when they attacked bawdy-houses. In 1668 the riots had lasted two days, and many brothels, including the two principal complainants', had been demolished. Whether because of Castlemaine's intervention, or, more probably, because in 1668 they went too far, eight of the unfortunate apprentices 'among whom a custom of attempting to pull down a bawdy house or two had long existed' were caught and prosecuted. At that time riot was equated with treason, and they paid for their exuberance with death.[19] The popular idea behind this demonstration seems to have been dissatisfaction with the bawdy state of London in general; it needed only one more step, to turn into a passionate denunciation of the Court and its ways, which would have been politically dangerous.

The number of whores (the usual seventeenth-century term, pronounced as in modern Scotland, hoors) trading on London streets has been estimated at 3,600,[20] to which must be added those with premises of their own. Remember that the population of the City was about 105,000, in 1660; assuming that only half of the population was female, of whom many were children, the proportion of whores to chaste females rises to startling heights.

Samuel saw 'abundance of loose women' standing at doors in a lane off Drury Lane.[21] Taverns were their stamping-ground, whence they invited their customers to the dark alleys outside, or the unlit expanse of Lincoln's Inn Fields, or as we have seen St James's Park, or the pleasure grounds nearby. They were often country girls lured to the big city by their own cupidity or the inducements of a brothel-keeper, always on the lookout for girls whom she could guarantee to be not only virgin but disease-free. Once these assets had been spent, the girl faced life on the streets until she died of disease or violence or starvation.

One rank up in the hierarchy were the 'jilts' who had managed to acquire their own premises, or worked from home for a madam. Some of these attained the next step and became the 'misses' of courtiers; and who knew what dizzy heights they might attain, by judicious bed-hopping. After all, Eleanor Gwyn's career had taken off from selling oranges.

Nevertheless there were two occupational hazards: pregnancy and disease. Although it is generally stated that there was no contraception, some of these women may have known something not open to their innocent sisters, according to a veiled hint in one of the pornographic pamphlets going the rounds in 1683, *The London Jilt*.[22] But if it was no more than the advice in *The Wandering Whore*, to urinate immediately after intercourse, it was unlikely to have been efficaceous.

But if a whore did become pregnant, she could still try to abort the foetus, or smother the infant. If a live child was born and survived, here, I suggest, is the source of the statistic we began with; the very few children who were born out of wedlock (excluding those whose parents subsequently married) were likely to have been born to whores. As to disease, there were plenty of germs and traumas waiting for these pitiful women, before starvation caught up with them. A minute number might find refuge in one of the 'foul wards' of the two hospitals, but most had no option but to trade until they could no longer walk the streets.

PART THREE

THE SOCIAL
CONTEXT

CHAPTER 11

THE HOUSEHOLD

To a seventeenth-century Londoner, 'household' meant the same as 'family': the collection of people who lived under one roof, whether they were linked by marriage, parentage, apprenticeship, employment or slavery. Since it is difficult to imagine all these people revolving round each other in the sometimes confined spaces of a seventeenth-century house and avoiding the birds and animals that got in their way, I have included pets in this chapter; and since seventeenth-century London contained a huge number of animals other than pets, they are here, too, to complete the scene, however illogically.

The master

The position of the head of the household was no sinecure. Samuel struggled to conduct morning prayers on Sundays, even when he was severely hungover. He took upon himself the physical chastisement of the servants, leaving Elizabeth to keep the household running smoothly when he had just beaten one of its members black and blue. He was also responsible for seeing that fiscal dues were paid. Leaving aside the inevitable vagaries of human nature, the head of the household was monarch of all he surveyed indoors. It was to him that the apprentices were bound; it was his membership of his guild or livery company that protected his family's livelihood, if he was one of London's innumerable craftsmen or traders; it was for him to assess the market and see that his family's productions were brought to the eyes of potential buyers.

169

[Fathers] may indeed have the benefit of the children's labour while they live with him and are maintained by him; but this is no more than he is entitled to from his apprentices and servants ... the legal power of a father (for a mother, as such, is entitled to no power, but only to reverence and respect) ... over the persons of his children ceases at the age of 21.[1]

These heavy demands on him no doubt frequently necessitated his presence elsewhere, such as in coffee-houses or the Exchanges, or on business trips further afield.

The mistress

During his absences, and usually after his death if she survived him, his wife took over. Mary Hull, widow of Charles's mercer, petitioned for payment of £3,932 due to her late husband for goods bought by Charles;[2] she may have continued to trade after his death, since membership of the relevant livery company was often extended to widows of members. But a woman should always remember that 'the whole world was made for man, but the twelfth part of man for women. Man is the whole world, and the breath of God; women the rib and crooked piece of man',[3] and she should behave accordingly.

When her husband's interests demanded that she drop this compliant Patient Griselda attitude and, *for his sake*, don an uncongenial mask of courage or efficiency, it was amazing how often she succeeded. During the Civil War, royalist husbands campaigned with Charles I; after his defeat they went on the run, or escaped abroad. Their property was preserved as far as possible, and managed, by their wives and daughters. The outstanding courage of some was recognised admiringly by their contemporaries as 'masculine'.[4] At the Restoration, as after the 1914–18 war when women had taken over men's jobs, the returning heroes expected women to move over, without demur, and resume their proper place in the home, which cannot have been easy.

We do have, however, an eye-witness view, that contradicts the subservient status expected by English men of their women. Magalotti was surprised to see how 'they [English women] live with all the liberty that the custom of the country authorises ... they go

London Bridge, pre-Fire. Note, on the extreme right,
the heads of executed criminals on poles over the first arch.

(above) River travel could be muddy.

(below) An ornate private travelling coach, with its leather 'curtains' let down.

(previous page) Some of John Evelyn's gardening tools, 1659. Note the 'four-poster bed' frame for tender plants.

(left) An early watering pot (see page 57).

A modern reconstruction (at Broughton Castle, Oxfordshire) of a seventeenth-century knot garden, designed to be enjoyed from upper storeys.

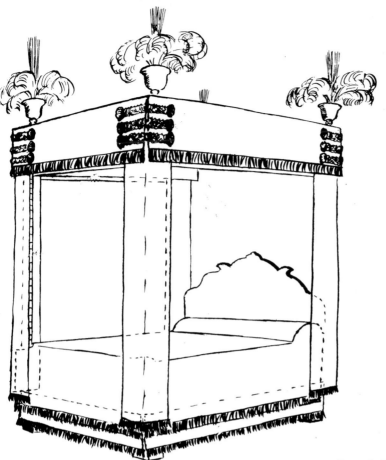

The complications of a 1660s bed.

A royal close-stool. Parliament voted
enough money to Charles II on his
return to buy a magnificent state bed
and a matching close-stool, as well as a
crown and sceptre.

(above) A Quack Doctor presenting his act on stage. The verse on this handbill vaunts his skill in curing anything from the pox to the pangs of love.

(below) Charles II touching for the King's Evil. Patients brought him various disabilities, not only scrofula (see page 80).

The Diseases and Casualties this Week.

Abortive	5	Imposthume	11
Aged	43	Infants	16
Ague	2	Killed by a fall from the Belfrey at Alhallows the Great	1
Apoplexie	1	Kingsevil	2
Bleeding	2	Lethargy	1
Burnt in his Bed by a Candle at St. Giles Cripplegate	1	Palsie	1
		Plague	7165
Canker	1	Rickets	17
Childbed	42	Rising of the Lights	11
Chrisomes	18	Scowring	5
Consumption	134	Scurvy	2
Convulsion	64	Spleen	1
Cough	2	Spotted Feaver	101
Dropsie	33	Stilborn	17
Feaver	309	Stone	2
Flox and Small-pox	5	Stopping of the stomach	9
Frighted	3	Strangury	1
Gowt	1	Suddenly	1
Grief	3	Surfeit	49
Griping in the Guts	51	Teeth	121
Jaundies	5	Thrush	5
		Timpany	1
		Tissick	11
		Vomiting	3
		Winde	3
		Wormes	15

	Males	95		Males	4095	
Christned	Females	81	Buried	Females	4202	Plague—7165
	In all	176		In all	8297	

Increased in the Burials this Week———— 607

Parishes clear of the Plague———— 4   Parishes Infected ———— 126

The Assize of Bread set forth by Order of the Lord Maior and Court of Aldermen, A penny Wheaten Loaf to contain Nine Ounces and a half, and three half-penny White Loaves the like weight.

A weekly Bill of Mortality, 1665. In this particular week 7165 people died of plague, but some still died of grief, lethargy, falling off a belfry or just 'suddenly'. Note, at the foot, the controlled price of bread.

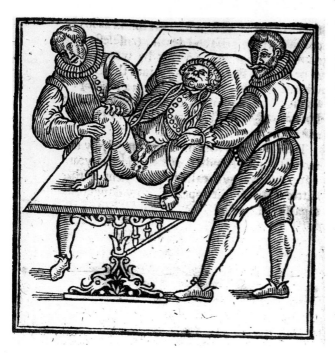

'Cutting for the stone'. The picture is earlier than Samuel Pepys's operation in 1658 (see page 89) but the surgical procedure did not change.

The Chamberlen family's gynaecological forceps and other instruments (see page 94).

whithersoever they please, either alone or in company, and those of the lower order frequently go so far as to play at ball publicly in the streets'. Again, he noted

> the liberty enjoyed by the ladies in London, who are not prohibited from walking in the streets by night as well as by day [here a faint doubt enters one's mind: was Magalotti perhaps misinterpreting the ladies?] without any attendance. By day they go on foot, or in their carriages, either incognito with masks, or without, as they think proper.

Indoors, 'such is the respect which the English entertain for their women, that in their houses the latter govern everything despotically, making themselves feared by the men'. Certainly Elizabeth terrorised Samuel when she had caught him *in flagrante delicto* with the maid.

Magalotti's account has to be discounted by an allowance for whatever conditions were observed by Italian women of his time; yet it remains that he thought the freedom of English women noteworthy. Perhaps there was a wider gap than at first appears between male expectations and female practice.

A few women carved for themselves a niche from which no man would attempt to dislodge them. Women could be street sellers, or peddlars, like Alice Dant who sold small textile wares and stockings from a back-pack, and left £9,000 to the poor.[5] At the other end of the scale, Samuel met a merchant's wife, Mrs Bland, herself a merchant. He was ingenuously surprised at how well she sustained her role: 'it seems she doth understand it and perform a great deal'.[6]

The ancient guilds and livery companies had admitted sisters as well as brothers to their mysteries. Some still did, although the Restoration trend towards masculine domination was as evident here as in property management. But wives could usually find a function in their husbands' businesses, such as buying and selling, and financial organisation,[7] which did not impinge on protected skills and processes. Defoe, looking back to the previous century from his time early in the eighteenth century, regretted that 'women servants are now so scarce ... an ordinary Tradesman cannot well keep one; but his Wife, *who might be useful in his shop*, or Business, must do the Drudgery of Household Affairs'.[8]

There is a thin scatter of female names in any contemporary list of traders. For instance, between 1635 and 1638 three women patented processes, two involving woodworking and one flower essences. None was taken out in a woman's name in our period. Six women issued trade tokens in the decade 1660–70; a minute proportion of the total. A few were printers: Anne Maxwell and Gertrude Dawson printed almanacs, and no doubt other publications.

Children

Toddlers erratically learned to walk in wheeled baby-walkers, where one least expected them, and small children ran about and got in the way, as is the wont of small children. But there was one sad difference from our day: at any time, one of them might be ailing or even dying. Neighbours and 'wise women' would come quietly in to help and advise and reminisce, and comfort, if they could.

Childhood lasted a very short time. In an artisan household, simple tasks could be given to children as young as three or four. Their little fingers could tie silk threads, and pick up buttons and pins.[9] But betweenwhiles they surely escaped sometimes to run and whip tops and play ball in the street. Older boys might be out of the house at school, but girls were likely to be at home and available to look after their siblings while adults got on with the business of living.

Every child had to learn the catechism, and repeat it every Sunday, as well as whenever adults requested a word-perfect recitation. 'My duty [is] ... to love, honour and succour my father and mother; to submit myself to all my governors, teachers, spiritual pastors and masters; to order myself lowly and reverently to all my betters ...'. Whether this lesson in submission really tempered the natural intolerance of youth may be open to question. But the catechism was ground into every child's mind as soon as it could think, and was the yardstick by which adults measured childish conduct – and, by repetition and approval, the yardstick by which, surely, many people continued to measure their own conduct when they were grown, and the emphasis had shifted from obedience to 'doing my duty in that state of life unto which it shall please God to call me'. If a child rebelled, or a young person struck out for herself, it was *against* these clear precepts.

A child should address an adult respectfully as 'Master' or 'Mistress' (a habit long obsolete with us, but only recently abandoned in France).

The pangs of romantic adolescent love could expect no sympathy. Marriage was deferred until the mid-twenties, and then more often contracted for sound reasons of compatibility and property than *le coup de foudre*.[10] As Hannah Wolley put it: 'of all the acts of disobedience, that of marrying against the consent of Parents is the highest. Children are so much the goods and chattels of a parent, that they cannot without a kind of theft give themselves away without the allowance of them that have the right in them.'[11]

Not all children were so fortunate as to grow up in a family; some were looked after by the parish, or placed in the only children's home in London, Christ's Hospital (here meaning a shelter, rather than a place where illness is cared for), which looked after them until they could be bound apprentices. In 1667 there were 267 children in the hospital; 130 had been apprenticed in the last year, and 18 buried.[12]

Apprentices

The apprenticeship system was still controlled by an Act passed under Queen Elizabeth, the Statute of Artificers. The system provided young people with a vocational education, in another household. They had already had years of repeating the words of the catechism about submission and obedience to masters, before they were 'bound apprentice' between twelve and sixteen. Parish children might begin their apprenticeship as early as eleven, and continue in it until they were *twenty-four*.[13] (Remember that the expectation of life at birth was then about 36 years.) The contract would continue for seven years or more, until the master was satisfied that the apprentice knew his trade. Apart from some public holidays, no home leave was given. The boy's parents might not see him again until his time was up.[14] Imagine the child of twelve leaving his home to live in strange surroundings with no parental love, withstanding the storms of adolescence and reaching physical maturity with only the recollection of his childhood and what support his master gave him to sustain him, and perhaps occasional letters from home if his parents could write.

A standard form of agreement was set out in Rose's *Almanac* for 1667. The master undertook to feed, clothe and instruct the apprentice, 'with a due manner of chastisement'. One of the very few justifiable reasons for an apprentice to walk out was if the master's wife took it upon herself to beat him as well.[15] Articles often excluded the master from any liability to look after the apprentice if he caught smallpox.[16] The clothes supplied by the master were plain and serviceable. The son of a rich father may have pined for the lace and velvet flaunted by his peers, but they were forbidden; sighing, he donned the blue apron that all apprentices wore.[17] And worse: 'fornication he shall not commit, matrimony he shall not contract, taverns or alehouses he shall not haunt' – although how he could have bought a drink is not clear; the master did not have to pay him a penny, throughout those long years.

Perhaps apprentices received some reward for their work in the form of presents at Christmas or the like; but the whole idea of apprenticeship was to protect the livelihood and status of master craftsmen – the narrowest of 'closed shops' – so it is unlikely that apprentices often had two pennies to rub together, unless their parents were rich and generous. Even so, this body of young men could present a threat to the established order. 'There being 3 or 4 apprentices to one master throughout the city, if they should resolve to arm, they could hardly be restrained by the trained arms ...'.[18]

The Act of Elizabeth had laid down the number of apprentices that each master might take, depending on the type of his trade, but these limits seem to have been relaxed by the 1660s. Masters in a prosperous line of business were taking up to six apprentices, for each of whom a premium of up to £100 was paid.[19] Goldsmiths and silk mercers could charge huge premiums, up to £1,000. On their public holidays – Easter, Whitsuntide and some others probably including Christmas Day – 'being free from all subjection towards their masters they do whatever they chose ... uniting together to the number of 10,000 [a Magalotti number] ... they spread over the different quarters of the city, meditating *and frequently accomplishing* the annoyance of the public'.[20] One of their favourite ways of annoying the public was to sack brothels – quite why is not clear, unless out of youthful frustration.

Girls, too, were apprenticed. Fly's *Almanac* for 1667 gives a precedent for binding a girl apprentice, by the parish, to a 'water-man'. This seems a curious choice for a female, but the waterman's only obligation is to keep her until she is 21. No mention is made of instruction, or chastisement, let alone fornication or alehouses.

The usual hours of work were long – as long as daylight lasted, except for Sundays, the day of rest and church-going. Defoe looked back to the good old days when 'the Apprentices of the Shop-keepers and Ware-house-keepers ... submitted to the most servile employments of the families in which they served ... such as cleaning their Masters' shoes, bringing Water into the Houses from the Conduits in the Street ... also waiting at table'.[21] Writing at about the same time as Defoe, Blackstone distinguished between the 'natural rights' of a slave, which by then magically became his when he set his foot on English soil, and the right of his master 'to the perpetual service of John or Thomas, this will remain in exactly the same state as before: for this is no more than the same state of subjection for life which every apprentice submits to for the space of seven years or sometimes for a longer term'.[22]

Servants

'All single men between twelve years old and sixty, and married ones under thirty, and all single women between twelve and forty, not having any visible [means of] livelihood, are compellable ... to go out to service, for the promotion of honest industry.'[23] No one was to be allowed to loll about at home doing nothing. If they were not apprenticed, they could find a niche as a servant. This was the theory, but one wonders how far up the social scale it was applied in practice.

Servants were recommended by friends and acquaintances. It was becoming usual to check references before engaging a servant, but this was not always done, which would seem to open the door to dishonest infiltrators and their accomplices.[24]

Samuel had a sister Paulina, whom both he and Elizabeth found hard to bear. The unfortunate woman lived in their household at intervals, in various capacities, from 'waiting woman' to menial. She had little choice, until Samuel at last managed to marry her off, when he could afford a modest dowry. A job as a waiting woman was similar to that of the Victorian governess, in providing the only means of livelihood open to gently bred, unmarried women. (Remember that a quarter of all women never married, in the 1660s.) A waiting woman acted as confidante, chaperone, companion, secretary and lady's maid. She should be able to sing and play an instrument. She was treated as being on the same social level – almost – as her employer, as in theory an *au pair* should be

175

nowadays; but no doubt waiting women were taken advantage of then, as young foreign *au pairs* are now. One suspects that Samuel was not the only employer with roving hands whose advances had to be repulsed while contemplating the alternative – unemployment in an unsympathetic world.

Below the waiting woman was a hierarchy of staff, mostly women. Unlike the waiting woman, they did not usually sit at the same table as the master and mistress. 'Cook-maids', chambermaids and general servants came and went in the Pepys household. One of them even left after she had been deloused, washed down and dressed (shades of Eliza Doolittle) by Elizabeth, but before contributing any labour in return. She was brought back the next day, stripped and dismissed, presumably in the clothes she had arrived in. The newspapers of the time constantly ran advertisements offering rewards for information leading to the recovery of absconding servants and various unconsidered trifles which had left their employers' premises with them.[25]

The spelling and punctuation of the following advertisement are as in the original:

A black haired maid, of a middle stature, thick set, with big breasts, having her face full marked with the smallpox, calling herself by the name Nan or Agnes Hobson, did upon Monday 28 May, about six a clock in the morning, steal away from her ladies house in the Pal-Mall, a mingle-coloured wrought tabby gown of Deer colour and white; a black striped satin gown with four broad bone black silk laces; a plain black watered French-tabby satin gown; also one scarlet-coloured and one other pink sarcenet petticoats, and a white watered tabby waistcoat plain. Several sarcenet, made and thin black hoods and scarfs; several fine white-holland shirts, a laced pair of cuffs and dressing; one pair of pink-coloured worsted stockings, a silver spoon, a leather bag, etc. She went away in a greyish cloth waistcoat turned, and a pink-coloured Paragon upper petticoat with a green tammy under one. If any shall give notice of this person, or things, at one Hopkins a shoomakers [his address is given] they shall be well rewarded for their pains.

Nan must have laid her plans carefully before she 'went away'. With this haul she would be hanged if she were caught.

Servants had no security. Theoretically they were hired from year to year, and could not be dismissed 'unless upon reasonable cause, to be allowed by a Justice of the Peace, but they may part by consent, or make a special bargain'.[26] In practice, their employers

176

often sacked them without going to a magistrate, at a whim, or for some minor misdemeanour, for which they might be beaten as well. Tragic instances of unmerited dismissal were the numbers of servants cast adrift to fend for themselves in London during the Plague, their employers having made off to the comparative safety of the country.

Their hours were long. The complicated laundry processes of the day could mean rising at 1 a.m. so as to be finished by supper time.[27] The maids had to sit up until their master and mistress came home at night. Elizabeth would expect help with undressing. There was less justification for Samuel to insist that his boy should help him to bed, but he felt hard-done-by if he had to manage for himself.

Servants' pay was low. They got their keep, of course, and their clothes; Elizabeth spent £7–8 on outfitting her new waiting woman, in 1666. They could hardly be expected to dress decently on their pay; in 1663 Elizabeth spent £4 on a mere 'country suit' for herself – the whole annual pay of a cookmaid. A less qualified general maid got only £3 a year. But at least 'by service all servants ... except apprentices became entitled to wages'.[28] They often moved on after a few years, to try another employer. The fortunate ones married, after perhaps ten years in service, during which a provident young person might have saved a modest provision towards setting up home.

There was no retiring age, and no pension. Bridget Holmes was in royal service from the reign of Charles I until her death at the age of 100 in the reign of William and Mary.[29] If a servant finally became incapable of work, there was no alternative for her but to apply to the parish.

But there were compensations. If a well-liked servant married, she could expect a modest dowry from her employer. An occasional tip might come her way, either from her employer or from guests in the household. Samuel advised a young man who had stayed only a few days in a grand house to leave the servants £10.[30] The custom applied to lesser homes in proportion. Servants were often remembered in wills, and left sums of money and a share of their mistress's wardrobe.

There were other positive aspects of domestic service then, which do not apply now. Since there was so little alternative employment for a woman, she did not feel *déclassée* if she went into service as a waiting woman; and instead of the lonely life of a living-in nanny where her employers are both out at work all day and come home too exhausted to talk to her, the seventeenth-century servant was part of a small companionable community, where she was valued, or at worst noticed, every day. The labour involved – particularly on washing day – could be taxing, but it was shared.

Samuel's boy was their only male servant. He was dressed in livery (uniform), and walked behind Samuel, to give him consequence in the outside world. At home, he ran messages and made himself generally useful. One of Samuel's forms of exercise seems to have been to beat the boy, with a cane or a birch or a whip or a rope's end, or even a salted eel, which happened to be handy. At least the boy survived, to sin again. The servant of the Rector of Halton was not so lucky: he died, after 'passionate and indiscreet correction' by his master, who was tried for manslaughter – and eventually pardoned.[31]

There were thousands of horses in seventeenth-century London. Many were hired out, from stables behind inns. It seems to have been comparatively rare for horses to be privately owned and privately stabled; but where they were, they would need appropriate servants. Where the master ran to a coach as well, a coachman would be needed too.

Slaves

Our national conscience was so salved by Wilberforce's crusade against slavery in the nineteenth century that we tend to overlook our part in it two centuries earlier. The Portugese had used their journey to the west coast of Africa to acquire labour for their possessions across the Atlantic in Brazil, in the fifteenth century. England put a toe into the water of this lucrative trade in 1562, when John Hawkins of Plymouth sailed to Guinea and 'got into his possession, partly by the sword and partly by other means', at least 300 slaves for sale to the Spaniards.[32] The popularity of slave labour *in England* increased so rapidly that Elizabeth decreed, in 1596, that all 'blackamoors' should be 'sent forth of the land' to Spain or Portugal, since they were upsetting the English labour market.

The advantages of black slaves over white indentured labour in the working conditions of the Caribbean colonies remained, however, and impelled English traders first to buy through Dutch slavers, then, from 1640–50, to acquire their stock direct from Africa.

William Penn's capture of Jamaica in 1655 gave a further boost to the English slave trade; so did the Navigation Act of 1660, which forbade English traders to use the Dutch as carriers. The Company of Royal Adventurers into Africa was chartered in 1660. In 1664 a Caribbean estate-owner complained of the expense he had been put to by late delivery of a consignment of '300 negroes bought by him of the Royal African Company at £20 a head'.[33] By 1672 the Royal African Company was exporting to the colonies 5,000 slaves per annum. 'Wastage' ran at about 25 per cent.

Although the seventeenth-century trade was to the sub-tropical colonies, it was inevitable that sugar estate-owners should bring a few slaves home. Small blackamoor boys made ravishing foils for their mistresses' fair complexions, as in Lely's portrait of the Duchess of Lauderdale; or added to the atmosphere of a cabinet, dressed in exotic costume to hand a dish of tea. Since they had a commercial value, they were liable to be stolen, even if they did not lose their bearings in the vast unknown city, or run away. 'Lost or absented, a little negro boy of about 13 years of age in a grey livery with a black and pink lace and a small cross in his forehead. He speaks Spanish and English indifferently well ...'.[34] The cross will have been a brand. At least he had only one. 'An East Indian tawny-black boy, long haired and slender, a mark burnt in his forehead and breast, his name Peter, in a Purple suit and coat, ran away ...'.[35]

Slaves were bought and sold in England as inanimate merchandise. The case of *Butts* v. *Penny* in 1677 decided that they could be recovered from someone whose possession of them was unlawful, just like any other goods. Part of the reasoning in that case was that they were 'infidels', hence, chattels. Legal theoreticians discussed for many years whether the position of slaves in law would be different if they were converted to Christianity, or, even more dangerously, whether mere entry into Britain, the Land of the Free, would *per se* emancipate them. It took another century for Lord Mansfield to hold, in the *Case of the Slave Somerset*, that it did. Meanwhile, to be on the safe side, better not let any interfering Christian visitor talk to your delightful young black; and, of course, return him to the plantation as soon as he grows out of his childhood charm.

Pets

Charles's troupe of spaniels needs no description. He also had – until they were lost or stolen, and he advertised for their return to the Porter's Lodge, Whitehall – a 'white bitch called Fymm, also a black lurcher with a cut tail called Gypsy'.[36] His brother James took his dogs to sea with him; in a dangerous shipwreck he shouted, 'Save the dogs and Col. Churchill'.[37] He lost a 'large white spaniel' in London, and a black greyhound wearing 'a collar studded with crowns and a plate engraved HRH James Duke of York', on a Yorkshire road. Their cousin Prince Rupert had a famous white poodle, in the 1640s.[38] He lost 'a brace of greyhounds, one black and one white', a young white spaniel and a Yorkshire buck-hound, all in 1667. The Duke of Albemarle lost 'a little fallow-coloured greyhound bitch, her ears cropped round', and two other grey-hounds.[39] One wonders if all these dogs just happened to stray, or whether the royal purse, so reluctant to open for dull things like tradesmen's bills and wages, might be relied on to ransom dogs.

Elizabeth's brother gave her a 'small black dog' – actually a bitch – which was unfortunately not house-trained. It is unusual to find Samuel indefinite about anything, but he does not identify the breed of the animal. It may have been a pug, which was a fashionable breed of lap-dog.[40] Elizabeth did indeed have it in her lap for her portrait by Savill.[41] Or it may have been a 'Pelitean' dog – 'these are little dogs also, which were accounted the jewels of Gentlewomen, and are no bigger than common ferrets or weasels'; or a 'spaniel gentle or the comforter ... A little pretty kind of spaniel of the least sort such as gentlewomen carry in their bosoms, lay in their laps, and kiss and dally withal'.

Randle Holme had also seen in his home town of Chester, 'kept by a certain gentlewoman, a dog so little that she would have carried it abroad with her in her muff',[42] as London ladies did. Nor does Samuel further identify a 'pretty little bitch' that its loving mistress – not Elizabeth – even took to bed with her, with disastrous consequences. Elizabeth was given a 'very fine spaniel puppy' by Sir William Batten, in November 1666; no doubt he made sure that Samuel knew what kind of dog it was, and properly appreciated his generosity.

There was a genre of Dutch painting popular in the seventeenth-century, showing the interiors of churches. In every picture there are several dogs. This would certainly not have been allowed in English churches, but Oxford colleges seem to have had a similar canine population.[43] During the Plague, the destruction of all dogs and cats in London was ordered. Defoe put the number of dogs destroyed at 40,000, 'and five times as many cats, few houses being without a cat, some having several, sometimes five or six in a house'.[44] The Monument recorded that 13,200 houses were burned in 1666. Some houses – say, for this purpose, 7,100 – survived, giving a rough total of 20,000 houses in the City within the walls; that, by a triumph of arithmetic, means that there was an average, before the Plague, of two dogs and ten cats for every house. This does seem rather excessive; can it be that some of the figures are not wholly reliable? It may be safer to say that there were a lot of dogs and cats about.

Monkeys had been imported as pets since the thirteenth century.[45] They frequently appear in Dutch seventeenth-century paintings of domestic interiors. Sure enough, there was one in the Pepys household. It got loose from its harness on one occasion, which led Samuel to apply his usual corrective – a sound beating 'till she was almost dead, that they might make her faste again'.[46] Considering that monkeys cannot be – or at least were not – house-trained, I can imagine few nastier fellow residents. Presumably the 'baboon' (probably a chimpanzee or gorilla)[47] that Samuel saw in Sir William Batten's house, and thought was a 'monster got of a man and she-baboon',[48] was also a domestic pet.

The theory of the 'great chain of being' – that God made the world solely for the use and pleasure of man, his most important creature – was ingeniously harnessed to prove that merchants could be treated, in *some* circumstances, as 'noble', since they supplied, as well as necessaries, 'those *sensus et animi oblectamenta* which the Almighty hath purposely for our solace and recreation, and for no other end, created, [such] as apes, parrots, peacocks, canary and all singing birds'.[49]

Samuel had two canaries,[50] and a blackbird worth 20s: 'he doth so whistle'.[51] King Charles had had a starling 'which he kept in his bed-chamber, and doth whistle and talk the most and best that ever [Samuel] heard anything in [his] life'.[52] Pigeons walked the roofs of London billing and cooing, as they still do; but the seventeenth-century birds were likely to be for eating rather than decoration.[53] Pigeons lived in pigeon-houses or dovecots. In Samuel's famous description of the Fire, 'the poor pigeons I perceive were loath to

181

leave their *houses*, but hovered about the windows and balconies till they were some of them burned their wings, and fell down'.[54] This could be read as either pigeon-houses, or pigeon-lofts in the roofs. Doves were also kept, in smaller numbers, as pets.

St John's College, Cambridge had a captive eagle.[55] I dare say it fulfilled some function of status symbolism in those grand surroundings. The strangest pet of all, in the *Diary*, was seen and coveted by kind Mrs Turner, the cousin who had put her house at Samuel's disposal for his lithotomy. I will quote Samuel's only reference to it, and leave you to imagine the situation before Mrs Turner took this mad idea: 'I to Mrs Turner in Salsbury Court, and with her a little, and carried her (the porter staying for me) our Eagle, which she desired the other day; and we were glad to be rid of her, she fouling our house of office mightily – they are much pleased with her.'[56]

Other animals

Mastiffs were accepted as watch-dogs. They were supposed to be tied up during the day, at least, but Aubrey describes what must have been a terrifying dogfight between two mastiffs, in Jermyn Street, in broad daylight.[57] In kitchens not yet modern enough to possess a smoke jack, there might be a turnspit dog, running round and round inside a wheel hung on the kitchen wall, without time or opportunity to relieve itself except as it ran.[58] There will have been the usual number of stray mongrels and cats eking out a living by scavenging and stealing. Cows and pigs shared their owners' homes, or wandered through the streets. Chickens roosted by the thousand in cellars and attics.[59] Horses varied as widely as motor-cars do. The stallion that Samuel rode to Hyde Park, and the 'managed' (*manège*) horses that he watched there, had little in common with the nags pulling hackney carriages, except their ability to release floods of urine and heaps of faeces in inconvenient places; let fly with any one of four large, hard feet; and bite.

CHAPTER·12

EDUCATION, LITERACY AND SPEECH

Education

When Charles II was twenty, his tutor William Cavendish advised him how to avoid his father's mistakes. 'The Universities abound with too many scholars, therefore if every college had but half the number they would be better fed and as well taught. But that which hath done most hurt is the abundance of grammar schools and Inns of Court.'[1] Charles concluded that education was a bad thing. It had encouraged unreasonable hopes in the middle and lower classes. Far better a good day's racing at Newmarket. The wide stream of Renaissance learning which had flowed so strongly in the Great Queen's days, and had still refreshed his father's Court, was diverted into the narrow channels of the Royal Society, where gentlemen stood about admiring the painstaking experiments of scientists. Education could expect no help from the throne.

Church instruction

More pervasive than Charles's cynicism, however, was the catechism repeated every Sunday after compulsory attendance at church, by every child and adolescent, whether or not they understood it or were able to follow it:

My duty towards my neighbour is to love him as myself, and to do to all men as I would they should do unto me; to love, honour and succour my father and mother, to submit myself to all my governors, teachers, spiritual pastors and masters; to order myself lowly and reverently to all my betters; to hurt nobody by word or deed; to be true and just in all my dealings; to bear no malice nor hatred in my heart; to keep my hands from picking and stealing, and my tongue from evil-speaking, lying and slandering; to keep my body in temperance, soberness and chastity; not to covet nor desire other men's goods; but to learn and labour truly to get my own living, and to do my duty in that state of life unto which it shall please God to call me.

Such unambiguous, practical advice. And so impossible to follow.

Formal schooling

A child's first contact with secular education was likely to be a nearby 'petty' school, where for a few pence a week she was kept out of harm's way, and sometimes as an optional extra picked up the skills of basic reading, writing and reckoning. Reading and writing were taught separately.[2] Reading began with learning the names of the letters, and the sounds they *usually* made.[3] (A French-speaking Swiss who came to England in 1661, and wrote a book on English grammar, lamented that 'though there have been many attempts made to reform the English way of spelling and purge it from its superfluous and excremental letters, yet there has hitherto been but little progress in it ... It is much to be wished, that the English way of spelling were brought nearer the pronunciation.')[4]

Thus, 'scummer', that useful kitchen implement for removing scum, was pronounced 'skimmer'; 'handkerchief' was pronounced 'henketcher'; 'chirurgeon' was pronounced 'surgeon'. A bright child might progress to the tricky heights of 'ou' as in 'cloud', but also in 'should' and 'journey' and 'double'. But the knack of putting the letters together and interpreting whole words and sentences was a long time in coming; sometimes so long that the child left her petty school without it.

The companion skill of writing, which to us goes hand in hand with reading, was taught only when the child had found her feet in reading. There was none of that glow of self-esteem that inspires the young pupil proudly tracing the letter she has just sounded, or producing a legible version of her own name. Mercifully, the crabbed, cryptic 'secretary hand'[5] which had ruled for a hundred years was going out of fashion by 1660, replaced by the graceful Roman or Italian hands, which we would recognise as akin to copperplate. 'These', said Randle Holme scornfully, 'are taught Women for their writing'; and a great improvement they were. Their swirls and squiggles are not easy to do with a quill pen. Many hours had to be spent in practising curly 'pothooks', to get the right pressure, without blots. Even the first step was laborious:

> Take a quill that is clear, the second or third in the wing, Scrape it with the back edge of your pen-knife, and slit it just in the back, and when you have equally shaved down your nibs, cut the ends of them sloping, so that the nibs towards the right hand may be shorter: round the ends of them a little, and when you have cut a place to receive the ink, wet it in your mouth, and hold your pen in your right hand between the fore-finger, middle-finger and thumb ... In writing, sit upright in Majestic posture...[6]

(I have to admit that ready-cut pens were sold by street vendors; I do not know whether schoolchildren were allowed to get away with that short-cut. Even ready-made ones would need trimming to the writer's own hand.)

So reading and writing were arid, painful fields, gladly forsaken as soon as possible by many. After all, who among the adults that a child knew could read or write? Very few, as we shall see. Many households possessed a Bible, but not necessarily for reading; it might come in useful in other ways, such as divining the whereabouts of lost objects and recording − written by someone else − family births, deaths and marriages.

Basic numeracy was more obviously useful. Grown-ups did a lot of sums, adding up the cost of food and taking it away from the coins in the household purse. I suspect that many children left their petty school with some ability to manage figures. Maidservants, for instance, were expected to be able to account for any housekeeping money they spent.[7] Apprentices minding their masters' shops had to give change. This was the only place where they may have learned how to do it, unless it came later by experience. (We tend to assume that reading and reckoning go together; that if you cannot read letters, you cannot 'read' figures either. But many an illiterate market trader can put a hand-held calculator to shame.)

Some petty schools were run by the families of immigrant weavers and other foreigners who increasingly affected London life. A child would acquire some knowledge of simple textile operations likely to be useful later, as well as or instead of reading, writing and reckoning. Some schools were fortunate in being under the care of a cleric who had lost his place in the religious upheavals, and who was available to transmit his skills in reading and writing. But, in general, elementary education did not reach a high standard.

For most girls, that was the end of schooling. 'Most in this depraved later Age think a woman learned and wise enough if she can distinguish her husband's bed from another's.'[8] Even if girls had almost reached the threshold of literacy before they left, they relaxed with a sigh of relief and got on with learning how to run the house from their mothers, who had felt no disadvantage in the honourable status of housewife from not being able to read or write. The main inducement to preserve, even to extend, reading skills was to be able to read the ballad sheets and chap-books, and the more accessible of the almanacs, that so proliferated; but sitting down with a good book was unthinkable. Writing had no demonstrable use at all.

Boys might still have some way to go, if they were to enter St Paul's, as Samuel did, or the charity-endowed schools such as the Greencoat school (founded 1633) or the Blackcoat school (founded 1656). They were supposed to be literate on admission at the age of eleven, but many were not.

St Paul's school was destroyed, with the cathedral, in 1666. The then High (head) Master moved to Wandsworth, and set up a school there which some Pauline boys may have been able to attend. The school reopened on its old site in 1671. Few things illustrate the small scale of seventeenth-century operations as vividly as the size of the school: St Paul's, the principal school in the City, had 153 scholars, and three masters, the High Master, the Surmaster and the Chaplain. There may at times have been a few more pupils, who paid fees, but the scholars paid nothing except an admission fee of 4d, 'to the poor scoler that sweepeth the school'. Masters may have occasionally taken a few boys into their homes, as boarders, but this was frowned on by the governors and frequently forbidden. The boys were taught Latin, Greek in the senior classes, and perhaps some Hebrew.[9] No science was taught, nor mathematics, nor geography, nor any living foreign language. The hours were long, the holidays short, the beatings frequent and painful.

The Act of Uniformity of 1662 provided that all teachers in

universities and schools, and the private tutors of the rich, had to be licensed and to conform to the Church of England. It does not seem to have been strictly enforced: some Nonconformists defied it and opened boarding schools taking between twelve and twenty boys,[10] outside the City limits. The Quakers opened a school for boys at Waltham in Essex in 1668, and another at Shacklewell, just north of Hackney, 'to instruct young lasses and maidens in what-soever things were civil and useful in the creation'.[11] By 1671 there were fifteen Quaker boarding schools, of which two were for girls and two were coeducational.

The sons of the nobility were usually educated at home by private tutors. They had the best chance of any, of acquiring a widely balanced culture, whether or not they took advantage of it. Very occasionally their sisters might be allowed to sit in on their lessons, but they would not be taken on the Grand Tours of European culture that their brothers set out on.

In 1650 Samuel had gone up to Cambridge, with an Exhibition (grant) from the Mercers' company tenable by St Paul's boys.[12] At Cambridge, once again, the syllabus was rooted in, and largely confined to, the classics. I shall not pursue a London boy to Oxford or Cambridge in the decade 1660–70, which would make a book on its own. Anthony Wood summarised the state of play: 'After the Restoration Oxford [and Cambridge] did in some manner decay in number. Presbyterians and Independence and other fanaticall [Nonconformist] people did forbeare to send their sons for feare of orthodox principles. Another party thought a University too low a breeding' – and sent their sons on a Grand Tour instead. As Edward Cocker put it in *The Clark's Tutor*, published in 1671, 'Paris Rome and Constantinople are the Court of the World: Venice Geneva and Lisbon, the City: Provence, Andalucia and Italy the garden: Africk and America the Desert and Wilderness.'

But where we may properly – that is, within the limits of this book – find young men being educated is at the 'third University'. There were then, as now, four principal Inns of Court: Gray's Inn north of Holborn, Lincoln's Inn along Chancery Lane, and Inner and Middle Temple along the river. Each had subsidiary Inns, and there were others for specialised branches of the legal profession. 'Men of estate ... left their patrimonial estates improved, to a Hopeful Heir, who pass[ed] from the free-school to the Colledge [Oxbridge] and thence to the Inns of Court acquainting himself with a competent tincture of the Laws of his Country', as John Evelyn put it.[13]

The competent tincture did not involve the exertion of being called to the Bar. But it would have the side-effect of imparting the metropolitan polish lacking in their distant home towns, or even in the fens or the Cotswolds, and – perhaps most important of all – they would make the acquaintance of other young men, who might have influential fathers or marriageable sisters. (This last is a supposition of my own, based only on one match I know of, between a young man from Derbyshire and a Kentish heiress. Like his father and brothers, he was admitted to Gray's Inn. The men in her family, too, tended to join Gray's Inn. How did he ever meet her, unless through this connection? Travel was difficult in those days; not lightly to be undertaken. He did not 'just happen to be passing', from Dovedale to Betteshanger.)

A very few girls, statistically speaking, went to one of the finishing schools clustered round Chelsea and Fulham, and, particularly, in the country village of Hackney. Mr Priest's school in Chelsea taught japanning [the newly fashionable lacquering] and other handicrafts, but, above all, dancing and music. Purcell wrote *Dido and Aeneas* for Mr Priest's girls to perform, in 1680. Mrs Perwich's school near Hackney Church had kept going throughout the Civil War. In 1661 it had 100 pupils, learning music, dancing, romance reading, lute, harpsichord, singing, violin playing and chamber music, with visiting masters 'of high standard'. Vivaldi would have approved: it had an orchestra of lutes and viols, with a harpsichord and organ. With all that, the pupils learned 'all other parts of excellent well-breeding', such as calligraphy, accountancy, housewifery, cookery, handicrafts and embroidery.

Hannah Wolley in Hackney offered instruction in

all works wrought with a needle, all transparent works, Shell-work, moss-work, also cutting of prints and adorning rooms or cabinets with them. All kinds of Beugle-works upon Wyers or otherwise [bugles were glass beads]. All manner of pretty toys for closets. Rocks made with shells or in sweets. Frames for looking-glasses, Pictures or the like. Feathers of crewel [wool] for the corner of beds.

Yet she was the author of those down-to-earth conduct books which insisted that women should understand, and be able to perform, all the practical tasks of a household. In *A Gentlewoman's Companion*, written in 1675 when she had been teaching for 30 years, she expressed her true feelings: 'Man is apt to think we were meerly intended for the world's propagation and to keepe its humane inhabitants sweet and cleane; but, by their leaves, had we the same Literature he would find our brains as fruitful as our bodies.'

There was a 'French school for young gentlewomen' in Longacre, 'where besides all fitting accomodations, they are taught the French Tongue with great advantage ... and have likewise all other kinds of education, as Writing, Dancing, Musick, etc., and with very good success, as many persons of Quality have had experience of'.[14]

If the rule for girls' education was the acquisition of useless accomplishments, there were shining exceptions. The Quakers believed in the intellectual as well as the spiritual abilities of women. And I cannot resist a reference to Mrs Basua Makin's school for girls at Tottenham High Cross, established in 1673, where eight-year-olds 'that can read well' could learn Latin, French, English grammar, Greek, Hebrew, Italian, Spanish and much else.

But there was a strong backlash. Once the Civil War and its aftermath were over, and the King safely back, men expected women to revert to their proper, humble status of admiring help-mate, who had no need of book-learning. In those days of high maternal mortality, an expectant mother often left directions as to how the child should be brought up, in case she should die in childbed. In 1661 Mrs Josceline wrote that if her baby was a daughter, 'I desire her bringing up may be learning the Bible as my sisters doo, good huswifery, writing and good work; other learning a woman needs not.' And the wife of John Evelyn, of all men, who when he married her at twelve years old was widely read, spoke French and understood Italian, thought that 'women were not born to read Authors and censure the learned ... all time borrowed from Family duties is misspent; the care of Children's education, observing a husband's commands, assisting the sick, relieving the poore and being serviceable to our friends, are of sufficient weight to employ the most improved capacities among us'.[15]

The result of girls' education can be seen, and enjoyed, in the Verney letters of the time.[16] In 1662 Betty Verney, who was restricting her marriage prospects because she insisted on having a lady's maid, wrote: 'As for the dressing my head myselfe, I must deal injenoiosely with you; I cannot yet doo it; I am confident going to plow would not mack me mor sick than the reaching up my armes does.'

Lady Hobart's request for some 'Jeseney and hunicuckells' for her garden was quoted in Chapter 4, but deserves another airing. Here she is describing the Fire of London, which stopped just short of her house in Chancery Lane: 'sure soe sad a sight was nevor seen be foare as that sitty is now lying in ashes besides the unimmajanable loos the hole kingdom receives buy it so trobled at the sad nuse of the distroction of Londone that I could not rit'. And about a young wife who was clinically depressed: 'Your por son will be a very misarabell man in his wif I fear ... She gros very malisas in hur toung to us all.'

Lady Hobart attacked written English through her ears, and wrote down exactly what she wanted to say, as she heard it in her mind. The familiar words came out easily – she remembered them from school – but faced with a word she had not learned to spell there, she sailed straight on undaunted. And once we, poor rule-bound readers with spell-checks in our computers, have got over our surprise, she carries us with her. (If not, try reading her aloud.) In any case, there was no proper or correct way of spelling. Printing was gradually imposing uniformity, but in our period it was no disgrace to spell phonetically, idiosyncratically or in the Verney style; as long as your readers were with you, that was all that mattered.

Self-improvement

We expect a reasonably educated person to have acquired some knowledge of arithmetic, geography, history and a foreign language. Both sexes are exposed to some form of tuition in domestic economy (or whatever the current subject description is) and woodwork or more useful practical skills. Girls no longer rely on their mothers for household experience, since those mothers are themselves likely to be earning a wage or salary outside the home. Most children now have an apparently innate knowledge of computers, although not of ironing.

The seventeenth-century picture is surprisingly similar, if you substitute individual tuition for schoolwork; assume that only a minute proportion of young people took the opportunities available; and for computers substitute shorthand and ready reckoners. But a seventeenth-century child would know much more than his modern counterpart about other subjects affecting everyday life, such as gardening, astrology and basic health care.

Samuel's knowledge of shorthand was not unusual for someone

of his background, in those days of elaborate handwriting. The idea that his *Diary* was written in an inscrutable code dies hard; let me repeat what so many have already said (but the truth is not nearly so interesting as an attractive fabrication): Samuel used an accepted system of shorthand, which had been invented by Thomas Shelton in 1626.[17] The name would be familiar to us if Pitman's system had not swept the board 200 years later. Shelton's was only one of a series on the market, beginning in 1588. Magalotti noted how both men and women wrote 'an abridgement' of sermons in church, meaning shorthand rather than a summary. Sometimes half the congregation would be busily scribbling away. In 1664 the 'books lately printed' advertised in an almanac included 'The psalms in Meeter ... written the shortest and exactest way by the rules and marks of Mr Shelton's book of short-writing'. Certainly shorthand would have baffled Elizabeth, if the unthinkable had happened and she had found Samuel's *Diary*. (She would not have been able to read the erotic passages, which were often in French, because they were in shorthand too.) But he may have used shorthand simply because it came easily to him.

Samuel's eager pursuit of other knowledge was characteristic of him. When he was 29 and a promising young clerk in the Navy Office, he realised that he was going to need mathematics, so he got the mate of the *Royal Charles* to give him eight lessons, beginning with the multiplication tables,[18] which his protracted and thorough education had not touched. His acquired ability to handle figures was rare outside the worlds of merchants, mariners and surveyors, and stood him in good stead years later when he justified to Parliament the Navy's expenditure of hundreds of thousands of pounds.

Those without Samuel's access to experts could attend the lectures at Gresham College, which had been founded in 1596 to enable Londoners to share in the new knowledge. Lectures on divinity, law, physic, astronomy, geometry, rhetoric and music were (and are still) given *free* and *in English*. 'Forasmuch as the greatest part of the auditory [audience] is like to be of such citizens and others as have small knowledge, or none at all, in the Latin tongue, and for that every man for his health's sake will desire to have some knowledge in the art of physic', the physic professor was told to deal with modern theories, and not recycle the ancient Greeks.[19]

Those who needed to manipulate figures could buy one of the ready reckoners advertised for sale in the almanacs, which often themselves gave tables of interest at 6 per cent (the maximum permitted rate) on sums from 5s to £100, for periods of one, three, six, nine and twelve months, and other useful data such as the value of annuities and leases.

Cocker's *Arithmetic*, which was a sore trial to many generations of schoolboys, was published in 1671. The multiplication tables 'must perfectly be learned by heart', but they only went up to 9 × 9, which was at least something. He set practical equations, which he called 'the golden rule' or 'rule of three'. Does this sound familiar? 'If 12 clerks can write 144 sheets in one day or 12 hours, how many must be employed to write the same number of sheets in 3 hours?'

In 1662 Samuel also 'perceive[d] that I am very short in my business by not knowing many times the geographical part of my business'.[20] Being Samuel, he set to and learned it, so well that by 1663 he could teach Elizabeth, using a 'payre of Globes'[21] – one of the Earth and one of the stars and planets – since she 'hath a mind to understand them', her perfunctory schooling having been deficient in this and many other respects. Samuel bought his from Joseph Moxon, his Majesty's Hydrographer, for £3 10s, a considerable sum in those days. Such pairs of terrestial and celestial globes, which could be works of art, were standard equipment in any cultured man's study.

Holland was the market leader in atlases. Mercator's *Atlas* (he was the first to use the name)[22] of 1595, and the superb *Atlas Major* published by Dr Blaeu in 1662, were both printed in Amsterdam. Blaeu's atlas ranges from Iceland to Japan, China to Brazil, in astonishing detail. (It is true that there are spaces in Africa filled in with elephants and ostriches; but when I worked in the Department of Lands and Surveys in Tanganyika in the 1950s there were still blank spaces on our maps, filled much less evocatively by the letters MBA, miles of bloody Africa.) The literate average man would not be able to afford those sumptuous productions, nor was he likely even to see them, but he could call into one of the many London map-sellers and, like Samuel with his pornographic book, have a free look at the multitudinous prints and maps of foreign places.

John Ogilby, whom we met when he produced the post-Fire map of London, was perhaps inspired by Blaeu's achievement when he planned an *English Atlas* in five volumes, which were to cover Africa, America, Asia, Europe and Great Britain. Advertisements inviting subscriptions for it began to appear from May 1669, but he seems to have bitten off more than he could chew. Only the Britannia volume achieved publication, and that after his death in 1676. Ogilby must have been an extraordinary man. He was born near Dundee in 1600. In the 1620s he had a dancing school conveniently close to the young gentlemen of Gray's Inn; then he went to Ireland, but lost everything he had in the Civil War. He set up as a publisher, in London, and again lost everything, in the Fire. Yet in 1667 he published *An Embassy From the East India Company of the United Provinces [Holland] to the Great Tartar Cham, Emperor of China.*[23]

The almanacs and news-sheets of the time frequently carried advertisements for books about foreign parts: for instance, *The Voyages and Travels of the Ambassadors from the Duke of Holstein to the Great Duke of Muscovy and the King of Persia 1633–39, with the Travels of John de Mandelsto* [sic: Mandeville?] *from Persia to the East Indies and thence into England 1633–50*; or *A Compleat History of Muscovy, Tartary and the Indies and the Adjacent countries … with divers maps and figures.* Almanacs themselves were an excellent source of geographical knowledge: for instance, they gave the following distances from London, which tended to vary depending on author; alternatives are in brackets.

Mexico	6,844 (5,710)
Calicut	5,214 (4,840)
Bermoudas	3,409
Babylon	2,724
Alexandria	2,169
Constantinople	1,547 (1,480)
Troy	1,605
Rome	857
Edinburgh	328
York	150
Calais	56

– and Quintzoy, 'the greatest city in the world', 7,272 miles away. (Where was Quintzoy? Where, come to that, was Troy? Yet Wing's *Almanac* for 1665 gives not only these distances, but the longest days in each place, and its meridian.)

Some geographical knowledge was assumed in any reader of a news-sheet. A random example, the *Weekly Intelligencer* for 2 November 1661, gave foreign news from Genoa, Madrid (where the young prince had died despite the bodies of Saints Isidore and Diego being brought to his room), Tangier, Dantzig (the Poles and Tartars had beaten the Muscovites), Rome, Alicante (the English had captured three Turkish pirate ships at Majorca), the Hague (Dutch privateers had captured two English ships bound for Portugal from Brazil; we wanted them back), and Venice (the pirates of Tripoli had captured three Christian trading ships).

It was no wonder that Jamaica was often in the news, when the King had promised in 1661 to allot 30 acres of 'improveable' land there to every person, male or female, over twelve years old, who went to live there in the next two years.[24] Twelve months later there was news of 'Surynam [Guyana] ... first settled in time of rebellion by banished Royalists [it] is yet coming to the highest probability of being the richest and healthfullest of all our foreign settlements'.[25] In 1668 William Lilley's *Almanac* carried advertisements for 'two books, of natural and moral history of Barbados, St Christophers, Mevis [sic], St Vincents, Antego, Martinico, Monferrat and the rest of the Caribby-Islands, in all 28', and 'a Book on the Ottoman Empire'. All this information about foreign places must have kept the coffee-houses buzzing and the globes turning.

Almanacs could also be relied on for a firm grasp of general history. Most of them gave a list of dates regarded *by the writer* as important, usually expressed as the number of years *ago* that something happened. Thus, counting back from, say, 1666:[26]

Creation of the world	5,670 years ago
Noah's flood	3,959
Brutus came to Britain and built London	2,773
Rome built	2,418

and from 1667:[27]

Joseph of Arimathea came to England	1,606 years ago
Painting and glazing first used in England	1,010
Coaches first used in England	92
Tobacco first planted in England	82
The great plague, whereof died 30,578	66
Smithfield paved	52
[Another] great plague whereof died 35,418	42

The plague outbreak we think of as The Great Plague, 1665, was not even mentioned. Perhaps two years was not long enough for the printers to reset the type.

Adam was, as we have seen, created 5,628 years before 1664.[28] He died 930 years later. The same almanac reminds us that the drawbridge which for many years had allowed ships to pass London

Bridge had been repaired in 1628 (it was obsolete by 1660).

One more almanac, this time George Wharton's for 1666. His memorable dates include:

1609: The making of Allum first brought to perfection in England, and silkworms first brought to England.

1659: Richard Cromwell [Oliver's son] his party deserting him consented to a commission and proclamation for dissolving his Parliament which was done accordingly. After which himself also was decently laid aside.

So much for history. Foreign languages could be acquired by personal tuition from the many foreigners at a loose end in London. The 'Ministers of the King's [actually the Queen Mother's] French Church ... will correct the accent of people who have learnt French from the Normans, Walloons etc., who may be taught in an hour to pronounce the sweetest way.'[29] The Flemish weavers spoke Walloon, and their heavy accent would grate on a Parisian ear.

If any person desireth to have either French gentlemen or gentlewomen or pages to wait, or other serving women of the same nation, as also Tutors to teach children at home, let them go to the French Church of the Savoy ... on Sunday, or any daies of the week to M. de Billon la Mare, in the Woodyard in Longacre ... and there they shall have information.[30]

Christianus Gravius, a gentleman that formerly taught the French Italian and Spanish languages in the famous university of Heidelberg, being lately come hither ... undertaketh to use such a method and give such directions therein that, according to the capacity of the Learner, they may suffice to bring him to a perfect knowledge of either of the said languages within 4 months or less.[31]

And occasionally those long years of Latin bore fruit, as when Samuel was able to converse with a prisoner in French and Latin (in confused circumstances – the prisoner was English) over 'a bottle or two of wine'.[32]

Where a seventeenth-century almanac reader would score over a twentieth-century reader of the popular press would be in gardening, astrology and medicine. Gardening we have already looked at. Our own popular press carries gardening articles, but not so pervasively as seventeenth-century almanacs, all of which insisted on proffering advice to their readers.

195

Certainly our popular press informs us of what our stars foretell; but in generally worded snippets. The seventeenth-century reader of almanacs could not but be aware of the yearly zodiacal progression of the stars and the career of comets, 'God's Ambassadors',[33] 'which God is pleased to send beforehand to forewarn us, that we may repent of our sins'.[34] He would need to know which sign of the zodiac applied to any current twinge, and whether the stars recommended a bath. John Tanner in his almanac noted that there would be an eclipse 'to be seen in both the Javas, Melair [Malaya?], Japonia, the Philippines and Molucca Islands', and another 'visible in Magellanica and other places very remote and unknown to us'. It was something to know that they happened, even if personal attendance was impossible.

The exactitude of almanac writers as to distances, so pleasing in geographical matters, is not lacking in astrology. Dade stated in his 1664 almanac the distances of the planets from Earth:

Saturn	47,708,750
Jupiter	26,030,920
Mars	7,558,540
Sun	5,025,303
Moon	208,290

And lastly medicine. Many Protestants, as well as Sir Thomas Gresham, held that any responsible man could and should doctor his own body, just as he could minister to his own soul. (It was for this reason that Sir Thomas had instituted his free lectures.) Culpeper had written in English, for the lay reader. The mass-market almanacs varied slightly in the emphasis of the standard information they provided. Not all of them gave tide tables, for instance, or the distances and dates I have abstracted above. But without exception they could be relied on for medical advice. An example at random: 'Diet after bleeding ... see that the moon be not in any of the figures that chew the cud ... for then the medicine will stay but little with the patient, causing him to vomit ...'. Possibly a quick look at Culpeper might be a useful cross-check.

Almanacs cost between 2d and 4d each.[35] No wonder that they sold so well – 400,000 almanacs were sold *annually*, in the 1660s.[36] Although they were mostly edited to fit each new year, much of the information in them remained as valid as when first printed, and most households would have several knocking about somewhere, to pass the idle moment, or to consult for horticultural or medical advice.

But reading, as we have seen, did not imply that the reader could also write. Literacy can be assessed in various ways; there is a difference of degree almost amounting to a difference in kind, between someone who can, with an effort, sign his name on a legal document, and someone who would think nothing of dashing off a newsy letter. Much academic midnight oil has been burned while an index of literacy that satisfactorily shows this difference has been sought. In the end, however, the stark difference between someone who signed documents with a mark, and someone able to write his name on them, has been adopted; and on that basis – admittedly imperfect, but at least consistent – 78 per cent of women were illiterate in the 1670s. Women were learning fast, however: twenty years later the figure had shrunk to 52 per cent.

Men in the great wide world had more need of literacy. An interesting table has been compiled[37] of the *il*literacy of various trades in London in the period 1580–1700, from which I have taken examples:

merchants	0%
goldsmiths	3%
drapers	12%
mariners	23%
sailors	29%
clothworkers	30%
butchers	35%
bricklayers	38%
carpenters	40%
watermen	67%

Bear in mind that these figures do *not* imply that six carpenters out of ten would sit down to read the latest book review; they mean only that one out of three watermen could at least sign his name. To my mind, this is still surprising, considering the little use watermen would have for such a skill.

Before embarking on the last aspect of this wide-ranging chapter, a small excursion: in 1669 William Holder described his new method of teaching the deaf and dumb. His method relied on infinite patience, a leather tongue and a plaster palate. As to lip reading, 'it is not impossible no nor very difficult to be done, even in those who were born deaf and dumb, but ... it is impossible to know infallibly by the Eye, what another speaks'.[38]

We have the City surroundings in place; we can imagine the traffic; we can smell the smells; we can make a rough guess at the intellectual background of most people; we can see their clothes and hairstyles. Now add a sound track.

How did they sound?

Stand for a while at a street corner in the City, and listen. That man with his young son are down from the Scottish Highlands, to bind the boy apprentice to a carpenter friend of his father's, who himself came to London when he was a child.[39] He has never lost his soft Gaelic cadences, but he has had to drop many dialect words because the sassenachs did not understand them. He will be glad to revive them with his new apprentice, who may well stay on in London when his time is up. If the boy goes home when he has served his time, he will find the Highland speech strange to his ear; some of its idiosyncrasies will have rubbed off in his years in London.

There is a flurry in the crowd, and a shout goes up, 'Stop thief!' But the man nearest us is a Cockney; he cries, 'Feef'. Cockney is a well-entrenched local dialect.[40] One of its habits, which still persists, is to use f or v where we would use th. Although it is less common now, we would recognise the Cockney habit of adjusting various vowels and consonants, so that Hislington 'as a haitch dropped from 'Ampton. Indeed, a Cockney gazetteer in the seventeenth century would be full of traps for the unwary. Try:

Gracyns Street *for*	Gracechurch Street
Vestmynster	Westminster
Powlls Cross	Paul's Cross
Wostrett	Wood Street
Sant Towlys	St Olave's
Stren	The Strand

'Fresh cress sold by a neighbour' came out as 'Fress cress sowld by a nighbower', none of which sounds too strange nowadays. One Cockney quirk which has died out explains that intolerably uncomic Samivel Veller in *Pickwick Papers*: the transposition of v and w.

A maid passes on her way to market. She came up from the

country, and her slow Essex accent sounds rustic to the quick-speaking Cockneys round her. She is no fool; she has so far rejected the blandishments of the madam over there, who speaks in a pseudo-refined tone faintly echoing what she thinks to be fashionable phrases, larded with French.

Groups of foreigners pool their experiences, in Walloon, or French, or Spanish, or Italian.

So much for the easily identifiable oddities. Now for that elusive character, the man in the street.

Have you ever heard a well-trained actor reading Chaucer aloud? He sounds like a drunken Cornish bumblebee trapped in a jar of honey – with impeccable erudition, I am sure. If you have missed this treat, perhaps you have heard Shakespeare read 'authentically', in purest BBC mummerset. Now turn your mind to the early years of our present Queen's reign; her broadcasts to the nation on Christmas Day could have cut glass at 50 paces. Between the two eras the Great Vowel Shift has occurred.[41] The *sound* of English vowels did not change after about 1700; what would seem odd to us is *where* they cropped up.

This is one of the fascinating aspects of the lack of rigid rules for spelling. If like Lady Hobart you spelled as you heard in your mind, what is written is a record not of bad spelling, but of how words were pronounced. All we need to find is someone who wrote them down. We cannot, for once, rely on Samuel, because Shelton's system left room for ambiguity, especially in vowels. Randle Holme, who as far as I know wrote in longhand, described a fancy waistcoat as a 'chate' because it che*a*ted by being all front and no back. Linings for breeches were 'loinings'. Mercury was 'quacksalver', not quicksilver. A 'scummer', logically enough, was a pierced ladle to remove scum. But it had made the transition to skimmer, in spoken English, leaving its excremental spelling to catch up.

Milton was justified in making 'end' rhyme with 'fiend' and 'God' with 'abode'. The poet Samuel Cowper (still pronounced Cooper) wrote about God moving in a mysterious way. It was not carelessness that induced him to rhyme 'way' with 'sea'; it did. 'Sea' was pronounced 'say', just as, notoriously, 'tea' was pronounced 'tay', for another hundred years. Rome and room sounded the same. In both Derby and Berkely, er is still pronounced ar by the English, although not by the Americans: but if we heard a plain seventeenth-century man saying that he had hard that sarvants could not larn to make tay, we would find it strange.

If it were possible to sort out the vowels, there would still be difficulties with consonants. How about gh? What of the poor ploughman, cuffing, as he ploffs the row ground? Why do we pronounce laughter as lafter, but daughter as dorter? It was in rural England that Fielding's countryfolk a century later dreaded that *Tom Jones* might seduce their dafters; in our period dafter was the normal London pronunciation.

Owen Price, whose method for cutting a pen I have quoted, was one of several contemporary writers who set himself the task of sorting out the English language. He tried hard to analyse the spoken language of his time, and deduce some rules; but he was defeated, and reduced to lists of words that were or were not pronounced as we would expect. (At this stage, if not before, we despair, along with foreigners such as M. Miège and George Bernard Shaw.) I will test your patience with only a few of Price's odder examples: 'o sounds oo in prove, forth, Rome, mushrom, afford, whore, custom, doth, go, love and mother ... ei sounds long in forfeit, leisure [the Americans are right], and neighbour'. It is as if a disc is malfunctioning; one can understand the words, but they sound distorted.

Owen Price explained that 'I have not been guided by our vulgar pronunciation, but by that of London and our Universities, where the language is purely spoken.' How hurt he would have been by a twentieth-century opinion which, contrary to my principles, I will gratefully adopt, leaving Owen to struggle:

> To speak with the accent of a rural district, even at Court, was not derogatory to the character and prestige of a Gentleman – what was not tolerated was to speak like a tradesman...
>
> There can be no doubt that could we hear the pronunciation of the politest circles in the age of Elizabeth, of the Charleses or of Anne, this would strike us as careless, slipshod and 'incorrect' in respect of the consonants just as the distribution of vowel sounds then current would produce on us the effect of rudeness and provincialism.[42]

What words did they use?

It is possible to date the entry of various words into the English language.[43] Some of them sprang from the emergent sciences, such as corpuscle (1660), rabies (1661), latex (1662), slide-rule (1663) and laminate (1664). Others which enriched the language in the decade 1660–70 are still familiar to us, such as illiteracy, genially, Bodleian, wet blanket, celibacy, whist, orangery, spick-and-span, shabby and newspaper. Some have fallen out of use, such as abigail (maidservant) and bedizen (over-dress). Some denote things we no longer use, such as speaking trumpets, glass coaches and privateers.

Few expressions are deader than outmoded catchphrases. Here again a dictionary has been compiled,[44] from which I have drawn some not-too-painful examples:

A d'autres: tell it to the marines (French catchwords were fashionable from 1660 to 1680).
Come aloft: cheers, let's have a party.
Go shoe the goose! never! (incredulously)
Her clothes sit on her like a saddle on a sow's back: she wears her clothes badly.
A bumble bee in a cow turd thinks himself a king: of a pretentious man.
Look you there now: you surprise me.
Snug's the word: keep it quiet. (When and why 'snug' changed to 'mum' I do not know.)
This is something like! approbation.
When hens make holy water: never.
His tongue runs on wheels (or *pattens*): of a talkative man.

My favourite two come from other sources. Dr Willis, in his *Oxford Casebook*, noted the sad case of a man with a hangover, 'hoping to cure himself with a hair of the dog that bit him'; and the Calendar of State Papers Domestic recorded a man who escaped the 1666 Fire 'with the skin of his teeth'.

Perhaps these examples should be categorised as adages, or proverbs. An adage is a 'saying in popular use, remarkable for some shrewd and novel turn'.[45] English used to be rich in them. They seem to have faded out, defeated by television. Some are so familiar to some of us that, if pressed, we would guess them to have originated in the usual places, the Bible or Shakespeare. Not so. In 1536, Erasmus published the latest of his collection of *Adages*, by then numbering 4,151. Among Erasmus's examples are:

a necessary evil
many a slip betwixt cup and lip
leave no stone unturned

God helps those who help themselves
putting the cart before the horse
a dog in the manger
one swallow does not make a summer
my heart's in my boots
he has one foot in the grave
sleep on it
call a spade a spade
up to the ears
to break the ice
to look a gift horse in the mouth
to blow one's own trumpet

And lastly: that mainstay of 'old-fashioned' English, the third person singular (he doth, she goeth), had disappeared from *spoken* English by 1653. 'Whensoever eth cometh in the end of any word, we may pronounce it sometimes like S and sometimes like Z.[46]

CHAPTER 13

HOBBIES, EXCURSIONS, FAMILY OCCASIONS AND ETIQUETTE

When the laundry was finished and dinner was over, and the children were at school or away, and it was still light enough to see, what did a leisured woman do to occupy herself? The answer, surely, was embroidery.

Embroidery

Hannah Wolley offered tuition (see page 188) in 'all works wrought with a needle ... frames for looking-glasses, pictures or the like'. This is a reference to an astonishing output of embroideries designed to cover mirror and picture frames, and books, and miniature chests, sometimes with drawers the fronts of which were covered individually. Many of these will have been produced at school, under the guidance of, and perhaps with contributions by, professional embroiderers, but surely pupils maintained their skills after they left school, and whiled away their time over their embroidery frames.

It was not a pastime for the long winter evenings: good eyesight and clear daylight were essential. The silk used was not twisted, but floss. Two or three very fine strands would be threaded into the needle at once. As they were drawn through the stiff satin base they would lie parallel − with luck and skill; if not, they would have to be gently teased into place with the needle. Twisting them together would have prevented much of the appalling tendency of the individual strands to tangle and knot, but it would have produced an entirely different effect.

Untwisted silks stitched in satin-stitch could merge from colour to colour, and could be subtly built up in thickness so that raised bits caught the light. Tent-stitch[1] could reproduce minute details. The colours were brilliant and fresh. Further effects were added by minute silver and gold spangles, gold and silver thread, mica panels and seed pearls. The silks have mostly faded now, and the precious metals have mostly tarnished, so that they scatter a blight of black specks instead of a dancing sparkle.

The designs were either produced by the embroideress herself, copying from a book of designs, or bought already drawn on the fabric. They were usually scenes from the Old Testament or classical mythology, or pictures of the monarch with or without his queen. Palaces and houses had tiny mica windows, kings and queens wore pearls and golden crowns, and needle-made gold and silver lace adorned their clothes. An endearing feature in most is the profusion of flowers and, especially, insects; great bumbling caterpillars and butterflies fill every vacant space, wildly out of scale. In one, a bird of a nightmarish size looms over the heroine of the picture: luckily for her she is unaware of it, as she paces through her flowery garden holding a microscopic bouquet, and shielded from the sun by a parasol with a chenille border.

Many of these elaborate works of art date from the peaceful era before the Civil War. But Peg Penn, the sister of the founder of Pennsylvania, produced an astonishing piece of work in the shape of a folded wallet or purse, $3\frac{1}{4}$ by 6 inches, on one side of which is a full-length portrait of her father in tent-stitch, boots, smile, buttons, curls and all, holding a pair of mariner's compasses over a neatly rounded globe, marked with lines of longitude, resting on a table with a checked tablecloth, and with a full complement of caterpillars and flying insects. His dog is wearing a collar on which can be read its name, 'Port' (or was it called 'Port Royal', the rest being on the other invisible side of the collar? Admiral Sir William Penn captured Jamaica, with its capital Port Royal, in 1655, so Peg was embroidering then, and I have assumed that the skill, so dearly acquired, was not abruptly laid aside on Charles's restoration.[2] The heyday of what the Victorians labelled stump work, but which its producers called raised work, was slightly earlier, but surely this skill too lingered on. Here again the dexterity and patience of the executant were astounding. The needle was used to weave Lilliputian free-standing garments and flowers.

Hannah also offered tuition in 'beugle works upon wyers'. There is a rare example of bugle- or bead-work in the Burrell Collection in Glasgow, which must be post-Restoration, since it shows a man dressed in Charles II's style of vest and coat. The border is made of flowers and leaves and fruit, all in beads mounted on twisted wires. Being coloured glass, they have not faded.

Bed hangings and curtains were embroidered in wool ('crewel') on linen, again plentifully scattered with hefty insects lumbering between curved stalks and branches rooted in a brown earth base; a style which unfortunately survives, in a bastard form, in 'Jacobean' – why not Carolean? – fire-screens and cushions nowadays.

Before embarking on such pieces, a girl completed an example ('sampler') of all the stitches she would need. Later ages transformed this necessary drudgery into pleasing designs in which the essential entomology had shrunk to a more reasonable size, executed in coloured wools or silk. Seventeenth-century samplers were more likely to be in white, on white linen, in long strips.

Drawing and painting

Charcoal or red or black chalks or crayons were used for drawing, pencils as we know them not having been invented. Colours could be bought ready-ground from a colour-man, and used with either water or oil as a medium. Some pigments, such as the richest and purest of all blues, ultramarine made from lapis lazuli, were so expensive that professional painters would charge up to 10 per cent extra if they were used; amateurs such as Elizabeth no doubt used smalt or indigo. Randle Holme, whose profession as a herald involved working with colours, listed 42, including ceruse (white) and arsenic (yellow; the artist's habit of shaping the brush point by the lips was better resisted).

Brushes, like pens, could be bought ready-made, and reshaped to suit individual tastes. The finest ones were made of squirrel hair. Randle Holme used the word 'pencil' for brushes 'of all bigness, from a small pin to the compass of a finger and thumb', and also for 'black and red lead pencils' (without the wooden casing of modern pencils), but the common usage seems to have reserved 'pencil' for the very fine brushes such as miniature painters might use.[3] The hairs or bristles were enclosed in quills which were mounted on wooden or ivory sticks.

Music

When the light began to fade, a leisured woman could move to her virginals. An almanac of 1665 advertised a 'new book of Lessons for the Virginals ... [and] instructions for singing after the Italian manner'. Virginals were as popular in seventeenth-century London as the piano in Victorian homes. As people desperately tried to save their furniture from the Fire, Samuel noted that one out of every three of the lighters full of household goods which he could see on the river had 'a pair of virginals' in it. ('A pair' was only one. At that time, virginals, the chest-shaped keyboard instruments on separate stands, were giving way to the more gracefully shaped spinets and harpsichords, but the term '[a pair of] virginals' was still used for the more modern instruments.)[4]

Stringed instruments go out of tune all too easily. Samuel, who had an accurate ear for pitch,[5] learned to tune his virginals himself,[6] but those not so gifted could enlist the help of a professional tuner. Samuel's passion for music, and his frequent references to it, may give a disproportionate picture of music in Restoration London; and yet, imagine the processions of dancing milk-maids preceded by musicians, and the ambulant ballad-mongers, and wedding processions through the streets, and the King's Music sounding across the river, and all those virginals ... (and remember that the ubiquitous transistor radio was mercifully absent).

Samuel took singing lessons. At that time, a 'trillo' or trill was not the alternation between two adjacent notes that we know, but a rapid reiteration of the same note. I like the thought of Samuel pacing Gray's Inn Walks, trying to master the trillo under his breath,[7] sounding like a constipated hen.

Asking friends round to make music was a normal way of entertaining in many families. Indeed, if the family could not muster enough musicians itself, this would be the only way of hearing pieces written for several instruments or voices, other than attending a church such as the Queen's or the Queen Mother's chapel, where the choristers were professionals. Public concerts did not begin until

1672,[8] unless you count the 'symphonies' to be heard at the theatre (see below).

Dancing

Samuel also took dancing lessons, from the dancing master who caused him such agonies of jealousy. Elizabeth knew the old-fashioned country dances, but not the fashionable ones that had come over from France with Charles. As she and Samuel rose up the social ladder, they had to learn the proficiency that they would have already acquired in a fashionable education.

Dancing classes were a respectable way for a woman to pass her time. 'Every evening there are entertainments at different places, at which many ladies and citizens' wives are present, they going to them alone, as they do to the rooms of the dancing masters, at which there are frequently upwards of forty or fifty ladies.'[9] Men could, and Samuel did, go and watch, 'although I do not in myself like to have young girls exposed to so much vanity'.[10] Randle Holme described the Art of Dancing 'opportunely and civilly used' as 'a commendable and rare quality fit for young Gentlemen and Gentlewomen ... much commended to be excellent for recreation after much study, making the Body active and strong, graceful in deportment, and is a quality very much beseeming a gentleman'. For once, he boggled at a detailed description, and referred his readers to Playford's *Dancing Master* for the steps.

The 1665 edition of Playford does not, disappointingly, give steps for 'the tunes of the French Dances and other new tunes', of which 85 had been added since the 1652 edition. The 'French Dances' include 'Lord Monk's March', which does not sound particularly French, thirteen 'corants', six 'jiggs' and six 'sarabands'. Samuel described a court ball, with 'bransles' and 'Corants' and unidentified French dances – but he found the dancing dull.[11]

The steps of Playford's English dances are arranged in fairly complicated sequences of orderly progressions. They are for sets of four, six or eight, 'longways' or in square or round dances, or for 'as many as will'. One figure from a dance 'longways for 6' reads: '1st man shake his own woman by the hand then the 2nd then the 3rd by one hand, then by the other, kisse her twice and turn her ...'. Another includes 'jumping up'.

I once had the good fortune to attend a performance of dances of the Restoration period, in the Banqueting Hall. The quiet music was accompanied by the gentle swish of the dancers' silk clothes and – a detail I had not anticipated – the clip and scrape of their leather-soled shoes on the wooden floor. The men looked supremely elegant, but I was not able to elicit from them a description comparable to that given me in the Ladies', of the technique of dancing. A woman leaned forward into her stays, her balance on her toes. The steps themselves were not complicated: short gliding steps to a rhythm of eight, with a change of balance and a pause, the toe turned out and the knees slightly bent outward, every third and seventh beat. From time to time the women ran round the men or each other, and both sexes did a little hop ('jumped up'?). The women held their arms at waist level in front of them and flexed, away from the body, and made consciously graceful hand and arm movements, as in classical ballet. The men were more static, and held their arms more simply, slightly flexed in front of them. The rowdiness of some Elizabethan dances was as lacking as the self-absorption of modern dancing; nor did there seem to be the sexual spice that gingered the ballroom dancing of my youth; but the spectacle provided both sexes with an inimitable occasion for display.

Other pastimes

There were domestic games of cribbage and gleek ('a game played without duces and treys ... played by three persons with counters, at a farthing etc. the dozen';[12] Samuel once managed to win 9s 6d at it)[13] and gaming for hundreds of 'guinneys'[14] at gaming houses, which Samuel thought 'poor and unmanly'.[15] After 1664 gaming was prohibited, to stop the 'debauch of many of the younger sorte, both of the Nobility and Gentry ... to the loss of their precious time and the utter ruin of their Estates and Fortunes'; but to make something illegal does not of course stop it.[16] It was always as well to examine the dice carefully before playing; in 1692 a patent was registered for making dice 'cutt perfectly square by a mold, with spots stained (instead of holes filled with wax) on them, to prevent deceits at play'.

Chess, draughts and backgammon had their exponents. Billiards was played on a table 'covered with fine green cloth', with ivory balls,[17] and shove-halfpenny was played on long tables such as John Evelyn remembered from his childhood. Ninepins, a form of skittles, was rather surprisingly played on board ship,[18] presumably in a calm sea, as well as in skittle alleys. Many large gardens had bowling alleys. 'Anyone for tennis?' could be heard already, in great houses; the game resembled squash or Real Tennis more than the Wimbledon kind. Randle Holme characterised it by 'a man cloathed all in white with a racket in his hand', but 'the manner of the play is so intricate that it is hard to describe', and he did not try.

Excursions

The non-virginal-playing and non-embroidering classes could go round to the friendly neighbourhood tavern or alehouse, 'to bring up young drunkards before the old ones die', as Randle Holme sourly observed. It has been calculated that in mid-seventeenth century there were 50,000 alehouses in England, one for every 100 inhabitants. Considering the density of population in London, this added up to a great many alehouses.[19]

Further up the social scale were inns, where you could get a drink and a meal at any hour except during service time on Sundays, and coffee-houses where you could be sure of catching up with the latest news. The first coffee-house opened in Holborn in 1650. By 1663 there were 82 of them in London.[20] Coffee-houses were male haunts, the origin of men's clubs. Respectable women could go to inns, or eating-houses. In 1667 Samuel and Elizabeth had a fixed-price dinner for 6s for two in the home of a French wig-maker.[21] Knowing in advance how much your meal would cost was a welcome innovation. Dinner for four cost 20s at another French 'ordinary' (*table d'hôte*) in 1668.[22] There was a floating restaurant called The Folly moored opposite Somerset House.

In fine weather, delightful journeys could be made to nearby villages, such as the Pepyses' favourite trip out to Islington via Kingsland, or to 'Foxhall' (Vauxhall) or the royal parks. 'Many carriages of ladies and gentlemen assembled in the evening to enjoy the agreeableness' of Hyde Park;[23] the King and Queen and various royal mistresses could often be seen there.

The *cognoscenti* could go to see:

an entire Egyptian Mummy with all the hieroglyphics and skutcheons on it ... lately presented to the view of His Majesty ... being not long since brought into England from the Lybean sands near ... Memphis. It is the body of a Princely young lady ... preserved in and with her coffin for 2,500 years without putrefaction ... [It] may be seen by any person of quality at Mr Savage's at the Head and Combe in the Strand.[24]

They might have the *entrée* to Arundel House, where the cabinet of curiosities included 'the skin of a moor, tanned, with the beard and hair white';[25] or pay to see Mr Tradescant's curiosities, including a Native American cloak, ornamented with shells.[26]

For less refined tastes there was cock-fighting in the cockpit in Shoe Lane,[27] 'a common amusement of the English, who even in the public streets take a delight in seeing such battles';[28] or the baiting of bears and bulls with dogs, 'very rude and nasty pleasure' in which the spectators, including women, risked having a bloodied dying dog land in their lap;[29] or prize-fighting with bare knuckles, at the Bear Garden in Southwark; or fencing matches where the teachers of fencing would try to drum up custom by taking on all comers;[30] or wrestling in Moorfields.[31]

The royal menagerie was housed in the Tower of London. Samuel took a party of children there to see the lions,[32] which had lived there since the thirteenth century and would stay there until they moved to the Zoological Garden in Regent's Park in 1834. He must have seen and admired them as a child, since he knew one of them by name – Crowly – which in 1660 'was now a very great lion and very tame'.[33] James I had refurbished their quarters in 1603, providing a cistern 'for the Lyons to drinke and wasche themselves in', fairly spacious cages and a viewing gallery above.

The menagerie was a convenient receptacle for those awkward four-footed tributes that foreign potentates thought the English monarch would enjoy, such as an elephant dispatched from Spain in 1623 which drank only wine – so its keepers said – and a tiger that arrived with the Ambassador Extraordinary of Savoy in 1613.[34] However, one can be sure that the pelicans, hawks and 'Persian' (Arab?) horse that the Russian Ambassador and his entourage presented to Charles in 1662 found better homes than the Tower. No doubt the bibulous elephant had died of cirrhosis of the liver by 1660, but the menagerie was still worth a visit, unless you were as intransigently rural as one visitor to the Pepys family: 'what a stir

210

Stankes makes with his being crowded in the streets and wearied with walking in London, and would not be woo'd by my wife ... to go to a play nor to Whitehall or to see the Lyons'.[35] There's no pleasing some people.

Those interested in zoology could try the 'India House' (Magalotti may be referring to East India House), 'which is full of rare and curious things ... birds of paradise, a serpent whose size is most remarkable, being more than 12 cubits [about 18 feet] in length ... and many other animals and curiosities which came from India and are kept there to gratify the curiosity of the public'.

Perhaps Stankes would have enjoyed a rousing execution. The phrase 'hung, drawn and quartered' trips off the tongue easily and ungrammatically. A man sentenced to this terrible fate was strung up by the neck, but not so as to kill him. Then his innards were taken out as if he were a carcase in a butcher's shop. This certainly killed him, if he had not died of shock before. The innards were burned, and the eviscerated corpse was chopped into four bits, which with the head were nailed up here and there throughout the City. There they stayed, rotting, until the kites and crows had picked them clean.

The men who had signed Charles I's death warrant and were still alive provided feasts for the birds. In October 1660 one of them was hanged, drawn and quartered at Charing Cross: 'he looking as cheerfully as any man could do in that condition'.[36] The huge watching crowd gave 'great shouts of joy' at the sight of his heart. A few days later 'the limbs of some of our new traitors were set upon Aldgate'.[37] On 19 May 1662 three more regicides were drawn on sledges over the bumpy roads from the Tower to Tyburn (near present-day Marble Arch: that is, right through London and beyond) and there hanged, drawn and quartered.[38] 'The heads and other remains of the persons who ... conspired to murder Charles I' were still adorning the various City gates *seven years later.*[39]

In June 1662 Sir Henry Vane was executed on Tower Hill. The 'very great press of people' pushed and jostled round the scaffold, so that he pleaded with them to 'let him die like a gentleman and a christian, and not crowded and pressed as he was'. As a royal favour 'the king had given his body to his friends', so that it could be buried decently.[40] On 9 May 1668, Charles was 'pleased' to permit all the quarters, and two of the heads, of four men hanged, drawn and quartered that day to be buried, 'the other two heads to be fixed on London Bridge'.[41]

Public executions were not limited to one site. In 1661 there were seven executions on Tower Hill, five at Tyburn, and twelve more in various places in the City. Samuel and Elizabeth both managed to see the public hanging of a robber, in Leadenhall Street, near the place of his crime and of his residence. Elizabeth had booked a good viewpoint. Samuel almost missed it because of official business, but 'got for a shilling to stand upon the wheel of a cart, in great pain, above an hour before the execution was done'.[42] He obviously thought the shilling well spent.

It was too late to execute Oliver Cromwell, for he had died of natural causes in 1658. It was not too late for him to provide a treat for Londoners. On 30 January 1661, Elizabeth and Lady Batten were able to enjoy the sight of his exhumed corpse, with two others, hanging at Tyburn until sundown, when they were cut down, decapitated and reburied under the scaffold,[43] except for their heads, which 'were set up on poles at the top of Westminster Hall'.[44]

If a criminal escaped hanging, he might provide some lesser treat. A handy missile could be chucked in passing at a miscreant immobilised in a pillory or the stocks. If you missed him in one place, you could catch up with him in the next; two men convicted of selling seditious books were 'stood in the pillory in Cornhill and the day following in Smithfield'.[45] There might be a public whipping of a vagabond or beggar[46] to show the children, with a stern admonition.

If all else failed, it might be worth seeing whether there were any amusing lunatics on show at Bedlam, or checking on the latest hit by the ballad-singers on London Bridge, or the puppet shows at Charing Cross.[47] The extraordinary nature of foreigners could be examined at close range. The Russian Ambassador and his entourage provided a running raree show in the winter of 1662, 'his attendants in their habits and fur-caps ... most of them with Hawkes upon their fists to present to the King';[48] and it was well worth keeping an eye on the Italian Grand Duke, who celebrated Charles's birthday in 1669 with a firework display 'which served to amuse the populace', especially when Cosimo 'distributed among them several casks of Italian wine and beer which called forth increased applause'.[49]

City occasions

Those spectacles were extras in the programme of entertainments for Londoners. The year would begin with the feasting of the twelve days of Christmas, culminating on Twelfth Night, 6 January. Then perhaps things were quieter, during the dirty cold days of January and February, but by mid-March Londoners could watch the fashionable parade of coaches in Hyde Park. May Day brought the maypoles into rollicking use, and Hyde Park saw 'great festivities and a vast concourse of people'.[50] About halfway through May came Ascension Day, when the choirboys and officials of each parish walked its boundaries with songs and rituals. The anniversaries of the coronation, 23 April 1661, and of the King's return, so opportunely on his birthday, 30 May 1660, were public holidays. Midsummer day was marked by gathering dew and greenery outside the City and bringing them home to beautify faces and homes. Bartholomew Fair was always something to look forward to, in September. Then the climax of the civic year arrived in October, when the new Lord Mayor was elected and went to Whitehall 'by water, with a grand procession of boats'.[51] There were also four separate and elaborate processions through the City, including Cheapside and St Paul's churchyard,[52] which delighted the populace (as the single surviving procession still does), although Samuel thought them 'very silly'.[53] Then Guy Fawkes's failure to blow up the monarch with his Commons had to be celebrated with whole-hearted royalism before Christmas came around again. And as well as general events, each livery company had its own calendar of jollifications.[54]

The Court

Between whiles the Court could often supply a splendid sight. After the delirium of Charles's first entry, he could often be seen and heard as his carriage and mounted escort of drummers and trumpeters and Gentlemen Pensioners with their gilt halberds[55] clip-clopped and jingled their way through the streets to some civic occasion or private function. If he was in a hurry, or the weather tempted him, he

213

would use his gilded royal barge to waft him and his musicians between Hampton Court, Whitehall and the City.

Royalty could be examined at even closer range. As Samuel became known to the royal brothers, they would recognise him and greet him – the world was smaller then, and a monarch would notice a rising civil servant. Elizabeth had no such claim to fame, but 'with two or three black patches on and well dressed' she could watch the Queen and her maids of honour in the royal presence chamber,[56] get a seat in Westminster Hall to see the royal celebration meal after the coronation,[57] enjoy the royal preacher,[58] and even watch a court ball.[59] A stray Welsh preacher with a scabby nose could count on personal contact with His Majesty in St James's Park (see page 81).

Anyone who looked respectable and could talk his way in could watch Charles dining, three times a week (Sundays, Wednesdays and Fridays),[60] which must have been penitential for the poor man at times, if the manners of the crowd at one superb supper he gave to mark Cosimo's departure were anything to go by. The meal ended with 'a most excellent course of confectionery ... but scarcely was it set upon the table when the whole was carried off and plundered by the people who came to see the spectacle of the entertainment ... so that His Majesty, to avoid the crowd, was obliged to rise from table and retire'[61] – and Magalotti never got one mouthful.

This ordeal was one of the penalties of kingship. The sight of a masticating monarch was available to his subjects in much of Europe and during much of the seventeenth and eighteenth centuries. After a decent show, he and his queen retired to their private apartments, to actually enjoy a meal.

The theatre

Charles was fond of the stage, or perhaps more accurately of the actresses who adorned it after the autumn of 1660, breaking all established shibboleths. The new theatres differed from the surviving buildings used for stage presentations, in having a roof, and a stage extending forward from the proscenium arch into the pit, which was filled with backless benches on to which most of the audience could be crowded. Capacity was probably between 700 and 1,000. A seat in the pit, however precarious and uncomfortable, cost 2s 6d. There was little or no standing room. A line of boxes, sometimes in two tiers, stretched round the house, 'divided into several rows of seats, for the greater accommodation of the ladies and gentlemen who, in conformity with the freedom of the country, sit together indiscriminately'.[62] One, or sometimes two, galleries took up the space above the front boxes and part of the pit. A seat in a box cost 4s, and in the gallery 1s or 1s 6d.[63]

There was no booking in advance. The doors opened at noon, when theatre-goers could pay their money, push their way to a seat and wait for three hours and more, as the boxes and rows of benches filled to capacity and beyond. 'Before the comedy begins, that the audience may not be tired with waiting, the most delightful symphonies are played: on which account many people come early to enjoy this agreeable amusement'.[64] Those unwilling or unable to waste so much time, such as Samuel by 1668 when he should have been busy on government work, could 'set a poor man to get a good place in the pit',[65] at noon, and go off to have dinner, sauntering back when the house was full.

At Christmas time Samuel was shocked at the number of 'ordinary prentices and mean people' who could afford a seat in the pit, 'so much the vanity and prodigality of the age is to be observed in this perticular'.[66] (It was not like that in his young days.) 'The house today was full of citizens, there hardly being a gentleman or [gentle]woman in the house, but a couple of pretty ladies by us, that made sport at it, being jostled and crowded by prentices.'[67] Samuel was not implying that the 'pretty ladies' were prostitutes. Elizabeth and her waiting woman could go to the theatre perfectly properly, without a male companion.[68]

Performances by the two licensed companies were daily, except on Sundays, Wednesdays and Fridays during Lent, Passion week, Christmas Day and while the Court was in mourning: for instance, on the death of Charles's mother (six weeks' closure) and his younger brother (four weeks). They were advertised by handbills posted in convenient places, and by word of mouth. The performance began by daylight, at 3 p.m. or 3.30, and lasted about three hours. Wax candles were supplanting tallow candles, which gave little light. One wonders just how much the people in the back row of the pit, let alone in the upper gallery, actually saw, even by wax candles; Magalotti found the King's Theatre 'sufficiently lighted on the stage and on the walls to enable the spectators to see the scenes and the performance', but he and his Duke were sitting in the royal box. There was no practicable way of dimming the house lights even further; nor the stage lights if the scene was supposed to be nocturnal.

The familiar words 'the scene opens with ... ' were a literal description of the scenery flats being pulled apart along grooves in the floor of the stage, and pushed together ('the scene closes') at the end. 'The scenery is very light, capable of a great many changes, and embellished with beautiful landscapes.'[69] The curtain was drawn back at the beginning of the piece and stayed open until it was over. Scenery was changed in full view, or behind a gauze. Its increased elaboration gave actresses an opportunity to show off their talents for singing and dancing during scene changes. Magalotti was much struck by 'a well arranged ballet ... with new and fanciful dances after the English manner, in which different actions were counterfeited ... so as to render intelligible the acts they were presenting ... this spectacle was highly agreeable from its novelty and ingenuity'. 'Machines' such as ropes for flying, trapdoors for appearing and disappearing, and parts of the stage which rose, were much used, provoking a burst of applause each time.

There was no respectful hush during the performance. Some people pushed their way out before the end of the first act, on the basis that the custom of seeing that much without charge still operated, and were pursued by the doorkeepers, assuring them that after 27 February 1664 it did not.[70] No sooner had everyone found his place again than latecomers pushed their way in, followed by the resentful comments of the already crowded occupants of the pit and the unfortunate doorkeepers trying to collect 'after-money', since the custom of seeing the last act or so for free no longer applied either. The eating (notoriously, of oranges, adding to the smell and convenient for throwing if the performance failed to please)[71] and discussion that had whiled away the time before the performance did not necessarily stop when it began. Perhaps because things could get rowdy, it was normal for fashionable women to wear a 'vizard', an oval mask held to cover the face.[72] Brawls between spectators, and robust criticism of performers, ensured interest even if the play itself was dull.

And Samuel, an inveterate play-goer, often did find the play dull. Here I shall follow the example of Randle Holme in dealing with dancing, and refer the reader who wishes to know more about the plays that were performed, and the actors and actresses who appeared in them, to standard works on the Restoration theatre, my aim being only to describe the theatre-going experience.

Family occasions

When did you last see your second cousin once removed? How many cousins german can you count? We have lost the habit of keeping personal regular contact with any relation more remote than a cousin, if that.

Hannah Wolley's advice to young wives builds to a climax:

> Be careful to keep your house in good order, and let all things with decency be in readiness when he comes home to his repast; let him not wait for his meals, lest by so staying his affairs be disordered or impeded ... show respect and kindness to what friends he brings home with him; *but more especially to his relations.*[73]

Elizabeth's immediate family unfortunately regarded Samuel as a source of clothes, money and jobs, so one can understand his keeping his distance. But Elizabeth had to put up with all the ramifications of her husband's family, and entertain and visit them frequently – even including the repulsive Uncle Wight, who proposed that, if she would have sexual intercourse with him, he would give her £500 and make any resultant child his heir. (If she did not conceive, he would presumably be entitled to go on trying, without a further downpayment. Samuel, unforgivably, was almost tempted by the idea.[74])

The birth of a child brought kin, neighbours and friends together in a 'gossiping', to give the mother moral support. Then the christening was an excuse for a celebration, as long as it had not been hastily done by the midwife if the infant was unlikely to survive. As far as I can see, confirmation was a quiet family occasion. There was no equivalent of Roman Catholic first communion, or Jewish bar mitzvah, with their social celebrations. The next family occasion was likely to be marriage, marked by uproarious ribaldry in some circles, with the bridal party in their new clothes[75] processing through the streets from church to the wedding feast, after which the happy couple took up residence in their own home, and were woken the next morning with music.[76] There were none of the agonies and ecstasies of a honeymoon in strange surroundings and artificial circumstances; nor was it likely that the newly-weds would have to live with their in-laws. They had deferred marriage so long expressly so that they could set up on their own.

Funerals could be elaborate and expensive. They might involve weeks of preparation. Sir Thomas Viner, the rich City alderman, died on 11 May 1665 and was not buried until 1 June. There being no refrigeration in those days, his body was embalmed.[77] The medieval pomp and ceremony of a rich man's funeral still survived in the processions of charity children whom he had benefited, and old men and women blessing his name – as many as he had years – followed with all available civic pomp by the Lord Mayor and the alderman.

Sir William Batten's hearse was accompanied from the Navy Office to his home at Walthamstow by 'a hundred or two' of coaches,[78] but Samuel was otherwise engaged. On the death of his cousin Edward, who was a member of the Middle Temple, Samuel borrowed Lord Sandwich's coach with six horses, and went as far as Shoreditch, on the outskirts of the City, in a cortège of 'about twenty coaches, and four or five with six and four horses': an impressive sight which must have blocked the traffic for miles round. The interment was to be in Norfolk, so Samuel felt he had done his family duty by then.[79]

For more ordinary mortals, the bereaved family had to assemble proper mourning clothes (see Chapter 7), and provide black enamel mourning rings for the chief mourners, and suitable refreshments for all those who attended. Samuel's brother Tom died on 15 March 1664. Samuel decided to have him buried in the aisle of Tom's parish church instead of in the churchyard – 'this costs me 20s more',[80] plus a 6d tip to the gravedigger. Samuel invited 120 people to come; 'though invited as the custom is at 1 or 2 a-clock, they came not till 4 or 5', with about 30 gatecrashers. They all got

> six biscuits a-piece and what they pleased of burnt [hot: it was March] claret ... Anon to church, walking out into the street ... and had a very good company along with the corps. And being come to the grave ... the Minister ... did read the service for buriall ... and so all broke up and I and my wife and Madam Turner and her family to my brother's, and by and by fell to on a barrel of oysters, Cake and cheese.

The funeral cost almost £10.

Fees for burials were an important part of parish income. It cost more to be buried at night, as some fashionables preferred. The chancel was the most desirable place, then the aisles. Coffins in the vaults might be 'jostled together', like Tom's, room being finite and the continental system of ossuaries (where in due course the bones are collected and stored and the burial space becomes available to the next comer) not being English. It cost less to be buried in the churchyard, and less in a shroud or sheet than in a coffin. 'As to that superstitious custom of burying in churches or having their dormitories in the very heart of cities where frequently churches are built, I neither think it decent nor sufferable', wrote John Evelyn,[81] but the custom went on.

The overcrowding of churchyards had become so unseemly, even before the Plague, that some churches acquired other plots not adjacent to the church itself, but parishioners still wanted to be buried in the churchyard, beside their parents, spouses and children. In 1569 a practical and generous Elizabethan, Sir Thomas Rowe, had given the City the site of the New Churchyard, outside Bishopsgate, stipulating that no burial fee should be levied save for 6d paid to the gravedigger. A hundred years later the poor were the main customers, especially for the burial of children, servants, strangers and the destitute.[82]

Two more cheerful markers in family life: Twelfth Night and St Valentine's Day. Twelfth Night was the principal day of celebration at Christmas. It was, as it still is, the day for taking down the decorations put up for Christmas, but instead of dusty plastic which has been up since mid-December, these were evergreen branches fixed in place only on Christmas Eve, and before taking them down people sang and danced and played childish romping games such as blind man's buff, and enjoyed themselves. There was a splendid cake – Samuel's cost him 20s for the ingredients alone, in 1668[83] – and a hired fiddler, and 'good fires and candles'; a really special occasion. The cake always had two charms in it, a bean and a pea. Whoever got them were King and Queen for the evening, and could order the other guests about, and a good time was had by all until the early hours.

We still celebrate St Valentine's Day, but only with saccharine cards, allegedly from anonymous admirers. The custom of taking as your Valentine the first person you saw that day still survived, just, in my childhood. Much to Samuel's amusement, Elizabeth took great care all morning, in 1662, 'that she might not see the paynters that were at work in gilding my chimny-piece and pictures in my dining-room', in case one of them should be entitled to be her

219

Valentine. He cannot have been so amused when one of his regular extra-marital partners turned up at his office in 1665 'with a hope to be in time enough to be my Valentine'.[84] St Valentine's habit of giving presents was taken seriously in Samuel's day. For her Valentine present in 1668, he gave Elizabeth a ring costing four or five pounds, which she had obviously had her eye on, and he also had to part with a guinea to her maid, who had had the foresight to call him first thing in the morning.

Etiquette

'Whenever you answer ... give always the titles of Sir, Madam or my Lord.'[85] A man bowed by moving one leg forward and bending both knees and his body. A woman curtsied bending both knees outwards, but keeping her body upright (remember her stays), which sounds ungraceful but was a great deal easier and safer than the Victorians' stately sinking with one foot behind the other. If a lady walking outdoors offered her cheek to be kissed – as was still the habit among Englishwomen, much enjoyed by continentals – the man should bow, kiss *his* hand, and then kiss her lips, if she were a social equal, or her hood (she was bound to be wearing one), if she were not.[86]

Ladies should not be seen in public more than they could help. According to Hannah Wolley: 'You think ... and intend no harm in your promenades or walks, but by so doing you give too often occasion for licentious amorists to meet with you, and may thereby be persuaded to throw off the veil of circumspection, to give attention to some wanton smutty story.'[87] (If Magalotti's dazzled view of free Englishwomen tripping along the streets by themselves, day and night, was at all realistic, this advice was not always followed.)

For men, hats were fraught with complications. Charles managed William Penn's Quaker reluctance to take his off with tact and charm (see page 123). Refusal to uncover could get on everyone's nerves very quickly, as George Fox knew. And what about Cosimo, soon to be the third Grand Duke of Tuscany, but at present incognito? When he met Charles, which of them should keep his hat on? This intractable problem was referred to the Queen Mother, who being French could give a final decision: Charles would not put his on at all, so Cosimo could decently (it seems) remain bare-headed.[88] Uncovering when not strictly necessary could convey a delicate compliment, as when Samuel drank the health of his wife's companion, 'which I pledged with my hat off'.[89] If, weighing one thing with another, you decided that it was up to you to take your hat off, it was vital to keep its inside to yourself and display only the outside with its decorative feather, which must have taken some careful manipulation.

Social calls on a lady should not be made in the morning, so that she had time to get the shopping and housework organised, and her hair in satisfactory curl. A visiting lady would pause outside her hostess's room, to take off her mask or vizard and unpin her outer skirts, if it had been a muddy walk; but she must keep her gloves on. She then sailed in, and shot a quick look round to check on the chairs. The seat of honour was the one with arms, facing the door. If two visitors were of equal rank, and were expected, there would be two arm-chairs, side by side, facing the door. The one to the right was the better. The hostess sat with her back to the door. After the usual dilemma about hats, a man could put his on again if pressed sufficiently. This at least got the unwieldy object and its feather out of the way, especially if the household had a pet monkey.

Since the demise of rush matting it was no longer acceptable to spit on the floor. Failing a spittoon, one should spit discreetly into one's handkerchief – and then remember not to wave it about.[90]

The real test came at the dining table. After the usual jockeying for position, you waited for grace to be said. Then you sat down and opened your napkin. (There was such an art in elaborately folding them that Samuel even had a man in to do them before a grand dinner.)[91] Hannah Wolley recommended 'pinning or keeping your napkin tite about you' to 'keep your clothes from greasing'.[92] At least you were not faced with the panoply of implements on a Victorian table.[93] At a magnificent state supper for seventeen, Magalotti carefully noted how 'there were as many knives and forks [i.e. a knife and fork each], which when they had sat down they found before them, arranged in a fanciful and elegant manner'. He obviously did not have the pleasure of dining with a Wolley-trained family, since he lamented the 'great want of that neatness and gentility which is practised in Italy, for on the [normal] English table *there are no forks*'.[94] Imagine, or even practise in cold blood, eating dinner without a fork; and a spoon was not used either, except for liquids like soup, so no spoons for your meat and two veg.

Now began the ritual of carving. Its importance was marked by a whole vocabulary peculiar to it.

> Breake that deere, leach that brawne, reare that goose, lift that swan, sauce that capon, spoile that hen, frush that chicken, unbrace that mallard, unlace that coney, dismember that herne, display that crane, disfigure that peacock, unjoint that bittern, untatch that curlew, allay that fesant, wing that partrich, wing that quaile, mince that plover, thie that pigeon, border that pastie, thie that woodcock, thie all manner of small birds

—and I will spare you the words for dealing with fish.[95] You were 'carved to' by your hostess. She put the best bits, or the bits she thought you would like, on to your plate and there was not a thing you could do about it.

> If you be carved with anything ... which you do not like ... it will show your civility to accept it, though you let it lie upon your plate ... In carving at your own table distribute the best pieces first, and it will appear very comely and decent to use a fork; if so touch no piece of meat without it ... Though the mistress of the house may out of compliment desire you to carve [horrors!] yet beg her excuse, though you are more able to do it than herself ... Being a guest, let not your hand be in the dish first

—fork or no fork. Drink was served glass by glass, the bottle being returned to the cystern (a large container like a foot bath) meanwhile. Toasts, 'being an indispensable appendage of English entertainment',[96] were a favourite way of imbibing more alcohol. 'When you have dined or supped rise from the table and carry your trencher or plate with you, doing your obeisance to the company.'

After the forkless dinner that appalled Magalotti, 'they dip the end of the napkin into the beaker which is set before each of the guests, filled with water [that is, a finger bowl, not for drinking], and with this they clean their teeth and wash their hands'. Not a pretty sight.

For the shy and nervous it must have come as a relief when the company moved to the withdrawing or banqueting room for dessert.

CHAPTER 14

DIVERS EVENTS
AND ACTS IN THE LAW

The nature of English law

Law impinges on present-day life at various points, and in different ways, sometimes depending on gender. When you marry, your legal status changes; if you later decide to divorce, your status changes again. If you do something which the state forbids, usually because it is wicked or antisocial (but not always), you may be prosecuted and punished. You may be harmed by someone, apart from the criminal law, and decide to sue him. You may enter into agreements. You may pay tax into the central kitty, or draw welfare benefits from it. When you die, your possession have to be distributed, either as you directed during your lifetime or according to general rules on intestacy.

This applied in the seventeenth century much as it does now. But whereas now it would be possible to arrive at the probable legal answer to any question that might arise, albeit after much burning of midnight oil and with many ifs and buts, it is remarkably difficult to do the same for the decade 1660–70, and probably was not much easier at the time.

A few more introductory notes (which can be skipped). English law differs from continental systems, in its reliance on the decisions of judges in individual cases, forming a body of precedents which have acquired such authority that they bind subsequent courts dealing with similar questions (common law). This has the merit of flexibility, but the disadvantage of uncertainty: will a judge think that running someone over with a Rolls-Royce is the same as flattening him with a coach and four? Another snag of medieval law as made by judges was that they sometimes painted themselves into a corner, whence they could only be rescued by another lot of lawyers who said, 'No, that can't be the law because it's so far from anyone's idea of justice.' So alongside the common law there developed an alternative system of 'equity', administered by the Chancellor of the time in his courts (Chancery). This too became ossified over the centuries, but in its prime served a useful purpose. The third strand in this confused picture was the ecclesiastical courts, which up to the Reformation had been the guardians of morals and thereby had carved for themselves a profitable monopoly in administering wills and dealing with matrimonial affairs. They were abolished during the Interregnum and, although revived on the Restoration, never regained their former status. There was also a scatter of minor local courts under the auspices of Justices of the Peace (magistrates), as now, which probably dealt with most of the legal problems of normal life.

The other members of the European Union have totally codified systems, which in theory enable one to look up any question and find the predetermined answer. The Romans, who did not stay with us for long, and Napoleon, who never got here at all, were adept at devising and imposing such systems. We are having some difficulty in adjusting ourselves to this way of thinking. Our own body of law has always included rules made by Parliament. But we tend to codify one field of law at a time, such as the Statute of Artificers of 1583 governing labour relations, the Poor Law of 1601, the Statute of Frauds of 1677, and the 1925 legislation governing the ownership of land, the common lawyers with the help of their Chancery colleagues having by then tangled the whole subject into a horrible mess.[1]

The legal status of women

At seven, a girl was old enough to become betrothed; at twelve, she could be legally married. 'If she be married younger she may dissent till she be fourteen.'[2] Until her marriage, a daughter was part of her father's family, and he was responsible for her. If her father died while she was still unmarried – and we have seen that in our period 25 per cent of women never married – she was handed on to the next head of the family. On marriage she became the responsibility of her husband,[3] and in the execrable law-French of the time changed from a *feme sole* to a *feme covert*. (Her husband was charmingly called her 'baron'.)

'By marriage the husband and wife are one person in law, that is, the very being or legal existence of the wife is suspended during the marriage, or at least is incorporated and consolidated into that of the husband.'[4] Her husband had the right to 'lawful and reasonable correction. How far that extendeth I cannot tell ... to the ... woman beaten by her husband, that retaliation [is] left to her to beat him again [back], if she dare.'[5] A *feme covert* was unable to enter into contracts (unless she was a merchant in her own right), or to make a will, without the consent of her husband. The titles of two sections in *The Laws Resolution of Womens Rights* say it all: 'That which the husband has is his own' and 'That which the wife has is the husband's'.

'A married woman perhaps may doubt whether she be either none or no more than half a person ... But let her be of good cheer ... in criminal and other special cases our law argues them several [separate] persons.'[6] A cheering thought indeed. And there were two ways of looking at it: 'we may observe that even the disabilities which the wife lies under are for the most part for her protection and benefit. So great a favourite is the female sex, of the laws of England.'[7]

But on widowhood everything changed.

Why mourn you so, you that be widdows? consider how long you have been in subjection under the predominance of parents, of your husbands, now you be free in liberty ... Maidens and wives vows [contracts] were all disavowable by their parents or husbands ... but the vow of a widow ... no man hath power to disallow of ... Then because a sober carefulness in business of profit or disprofit doth mitigate greatly the sorrowing for such actions as opinions or fancies makes thus grievous, let her looke to her affairs as cause and need requireth[8]

— always assuming that the years of subjection have not irredeemably sapped her energy.

Marriage

Holy matrimony ... is an honourable estate ... not by any to be enterprised, nor taken in hand, unadvisedly, lightly or wantonly, to satisfy men's carnal lusts and appetites, like brute beasts that have no understanding, but reverently, discreetly, advisedly, soberly, and in the fear of God; duly considering the causes for which Matrimony was ordained.

First, it was ordained for the procreation of children, to be brought up in the fear and nurture of the Lord, and to the praise of his holy Name.

Secondly, it was ordained for a remedy against sin, and to avoid fornication; that such persons as have not the gift of continency might marry, and keep themselves undefiled members of Christ's body.

Thirdly, it was ordained for the mutual society, help and comfort, that the one ought to have of the other, both in prosperity and adversity.

These reverberating words are taken from the 1662 Book of Common Prayer. The man undertook to 'love [his wife], comfort her, honour, and keep her in sickness and in health; and forsaking all other to keep [himself] only unto her, so long as [they] both shall live'. He declared that he worshipped her with his body, and he endowed her with all his worldly goods. The woman's first undertaking was to obey and serve her husband; she made no promise to comfort him, despite the 'thirdly' the minister had only just said, and she did not refer to her sexual or financial circumstances. The service ended with an unequivocal reminder to the bride and any other married woman in the congregation: 'ye wives, submit yourselves to your husbands ... be in subjection to your own husbands'.

There was a third person involved, who had an important walk-on role: the bride's father, from whom, in the old days and in fairy stories, her suitor had 'asked for her hand in marriage'. When the minister asks, 'Who giveth this woman to be married to this man?', the bride's father wordlessly gives that hand to the minister for onward transmission to the bridegroom, and steps back, his duty done without so much as an 'I do'.

So much for the general picture. Now to look in more detail; and the first question must be, what was a valid marriage?

Imagine a church full of friends and relations dressed uncomfortably in clothes thought to be appropriate. The parson does his stuff, the happy couple and the witnesses retire to the vestry to sign the register. So far, no essential difference between now and the 1660s. Even if something should happen to destroy every written record of the ceremony, people were there who would remember it years later, and could give evidence that it had happened. Bigamous or incestuous marriages were discouraged by the requirement to give public notice three separate times, in the parish church of each party, of their intended marriage, so that anyone who knew of any reason why 'these two persons should not be joined together in holy matrimony' had a chance to say so (calling the banns: that is, summoning anyone who could prevent or 'ban' the marriage).

Many people, then as now, preferred to avoid all that publicity and be married in church with the permission of the bishop of the diocese in which they lived ('special licence'), but without any calling of banns. Some element of publicity still existed, in the shape of two necessary witnesses to the ceremony, but they could be casual passers-by who might even sign with a mark, and would be untraceable if any question arose later. The bishop's records were preserved, however, to prove the marriage if necessary.

Nowadays we may opt for a quiet affair in the local register office. That too had existed, during the Interregnum when the Puritans treated marriage solely as a matter for the parties and the state in the person of a Justice of the Peace, not involving God. One of the first things Parliament did after Charles's return was to reassure people who had been married in that way 'during the late troubles'. They were just as married as if they had been united 'according to the rites and ceremonies established in the Church or Kingdom of England',[9] but that particular route to married bliss was blocked from 1660 on.

The plot now thickens. You may remember that Henry VIII's first wife, Catherine of Aragon, was discarded because Henry suddenly noticed – after many years together, during which she had suffered five stillbirths and one neonatal death as well as producing a daughter, Mary, who would succeed him – that he had been living in sin with her. She had been lawfully married to his older brother, Arthur, who had died, and her failure to bear Henry a son was God's judgement on *him* for this sin. (At that time and for many years after, it was incest to marry your deceased brother's widow.) Had she been Arthur's wife? She said, no.

227

It was perfectly possible to get lawfully married without going near a church. All that was needed was a declaration *in the present tense* by each of the parties that he or she took the other in wedlock ('espousals'). 'There needs no stipulation or curious form of contract in wedlock making ... It may be made by letters.'[10] It would be difficult to prove unless there were witnesses present who could be called to give evidence later, but technically the mere declarations sufficed. If the declarations were in the future tense – 'I *shall* marry you' – it was not a valid marriage until it was consummated, or superseded by declarations *de praesenti*. Catherine said she and Arthur had exchanged promises to marry – indeed, a large part of her dowry was paid over to the English Crown on that basis, and was never returned – but that they had never had sexual intercourse. In the face of Henry's desperate desire that the child Anne Boleyn was carrying should be born in lawful wedlock to be his heir, poor Catherine stood little chance.

That was past history. But the potential confusion between declarations *de praesenti* and *in futuro* persisted as ineradicably as lawyers' liking for Latin. And considering that a girl of twelve and a boy of fourteen were old enough to be validly married, the scope for unscrupulous adult machinations was wide. The following is so clear an illustration of the difference between betrothal and marriage that I include it even though it is ten years after our period. On 8 June 1680, Samuel Jeake asked Mrs Hartshorn for permission to marry her daughter Elizabeth, then aged twelve years and eight months. The next four months were passed in hammering out the marriage contract, but finally Samuel Jeake was able to enter in his diary: 'I was betrothed or contracted to marry ... Mistress Elizabeth Hartshorne', by saying, 'I Samuel take thee Elizabeth to be *my betrothed wife* and promise to make thee *my wedded wife in time convenient* in token whereof is this our holding by the hand.'[11] All was not yet plain sailing. Relations between Samuel Jeake and both ladies deteriorated into 'great displeasure and indifference', but at last, on 11 February 1681, 'I moved [Elizabeth's mother] about 3 hours p.m. [Samuel was a careful man] for the consummation of my marriage with her daughter', and on 1 March 1681 'about 9 hours 35 minutes I was married to Mistress Elizabeth Hartshorne. The day was cloudy but calm. Devirg 3 Thursday night.'[12]

Marriage by declaration was popular among the poor, since no fees were involved. It was used by the Quakers, since it avoided any swearing, which they refused to do. George Fox relates a lawsuit in

228

1661, in which the legitimacy of the child of such a marriage was in issue; the judge relied on an earlier case.

> A man that was weak of body, and kept his bed, had a desire in that condition to marry, and did declare before witnesses that he did take such a woman to be his wife, and the woman declared that she took that man to be her husband. This marriage was afterwards called in question; and (as the judge said) all the bishops at that time concluded it to be a lawful marriage.[13]

Finally, there was the clandestine marriage. There was no need to go as far as Gretna Green. The parson of St James's in Duke Place, or the minister out at St Pancras, would oblige, without licence or bans, in their churches or in a convenient inn or a private house, and at any time of the day or night. The clergyman and everyone who attended the event risked prosecution; but the clergyman could afford a fine, considering the fees he exacted from the happy couple – or, more often, from the bridegroom, who had abducted a young heiress and married her without her parents' consent.[14] Clearly this was reprehensible: 'all ravishments and wilful taking away or marrying of any maid, widow or damsel *against her will* or without the assent or agreement of her parents' were capital offences.[15] But nevertheless as long as the bride was at least twelve, and could be shown to have consented, the marriage was legal.[16] The unfortunate girl was as irrevocably married as if she had sat through her banns and gone to church through the streets in a bridal procession.

The goal in some cases was money. That silent handing over by the bride's father, in the marriage ceremony, was more important than it looked, and certainly more important than the husband's undertaking to endow his wife with all his worldly goods, which seems to have sunk without trace. In affluent families, marriage would normally be the culmination of months of hard bargaining by both sides, as to the capital the bride would bring with her ('dowry' or 'marriage portion'), which went into the husband's family funds, and the annual income ('jointure') and/or capital sum ('dower') she could expect *if* (a 50/50 chance) he died before she did.

The negotiations were usually carried out, and the sums provided or promised, by the parents of the engaged couple. The dowry might go straight out of the husband's family again, in the shape of a dowry for one of his sisters. If the parties were young, the widow's entitlement, if it came to be payable at all, might be so far off as to be hardly worth thinking of seriously, from the husband's advisers' point of view; it was up to the wife's side to insist that it should be tightly tied up beyond the reach of her husband, which was easier said than done.

Landed families have always made elaborate marriage settlements, even where the parties married for love. Advice to a young gentleman: 'First, then, as soon as you shall be able, look into your estate, labouring not only to conserve it entire but to augment it either by wise forethought, marriage or by some other thrifty means.'[17] But the negotiated dowry spread far down the social scale. Samuel finally disposed of his disagreeable sister Paulina for £600,[18] after hawking her round several possibles who declined her. He himself had married a portionless girl of fifteen because he fell in love with her, but he did not let her forget that she had come to him with nothing.

Clandestine marriages were not always a matter of unscrupulous adventurers carrying off innocent heiresses. There were many others who did not want their married bliss to become public knowledge, such as apprentices who married against their articles, maidservants who would be dismissed if their mistress knew they had another loyalty, widows whose jointure would cease if they were known to be the responsibility of a new husband, and even pregnant girls doing what they could to redeem their reputation (although children conceived before marriage were still penalised, in that they would not inherit with children conceived and born in wedlock). And there was the added advantage of not being the subject of gossip in the local tavern, or the unwilling host to uproarious merrymaking after the ceremony, the costs of which, with the various fees payable for a wedding with banns, could mount up alarmingly.[19]

Samuel's marriage was unusual in being prompted solely by love on his side. Love has no financial worth or legal significance. Marriages were arranged as financial investments, but if one party really could not bear the prospect of spending the rest of his or her life with the proposed spouse, he or she was allowed to cry off, especially if the bride's repugnance would prevent the birth of issue, in a dynastically motivated match. For a woman to reject an apparently suitable spouse would need careful thought, considering parental pressure, the possible scarcity of alternative mates and the lack of any alternative to marriage other than domestic service. The option of entering a nunnery, a comfortable shelter for many pre-Reformation women disinclined to marriage in general or one spouse in particular, was no longer open. Many women would not have the fortitude, or the confidence in their lovers' constancy, that supported Dorothy Osborne between 1648 and 1654, while her brothers refused their consent to her marriage to William Temple and pressed her to take various suitors, each of whom was financially appropriate but unloved.[20]

Divorce

After all these complications, at least there was no doubt about divorce: there was none.

For the rich and desperate, whose family line faced extinction when a bride produced no heir, there was a remedy. They could apply to Parliament for a private Act to dissolve the marriage. There were none in our period. A famous case that eventually came to Parliament in 1670 provided that Lord Roos, the heir to the Earl of Rutland, could remarry, but it did not dissolve his marriage to Anne Pierrepont, the flighty co-heiress of the Marquis of Dorchester. The case dragged on through various courts for years. Charles often dropped in to hear the lastest permutation, commenting that it was 'as good as a play'.

The ecclesiastical courts might impose a legal separation and order alimony, where one party had been guilty of adultery or life-threatening cruelty. This was rarely invoked after the Restoration.

The spouses might come to an agreement to live apart. But the wife normally had very little bargaining power, especially since the husband could deprive her of all access to her children. Such an agreement merely absolved the parties from their ecclesiastical duty to live together. Neither of them could remarry. So a wife was irrevocably tied to a husband who turned out to be a violent, drunken, syphilitic, promiscuous lout who dissipated her dowry, brutally exercised his matrimonial rights, and abused her children.

On one occasion Charles set up as a marriage guidance counsellor/matrimonial judge, which he must have regretted. A wife had managed to get an order for alimony against her husband, in his absence – so he said. Charles was on the wife's side, and ordered the husband to pay £500 arrears, but the wife 'declined His Majesty's extra-judicial judgement', which must have been mortifying for him, so the case went back to the Master of the Rolls to determine.[21]

If there was no legal divorce, what did ordinary people do? The answer must be, they parted and went their own ways. Sometimes they formalised their separation (as the Mayor of Casterbridge did in Hardy's novel) by the husband's 'selling' his wife in the market place, usually with her consent and to a previously identified partner.[22] If there was no agreement, the husband upped and went. (I have assumed a deserting husband. It would be more difficult, but by no means impossible, for the wife to disappear into thin air, but she might be encumbered by pregnancy or children.)

The deserted wife was fortunate if she was able to call on family resources or her own earning capacity, to keep her from destitution or the Parish. She had little chance of finding her husband again, in those days of difficult travel and no central records. Even if she did, what could she do except – if she were strong enough – wallop him? If later one or other spouse wanted the comfort of a church wedding, as long as the church was far from the site of their previous married life, who would know? Anyway the danger of the second ceremony being banned could be obviated by marriage by declaration. Bigamy was a capital crime;[23] but how many bigamous couples happily lived out their lives together has not, unsurprisingly, been recorded.

One girl married her love, Thomas Witham, and then 'in obedience to her father, married Gilbert Cooper'. I am glad to say that she was pardoned, 'on condition of her adhering to the first marriage'.[24]

'It falleth out not seldom [the husband] to be taken captive ... or it is uncertain whether he live or no.'[25] Seamen who had the bad luck to be captured by Barbary pirates, for instance, might not be ransomed, or rescued, for years, if ever. In theory their spouses could not remarry without proof of their husbands' death. In practice this seems to have been presumed after seven years.

Crime

Pick-pocketing was rife, in those crowded streets. A prosperous-looking man shouts, 'Stop thief!' and raises the hue-and-cry, but the villain zig-zags through the lanes and passageways, and escapes. Maidservants, suspiciously thickly dressed, make off with their mistresses' clothes, apprentices with their masters' goods, manservants with their horses and anything they could carry. In a dark alley, three figures bend over a body; dead men tell no tales, best dispatch him. In another alley, a prostitute's hands flicker from codpiece to pockets, but her customer is too engrossed to notice. A scream; a woman is being raped ('ravished'), but as little attention is paid to her then as now.

Just outside the built-up area wait the highwaymen, on the dark slopes where the horses labour and what security may lie in the City streets is far behind. Highway robbery was on the increase.[26]

Stealing, from people or houses, with or without violence, was the most common crime. If the value of the stolen goods exceeded 12d, theft was punishable by death. The other crimes that filled the gaols were the semi-political offences such as refusing to swear the oath required by the Crown to weed out dangerous elements such as Quakers and other dissenters.

It would be tedious, even if it were possible, to set out all the crimes on the statute book and their appropriate sanction. Suffice it to say that there were very many capital offences which we would not treat as serious crime. A disconcerting aspect of criminal offences was the power of the Crown to declare that some act was criminal: for instance, to say that the new currency might devalue national funds was declared to be treason, by extension of the Treason Act which applied to counterfeiting money; hence it was punishable by death. During the Plague, 'persons who, though of infected families, refused to remain shut up' in their plague-stricken houses were declared liable to be committed to Newgate,[27] where they would probably die anyway; it hardly mattered whether it was the plague or typhus that finished them.

What is missing from the picture is the kind of crime that our society suffers from so grievously: sexual perversions involving the abuse of its weaker members. No doubt examples occurred, but not on the organised scale that provides a dungheap for the modern gutter press. Nor did our other scourge, drug-related crimes, afflict seventeenth-century Londoners. And the complicated company frauds of our day did not exist, there being, in our terms, no companies.

There was no police force. The constables of each parish did their best to apprehend criminals, with the help of honest citizens with their eyes on the rewards offered, and the parish watchmen, who were not always conspicuously energetic. Constables were the lowest grade of local authority office-bearer. They were appointed by the parish – that is, by the incumbent and his churchwardens – for a fixed term, and paid, but at so low a rate that a busy man hoped not to be appointed. It was, however, his public duty to accept. There would be three or four constables to a parish, depending on its size and prosperity.

Once caught and brought to trial, the prisoner's best chance was to object straight away to the indictment (the description of the crime with which he was charged). It had to be technically correct; and unless George Fox's experience in 1664 was atypical, it was often full of mistakes. On at least one occasion he managed to tie the court up in knots, demonstrating five separate errors in one indictment. (This did not get him very far; he was imprisoned anyway, but illegally.)[28]

If a prisoner was validly charged with a capital crime, he had two choices. He could

> reply that he wished for the judgement of god, in which case the trial is finished, for, guilty or not, he is irreparably doomed to death; yet this does not render the family infamous, as he has not been declared guilty; and on that account the customary public method of punishment is not made use of with him, *nor are his effects confiscated, but descend to the natural heir.*[29]

A devoted family man who assessed his chances of acquittal at nil might take this course, although its sequel, *peine fort et dur*, was barbaric:

> He is then stretched upon the ground on his back, having a stone underneath him, which raises his loins upwards, and is covered with a table [more usually a board or flat stone] loaded with heavy stones, which are not all laid upon him together to crush him at once, but one after another, so as to prolong his death to a great length of time.[30]

This graphic description comes from Magalotti, who is extremely unlikely to have witnessed such a scene. It is correct; indeed he missed one or two trimmings, such as that the prisoner was sentenced to be confined in a 'low dark chamber ... and have no sustenance, save only on the first day three morsels of the worst bread and on the second day three draughts of standing [stagnant] water ... this should be his diet alternately till he died'.[31] (Hence the scene in Arthur Miller's play *The Crucible*, where the prisoner pleads for a quicker death by 'more stones'. This barbarity was exported to New

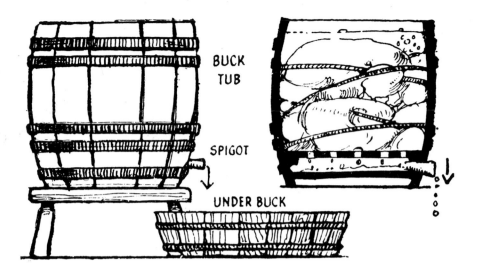

BUCK TUB

SPIGOT

UNDER BUCK

(above) Laundry: linen soaking in a buck tub (see page 134).

(right) A kitchenmaid. She is wearing pattens attached to her shoes and carrying home the vegetables in a basket.

Some street-cryers' trades: the chimney sweep (above left); the orange-seller (above right); the mop-seller: 'maids buy a mapp' (below left); and the oyster-man: 'twelve pence a peck oysters' (below right).

From *The Accomplisht Ladys Delight* (1677). This paragon is stirring a delicate preserve (top left), distilling medicinal spirits (top right), and trying out her own brand of cosmetics. In the kitchen one maid is ready to put loaves or pies into the oven (on the left), while the other is about to stir the contents of a cauldron. Two joints are roasting on a spit.

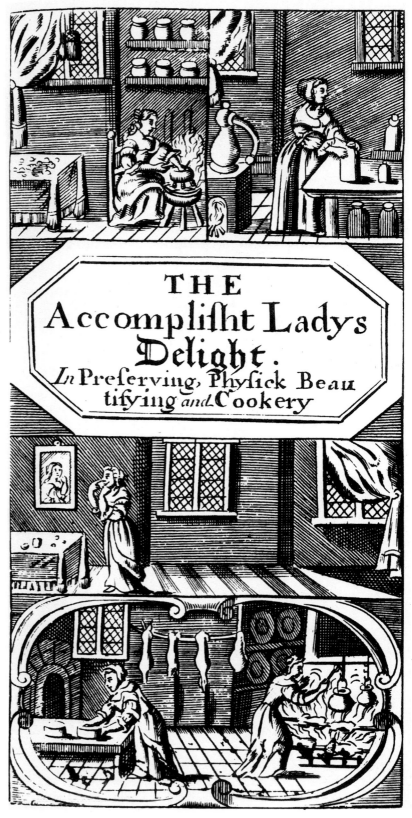

THE
Accomplisht Ladys
Delight.
In Preserving, Physick Beau
tifying and Cookery

From Archdale Palmer's *Recipe Book 1659-1672*:

(above) To Gett away Warts. Given mee 12th Jan: 166½ by Baron Hill. Take blacke Snayles & Gash and cutt them with yr Knife, then take ye Liquor wch comes from them & anoynt yr warts wth this liqor 3 or 4 times every day till all bee gon.

(below) For sore Eyes. Take 350 sowes [woodlice], & bruise them & straine them wth an handfull sage & of Rice & of Betony & Ground Ivy, let them bee putt into a thinne Canvas bagg & hung in 3 or 4 Gallons Ale, & after it hath stood 5 or 6 dayes, then draw it forthe, & drinke of it in ye Morning at 8 Clocke, & fast after it an houre & then at 4 Clocke againe in ye afternoone.

Pepys's *Diary*. Samuel Pepys
used Shelton's shorthand
system, invented in 1626,
with a few words written
out in full.

Globes showed the known world more
clearly than flat projections in atlases.

(above) This is a very grand virginal, made by Adam Leversidge in 1666. The lid would shut down over the strings and the lower panel would fold up to enclose the keyboard. Most were 3 to 4 feet long. The stand was separate.

(below) Tennis. Charles II played a keen game. He even took off his hat and jacket to do so.

The Red Bull theatre.
Some theatres dating
from before the Civil
War, like this one, were
brought back into use.
Note the audience
behind the stage, and
the lighting – hanging
'branches' and candle
foot-lights.

A stage set in the Duke's Theatre in
Lincoln's Inn Fields.

Embroidered frame
for a mirror, c.1665.

England with the rest of English law.) The trouble with Magalotti was that he believed everything; *peine fort et dur* was rarely carried out in practice.[32]

Alternatively, the prisoner might elect to go for trial. Jurymen were then summoned (no women, of course). The prisoner had the right to object to ('challenge') 35 jurymen whom he did not like the look of, and more if he could 'show cause'. Eventually twelve men were chosen and sworn, whose function was to listen to the evidence and decide, subject to the judge's directions on law, whether the case against the prisoner had been proved. Their task was not easy. They were shut up without rest, food or drink until they reached a unanimous verdict, and if in the judge's view it was the wrong one, he could send them back, still without food or drink, until they saw reason. One stalwart jury even then refused to convict two Quakers of unlawful assembly, so the judge fined all twelve of them and sent them to Newgate, a notoriously squalid prison where they risked death from 'jail fever' (typhus). They were not released until they managed to get writs of Habeas Corpus, which forced another judge to release them.[33] If a case being heard on assize – that is, outside London – lasted longer than had been expected, the judge went off to the next assize town in considerable state – and the jurymen wrestling with the part-heard case followed him, in carts. All in all, a juror's life was not a happy one.

Juries in murder trials could bring in a verdict of manslaughter, in cases of provocation, such as when a man found his wife in the act of adultery with her lover, whom he killed. The penalty for manslaughter was only imprisonment with branding on the hand, and 'the court directed the executioner to burn him gently, because there could not be greater provocation than this'.[34] Self-defence could reduce murder to excusable homicide, in which case the prisoner's goods were still forfeit, but pardon was automatic.[35] Juries also persistently undervalued the value of stolen goods, so that they fell below the limit at which theft became punishable by death.

The prisoner's chances of acquittal were minimal. He could not compel the attendance of any witness he wanted to call, and it would take a brave man voluntarily to confront the majesty of the law arraigned on the prosecution side to give evidence for the accused. He was not allowed Counsel. He could only try to undermine the evidence of the Crown's witnesses, who in any important case would have been well rehearsed. Sometimes the witnesses were not even in court. Two widows were condemned to death for witchcraft, in 1665, on the statements of the children they were said to have bewitched, who were too young to give evidence; the quality of these statements is demonstrated by a description by one of the children of throwing an invisible mouse into the fire, where it exploded.[36]

There was no right of appeal; indeed, sentences were carried out so fast that there was little time between verdict and execution to do anything except pray. But it was often possible to apply to the King for a pardon, an arbitrary use of the royal prerogative which served the purpose of an appeal system to some extent – as long as, in those days of bad roads and poor communications, it arrived in time. Presumably in cases of justifiable homicide someone wrote on the papers, 'Do not execute before pardon arrives.'

Punishments varied from death by burning at the stake or hanging, with or without drawing and quartering, to imprisonment, branding, public whipping, or a spell in the pillory or stocks. For a wife to kill her husband, or a servant his master, was so against the natural order of things that it was treason, under the Treason Act of 1351, punishable by being burnt alive. Suicide (*felo de se*) and many other crimes entailed the automatic forfeiture of the criminal's property.

Prisons seem to have been chronically full. They housed prisoners on remand, as well as debtors and condemned criminals. Typhus was endemic, hence the nosegay of aromatic herbs carried by Old Bailey judges to ward off the evil humours wafted towards them from the prisoners in the dock. The horror of imprisonment in Newgate, London's principal prison, emerges almost casually from a contemporary account:

> When we first came into Newgate there lay (in a little by-place like a closet near the room where we were lodged) the quartered bodies of three men who had been executed some days before. [The relatives eventually got permission to bury the quarters, but it took time. The heads] were ordered to be set up in some part of the City. I saw the heads when they were brought up to be boiled ... the Hangman put them into his kettle and parboiled them with bay-salt and cummin seed, that to keep them from putrefaction and this to keep the fowls from seizing on them.[37]

At least modern prisoners do not have that stench in their nostrils; but there is an uncanny echo of contemporary drug culture in modern prisons, in this 1669 complaint: 'So bold were the coiners [forgers of coinage], that the manufacture went forward even within the walls of Newgate.'[38]

The Tower of London was still used as a prison, for important offenders such as Sir William Coventry, who was sent there for challenging the Duke of Buckingham to a duel,[39] illegal since 1666.

Those harmless, obstinate Quakers who for religious reasons refused to swear the Oath of Allegiance had to serve their sentences cheek by jowl with violent criminals. Chains and manacles were in common use. If the prisoner could raise any money, he could alleviate his misery, but the common case of the debtor incarcerated until he could satisfy his creditors hardly allowed for this. 'Neither the plaintiff nor the sheriff is bound to give him meat or drink ... if he has no goods he shall live of the charity of others, and if others will give him nothing let him die in the name of God.'[40] Not until 1670 was an Act passed 'for the reliefe and release of Poor distressed Prisoners for debt:

> forasmuch as very many persons now detained in Prison are miserably impoverished either by reason of the late unhappy times, the sadd and dreadful Fire, their owne misfortunes, or otherwise soe as they are totally disabled to give any satisfaction to their Creditors, and soe become without advantage to any a Charge and Burthen to the Kingdome, and by Noisomnes (inseparably incident to extreme poverty) may become the occasion of Pestilence and contagious diseases.

The commonsense idea was adopted of avoiding such risks to public health by letting the debtor out if he had less than £10, could not pay the debt which had landed him inside, and had not defrauded his creditors. If a bloody-minded creditor insisted that he should stay in prison, the creditor had to pay for his keep, at the rate of 18d a week; if he stopped, the debtor was released.

There is an occasional whiff of torture, although I have found no official reference to it. A midwife imprisoned in Newgate heard such screams that she thought a woman was in labour, and misguidedly offered her services. An awkward witness might be more amenable if he were 'shown the rack'.[41]

Cases where the executioner 'burned gently' were perhaps equalled by the zeal with which some executioners dealt with prisoners condemned to the pillory. Nailing the prisoner's ears to its wooden framework was an optional extra; sometimes the unfortunate man had to leave his ears there when his sentence was over. It was accepted, in general, that physical violence to the criminal, inflicted in public, was salutary and justified.

Sometimes the full rigour of the law could be avoided. A woman might 'plead her belly'. It would be unconscionable to kill her unborn child as well. But the pregnancy had to be sufficiently established to be confirmed by a 'committee of matrons'; a mere half-hour's worth would not do.

Or she might claim benefit of clergy, open to women as well as men.[42] In the Middle Ages, the Church had looked after its own. Clerics were protected from the secular arm of government. And since generally it was only the clergy who could read, it was easy to tell a cleric from a layman. If he could read, he was home and dry; he 'had his clergy'. Time moved on, and many clerics moved out with their monastic orders; also, literacy spread among the laity. The pretence that benefit of clergy had anything to do with the Church withered away, and the list of offences in which it could *not* be claimed grew longer. An Act of Henry VIII excluded 'petit treason, murder of malice prepensed, robbing churches or persons in their dwelling houses or in or near the highways [highway robbery] or burning houses or barns containing corn', with the aiders and abettors of those offences. An Act of 1670 added to the list of excluded offences, stealing cloth at night 'from the racks or tenters where the said cloth is put for the drying thereof ... to the utter undoing of many clothiers [cloth merchants]'.

The prisoner who claimed benefit of clergy was required to read a passage from the Bible, usually the 'neck verse' in psalm 51: 'Have mercy upon me, O God, after thy great goodness: according to the multitude of thy mercies do away mine offences.' (Surely any habitual male criminal would take care to commit the neck verse to memory before his trial, just in case? Like spotting examination questions, he might be unlucky if the judge put another passage to him, but it was worth trying.) Women were not asked to read anything, which was remarkably fair considering the high level of female illiteracy. If the prisoner passed the test, he or she did not get off scot free, but the punishment was reduced to manageable levels, such as branding 'on the brawn of the left thumb the said mark to be made by the gaoler openly in the court before the judge', plus any other appropriate punishment such as whipping or stocking.[43] Just as the absence of an appeal system was tempered by the royal prerogative of pardon, benefit of clergy provided in practice, if not in logic, a means of sparing first offenders.[44] An attenuated version of it lingered on until 1827.

Transportation hovered in the background of many sentences. We had not yet discovered the usefulness of Australia for dumping unwanted citizens, but the idea was the same: out of sight, out of mind. The dominions ('plantations') on the east coast of America and the Caribbean islands needed hands, especially before the African slave trade was fully functioning; what better source of slave labour than the dock?

In 1667 a woman who had already been branded for a previous offence was found guilty of stealing two shirts and four smocks, value 6s 8d. This time she faced the death penalty, but an application for pardon was made to the King; 'the felony was of small value, and she and her husband are very desirous for her to be transported to the plantations', where presumably her husband was able to join her.[45] Two years later Margaret Griffith, sentenced to transportation, petitioned to be sent to Virginia, where she could serve under her brother; and Richard Charnut petitioned to be transported instead of dying for the theft of two pewter plates. Thomas Poulton, convicted for house-breaking, was included in 'the next transportation pardon, on account of his youth and penitence and his having been seduced by evil company'.[46] Quakers found guilty of a third offence were liable to be transported, which must, if they survived the Atlantic crossing, have been welcome indeed.

Civil law: tort

This amorphous concept (named from the French *tort*, a wrong) gave rise to the doctrine of negligence, which is what you would rely on if you had to sue someone who had run you over. Any modern legal adviser would recognise the following situation: the plaintiff suffered damage through the acts of the defendant, who *knew or ought to have known* that he might hurt other people by what he was doing. In 1676 what the defendant was doing, according to the plaintiff, was training two ferocious unbroken mares to pull a coach, in the middle of Lincoln's Inn Fields; or, putting it another way, '*duas equas feroces et minime domitas in trahendo currum ... improvide incaute absque debita consideratione ineptitudinis loci illius*'.[47]

239

Another kind of wrong is damage to your reputation, if someone speaks (slander) or writes (libel) bad things about you. Some reports of decisions were short, if not sweet. It was slanderous to say, 'I know myself, and I know you, I [presumably the speaker stressed the pronoun] never buggered a mare.'[48] The law of defamation has, like the law of negligence, become vastly complicated, but one factor already present in the 1660s was that the defamatory statement must have been heard or read by ('published to') a third party. Here is another sample of 1660s legalese, this time in what passed as Norman French, with gaps where the reporter's vocabulary failed him: '*cestuy que laugh quant il oye un auter a lier le libel n'est un publisher sil ne fait pluis*',[49] which I think means, if you hear a defamatory statement but it only makes you laugh, and you don't say anything, you haven't passed it on or 'published' it yourself; but I could easily be wrong. I cite it mainly to show how incomprehensible most legal proceedings must have been to the average man and woman in the street. And as if the garbled language were not enough, there was a peculiar way of writing legal documents, 'court hand', which made it difficult or impossible for a non-lawyer to read them.[50]

Analogous to slander was a quasi-criminal offence created by the 1660 Act of Oblivion: 'If any person ... within three years ... shall presume maliciously to call any other person ... any name or other words of reproach any way tending to revive the memory of the late differences ... then [he] shall pay ... the party grieved ... [if the aggrieved party is a gentleman or above] £10, and if under that degree, 40s.' A worthy idea, but certain difficulties in proving the offence might hinder any windfall.

Contract

The law was tidied up in 1677 by the Statute of Frauds, which provided, for example, that a sale of land had to be evidenced in writing. Without statutory provisions most people got by with common sense and custom, such as the 'earnest money' paid to seal a bargain (often paid as part of marriage betrothals). The traditional 'luck-penny' was not enough in serious transactions; the payment had to bear some relation to the value of the contract.[51] Although a sale of land might well be legally valid if buyer and seller merely agreed and shook hands on the bargain, it would be a foolish man who undertook such a major transaction without a formal record of it under his seal and witnessed, in case he needed to enforce it later. Commercial dealings came within the international Law Merchant, which had evolved from medieval times.

Tax

Charles came back to an empty treasury and a mountain of commitments, claims and debts. It was hardly his fault that contemporary thinking failed to solve all his financial problems immediately. The situation was made no easier by his dislike – following in his father's footsteps – of summoning an increasingly recalcitrant Parliament.

The first expedient was the Poll Tax. It was not a new idea; it had provoked the Peasants' Revolt 300 years earlier, which surely was hardly a recommendation. But it had an attractive simplicity for administrators: if you had a head ('poll'), and an income above a modest threshold, you were liable. There was no assessment of income, with all the consequent difficulties with which we are so familiar. Liability depended on social status. The nobility and gentry paid between £20 and £100 a year. Most people paid 6d a year. Various categories of office-holder paid more. The assessment machinery was simplicity itself:

> This afternoon there was a couple of men with me, with a book in each of their hands, demanding money for polemony [*sic*]; and I overlooked the book and saw myself set down *Samuel Pepys, gent., 10s for himself and for his servants 2s*. Which I did presently [immediately] pay without any dispute; but I fear I shall not escape so [Samuel was liable to pay £10 as an esquire, one step higher than a gentleman], and therefore I have long ago laid by £10 for them; but I think I am not bound to discover myself [disclose his actual liability].[52]

The idea familiar until recently to married taxpayers, that a man and his wife are one person for income tax purposes, cropped up in 1667; the JP who thought of it, and ruled that therefore a couple need pay only one lot of poll tax, was sent to reconsider this interpretation of the law in prison.[53]

It was possible to avoid the poll tax by staying one jump ahead of the men with the books in their hands. Perhaps something more static might work better. In 1662 a form of capital tax was tried: 2s a year on every fireplace ('hearth') in the house. So wealth – that is, the size of the house – was the determinant, instead of social status. But alas some mean-minded citizens responded by blocking up their chimneys.

The country had generally welcomed Charles back with enthusiasm. Now was the time to express their feelings in £ s d, and make appropriate donations. Samuel wrote, 'I think it will not come to much',[54] and he was right.[55] The old system of 'subsidies' was brought back in 1663, but did not fill the yawning gap between income and expenditure. By 1664 war with the Dutch was imminent. Parliament voted £2,500,000 to be raised in the form of secured loans, paid over three years, and earmarked for the Navy.[56] This began at last to make inroads into the financial chaos of the time.

The other way in which taxes affect the citizen is indirect taxation on commodities that he can choose – to some extent – whether to buy or not. Charles and his parliaments were always trying to balance the need for money, the interests of the plantations and of the merchants trading with them, and the desirability of encouraging home production and discouraging foreign imports. The fourth Act of his reign contains a fascinating list of dutiable goods, such as

Alphabets, the set containing 24
Armour, old, the 100weight
Babies [dolls] or puppets for children, the gross
Balls – tennis – the 1,000
Caviare the 100weight
Chairs of walnut tree
Elephants' teeth
Juice of lemons, the pipe [as in port; convenient for long voyages]
Playing [card] tables of walnut tree, the pair

The poor rate

The parish exacted from anyone of any substance, a payment to support the parish poor, or – which was much resented – to help the poor in a neighbouring parish. This is considered further in the next chapter, in the section dealing with the poor.

Wills and intestacy

By the Custom of London, a testator wishing to leave property away from his natural heirs – that is, his wife and children – was free to do so only to the extent of one-third of his personal property, or half if he had no children.[57] Most rich men found a way round this, if they wanted to leave a substantial legacy to a friend, a more distant relation or a mistress.[58]

It was usual to delay making a will until death was hovering. The example given in Fly's *Almanac* for 1667 was succinct. It gave a life interest to the widow, after legacies to any children, the widow being sole executrix; remainder to the children. It does not give any advice on witnesses or other formalities, perhaps because everyone was taken to know about them. It was more usual to pad out the bare bones with introductory phrases on the lines of:

> In the name of God amen. This — day of — in the —th year of the reign of our sovereign Lord Charles ii by the grace of God of England Scotland France and Ireland and Defender of the Faith anno domini 16— I — , in the county of — , husbandman [it was usual to state the calling or profession of the testator], being weak in body but of sound and perfect memory and knowing the certainty of Death, do therefore ordaine and constitute and make this my last will and testament in manner and forme following viz first I commend my soule into the hands of Almighty God my creator and to Jesus Christ my redeemer by and through whom I hope to have forgiveness of all my sins and life everlasting and my body to the earth from whence it came and for my temporal estate I give and bequeath as hereinafter following...[59]

Only then need the relatives sit forward on the edge of their chairs.

Unless a copy of a helpful almanac could be found, there must have been someone who could be reached quickly, who had a workable precedent of a will. In the pre-Reformation days it would have been the local priest. Now, I suggest, it was the parson or the schoolmaster who was hurriedly summoned; or a precedent of a will that had worked in other cases could be borrowed, or was available in the family archives. In the country, perhaps the legal knowledge acquired by the local squire at the Inns of Court when he was young could be tapped.

Wills were usually witnessed, by at least two people. It is not unusual to find one or more of the witnesses, and even the testator, making their mark, being illiterate. As well as the executor or executrix of the will, the testator often appointed 'overseers' to see that all was done properly, especially if the executrix was the widow. Unmarried daughters were often left an annuity to be paid by the principal legatee, usually a brother, who would have to feed and clothe them as well, as long as they behaved themselves. Sometimes the overseers could discourage a daughter from marrying someone they thought undesirable, by taking her annuity away.[60]

If matters had been left too long and there was no time to write out even the shortest form of will for the dying man to sign, he could dispose of his personal property (not interests in land) orally, by words showing 'an intent to bequeath, not any loose idle discourse in his illness; for the sick man must require the by-standers to bear witness of such his intentions'.[61] Someone present would write it down and sign it on his behalf (a 'nuncupative' will).

If a testator really wanted to cause a family row, he could leave a holograph will: that is, one written in his own handwriting. This need not be witnessed at all, but was only valid 'if sufficient proof can be obtained of the handwriting'.[62]

If there was no will of any kind, the rules of intestacy applied. They varied from place to place, according to local custom. The Custom of London, the most usual one, gave one-third to the widow, two-thirds between the children, the widow being appointed administratrix. If there were no children, the widow would take the whole. She might be deterred from deserting her husband for a lover, by the thought of losing her rights to his estate ('forfeiture').

> Here wanteth equality in the Law ... a poore woman shall have but the third foote of her husband's lands when he is dead, for all the service she did him during the accouplement (perhaps a long time and a tedious) and if she be extravagant with a friend [a delicate euphemism for going to live with her lover] this is an elopement and a forfeiture ... But men may lope over ditch and dale, a thousand out-ridings and out-biddings is no forfeiture.[63]

It was safer to get her husband to make a will. 'Though our lawe may seem somewhat rigorous to wives, yet for the most part they can handle their husbands so well and doucely, especially when they are sick, that ... their husbands at their death of their goodwill give them all.'[64] She should go about it carefully, however. 'If a man made a will in his sickness, on the over-importunity of his wife, contrary to his own wishes and desires, and merely that he may be quiet, this is a will made by restraint, and shall not be good.'[65]

CHAPTER 15

MONEY, POVERTY
AND CLASS

The rich

A few people were very rich indeed. Alderman Sir Robert Viner[1] advanced £30,000 to provide regalia for Charles's coronation, and still had another £30,000 available to pay the army in Ireland. With three other people he stumped up £250,000 to keep the state liquid, and himself provided another £300,000 to pay the Navy in 1665. In 1667 he and Alderman Backwell, another City financier, offered £800,000 up front, for the right to collect the poll tax, which was estimated as likely to produce only £480,000. (This system of tax collection, called 'farming', had been in use for many centuries.) His loans were mostly secured on something, such as the *future* produce of the hearth tax or the excise duty, but Sir Robert must have known he was taking appalling risks. It is sad to relate that when the Crown reneged on all its monetary obligations by 'stopping the exchequer' in 1672, he was ruined.

As with the immense salaries drawn by some heads of enterprises nowadays, one wonders how anyone could spend all that money. A medieval baron would have shown off his wealth in the size of his private army of retainers, all dressed in his livery, swaggering about the countryside terrorising lesser mortals, and forming endless processions on state occasions and funerals. Tastes had changed. As an alderman, Sir Robert could not move out of the City to the suburbs, or a country estate, where he would anyway have pined for his counting house and the insider gossip of the Exchange. But money could buy elegant objects for display in the houses of the rich, wherever they were.

The palatial mansions south of St James's Park and on either side of Piccadilly cried out for elegant furniture and *objets d'art*. The unruly crowds of medieval retainers gave way to musicians and velvet-lined gilded coaches drawn by matched horses. With care and attention to detail, it was no doubt possible to spend quite a large proportion of one's income. Then perhaps a country estate could be picked up, 'the property', as the auctioneers say, 'of a gentleman' ruined in the late troubles and inadequately recompensed by his sovereign.

Gregory King

Who were these rich men? Alderman Viner was a gold merchant and banker. Despite the wars abroad and the disasters of plague and fire at home, money could still be made by energetic entre-preneurs with capital. To have any idea of their number, we can consult a seventeenth-century analysis, Gregory King's 'Scheme of the income and expense of the several families of England' (reproduced on pages 248-9). This sounds promising; but large pinches of salt have to be scattered over it. For one thing, his calculations concerned the year 1688. How much had changed since 1660? Perhaps not much. But more drastically, King's figures and working methods have been demolished by modern historians.[2] He wrote in the context of a debate which had been brewing since the dissolution of the monasteries, on the best way to deal with poverty and unemployment. He is now thought to have bent his figures to suit his theories. However, we can take a sideways look at him using his 'Scheme' as evidence of what, in the last two decades of the century – and probably in our period – was at least acceptable to current thinking without vehement demur.

Above the line in King's table,[3] he listed various categories of people who contributed to the national wealth, such as 'eminent merchants and traders by sea' (Alderman Viner would have fitted in here) and 'persons in greater – and lesser – offices and places' (the predecessors of the civil service, such as Samuel). Below the line came 'common seamen', 'labouring people and out servants', 'cottagers and paupers', 'common soldiers', and 'vagrants; as Gipsies,

Number of families	Ranks, degrees, titles and qualifications	Heads per family	Number of persons
160	Temporal Lords	40	6,400
26	Spiritual Lords	20	520
800	Baronets	16	12,800
600	Knights	13	7,800
3,000	Esquires	10	30,000
12,000	Gentlemen	8	96,000
5,000	Persons in greater Offices and Places	8	40,000
5,000	Persons in lesser Offices and Places	6	30,000
2,000	Eminent Merchants and Traders by Sea	8	16,000
8,000	Lesser Merchants and Traders by Sea	6	48,000
10,000	Persons in the Law	7	70,000
2,000	Eminent Clergy-men	6	12,000
8,000	Lesser Clergy-men	5	40,000
40,000	Freeholders of the better sort	7	280,000
120,000	Freeholders of the lesser sort	$5\frac{1}{2}$	660,000
150,000	Farmers	5	750,000
15,000	Persons in Liberal Arts and Sciences	5	75,000
50,000	Shopkeepers and Tradesmen	$4\frac{1}{2}$	225,000
60,000	Artizans and Handicrafts	4	240,000
5,000	Naval Officers	4	20,000
4,000	Military Officers	4	16,000
500,586		$5\frac{1}{3}$	2,675,520
50,000	Common Seamen	3	150,000
364,000	Labouring People and Out Servants	$3\frac{1}{2}$	1,275,000
400,000	Cottagers and Paupers	$3\frac{1}{4}$	1,300,000
35,000	Common Soldiers	2	70,000
849,000		$3\frac{1}{4}$	2,795,000
	Vagrants; as Gipsies, Thieves, Beggars, &c		30,000
	So the general Account is		
500,586	Increasing the Wealth of the Kingdom	$5\frac{1}{3}$	2,675,520
849,000	Decreasing the Wealth of the Kingdom	$3\frac{3}{4}$	2,825,000
1,349,586	Neat Totals	$4\frac{1}{13}$	5,500,520

Source: Peter Laslett, *The World We Have Lost* (London, 1965), pp. 32–3.

the several families of England' calculated for the year 1688

Yearly income per family		Yearly income in general	Yearly income per head			Yearly expense per head			Yearly increase per head			Yearly increase in general
£	s.	£	£	s.	d.	£	s.	d.	£	s.	d.	£
3,200		512,000	80	0	0	70	0	0	10	0	0	64,000
1,300		33,800	65	0	0	45	0	0	20	0	0	10,400
800		704,000	55	0	0	49	0	0	6	0	0	76,800
650		390,000	50	0	0	45	0	0	5	0	0	39,000
450		1,200,000	45	0	0	41	0	0	4	0	0	120,000
280		2,880,000	35	0	0	32	0	0	3	0	0	288,000
240		1,200,000	30	0	0	26	0	0	4	0	0	160,000
120		600,000	20	0	0	17	0	0	3	0	0	90,000
400		800,000	50	0	0	37	0	0	13	0	0	208,000
198		1,600,000	33	0	0	27	0	0	6	0	0	288,000
154		1,540,000	22	0	0	18	0	0	4	0	0	280,000
72		144,000	12	0	0	10	0	0	2	0	0	24,000
50		400,000	10	0	0	9	4	0	0	16	0	32,000
91		3,640,000	13	0	0	11	15	0	1	5	0	350,000
55		6,600,000	10	0	0	9	10	0	0	10	0	330,000
42	10	6,375,000	8	10	0	8	5	0	0	5	0	187,500
60		900,000	12	0	0	11	0	0	1	0	0	75,000
45		2,250,000	10	0	0	9	0	0	1	0	0	225,000
38		2,280,000	9	10	0	9	0	0	0	10	0	120,000
80		400,000	20	0	0	18	0	0	2	0	0	40,000
60		240,000	15	0	0	14	0	0	1	0	0	16,000
68	18	34,488,800	12	18	0	11	15	4	1	2	8	3,023,700
									Decrease			*Decrease*
20		1,000,000	7	0	0	7	10	0	0	10	0	75,000
15		5,460,000	4	10	0	4	12	0	0	2	0	127,500
6	10	2,000,000	2	0	0	2	5	0	0	5	0	325,000
14		490,000	7	0	0	7	10	0	0	10	0	35,000
10	10	8,950,000	3	5	0	3	9	0	0	4	0	562,500
		60,000	2	0	0	4	0	0	2	0	0	60,000
68	18	34,488,800	12	18	0	11	15	4	1	2	8	3,023,700
10	10	9,010,000	3	3	0	3	7	6	0	4	6	622,500
32	5	43,491,800	7	18	0	7	9	3	0	8	9	2,401,200

Thieves, Beggars, &c.', whose income was less than their expenditure. The conclusion King drew was that, of the population as a whole (roughly five and a half million), more than half were 'decreasing the wealth of the kingdom' because they spent more than they got (quite how is not clear to me).

One column of his table is headed 'yearly income per head'. The amounts are startling, no matter how one has been trying to make adjustments to seventeenth-century figures to produce remotely comparable 1990s figures. One hundred 'temporal lords' top the list, with annual incomes of only £80 each. Choosing from his categories people who were likely to live in London, a large number of 'gentlemen' (that is, men who did not have to earn their living) had incomes estimated at £45; merchants, between £50 and £33; office holders, between £30 and £20; 'persons in liberal arts and sciences', £12; shopkeepers and tradesmen, £10; and 'artizans and handicrafts', £9 10s.

Perhaps it is reasonable to assume that London incomes were higher than in the rest of the country. Even so, Alderman Viner's wealth is hard to reconcile with King's figures. Nevertheless, his 'Scheme' may at least give us some shaky guide to the hierarchy, if not the amounts, of incomes.

The middling sort

The terms 'middle class' and 'bourgeoisie' had not yet been coined. Clearly there was a gap between the rich and the poor; very logically, its occupants were described as 'the middling sort'. Samuel was a pre-eminent example. Because his description of domestic life is so vivid and detailed, it is hard to avoid treating him as typical of Londoners; but there were more poor folk than the middling sort, and they were not half as comfortable as Samuel.

The poor

They thronged the London streets. They begged, and starved, and quarrelled, and bred. They were the most numerous component of any crowd, yet the hardest to imagine,[4] since none of them wrote diaries, so far as we know.

The common seamen, at least, can be discerned in the crowd. Oliver Cromwell had already laid up trouble for Charles, in the shape of his naval wars; he may have captured Jamaica from the Spanish, but ships are expensive to keep at sea, and when they are brought home their crew need to be paid their accumulated wages as soon as possible, which he did not do. One of the first laws passed by the Parliament that welcomed Charles back provided that the Navy should be paid off from the proceeds of the poll tax.[5] It was then thought that 40 ships were involved, with 3,681 men owed £128,982 4s.[6] But there were 65 ships 'out of employment' from 14 March 1658, and 36 more 'who entered into His Majesty's pay on 24 June last', all of which needed to be paid off.[7] Some were paid off in Portsmouth, most in London. By March 1661 the Commissioners were paying off two ships a day, at the Guildhall, from 7 a.m. till 10 or 11 p.m., the total amount for each ship averaging about £4,000. Sometimes they called a halt because of some civic function 'which the mariners' presence would have disturbed';[8] first things first. But the poll tax was slower to come in than had been anticipated, and the ships still waited off shore, unable to dock because there was no cash to pay their crews.

Painfully, one by one, the ships came in and the seamen were paid. But not always with cash. They were given 'tickets', redeemable at the Navy Office, with more form-filling and delay. Tickets would not fill bellies. So the seamen rapidly found middlemen – or, frequently, women – who would advance cash to them in exchange for their tickets. 'There are women brokers who stand about the Navy Office offering to help seamen who have any tickets to ready money ... at 5s per £ or more loss to the seaman.'[9] The starving sailors were thankful to get even that pittance, as long as it bought them a drink and placated their wives. By June 1661, 'all such tickets as have been produced and have been approved and allowed to be due and right' had been paid, so it was said, but 'many tickets are pretended to be unsatisfied which have not been produced or claimed', and a deadline was set, 13 June 1661, after which any ticket produced would be treated as a forgery,[10] cold comfort for a starving, illiterate seaman.

The scandal dragged on. In 1666 the obvious, cynical remedy was applied: an Act was passed 'To prevent the disturbance of seamen; Whereas divers Fightings Quarrellings and disturbances do often happen in and about His Majesty's offices ... for His Majesty's Royal Navy, and frequent Differences and Disorders are occasioned ... on pay-days in London ... by the unreasonable Turbulency of Seamen', the Navy Commissioners and their Clerk of the Acts (Samuel) were authorised to imprison offenders for seven days, or fine them 20s, which, of course, these unreasonably turbulent sailors did not have.

In 1667 the officers and seamen of the frigates *Harp* and *Mary*, off the coast of Ireland, humbly petitioned the Principal Officers and Commissioners of His Majesty's Navy:

> That your poor petitioners having sent several petitions to your Honours, but receiving no answer, there being above 52 months pay due to them, and having neither money nor credit nor wherewith to buy bread for their wives and children, who are now in a starving condition, being forced also to lie on the streets by reason their landlords will trust them no longer, and your petitioners going naked for want of clothes, which together are a thousand times worse than to die by the hands of an enemy, for what can be more grievous than for men to see the starving of their wives and children, therefore the humble request of your poor petitioners is that Your Honours will be pleased to take the miserable condition of themselves, their wives and children so into consideration as to order them their pay, that their families may not be altogether starved in the streets, and themselves go like heathen, having nothing to cover their nakedness.[11]

And this was a plea not for charity, but for bitterly earned pay, due for more than four years. In another petition, seamen's wives *and widows* pathetically pleaded 'for order for speedy payment of their moneys; their tickets have been long in the office, and many of them have come 200 miles for their money'.[12]

There were rumours that the discount rate had gone up to 8s in the pound, and that thousands of tickets were not being paid at all, the luckless presenters being promptly drafted ('pressed') for further service in other ships, without tickets or money.[13] No wonder that in the Dutch wars many English seamen served the Dutch, who paid cash. ('We did heretofore fight for tickets; now we fight for dollars.')[14] It is still shaming, to this day, to find that in 1668 Charles spent nearly £11,000 on two pairs of earrings,[15] and a year later £2,800 on a jewel for the Queen, and £6,000 for two large diamonds – recipient unknown.[16] That would almost have paid off five ships, in cash.

Meanwhile, how did the seamen live? They enlisted abroad. They stayed, and rioted in their hundreds[17] for the wages they had so desperately earned. They begged. They stole. They starved.

King's next category was 'labouring people and out servants'. They were not unemployed so much as underemployed. No matter how hard they worked, they could not earn enough adequately to keep themselves and their families, and they were often employed in seasonal trades which left them penniless in the slack season: for instance, those engaged in producing and selling luxury goods for which there was no demand during the summer, when the smart set left London if they could. These people might apply to the parish together with those who had no form of income at all.

'Cottagers' did not live in London. 'Paupers' did, all too many of them. 'The people are in a desperate condition ... [they] curse the king, wish for Cromwell, and say come Dutch come Devil they cannot be worse.'[18] There was, in theory, an elaborate welfare scheme in place, remarkably similar to the benefit safety net which operated until 1988, when it was rejigged. A distinguishing feature of the 1660s welfare scheme was the all-importance of 'settlement'. The preamble to the Poor Law Amendment Act of 1662 identified the problem: 'Whereas the necessity, number and continued increase of the poor ... is very great and exceeding burthensome, being occasioned *by reason of some defects in the law of relief and employment in such parishes ... as they are legally settled*, which doth enforce many to turn [into] incorrigible rogues and others to perish for want'[19] – not, of course, just naked, hopeless poverty.

Benefits were doled out by parishes, and a claimant had first to satisfy the parish authorities that she – women more often needed help than men – belonged to that parish.[20] One of Charles's earliest Proclamations had deplored the habit of 'Rogues Vagabonds Beggars and other idle persons from all parts of the nation [resorting to] the cities of London and Westminster and the suburbs ... where they get their living by begging, stealing and other lewd practices'. They were all to be 'sent to the place of their birth or last abode to be kept as impotent [i.e. those who could not work would be supported] or made to labour [if they could work] ... At their peril they [must] forthwith depart to the place of their birth or abode.'

So the first hurdle for a claimant was to prove 'settlement' in the relevant parish – preferably a rich one. Up to 1662 a claimant had to show three years' residence in a parish before she could claim from its funds; after 1662 only 40 days sufficed.

To prevent a child from being born in a parish, it was not unknown for the parish overseers to hustle a pauper woman in labour over the parish boundary into the next parish. The real problem was foundling children, left abandoned in the streets. No one could argue that they had a prior settlement elsewhere. Some astute and selfless mothers would even deliberately abandon their children in a prosperous parish, and disappear. They were not always poor. 'Whereas the putative fathers and lewd mothers of Bastard Children run away out of the Parish, and sometimes out of the County, and leave the said Bastard upon the charge of the parish where they are born, although such Putative Fathers and lewd Mothers have estates sufficient to discharge [indemnify] such Parish',[21] the parish officers were empowered to seize the property of either parent and sell it, to cover the cost of rearing the child.

These children did not do too badly, considering the standards of the time. Some parishes sent their foundlings out of London to healthy country parishes. The parish officer would visit them there at least once a year, to check that the payments to their nurses were being properly spent. When they were old enough, they were apprenticed, rather earlier perhaps than some other children, but their parish would fork out a premium and a suit of clothes. There is a list[22] of the apprenticeships to which one inner-city parish despatched its children, in the period 1677 to 1711, which I quote despite its being outside our period. Of 28 children, nine girls went to 'housewifery', sometimes combined with other trades. Others went into various textile trades. Of the boys, three went to sea, one was bound to a chimney sweep, one went to Jamaica, and one became a gardener.

It is the variety of these trades that is heartening. There would be no point in sending a passionate gardener to sea, or in forcing a boy with the sea in his blood to bend over seedlings all day, so surely one can hope that even parish children were allowed some say in their destinies? And if the worst happened, and their disastrous beginning led to early death, the parish was not too hard-hearted. It buried them with shrouds and coffins, and rosemary, and even a decent drink for the pallbearers.

Some poor folk did not meekly return to their place of settlement, or disputed it. The parish authorities, which were of course concerned to minimise the number of claims on their resources, could

cause such persons to be apprehended, publicly whipt, and sent away (except such as are willing to go to the English plantations) ... no poor to be permitted to beg, and the impotent provided for, so as to live comfortably and yet to be kept from profes'd idleness [this was the balance that still evades social reformers] and such as are able may have means provided to set them on work.[23]

For three years after the new Poor Law, Justices of the Peace could send 'rogues vagabonds idle and disorderly persons and sturdy [able-bodied] beggars *as they think fit* to be transported to the English plantations ... there to be disposed of in the usual way of servants for a term not exceeding seven years':[24] in other words, enslaved, with no right of appeal.

Nowadays welfare benefits necessitate interminable form-filling. Then, it was a matter of direct application in person to the vestry, the quorum of parish officers who wielded a large measure of authority over the destinies of the poor. In theory, each parish kept a stock of wool, hemp and flax, so that the deserving poor could be usefully employed. It seems to have been assumed that anyone could turn a heap of unspun wool into a marketable commodity to the credit of the parish chest. But in practice, and not surprisingly, the more usual course seems to have been to pay a small pension, enhanced by single payments to meet temporary crises such as fires, illnesses and childbirth. A single payment could even redeem goods in pawn, or pay arrears of rent. The going rate of basic pension was between £1 12s 6d and £3 18s a year, which might be temporarily made up to more than £7.

An unsuccessful claimant could go straight to the Lord Mayor's house, and appeal to him to reverse the decision of the vestry. She was often heard there and then, and stood a good chance of being awarded at least something to tide her over, since it was in the City's interest to cut short litigation and argument. Perhaps, even, the Lord Mayor enjoyed being able to temper justice with mercy.

As well as the poor rate assessed by the vestry on every householder above a certain level of prosperity, the parish administered private charities such as bequests and gifts for charitable purposes. 'Decayed' members of livery companies, and their widows, might rely on the charity of their fellow-members. There were alms-houses, for the fortunate; but the occupants must have represented a minute proportion of those without a roof over the heads.

A time-honoured expedient of the poor has always been to pawn their possessions. 'Uncle's', with its well-known three balls, was a later creation.[25] But individuals would lend on the security of clothes and tools, often at unconscionably high rates of interest, defying the legal limit of 6 per cent. Samuel recorded that 'old Hardwicke came and redeemed a watch he had left with me in pawn for 40s seven years ago; and I let him have it'[26] – without any mention of interest; old Hardwicke was lucky. In December 1660, Viscount Grandison petitioned for a licence 'to erect seven large houses in London and Westminster for registering and securing all pawns' at the rate of 3d per month for every 20s, 'instead of 6d as now usually exacted. Many poor are driven to beggary because they are obliged to pawn their clothes etc. to buy [trading] stock'. The idea was commended, but the petition was refused because the rate of interest, which was an annual rate of 15 per cent, exceeded the permitted 6 per cent. In 1662 the Earl of Bristol was commissioned 'to erect in London and other counties, banks and *monts de piété*': in other words, state-controlled pawnshops.[27] Nothing seems to have come of the idea.

Layabouts who persisted in idleness might be braced by a spell in a house of correction. Henry VIII's palace of Bridewell[28] at the confluence of the Fleet and the Thames rivers, which had perhaps become too malodorous even for the noses of sixteenth-century royalty, was donated as the first correction centre, in 1553, 'to be a workhouse for the poor and idle persons of the city'.[29] Each parish was supposed to provide itself with one, to which a Justice of the Peace could consign such idlers. There was a workhouse in Clerkenwell, which accommodated 600 able-bodied and 100 impotent poor between 1663 and 1672, when it closed.[30] The idea was ahead of its time. The normal practice was to give poor women who had housing, but who could not afford their rent, employment and income by lodging with them the indigent poor whose rent the parish paid, giving the lodgers either work or an allowance; a much more human treatment.

After the paupers in King's 'Scheme' come 'common soldiers'. They were a different problem from the common seamen; they were here, on land, and practised in the fighting skills. They had to be, and were, dispersed as quickly as possible, before discontent turned into rebellion. Soldiers could beg their way home – they had a special exemption from the prohibition against begging – in small numbers which did not pose the threat of mutiny when a whole ship's crew landed and was not paid.

That leaves us with 'Vagrants; Gypsies, Thieves, Beggars, &c.' Gypsies upset the authorities then as now; they were 'lewd persons calling themselves Egyptians and pretending to tell fortunes'.[31]

Theft from the person – that is, pick-pocketing – was the preferred option of thieves, closely followed by theft from buildings and misappropriation from employers. Often gangs worked together. Randle Holme listed the 'canting terms' (thieves' slang) they used. The modern plague of shoplifting had little chance in those cramped shops, with at least one apprentice standing guard at the entrance; but the days of such innocence were shortened as the practice grew of displaying goods on the outside counter.

And as for beggars, no matter what the statutory prohibitions said, 'neither walking riding nor in coach is it possible to make the least step without being thronged by all sorts and tyred by their importunities',[32] which has the ring of truth.

Class

The English system of primogeniture, whereby the family property devolved on the eldest son and the others had to make their own way in the world, may have led to unhappy marriages as those sons harvested the crop of heiresses; but it had the salutary effect of making a career in trade for the younger sons, in default of convenient heiresses, perfectly acceptable to the upper echelons of society. The alternatives available to later generations – the Army, the Church, India and the colonies – were not open. The Civil War had shaken the foundations of many stately homes. The boom in trade post-war, and especially post-Restoration, made the City an attractive prospect to many younger sons, and indeed, one would think, to many eldest sons, contemplating derelict estates burdened with jointures and debts.

If a younger son made his fortune, he could rise up the ladder again – so far as he had gone down it by donning the apprentice's blue apron – and buy himself a title. In 1668 a baronetcy cost £1,095.[33] If a man could show an annual income *from land* – still the touchstone of nobility – of at least £1,000, he could get himself a peerage; the titles of over half the 135 peers in the House of Lords in 1640 had been bought since 1603,[34] and the system was still in place. Then perhaps it is relevant to glance at the summit of the English social hierarchy: a man could not choose to be born to one of the King's mistresses, but if he was, he was fairly sure of a resounding title.[35]

A man's social status was worth determining. A gentleman or above stood to make more (£10) if his noble feelings were hurt by animadversions about his conduct in the 'late unhappy differences' than if he were a mere citizen (£2). If he were a peer, he was automatically absolved from 'all offences then clergiable to commoners, and also for the crimes of housebreaking, highway robbery, horsestealing and robbing of churches',[36] which perhaps accounts for the folk memory of gallant, handsome, titled highwaymen. He did not even have to read anything, and he was not 'burnt in the hand'. On the other hand, he stood to pay more poll tax.

For women whose worlds had collapsed in the Civil War or the Plague or the Fire, there was no way out save domestic service, which at least provided a roof over their heads. The Victorian expedient of becoming a governess, hateful thought it was in some instances, did at least in their own eyes preserve a vestige of their middle-class self-respect and save them from demeaning manual work; but no one wanted governesses in the 1660s. Samuel's sister Paulina faced the prospect of living in his household as a menial servant, not even as a waiting woman, since she had antagonised Elizabeth; she was lucky that he found a dowry and a husband for her.

This stark choice is difficult to imagine. There were no secretarial jobs, no clerical jobs, no nursing jobs, no women teachers, no women in the other professions. A woman could not earn an independent living by hard work. Of course, there were exceptions. Women searchers recorded the cause of death for the bills of Mortality. Women kept petty schools. Midwives and 'wise women' made a reasonable living. But these women were exceptional. The normal path to employment led through the front door of a man's house, as a wife, or the back door, as a servant.

Two pendants to this consideration of class. In the twentieth century, one of the easiest ways of assessing someone's social class – such an essential exercise in English life – is his accent. Not so in the seventeenth century. Regional accents flourished. One of the advantages of joining an Inn of Court and spending part of one's youth in London was that rougher speech habits gave way to some extent to the speech of the (royal) Court and the (legal) courts; 'received pronunciation' was on its way. But it had a very long way to go, and meanwhile accent was no guide to status.

Nor was dress. The Middle Ages had insisted that no one should dress above his station. These sumptuary laws were obsolete by the seventeenth century, but it is interesting to see that their spirit faintly lingered on. When the great day came that Samuel and Elizabeth could sally forth in their own carriage, Samuel at first had cold feet about wearing his 'fine [summer suit] of flowered tabby vest and coloured camelot tunic, because it was too fine with the gold lace at the hands [wrists]', but his wife insisted, and off they went, Elizabeth 'extraordinary fine' too, in the spanking new chariot. Naturally the fine horses and coach provoked ill-natured jealousy; but 'Povy told me of my gold-lace sleeves in the park yesterday, which vexed me also, so as to resolve never to appear in Court with it, but presently to have it taken off, *as it is fit I should.*'[37]

PART FOUR

HORIZONS

CHAPTER 16

RELIGION AND POPULAR BELIEFS

The Church of England

For centuries the Christian Church justified its existence by Christ's saying to Peter, 'Thou art Peter, and upon this rock will I build my church.'[1] For almost as many centuries dissidents protested that there was no divine justification for the Church to exact income from Christ's followers in return for interceding on their behalf to God; they were entitled to stand before their God with only their conscience for guide.

The Protestant ethic had flowed strongly during the Civil War and the Interregnum. In its heyday the Puritan Church imposed as strong a constraint on its members as ever the Roman Catholic Church had done: not, it was true, in the capacity of intermediary, but as the arbiter and controller of that very conscience the freedom of which it purported to protect. The Church of England, headed by the monarch, lost its position with his head.

Charles committed himself to re-establishing the Church that his father had, in the view of some of his subjects, died for. After the Puritans, the Church of England was comparatively mild: but even that Church required more of its congregations than we would find congenial. The seventeenth century, and in particular the period following Charles's return, is so consistently regarded as a period of abandon, of kicking over the traces at last, that it is a surprise to find the strength of the constraints still tolerated when the rule of the Saints was over.

First, it was necessary, and normal, to go to church at least once every Sunday. Each non-attender 'without reasonable excuse' – that favourite phrase of law-makers – was fined a shilling.[2] For women, church-going provided a weekly outing at which other women's clothes could be noted and possible social contacts assessed. But there is no need to belittle the place it had in the lives of ordinary people. They needed, and wanted, to be told what they should think, and believe, and aspire to. Those whose lives were painful because of illness or poverty were glad of reassurance that their time would come eventually, in the next world.

Then, the form of the service (liturgy) was predictable. Year by year the congregation heard the stories of the Old and New Testaments; incomprehensible, perhaps, but there must be some meaning in them or the world made no sense – which would be unthinkable. The only chance of free expression open to the parson was his sermon. The Book of Common [i.e. unified] Prayer had been compiled in the reign of Edward VI. Mary Tudor had done away with it, 'to the great decay of the due honour of God and discomfort to the Professors of the truth of Christ's religion',[3] but Queen Elizabeth had reimposed it. As for more recent history, 'by what undue means, and for what mischievous purposes the use of the Liturgy (though enjoined by the laws of the land, and those laws never yet repealed) came, during the late unhappy confusions, to be discontinued, [was] too well known to the world'[4] in 1660.

While Charles was still in Breda awaiting the call, various Protestant divines went over to Holland to pressure him into at least retaining various loaded Puritan expressions in the liturgy, since he could not be shifted from his loyalty to the Church of England. They were so persistent that Charles appointed a committee to consider their suggestions. The 1662 Book of Common Prayer was the result. Next time you have time, a good light, a 1662 Prayer Book and a magnifying glass, read the Preface. Pending that occasion, here is a sample:

> When, upon His Majesty's happy restoration, it seemed probable that, amongst other things, the use of the liturgy would return of course (the same having never been legally abolished) ... those men who under the late usurped powers made it a great part of their business to render the people disaffected thereto [that is, to the Book of Common Prayer] saw themselves in point of reputation and interest concerned (unless they would freely acknowledge themselves to have erred, which such men are very hardly brought to do) with their

utmost endeavours to hinder the restitution thereof ... Great importunities were used to His Sacred Majesty, that the said Book might
be revised ... as should be thought requisite for the ease of tender
consciences; whereunto His Majesty, out of his pious inclination to
give satisfaction (so far as could be reasonably expected) to all his
subjects of what persuasion whatsoever, did graciously condescend...

Of the sundry alterations proposed to us, we have rejected all such
as were either of dangerous consequence ... or else of no consequence
at all ... But such alterations as were tendered to us ... as seemed to
us in any degree requisite or expedient, we have willingly and of our
own accord assented unto ... Our general aim therefore in this
undertaking was not to gratify this or that party in any their unreasonable demands; but to do that, which to our best understandings we
conceived might most tend to the preservation of Peace and Unity in
the Church; the procuring of reverence and exciting of Piety and
Devotion in the publick Worship of God; and the cutting off occasion
from them that seek occasion of cavil or quarrel against the Liturgy
of the Church.

Under a separate heading, 'Of Ceremonies, why some may be
abolished and some retained', the committee dismissed the views of
both those who were too set in the old ways and those 'so new-
fangled that they would innovate all things', and explained why it
had pruned 'the great excess and multitude' of ceremonies, 'many
of them so dark, that they did more to confound and darken than
declare and set forth Christ's benefits to us'. The ceremonies that
remained included morning and evening prayer; the service of
baptism with a new form suitable for 'those of Riper Years' to
welcome in any anabaptists; marriages; burials; the churching of
women to give thanks for their safe deliverance from the 'great
danger of child-birth'; and prayers for the Navy to use as well as
the daily morning and evening service, asking God to 'stir up thy
strength and come and help us', with 'short prayers for single persons
that cannot meet to join in prayer with others by reason of the fight
or storm'.[5] With the addition of prayers 'upon several occasions',
such as asking for rain or fair weather, and that Parliament when
in session should act so 'that peace and happiness, truth and justice,
religion and piety may be established among us for all generations',
the Book of Common Prayer covered all eventualities, leaving no
room for ad-libbing.

What did the members of the Church of England believe? There are the creeds, each more incomprehensible than the others; but the curious reader, if she still has the magnifying glass, should refer to the Articles of Religion that come almost at the end of the book, just before the riveting Table of Kindred and Affinity which prohibits her from marrying, for instance, her grandfather. The Thirty-nine Articles 'contain the true doctrine of the Church of England', and must be read 'in the literal and grammatical sense'.[6] They are reassuringly plain, and almost comprehensible. Article 28, for instance, is perfectly clear about the doctrine of transubstantiation that had bedevilled religious thought for so long. No need any longer for Queen Elizabeth's adroit sidestepping:

> His was the word that spake it
> And what that word did make it
> That I believe, and take it.

The doctrine is 'repugnant to the plain words of Scripture ... The Body of Christ is given ... only after a heavenly and spiritual manner.'

Everyone knew where they were, and there was no room for divergence.

The Church of Rome

It is easy to forget the role of nationalism in England in the religious troubles of the seventeenth century. Behind every Catholic[7] lurked the hostile forces of France and Spain – in popular thought. The Stuart habit of marrying Catholics (Charles I married Henrietta Maria of France; Charles II married Katherine of Braganza, in Portugal; James II's second wife was Mary of Modena, but by then he was Catholic too) seems now almost consciously perverse. These ladies at least brought dowries. Perhaps they were the best offers on the market at the time. They also brought priests and chaplains with them, and they naturally stipulated that they and their household must be free to practise their religion in their new country: an unending source of trouble in xenophobic London. The Great Fire was said to have been started by a Catholic foreigner; it was just the sort of thing they would do.

Charles I was all too aware of the trouble that his adored but bigoted wife would create if she tried to make their eldest son a

Catholic. In letter after letter to her during the Civil War, he forbade her to 'endeavour to alter him [their son] in religion, nor so much as trouble him upon that point'.[8] Charles II managed to come back to England unscathed in that respect at least, but he never shared his subjects' xenophobic antipathy to Roman Catholicism. He was received into the Roman Catholic Church on his deathbed, by the same priest, Father Huddleston, who had saved his life while he was on the run from Worcester in 1650.

But on lower levels, membership of that Church still carried such opprobrium that when Elizabeth 'talked of her being and resolving to die a Catholique', Samuel was deeply perturbed.[9] She was not, and did not; but it was a useful weapon in their matrimonial arguments.

The Society of Friends in Truth

George Fox's father was a Leicestershire weaver, the epitome of rural England. George was born in 1624. When the Civil War broke out, he refused to fight for either side. His ministry is usually dated from 1647.[10] By 1659 the nascent religion had acquired its necessary libation of the blood of martyrs: 21 Quakers[11] had died in prison, or because of ill usage. By 1660 there were more than 35,000 Quakers, mostly of the 'middling sort' and mostly in the shires[12] – an astonishing increase from a standing start.

Their doctrine was founded on Fox's teaching: 'All wait patiently upon the Lord, whatsoever condition you be in; wait in the grace and truth that comes by Jesus; if ye do so, there is a promise to you, and the Lord God will fulfill it to you.' It needs no intermediary, nor a liturgy, to sit in silence until your spirit is moved by God.

The Quakers refused to take the easy course, and give at least lip service to the established order. They persisted in wearing their hats in unsuitable places, making their loyalties visibly obvious; and as soon as they opened their mouths, even a blind man could spot them. It was as if they invited punishment. 'Oh the daily reproaches and beatings in highways because we would not put off our hats, and for saying "thou" to people.'[13] Even more serious, they refused to pay tithes to maintain the established Church in its 'steeple-houses'.

Inevitably, their huge numbers soon required some kind of organisation. Arguably differing in this from either of the above two churches, they exercised 'exemplary sobriety, plainness ... and circumspect care in the government of church affairs',[14] which was so efficiently organised that, for example, they had their own communications system; although 'all the posts were laid open to search all letters, so that none could pass, we heard of several thousands of our Friends that were cast into prison'.

We must not attribute to the Quakers of the seventeenth century that peaceableness and sobriety that came to characterise them later. Cromwell had found them most troublesome, although he seems to have liked and respected Fox himself. Early adherents encouraged rebellion against the established order, by interrupting solemn Puritan services with shouts of 'hireling' and 'deceiver'.[15] Where would such lack of respect end?

In 1660 Fox appeared in Westminster Hall on charges that 'I and my faculty were raising a new war to imbrue the whole nation in blood'. (At least it was home-grown; no foreign influence was alleged.) The prosecution failed to attend, so 'it was the king's pleasure that I be set at liberty'. Charles too seems to have had a soft spot for Fox. He set free 700 Friends imprisoned by Cromwell, and declared, according to Fox, that 'none should molest us so [long as] we lived peaceably, and promised it upon the word of a king to us'.

This gentle climate changed abruptly after the abortive – indeed, risibly hopeless – rebellion of the Fifth Monarchy Men in January 1661. Once again 'all the prisons were soon after filled with Friends and many died in prison, they were so thronged up'. The national jitters about foreign warmongers and eccentrics generally produced a savage bunch of laws miscalled the Clarendon Code (it had little to do with Clarendon, and nothing to do with a code). So much for the word of a king.

Nonconformists, including the Quakers, had an Act to themselves in 1665: after all, they 'obstructed the administration of justice' by refusing to take oaths, and 'they often assemble themselves in great numbers ... to the great endangering of the public peace ... and to the terror of the people, by maintaining a secret and strict correspondence among themselves'. A gathering of more than five adults for worship was declared to be an unlawful assembly, punishable by fines, but for the third offence by transportation. The Act of Uniformity enforced the use of the revised Book of Common Prayer, and required all parsons and schoolteachers to swear that 'it is not lawful upon any pretence whatsoever to take Arms against the King'. (That surely discouraged the dyed-in-the-wool anarchist.) 'Conventicles' were generally forbidden, and dissident ministers and teachers who had been ejected from their livings and schools because they refused to take the Oath of Supremacy had to move at least 5 miles away, and stay out of any borough. This led to the founding of many Nonconformist educational establishments just outside borough boundaries. The Licensing Act enabled religious, as well as seditious, tracts and pamphlets to be suppressed.

The Jews

In all this popular, and slightly manufactured, indignation against Quakers in particular and dissidents in general, the Jews for once avoided persecution. They had been expelled from England centuries ago for their well-known practice of eating Christian babies (more probably for their reasonable hopes of repayment of the loans they had made to those in power). Cromwell had recalled them in 1657 because he needed their financial expertise. Samuel went to a synagogue of Sephardic Jews.[16] He described the service, 'but Lord, to see the disorder, laughing, sporting, and no attention, but confusion in all their service, more like Brutes than people knowing the true God, would make a man forswear ever seeing them more'; yet his mind was 'strangely disturbed with them'.

Providences

There was a general feeling that God was not only omnipresent, but very practical. As well as signposting the usefulness of various plants which he had created for the benefit of man (the doctrine of signatures: see Chapter 6), he was in the habit of giving broad hints to individuals. The country parson Ralph Josselin was constantly aware of his attention. 'I observe a Providence. A man I was hiring declined me to go to a Quaker, I know not his motives, there he fell ill of the smallpox ... and died, the lord watched over me and mine for good.'[17] Hard luck on the Quaker, let alone the hired man, but still.

The Lord was not too grand to deal with humbler cases. A young man was courting a girl called Mary Naylor; 'when I came home there was a direct N and half of M *providentially* made upon my breeches, plain to view in any man's sight, made of mire from leaping. I looked upon it to be from providence ... The smaller of God's providences should not be passed by without observation.'[18] But I have to say that he married someone else.

Other-worldly intervention was not always benign. In 1665 a maid stole £2 from her mistress. Her defence was that she was owed more than £2 in wages. 'The devil fetch her', she said, 'if there was not £8 owing for' − and he did; she died, 'her body black as pitch' where the infernal claws had gripped her.[19]

Portents

From a newspaper of 1661:

> We must now tell the Reader (for we can hold out no longer) how strangely impudent the lying faction have been in forging Prodigies ... They say (and in print too) that in several places in England it lately rained blood, frogs and other animals ... be it known that we have sent to those severall places and have it under the respective Magistrates' hands that there is not the least colour or pretence for any [such statement]. Whereof the publishers and disposers being now detected some of them are already in custody.[20]

An early piece of investigative journalism. But it was much more fun to believe in such things, and have your blood run cold. There were an astonishing number of comets in those days. (Do we no longer see them through the urban murk, or have we become blasé?) And each one foretold something, to the seer. A comet in 'merryland' (Maryland) was closely followed by disaster: 'the Indians slaughtered many of the English planters', who should presumably have taken adequate precautions after such a warning.[21]

Eclipses, too, 'are the forerunners of great Evils as Sickness Pestilence Death and Warr',[22] so it was as well to be equipped with an almanac to tell when the worst would happen. The best almanac for this might have been the series compiled by that well-known astrologer William Lilly, but he somehow managed to lead from the back, reviewing each year the events of the previous year. And when he was undeniably adrift it was not his fault, but 'the all-disposing Providence of God [which] had otherwise determined it, without doubt our heinous sins thereunto moving him'; hardly fair to a poor mundane soothsayer.

Astrology

We have already looked at astrology in connection with medicine, and I will not labour the point that it was generally treated as an essential and useful branch of knowledge. John Gadbury, another almanac-writer prophesying backwards in 1666, explained that 'divers Doctors and Professors of Physick published their opinion of the causes and cures of that most unwelcome and devouring Guest [the Plague] ... the most part for want of skill in Astrology missed the true Causes [i.e. sin] ... let us give the Stars that honour is their due, as being God's Ambassadors'.

Superstitions

In that climate of thought, superstitions must have proliferated, but I have to admit that I cannot cite contemporary instances. Even Samuel is silent. Short of a laborious market survey, they are not the kind of thing that people write down. Touching wood, and crossing our fingers, and throwing salt over our left shoulders, have averted ill luck for centuries, and still may do. We are not so strong nowadays on the many arrangements enabling a maiden to see the face of her future husband in a mirror, or a sheet of water, or the embers of the fire. Computer dating has taken over.

Life was more interesting when seeing the new moon through glass brought bad luck, and so did a broken mirror, and dropping a fork meant that your sweetheart was thinking of you – but there were few forks about in our period – while dropping a knife foretold a death, and putting shoes on a table was not only insanitary but downright dangerous, and blue and green should never be worn together, and hawthorn should never be brought into the house, and if you put a garment on inside out in the morning you had to stay that way for the rest of the day.[23] Everyday life was for many people permeated with superstitions, providing a dimension we have lost.

Witchcraft

Charles's grandfather had written a book condemning it. Doctors and lawyers did not disbelieve in it. Newton, who discovered the force of gravity, was persuaded of it. Present-day tabloids disapprove of it. Were there witches?

In 1664 Sir Matthew Hale, a much respected judge, presided over the trial of two women accused of witchcraft. 'That there were such creatures as witches he made no doubt at all; for, first, the scriptures had affirmed so much. Secondly the wisdom of all nations had provided laws against such persons, which is an argument of their confidence of such a crime.'[24] His first argument was still current a century later: Samuel Wesley agreed that 'the giving up of witchcraft is, in effect, giving up the Bible'.[25] Hale's second argument did not convince his fellow-lawyer Lord Selden: 'the law against Witches does not prove there be any; but it punishes the malice of those people that use such means to take away men's lives'.

This rational view was shared by Hobbes, the political philosopher: 'As for witches, I think not that their witchcraft is any real power; but yet that they are justly punished for the false belief they have that they can do such mischief, joined with their purpose to do it if they can.' In other words, witches mistakenly thought they were witches, and persuaded others that they were right. But just in case, the Act of Free and General Pardon, Indemnity and Oblivion which was a main plank of Charles's restoration programme excepted from forgiveness 'all offences of invocations, conjurations,[26] witchcrafts, forceries, inchantments and charms'.

So much for the educated classes. Folk memory has such a clear picture of witches[27] – surely they must have sometime been real? The answer seems to be that the belief in witchcraft flourished in rural districts, and in poverty, and in close contact with natural and unpredictable phenomena which hardly affected city-dwellers. An old, poor, widowed, ugly crone broods on a grievance and mutters to herself, watched by the only companion she has, her cat. The subject of her grievance, or his cattle or crops, suffers some mischance. She is satisfied. He is not. An everyday story of country folk. But it belongs in the country, not surely, in bustling London.

CHAPTER 17

THE WORLD PICTURE

Think of a child of ten, in 1660, at his grandfather's knee; not a usual picture, because generations did not often live in the same house. But this child has gone to listen to grandfather's stories, and grandfather was ten in 1600. He remembers the Great Queen dying, and everyone grieving and praising her courage in withstanding her Spanish brother-in-law's overtures, first peaceful then warlike. England, and a favourable wind, vanquished the Spanish battle fleet. England had cause to be proud, in those days.

Then James came down from the wilds of Scotland, with his Danish wife. A queer man, by all accounts, but that was because he never saw his mother and had been brought up to despise her. She was the first monarch that grandfather knew of, to lose her head.

Next came James's son Charles and his French wife. Things went from bad to worse. English men wanted to govern themselves through Parliament, but the King wanted the power himself, and in the end there was war. A terrible affliction in which men – and women too, come to that – fought against their brothers for the cause they thought right. Too difficult for a boy of ten to understand. Grandfather was living in the country then, and managed to some extent to stay out of all the conflict, but money and food were very tight; both sides took everything they could find, so that sometimes the ploughing had to be done by pulling the plough yourself if all the horses and oxen had gone. And what had been unthinkable before Mary Queen of Scots died happened again: his subjects killed our king.

Then there were years when life was grey and quiet, and Oliver was our Protector; a new-fangled kind of title for a ruler. Suddenly, so it seemed, he and his son disappeared. We have a King Charles again, and a very likely looking lad he is. Let us hope, says grandfather, that we never have war in the land again, and that the King will have a son who will be sitting on his throne when you, my boy, are as old as I am.

The generation game is fascinating. History books are apt to divide history into 'ages' – 'the Tudor age', 'the Stuart age' – as if no one survived from one to the other, or heard in his childhood stories told by his grandfather. Granted, people live much longer now. My son when small was patted on the head by a lady who remembered Queen Victoria's jubilee. But the scene I have imagined was easily possible, and that child might talk about his grandfather's reminiscences to his friends, and even, in due course, tell *his* children about them; so that the pride of Elizabethan days and the horror of two royal executions and a war resonated in the minds of those who came later.

The war had one unforeseen result: countrymen whose lives had been limited to a few fields and a visit to the local market were suddenly gathered up and marched briskly to and fro, seeing parts of the country they never would have seen otherwise, and slowly, laboriously, thinking, and even expressing and exchanging ideas with their fellow-soldiers.

And the world itself was expanding. Most people agreed by then that it was shaped like an orange, not a plate. There were rumours of two huge land masses over the Atlantic, beginning with the parts everyone had heard of and some people had gone to, such as the plantations and the Caribbean islands, but stretching west for thousands of miles where no Englishman lived.[1] English merchants rounded the Cape of Good Hope and traded in the Spice Islands, and if they met a Dutch merchant ship, they knew who had the right of way. Russian markets were newly open. India was only three months away.

There were a few awkward corners. It was inadvisable to be captured by an Algerian or Tunisian pirate. Occasionally a well-wisher,[2] or a passing sea captain short of hands, would ransom Englishmen enslaved by them. One of the terms of the treaty of 1662 with Algeria provided that

all subjects of the King of Great Britain now slaves in Algier ... be set at liberty and delivered upon paying the price they were first sold for in the market [Who produced the money? The English Crown was chronically short of cash] and for the time to come no subject of

275

His Majesty may be bought or sold or made slaves in Algeir or its Territories.[3]

But old habits die hard, and who was going to look? At least the English debtors enslaved in the plantations had better conditions, one hopes, and only had to serve seven years.

Not only were Englishmen travelling the globe, but foreigners were coming to England. A queer lot, foreigners; always were and always will be, with their incomprehensible languages and outlandish clothes. Good for a laugh, though, over a pint of ale in the tavern.

In more cultured circles, the Grand Tour was a part of the education of every gentleman. Men of science and learning, such as Charles himself and his cousin Rupert, and not forgetting Samuel, all members of the Royal Society, watched experiments which nearly succeeded in transfusing blood from one animal to another. It was only a matter of time.

For the man in the street – if such a person ever existed in that crowded throng – life was on the whole more comfortable, after 1666. And his wife could count on help with the housework, in the shape of another pair of human hands. Maidservants fell ill, and left unexpectedly, and were rude and uncooperative; but such is domestic life. Do washing machines never go wrong?

EPILOGUE

The room is quiet. The child burps gently, the cat purrs, the fire rustles. The sleepy woman has time to think. What will be her daughter's life? A good man, who does not beat her and provides for her properly, and keeps his hands off other women, is the best she can hope for, and smallpox early on, and slightly, so that her skin is not spoiled. Heaven knows, such men are few and far between.

At least the King is back, and there will be no more argument and fighting about who should rule.

The girl might see in the next century. How strange it sounds, 1700. But life is unlikely to change much, while men control it. Hardly likely they would ever allow a woman to be a physician, say, or a teacher. If she doesn't find a man, she could try the stage, but there are too many pitfalls there for any girl.

The woman should go and see whether the maids are preparing dinner and not lazing about and teasing the apprentices. But she takes a few more moments' peace.

ABBREVIATIONS
AND EXPLANATION

For further information, see the Foreword.

CSPD = *Calendar of State Papers Domestic.* It is usually possible to give the day and month, as well as the year. Where only the month is given, it is because the day is not clear. Where neither is given, it is usually because the reference is to a petition, which were lumped together with miscellaneous notes at the end of the year's entries.

Diary = *The Diary of Samuel Pepys,* edited by Robert Latham and William Matthews, in eleven volumes, London, 1970–83.

Magalotti = *Travels of Cosmo the Third Grand Duke of Tuscany Through England During the Reign of King Charles* II *1669,* by Count Lorenzo Magalotti, edited by J. Mawman, London, 1821. Magalotti's style is conversational, not neatly divided day by day, as Samuel Pepys kept his diary. It would not assist the reader if I were to give the date of an entry: it would only involve searching back several pages to find the day, but not the month, buried in the middle of a paragraph. He and his master were in England from April to June 1669, mostly in London.

'The City': where this appears with a capital initial, I mean the area covered by the old Roman city and bounded by its walls: the 'square mile' inhabited today by bankers and financiers, and governed still by the Lord Mayor of London and his Common Council.

NOTES

Preface

1 I have taken the information on Cosmo and Magalotti from the preface to Magalotti, and J. P. (daughter of G. M.) Trevelyan, *A Short History of the Italian People*, London, 1919. Nicholas Culpeper appears in the *Dictionary of National Biography*. John Aubrey's life is summarised in the introduction to the Folio edition (London, 1975) of his *Brief Lives*.

Chapter 1: London

1 W. G. Hoskins, *The Making of the English Landscape*, London, 1955.
2 A. L. Beier and R. Finlay, *The Making of the Metropolis, London 1500–1700*, London, 1986.
3 A. M. Hind, *Wenceslaus Hollar and his Views of London and Windsor in the Seventeenth Century*, New York, 1972.
4 CSPD, 25 March 1663.
5 CSPD, petition 1664.
6 C. G. Clay, *Economic Expansion and Social Change: England 1500–1700*, Cambridge, 1984, vol. II, on which I have drawn extensively in this section.
7 CSPD, 6 March 1664.
8 This account of the herald's predicament occurs only in 1668, in a note by that herald's son, on the death of his father.
9 Harry Margary, *A Collection of Early Maps of London 1553–1667*, Lympne, Kent, 1972.
10 Highways and Sewers Act 1662.
11 Ibid.

12 CSPD, petition 1667.

13 John Evelyn, *London Revived*, London, 1666.

14 *Diary*, 1 February 1664.

15 D. Davis, *A History of Shopping*, London, 1975.

16 John Aubrey, *Brief Lives* (Folio Society edition), London, 1975.

17 Contemporary pamphlet, *The Citie's Loyalty Displayed*.

18 Ambrose Heal, *Sign Boards of Old London Shops*, London, 1957.

19 Magalotti.

20 London Topographical Society, *A Survey of Hatton Garden*, London, 1983. 'Carpenter' conveys to us a skilled craftsman. In Arlidge's case it meant that he was a member of that City company. If he were described nowadays, 'property developer' would be more appropriate.

21 Rosemary Weinstein, 'New urban demands in early modern London', *Journal of Medical History*, supplement no. 11, London, 1991.

22 CSPD, 23 June 1669.

23 Magalotti as to the one by Somerset House. I have assumed that the other was a two-horse-power one as well.

24 CSPD, 16 November 1663.

25 CSPD, July 1663.

26 *Davis*, op. cit.

27 CSPD, 18 February 1662.

28 Keith Thomas, *Man and the Natural World*, London, 1983.

29 Clay, op. cit.

30 S. D. Chapman, 'The last of the old London textile printers', *Journal of Textile History*, vol. 14, Guildford, 1983.

31 Magalotti remarked on 'the salubrity of the air, which is almost always clear: that thick atmosphere which is seen from a distance hovering over London not being caused by corrupt vapours but arising casually from the smoke of the mineral coal'.

32 Evelyn, op. cit.

33 V. Harding, 'Location of burials in early modern London', *The London Journal*, vol. 14, 1989–91.

34 CSPD, 1665.

35 CSPD, 12 November 1666.

36 Weinstein, op. cit.

37 The small compass of the two cities is demonstrated by this twice-weekly collection, compared to the elaborate arrangements needed now.

38 *Diary*, 1 July 1667.

Chapter 2: The houses

1 John Schofield, *The London Surveys of Ralph Tresswell*, London, 1987.

2 CSPD, 26 August 1663.

3 John Stow, *The Survey of London* (Everyman edition), London, 1912.

4 CSPD, October 1664.

5 In *The London Surveys*, Schofield suggests that since pronounced jetties were going out of fashion by the second half of the sixteenth century, the houses surveyed by Tresswell, which tended to be jettied, were already standing by 1550: corroborative evidence of the longevity of London houses as long as fire did not intervene.

6 John Schofield, *The Building of London*, London, 1984.

7 Stow, op. cit., on which I have drawn for most of the information in this section.

8 London County Council, *Survey of London*, part two, London, 1937.

9 Schofield, *The Building of London*, op. cit.

10 W. S. Page, *The Russia Company 1553–1660* (undated, published before 1912 by William Brown and Co. Ltd).

11 Illustrated in Ambrose Heal, *Signboards of Old London Shops*, London, 1957.

12 British Library, Additional Charters, 40389–91.

13 Public Record Office, SP 25/71 f137.

14 Magalotti.

15 Schofield, *The Building of London*, op. cit.

16 To anyone who has wondered how Mr and Mrs Jones thought of the name Inigo, I can only say that in Latin his name was Ignatius. How that turned into Inigo I do not know.

17 One of the very few buildings in London of which Magalotti approved, it being decently Italianate.

18 *Diary*, 26 July 1666.

19 CSPD.

20 CSPD, 30 June 1666.

21 Magalotti. This was the only other contemporary house of which he approved.

22 *Diary*, vol. X (Companion volume).

23 CSPD, 1 October 1664.

24 CSPD, 14 August 1663.

25 Samuel Pepys's account of the Fire is the most famous, but John Evelyn better conveys the anguish and terror of the onlookers. For it and other vivid accounts and for details of the devastation, I have relied on Gustav Milne, *The Great Fire of London*, London, 1986.

26 A. M. Hind, *Wenceslaus Hollar and His Views of London and Windsor in the Seventeenth Century*, New York, 1972.

27 Milne, op. cit.

28 Rebuilding Act.

29 CSPD, 13 September 1666.

30 CSPD, Addenda, 8 September 1666.

31 CSPD, 4 September 1666.

32 CSPD, 24 January 1667.

33 *London Gazette*, 13 December 1666.

34 CSPD, 10 September 1666.

35 *London Gazette*.

36 One of the few things Richard Cromwell did before he, and everyone else, decided that he could not step into his father's shoes was to order the Captain of the good ship *London*, accompanied by the *Marmaduke*, to go to St Helena, 'repair on shoare, and in the name of His Highness Richard, Lord Protector of England, Scotland, and Ireland, and the Dominions thereunto belonging, and for the use of the Honourable English East Company, [to] take possession of the island and with drum and trumpet proclaim the same'. There were few human ears to hear the fanfare. The East India Company hoped to develop a station there on the route to India, since the Dutch had taken over the obvious staging post at the tip of Africa, but the little settlement never prospered. The 30 'burnt Londoners' who accepted the company's offer of free passage and land, in 1667, replaced earlier settlers who could not bear the conditions any longer. In 1670 the total population was 48 English settlers and 18 African slaves. Philip Gosse, *St Helena 1502–1938*, London, 1938.

37 Milne, op. cit.

38 Magalotti.

39 CSPD, 10 August 1668.

40 *London Gazette*, 3 September 1666.

41 *London Gazette*, 8 October 1666.

42 CSPD, 19 September 1666.

43 *London Gazette*, 29 September 1666.

44 *London Gazette*, 20 September 1666.

45 *London Gazette*, 22 December 1667.

46 *London Gazette*, 22 December 1666.

47 *London Gazette*, 13 September 1666.

48 CSPD, 21 March 1667.

49 H. Hobhouse and A. Saunders, *Good and Proper Materials*, London, 1988.

50 Magalotti cannot have been wrong in his dates here, since he and his prince left England in June 1669. But other authorities give a later date.
51 CSPD, 29 March 1667.
52 Reproduced in Walter Besant, *London in the Time of the Stuarts*, London, 1903.
53 Misson as translated by Ozell and quoted in Letts, *As the Foreigner Saw Us*, London, 1935.

Chapter 3: Interiors

1 *Diary*, 24 April 1663.
2 'Banquet' has travelled to China, where no Sino-English meeting is complete without one. In 1667 Lord Ossory, on his way to Ireland, was entertained by the Mayor and Corporation of Lichfield to 'a noble banquet of better sweatmeats than are usually found in such corporations, and wine in plenty', CSPD, 10 February 1667.
3 Clarendon, *Life of Himself*, Oxford, 1978.
4 William Cobbett, *Parliamentary History*, vol. IV, London, 1808. The Commons 'did walk on foot from Westminster to Whitehall ... they went up into the Banqueting House and there attended His Majesty's coming to Whitehall which being about 7 of the clock His Majesty, about half an hour after, came into the Banqueting House and there placed himself upon his chair of state'.
5 CSPD, 16 November 1664.
6 C. L. Kingsford, 'Some London houses of the early Tudor period', *Archeologia*, vol. 71, Oxford, 1921.
7 This was the only significant change, I suggest, between Tresswell's time and our period.
8 Randle Holme, *The Academy of Armory*, Chester, 1688.
9 For a splendid example, I recommend Bolsover House in Derbyshire.
10 Peter Thornton, *17th Century Interior Decoration in England, France and Holland*, Yale, 1978, on which I have drawn extensively in this chapter.
11 CSPD, petition 1665.
12 Holme, op. cit.
13 I. Brett, *History of Chintz*, London, 1970.
14 *Oxford English Dictionary*.
15 Christina Hole, *English Home-life*, London, 1947.
16 Cobbett, op. cit. Tenter hooks kept fabric stretched and taut, on walls or on frames used by textile finishers (see, e.g., the top right corner of Newcourt's map, the first illustration in this book).

17 CSPD, 2 June 1663.

18 *Mercurius Publicus*, 29 December 1659–7 June 1660.

19 Mary Evelyn, *Mundus Muliebris* (Latin for *Women's World*), edited by her father, John Evelyn, London, 1690. There are still some silver ('plate') fire-irons in Knole and in Burghley House.

20 Farlie, *Emblem Book*, London, 1638.

21 *Weekly Intelligencer*, 1 April 1661.

22 G. V. Blackstone, *A History of the Fire Service*, London, 1957.

23 The part of the deed which described the property, nowadays done by referring to an official agreed map, demonstrates how necessary Tresswell's surveys had been. Plots were identified by reference to surrounding plots. If the neighbours did not agree, what then? One example from 1669 conveyed a plot which 'abutteth on the south a garden belonging to [illegible] and afterwards to Sir Francis Walsingham's house now called the Navy Office and upon the street called Hart Street or Crutched Friars on the north a house ... now of Daniel Skinner and on a yard called Burnt Yard and a certain yard or garden within the great gate leading out of Hart Street'.

24 A shovel-board table was marked with lines on its surface, from end to end, and distances or 'scores' along one long side. The players stood at one end and took turns to knock a coin along the table between the lines, with the side of one hand, to get the highest score. A penny or a halfpenny was the usual coin – hence 'shove-ha'penny board', or more rarely, 'shove-penny board'. It was still being played in country pubs in my youth, but has given way to one-armed bandits.

25 Cobbett, op. cit.

26 Holme, op. cit.

27 Thornton, op. cit.

28 *Diary*, 18 May 1664.

29 The word 'virginals' was often applied to harpsichords.

30 *Diary*, 13 July 1660.

31 E. Walsh, *The Excellent Mrs Beale*, London, 1975.

32 Ashmolean Museum, Oxford.

33 *Diary*, 21 November 1662.

Chapter 4: Gardens, parks and open spaces

1 J. Taboroff, 'Wife, unto thy garden', in *Journal of the Garden History Society*, vol. 2, 1974.

2 Magalotti seems to have been much struck by these: 'a stone cylinder

through the axis of which a lever of iron is passed, whose ends being brought forward and united together in the form of a triangle, serve to move it backwards and forwards'. Perhaps Italian gardeners did not use them, not having much in the way of greensward.

3 Platt, *The Garden of Eden*, London, 1652.

4 Keith Thomas, *Man and the Natural World*, London, 1983.

5 John Parkinson, *Paradisi in Sole*, London, 1656.

6 *Diary*, 21 May 1662.

7 Michael Gibson, 'The history of the yellow rose', *The Garden, Journal of the Royal Horticultural Society*, June 1989.

8 Sir Henry Wootton, the man responsible for the quip that 'an ambassador is a man sent to lie abroad for his country', sent a double yellow rose bush home from his embassy in Venice, in 1623. Perhaps it died on the way; nothing more seems to have been heard of it.

9 John Harvey, *Early Nurserymen*, London, 1974, on which I have drawn for much of the information in this paragraph.

10 F. P. Verney and M. M. Verney (eds), *Verney Memoirs*, London, 1904.

11 *Diary*, 25 June 1666.

12 Harry Margary, *A–Z of Restoration London*, Lympne, Kent, 1992.

13 T. Girtin, *The Triple Crowns: A History of the Drapers' Company*, London, 1964.

14 I am grateful to Mrs Mavis Batey, President of the Garden History Society, for allowing me to quote from her monograph on London royal parks, as to the early history of Hyde Park and St James's Park.

15 *Diary*, 1 May 1660.

16 CSPD, 29 April 1664.

17 CSPD, 23 April 1664.

18 *Diary*, 18 August 1661.

19 CSPD, August 1664.

20 *Diary*, 12 September 1661. There were four gondolas in all.

21 CSPD, petition September 1665. All the gondolas were sold in 1666 to fund a change in Charles's taste, from French to Italian music. It seems a bit hard on the Venetians to use their splendid present as a source of cash. *Diary*, Companion volume, 'Music'.

22 CSPD, 27 February 1662.

23 CSPD, 14 May 1667.

24 Rochester's poems were often so filthy, and so topical, that they were not published in full in his lifetime. 'A ramble in St James's Park' is included in *The Golden Stolpe Manuscript*, ed. B. Danielsson and D. M. Veith, Uppsala, 1967. A whore of the bulk would use any convenient

base or mass (bulk). A whore of the alcove preferred somewhere less public.

25 *Diary*, 20 May 1668.
26 CSPD, 15 August 1668.
27 *Diary*, 26 May 1667.
28 *Diary*, 21 January 1661.
29 *Diary*, 27 March 1664.
30 *Diary*, 23 April 1665.
31 *Diary*, 25 May 1662, 28 May 1667.

Chapter 5: Communications

1 Much of the information about the river is taken from M. Leapman, *London's River*, London, 1991.
2 Magalotti: he is not always totally reliable on figures, accepting, naturally enough, what he was told.
3 *Diary*, 7 December 1663.
4 *Diary*, 18 May 1661.
5 *Diary*, 24 March 1662.
6 *Diary*, 15 September 1662.
7 *Diary*, 18, 20 and 22 December 1665.
8 *Diary*, Companion volume, article on Weather by D. J. Schove. Although the sixteenth and seventeenth centuries are sometimes referred to as a 'little ice age', Schove states that the weather in the *Diary* period 'was not greatly different from that of our own day'.
9 *Diary*, 4 April 1662.
10 William Cobbett, *Parliamentary History*, vol. IV, London, 1808.
11 *Diary*, 27 December 1664.
12 *Diary*, 23 May 1664.
13 John Evelyn, *London Revived*, London, 1666.
14 *Diary*, 6 February 1668.
15 *Diary*, 10 September 1661.
16 *Diary*, 1 May 1663.
17 *Diary*, 17 September 1661.
18 *Diary*, 16 February 1663, 15 November 1666.
19 Magalotti: 'There are found at every corner decent coaches, well equipped ... of these there are reckoned to be 800.' Either he or his informant was exaggerating, or the limit was being ignored.
20 The fact that these were the only rates specified in the Act shows the importance of the Inns of Court in London life.
21 CSPD, 1667, Case of the Hackney Coachmen of London (undated).

22 CSPD, 3 March 1662.
23 John Evelyn, *A Character of England*, London, 1659.
24 J. Crofts, *Packhorse and Wagon*, London, 1967.
25 Elias Ashmole, *Diary*, Oxford, 1966.
26 F. P. Verney and M. M. Verney (eds), *Memoirs*, London, 1904.
27 L. Weatherill, *Consumer Behaviour and Material Culture in Britain 1660–1760*, London, 1988.
28 *Diary*, 1 May 1667.
29 *Diary*, 10 November 1661.
30 *Diary*, 12 November 1666.
31 T. Firmin, *Some Proposals for the Employment of the Poor*, London, 1678; quoted in H. Perkin, *Children in English Society*, London, 1969.
32 *Diary*, 23 April 1662.
33 *Diary*, 16 and 18 January 1661.
34 All this information came from the statute setting up the Post and scattered entries in CSPD. I doubt whether it worked quite as it claimed.
35 Crofts, op. cit.
36 Ibid.
37 Hannah Wolley, *Guide to the Female Sex*, London, 1682.
38 Ravenscroft, *The Italian Husband*, London, 1698.
39 CSPD, 24 September 1668.
40 CSPD, April 1662.
41 N. Penney (ed.), *Journal of George Fox* (Everyman edition), London, 1924.
42 CSPD, September 1667.
43 CSPD, December 1666.
44 Crofts, op. cit.; quoting Sir William Petty.
45 CSPD, 22 November 1667.
46 CSPD, note at the end of the 1667 volume.
47 *Diary*, 25 March 1667.
48 Crofts, op. cit.
49 CSPD, 19 April 1669.
50 CSPD, 19 April 1669.
51 CSPD, 2 July 1666.
52 CSPD, May 1667.
53 CSPD, 5 July 1667.

Chapter 6: Medicine and dentistry

1 Peter Laslett, *The World We Have Lost Revisited*, London, 1971.
2 Anne Lawrence, *Women in England 1500–1760*, London, 1994; drawing on E. A. Wrigley and R. S. Schofield, *The Population History of England 1541–1871*, London, 1989.
3 Sir Kenelm would not have been gratified by the reference to his weapon salve in J. G. Frazer's *The Golden Bough*, London, 1922. The author cites Bacon, who died in 1626:
'It is constantly received and avouched that the anointing of the weapon that maketh the wound will heal the wound itself. In this experiment, upon the relation of men of credit (though myself, as yet, am not fully inclined to believe it) you shall note the points following: first, the ointment wherewith this is done is made of divers ingredients, whereof the strangest and hardest to come by are the moss on the skull of a dead man unburied, and the fats of a boar and a bear in the act of generation.'

Frazer, in his inimitable style, added to this example of sympathetic magic similar practices then (1922) still current in Suffolk, Cambridgeshire, Essex and the Hartz Mountains, and among the savages of Melanesia and America.
4 This advertisement appeared regularly in, for example, *The Kingdom's Intelligencer*.
5 Keith Thomas, *Religion and the Decline of Magic*, London, 1971. This very learned author argues that Ashmole 'was not resorting to magic, but employing a purely physical form of treatment'. The treatment was so obscurely related to science, however, that for my purpose I have chosen to treat it as magic.
6 W. J. Bishop, *Early History of Surgery*, London, 1960.
7 B. Inglis, *A History of Medicine*, London, 1965.
8 CSPD, 19 April 1669.
9 *Weekly Intelligencer*, 14–21 January 1661.
10 William Cobbett, *Parliamentary History*, vol. IV, London, 1808. The order of service provided for the King to 'lay his hand upon the sore of the sick person', which if he really did must have set up an incomparable bank of cross-infecting bacteria, and then 'the sick person [is] to have [an angel of gold noble] hang'd about his neck and to wear it until he be full whole'. Walter Besant, *London in the Time of the Stuarts*, London, 1903, in which the whole order of service is set out.
11 A nickname given to Charles because of his sexual prowess: the name of a famous stud horse.

12 *London Gazette*, 24 March 1662.
13 Elias Ashmole, *Diary*, Oxford, 1966. Although 'Arise' sounds like the beginning of a text, as in If-Christ-had-not-died-for-thee-thou-hadst-been-damned Barebones, it was simply an Anglicised version of Rhys. He was a prophetic Welshman who insisted that Charles would be restored in 1653. Oliver Cromwell seems to have tolerated him despite his overt royalism. Those who would like to know more about Arise may find him in Christopher Hill's *Change and Continuity in Seventeenth Century England*, London, 1974.
14 Reported in *Mercurius Publicus*, 25 May 1660.
15 John Gadbury's *Almanac* for 1666.
16 Thomas, op. cit.
17 Ibid.
18 L. R. C. Agnew, 'Quackery', in *Medicine in 17th Century England*, ed. A. G. Debus, Berkeley, California, 1974.
19 Archdale Palmer, *The Recipe Book 1659–1672*, Wymondham, Leicestershire, 1985.
20 Ibid.
21 Bishop, op. cit.
22 CSPD, 7 January 1667.
23 A. H. T. Robb-Smith, 'Cambridge medicine', in Debus.
24 Henry Peacham, *The Complete Gentleman*, London, 1622.
25 Anthony à Wood, 10 January 1662. *The Life and Times of Anthony Wood*, Oxford, 1891–1900.
26 Wood, op. cit., 28 February 1666.
27 Antonia Fraser, *King Charles II*, London, 1979.
28 F. H. Garrison, *An Introduction to the History of Medicine*, Philadelphia, 1929. The list of dutiable goods in the Tonnage and Poundage Act of 1660 included under 'drugs':

alum	marmelade
arsenic	mummia
frankincense	opium
horns of harts or stags	pistachio
lapis lazuli	rhubarb
manna	turpentine

Mummia was still in the average witch-doctor's pharmacopoeia in East Africa in the 1950s. It is, or purports to be, ground-up mummies. Rhubarb was long regarded solely as a medicine. What marmalade is doing in this list I do not know.
29 Thomas, op. cit.
30 Nicholas Culpeper, *Complete Herbal and English Physician*, London, 1653.

Most almanacs included a chart of which body parts went with which signs.

31 Garrison, op. cit.
32 CSPD, July 1667.
33 CSPD, 11 April 1665.
34 CSPD, August 1667.
35 CSPD.
36 L. M. Zimmerman, 'Surgery', in Debus.
37 I am indebted to Dr de Raeve of Oxford for this information, and for causing me to see the whole seventeenth-century medical scene in a more realistic light.
38 Ralph Josselin, *Diary 1616–83*, ed. Alan Macfarlane, 1976.
39 CSPD, 12 February and 21 February 1667.
40 For this I am indebted to Emma Kirkby, who included it in a concert in Oxford.

When John Evelyn was in Paris waiting out the Civil War, he went to 'the hospital of the Charity, [where] I saw the whole operation of Lithotomie ... There was one person of 40 years old had a stone taken out of him, bigger than a turkey's egg. The manner thus: the sick creature was stripp'd to his shirt, and bound armes and thighs to an high Chaire, 2 men holding his shoulders fast down: then the Chirurgion with a crooked Instrument prob'd till he hit on the stone, then without stirring the probe which had a small channel in it, for the Edge of the Lancet to run in, without wounding any other part, he made Incision thro the Scrotum about an inch in length, then he put in his forefingers to get the stone as near the orifice of the wound as he could, then with another instrument like a crane's neck he pull'd it out with incredible torture to the Patient, especially at his after raking so unmercifully up and down the bladder with a third Instrument, to find any other Stones that may possibly be left behind: the effusion of blood is great. Then was the patient carried to bed, and dress'd with a silver pipe accomodated to the orifice for the urine to pass, when the wound is sewed up. The danger is feavour, and gangreene, some wounds never closing ... After this person came a little child of not above 8 or 9 years of age, with much cheerfulnesse, going through the operation with extraordinary patience, and expressing great joy when he saw the stone was drawn. The use I made of it was to give Almighty God hearty thanks, that I not ben subject to this infirmity, which is indeed deplorable.' (John Evelyn, *Diary*, 3 May 1650).

41 I owe the information in this section to the kindness of the Archivist of St Bartholomew's Hospital and his staff, who produced for me: N. Moore, *The History of St Bartholomew's Hospital*, London, 1918; V. C. Medvei and J. L. Thornton (eds), *The Royal Hospital of St Bartholomew 1123–1973*, London, 1974; G. Whitteridge and V. Stokes, *A Brief History of the Hospital of St Bartholomew*, London, 1961; and the *Journals* of the hospital.

42 Hospital *Journal*, 14 October 1661.

43 Hospital *Journal*. Italics added.

44 CSPD, petition 1668.

45 Thomas, op. cit.

46 S. X. Radbill, 'Pediatrics', in Debus.

47 Ibid.

48 Dr Gillian Clarke, 'Infant Death During the Early Modern Period', lecture, Oxford, 1993.

49 Radbill, op. cit.

50 Laslett, op. cit. A contemporary midwife, Jane Sharp in *The Midwives Book*, London, 1671, put it at about fourteen years. One has a feeling that she is likely to know, since she had been a 'Practitioner in the art of Midwifery above 30 years'.

51 P. Crawford, 'Attitudes to menstruation', *Past and Present*, vol. 91, 1981.

52 Ibid. This belief that a menstruating woman could by her very presence make wine and food undrinkable/uneatable is still with us. I have even heard the argument seriously advanced, by an Anglican cleric, that it would be self-evidently impossible for women to be ordained because it would be impossible for a menstruating woman to administer communion. At least the seventeenth century did not have to confront that problem.

53 Thomas, op. cit.

54 For this, see further in Chapter 10.

55 For the possibility that some women knew some means which might inhibit conception, see Chapter 10.

56 *Observer*, 13 November 1993.

57 Dr Irvine Loudon, 'The Most Dreadful of All Diseases', lecture, Oxford, 1993.

58 This is Jane Sharp's figure – see note 50 above.

59 Inglis, op. cit.

60 D'Arcy Power, 'Clap and the pox in English literature', *British Journal of Venereal Diseases*, vol. 14, 1938.

61 For an example of a bride who was not so lucky, the reader may like

to try Charles Dickens' *Bleak House*, in which Esther Somerson lifted her veil and showed her 'ravaged countenance' to her suitor, Mr Guppy, who recoiled in horror – and left.

62 R. Houlbrooke, *English Family Life*, Oxford, 1988.

63 Lists of deaths and their causes. They were only as reliable as the returns from which they were compiled. 'Searchers', usually old women receiving parish relief, were employed to inspect each corpse and give their opinion of the cause of death, which could include such fatal diseases as Ageing, Grief and 'disappointed in love', not to mention 'suddenly' and 'killed by a fall from the belfry at All Hallows the Great'. The figures of deaths from venereal diseases were particularly unreliable, since grieving relatives preferred their nearest and dearest to have died from some other cause. A small *pourboire* could often rectify the diagnosis.

64 John Graunt, *Observations on the Bills of Mortality*, London, 1662.

65 R. Saunders, *The English Apollo*, London, 1666.

66 J. Stardmare, quoted by Radbilt, op. cit.

67 Edmund Verney's wife was 'melancholy-mad'. He was recommended several women who would look after her in their homes. F. P. and M. M. Verney (eds), *Verney Memoirs*, London, 1925.

68 CSPD, 8 April 1667.

69 John Aubrey, *Brief Lives* (Folio edition), London, 1975.

70 Rachel Field, *Irons in the Fire*, Ramsbury, Wiltshire, 1984.

71 Debus, 'Paracelsian medicine', in Debus.

72 J. S. Curl, 'Spas and pleasure grounds of London', *Journal of the Garden History Society*, vol. 7, 1979. Many other spas were developed just after the decade 1660–70.

73 Verney, op. cit.

74 CSPD, 31 July 1669.

75 M. Smith, *A Short History of Dentistry*, London, 1958.

76 J. Woodford, *The Strange Story of False Teeth*, London, 1968.

Chapter 7: Clothes, jewellery, cosmetics, hairdressing, washing and so on

1 C. G. A. Clay, *Economic Expansion and Social Change 1500–1700*, Cambridge, 1984.

2 Randle Holme, *The Academy of Armoury*, Chester, 1688.

3 *Diary*, 28 March 1664. The phrase is a quotation from a popular ballad.

4 CSPD, 10 June 1661.

5 CSPD, 16 February 1662.

6 *Diary*, 11 November 1661.

7 'Case of St Giles, Cripplegate' quoted in Alice Clark, *Working Women in the Seventeenth Century*, London, 1919. Unfortunately, Miss Clark did not give the date of this case, and I have been unable to trace it. I have assumed that it applied in the decade 1660–70, when such lace was most fashionable.

8 The quotation is from Christie's catalogue.

9 Louise Taylor, *Mourning Dress*, London, 1983.

10 A few Dutch and Walloon Protestant refugees began to arrive in England from 1560. The French Huguenots took flight across the Channel after the Massacre of St Bartholomew in 1574. The main influx was after the revocation of the Edict of Nantes in 1685, but by then there was already a steady flow. I have taken the dates from Clay, op. cit.

11 Alum is a curious substance. In the days before synthetic chemicals, it was essential to textile finishers as a mordant, to 'fix' dyes and make them fast. Until the fifteenth century, almost the whole of Europe's textile trade depended on supplies from Turkey, where it occurred in an easily mineable form (hence the Turkish pre-eminence in the production of silk fabrics and wool carpets). By a series of lucky breaks, Pope Pius II was able to cash in on a discovery of alum near Civitavecchia, and in his turn he was able to hold the European market to ransom, which, for England, became increasingly unnerving – English prosperity depending on its textile export trade – as relations with the papacy deteriorated with Henry VIII's matrimonial imbroglios. Alum occurs in the form of alum-bearing shale in England, principally in two places, near Bournemouth and on the Yorkshire coast near Whitby. This was known, but the trouble was that the technology needed to produce viable alum from shale was not the same as that used to extract the pure mineral occurring in Italy and Turkey. It took years, and several fortunes, before the problem was solved.

12 Copy of a family will in my possession.

13 Taylor, op. cit.

14 Quoted in A. D. Briscoe, *A Stuart Benefactress*, Lavenham, Suffolk, 1973.

15 The increasingly rare sight of a mature Swiss lady wearing the charming local dress of her girlhood demonstrates the versatility of the laced fastening, as the sides of the bodice, which nearly met when she was young, gradually part company, kept in contract only by an expanse of lacing. But the dress is still wearable.

16 *Antiquaries' Journal*, 1979.

17 *Diary*, 16 February 1669.

18 J. Arnold, *Patterns of Fashion*, London, 1972.

19 F. P. and M. M. Verney (eds), *Verney Memoirs*, London, 1925. Richard Verney had managed to marry an heiress. He promptly had to supplement her trousseau with a wadded cloak and a silk mantle, at London prices – 43 shillings each.

20 Those who enjoy words, or Jane Austen, or both, may like to know that a galloshio had given birth to a verb, by her time. In an early fragment, *The Watsons*, Lord Osborne observes that 'nothing sets off a neat ankle more than a half-boot; nankin galoshed with black looks very well'.

21 Holme, op. cit.

22 *Diary*, 24 January 1660.

23 Magalotti.

24 Information from the Platt Hall Museum of Costume, Manchester.

25 Contemporary correspondence included in W. Ramsay, *The Worshipful Company of Glass Sellers of London*, London, 1898.

26 CSPD, undated, at the end of 1668.

27 CSPD, 22 September 1669. Neither the Curator of the Jewel House in the Tower of London nor the Crown Jeweller can throw any light on the subsequent history of these pieces.

28 *Diary*, 9 January and 3 April 1667.

29 *Weekly Intelligencer*, February 1661.

30 Ibid.

31 Ibid.

32 But they certainly rang, like our modern pestilential mobile phones. At least the latter are unlikely to give rise to the embarrassment suffered by a seventeenth-century whore, who stole her client's alarm watch and hid it in her 'commodity' without first turning off its alarm. *The Wandering Whore*, quoted in R. Thompson, *Unfit for Modest Ears*, London, 1979.

33 *Kingdom's Intelligencer*, 31 December 1660–1 July 1661.

34 William Cobbett, *Parliamentary History*, vol. IV, 14 May 1660.

35 CSPD, 8 August 1667.

36 Antonia Fraser, *King Charles II*, London, 1979.

37 CSPD, 14 November 1668: a copy of a letter written by Charles 'when His Majesty was at Brussels'.

38 Lord Clarendon's *Life of Himself*, quoted in a footnote to the entry for 29 May 1660 in Cobbett's *Parliamentary History*, vol. IV. Clarendon, who rode so near to Charles on that journey (and was so abysmally

let down by him later), gave a vivid account of Charles's journey from Dover via Canterbury to London. At Canterbury the weary young man was unmercifully jostled by petitioners who 'forced him to give them present [immediate] audience ... the King was extremely nauseated by their suits ... he never afterwards received their addresses with his usual grace and rarely granted anything they desired'. One can see why, but it led to accusations of ingratitude that cloud his reputation still. He was only 30, and under the most extreme stress imaginable.

39 *Antiquaries' Journal*, 1979.

40 CSPD, 10 April 1661.

41 Quoted in Cobbett, op. cit.

42 CSPD, August 1667.

43 *Diary*, 6 April 1661.

44 V. Cumming, *A Visual History of Costume: The Seventeenth Century*, London, 1984.

45 Pinking had been a favourite decoration for centuries. It involved slashing the outer layer of fabric so that a contrasting lining showed through. Sometimes the lining was pulled through into little puffs. To prevent the outer fabric from fraying too much, it was usually cut on the bias, with special scissors with zig-zag edges. Pinking shears are still used today, but not merely to produce this orgy of conspicuous consumption.

46 I cannot resist relaying Magalotti's description of Charles's costume early one morning in 1669, when he had gone for a walk by himself in Newmarket. Cosmo met him coming back. He was 'in a plain and simple country dress, without any finery, but wearing the badges of the order of St George and of the Garter'. Some countryman!

47 CSPD, 11 October 1666.

48 *Diary*, 4 November 1666.

49 *Diary*, 26 June 1667.

50 *Diary*, 18 March 1664.

51 Taylor, op. cit.

52 C. Willett and P. Cunnington, *The History of Underclothes*, London, 1951. These effigies were of an unnerving verisimilitude. The authenticity of their underclothes was perhaps analogous to the genuineness of the Irish lace with which Mr Cochrane insisted that his dancing Young Ladies' lingerie be trimmed – but their lace was more on public view.

53 *Diary*, 15 October 1664.

54 CSPD, 30 July 1664. One of the last ships to reach Malta, before the siege closed round it in the last war, was HMS *Manxman*. As she

steamed towards Valetta, she displayed the silk flag which had been embroidered for her by the ladies of the Isle of Man.

55 S. D. Chapman, 'Genesis of the British textile industry', *Textile History*, vol. 3, Westbury, Wiltshire, 1972.

56 Holme, op. cit.

57 *Diary*, 21 May and 27 June 1661.

58 D. de Marly, 'Fashionable suppliers 1660–1700', *Antiquaries' Journal*, 1979.

59 Mary Evelyn, *Mundus Muliebris*, ed. John Evelyn, London, 1690.

60 Hannah Wolley, *Guide to the Female Sex*, London, 1682. Hannah 'knew not how to excuse the vain custom now so much in fashion to deform the face with black patches'.

61 Taylor, op. cit.

62 *Diary*, 29 October 1666 ('a new fair pair of locks'), 11 May 1667 ('fair hair' and 'white locks'), 12 May 1667 ('white locks'). The learned editors of the *Diary* have, perhaps, conflated the two fashions, making wired locks white: see their note 2 to the entry for 11 May 1667. I am not sure that this is right. The only representation I have seen of wired locks is a miniature by Samuel Cooper of Henrietta Duchess of Orleans, *c.*1661, in the Victoria and Albert Museum. As it happens, the lady is fair. I do not think Elizabeth would have dressed 'mighty fine' in 1666, in such a *déja vu* fashion. I think she was wearing added side ringlets of fair hair, in which – assuming she was a brunette – she must have looked very striking. Perhaps this was what really upset Samuel.

63 *Diary*, 2 November 1663.

64 *Diary*, 27 March 1667.

65 *Diary*, 25 May 1662.

66 Holme, op. cit.

67 *Diary*, 12 November 1664.

68 *Diary*, 5 September 1662.

69 Hannah Wolley, *The Accomplish'd Lady's Delight* (2nd edition), London, 1677.

70 L. Wright, *Clean and Decent*, London, 1960.

71 *Diary*, 21 February 1665.

72 *Diary*, 25 February 1665.

73 Neve's *Almanac* for 1667. Most almanacs gave similar advice.

74 Magalotti.

75 The list also included 'an Italian lock, *custos pudicitiae*'. Neither, so far as I know, is there now.

76 Hannah Wolley, *The Queen's Closet Opened*, London, 1655.

77 Hannah Wolley, *Guide to the Female Sex*, London, 1682.
78 Charles Allen, *Curious Observations on the Teeth*, Dublin, 1686.

Chapter 8: Housework, laundry and shopping

1 John Evelyn, *Fumifugium*, London, 1661.
2 Reproduced by gracious permission of the Queen in Caroline Davidson, *A Woman's Work is Never Done: A History of Housework in the British Isles 1650–1950*, London, 1982.
3 Sean Shesgreen (ed.), *The Cries and Hawkers of London*, Stanford, California, 1990.
4 Erasmus described the average English manor-house floor, in 1530, in Latin. It had a foundation, undisturbed for maybe twenty years, of '*sputa, vomitus, mictum canum et hominum, projectam cervisiam, et piscium reliquias, atque sordes non nominandas*'. A non-Latinist will get the general idea.
5 Dorothy Hartley, *Water in England*, London, 1964.
6 Archdale Palmer, *Recipe Book 1659–1672*, Wymondham, Leicestershire, 1985.
7 Hannah Wolley, *The Cook's Guide*, London, 1664.
8 *Diary*, 22 February 1664 and 4 April 1666.
9 Hartley, op. cit. I have drawn most of the information in this section from that delightful book.
10 *Diary*, 21 May 1662.
11 Dorothy Hartley makes the intriguing suggestion that washing was dried on that mysterious linear measure, a 'rod, pole or perch', also used for drying armour – how else? – and accommodating roosting birds. The measure was five and a half yards long. Its disappearance in metrication relieved many a schoolchild.

   If drying rods were fixed in a loft, as in the Dutch seventeenth-century doll's house in the Folk Museum in Amsterdam, they would be easier to use than ropes, but they still lacked the element of mobility solved by the Victorians' racks on pulleys.
12 Hannah Wolley, *Observations in Physic and Chirurgery* and *The Queen-Like Closet*, London, 1662.
13 Tonnage and Poundage Act 1660.
14 CSPD, 3 August 1661. A Royal Proclamation provided for the punishment of 'smuckellors'.
15 CSPD, 2 October 1669.
16 Samuel collected prints of street vendors of his time. As well as three Italian sets and one French set, he had three sets of English ones: all

superbly reproduced in *The Cryes of London*, Cambridge, 1994.

17 To show the multiplicity of the street cryers' trades, I have divided the English ones in Samuel's collection into categories:

Perishables: fish, such as oysters, mackerel, smelts, flounders, mussels, dried cod ('poor jack'), crabs and eels; fresh fruit and vegetables, such as strawberries, cooking pears, oranges and lemons, cherries, onions, rosemary and bay, radishes and lettuces, cucumbers, artichokes and asparagus; cooked food, such as 'hot pudding pies' and 'hot codlings' (apples); dairy products, such as milk, cheese and cream; others such as vinegar (the only vendor with transport, a donkey), live chickens, 'colly molly puffs' and Dutch biscuits.

Household goods: such as bed mats and door mats, rope (for clothes lines), marking stones, toasting forks, ink and pens, drinking glasses, steels and tinder boxes, measuring sticks (yardsticks and ellsticks), 'screens' (hand-held fire-screens 'if you desire/to keep your beauty from the fire'), 'small coal, a penny a peake' (a pan the size of a large saucepan), small brushes and notebooks, papers of pins, knives, combs and inkhorns, trumpery jewellery, spectacles, fire-irons, wax and wax wafers (for closing letters), straw baskets and hats, mops, matches and 'savealls' (to use up the ends of candles).

Clothes: such as shoes, bandstrings (the tasselled ties at the neck of shirts) and thread laces (almost the only time children are shown).

Services: such as a chimney sweep (a man with a small boy), water sellers, both New River and Thames, knife grinders, tinkers, menders of brass and iron pots and rush- and cane-seated chairs and barrels, a sow-gelder (how do you geld a sow?), the watchman crying the time at dawn and dusk, and two whores, Mother Cresswell and Mrs Russel (the first was 'the town bawd', the second with the more honorific title was labelled a 'courtesan').

Dealers: in 'kitchen stuff' (especially dripping from spit roasting), 'ends of gold and silver' (odd bits of bullion lace?), old boots and shoes in exchange for new brooms, any old iron, old clothes and other textiles, and rabbit skins.

Entertainers: such as a fiddler, sellers of children's whirligigs, singing glasses (long trumpet-shaped glasses: a most fragile stock in trade) and singing birds, a mountebank with a monkey selling medicines, ballad singers, an acrobat, and a lady tightrope walker showing off her legs.

Others: such as sellers of almanacs and the *London Gazette*, a man begging food for poor prisoners, and a beggar-woman with two children. The little one on her back is the only figure that does not wear some sort of head covering.

18 Magalotti.

19 *Diary*, 26 April 1664.

20 Magalotti explains that the Court of Chancery and the King's Bench were at one end of Westminster Hall, with other unspecified courts. The rest of the space 'serves for the people who assemble there on the business of the law-suits and for the accommodation of many moveable shops which are placed round it'.

21 *Diary*, 5 February 1661.

22 *Diary*, 29 July 1667. Solomon turns up again later, in George Fox's *Diary*. He emigrated to Jamaica in 1671, settling there while Fox and others went on to New England.

23 Dorothy Davis, *A History of Shopping*, London, 1966.

24 Ibid.

25 Ibid.

26 Ambrose Heal, *Signboards of Old London Shops*, London, 1957.

27 *Diary*, 8 September 1663.

28 CSPD, 1666.

29 I have taken the information on City markets from B. R. Masters, *The Public Markets of the City of London Surveyed by William Leybourne in 1677*, London, 1974, although this is slightly outside the decade 1660–70.

30 St Mary Woolchurch, hence the alternative name of the market after rebuilding – Woolchurch market.

31 B. Clarke, *Glimpses of Ancient Hackney*, London, 1894. This fascinating book, written at the end of the nineteenth century by a long-lived, antiquarian-minded doctor, vividly illustrates the theory I have aired earlier, that houses used to survive for centuries.

32 CSPD, 9 March 1664.

33 CSPD, 4 April 1664.

34 CSPD, August 1661.

35 CSPD, 9 April 1662.

36 *London Gazette*, 24 August 1667.

37 CSPD, 7 June 1661.

38 For this section I have drawn on W. Boyne, *Trade Tokens Issued in the Seventeenth Century*, London, 1889.

39 T. Girtin, *The Triple Crowns: A History of the Drapers' Company*, London, 1964.

40 CSPD, 11 March 1668.

41 William Cobbett, *Parliamentary History*, vol. IV, London, 1808. Cobbett

comments that 'the copper farthings were called Lucas farthings to this day'.

42 *London Gazette*, 4 October 1666.

43 *Abstract of British Historical Statistics, the Schumpeter–Gilboy Price Indices*, Cambridge, 1962.

44 Anthony à Wood, *The Life and Times of Anthony Wood*, Oxford, 1891–1900; and in the case of the Flanders lace, *Mercurius Publicus*, 18–25 April 1661.

45 From scattered references in the *Diary*, and Caroline Davidson, *The Ham House Kitchen*, London, 1986.

46 CSPD, 1666, note on the Bills of Mortality, which also gave the permitted bread prices, at the end of the volume.

47 Boyne, op. cit.

Chapter 9: Cooking, meals, food and drink

1 *Diary*, 23 December 1660.

2 *Diary*, 13 December 1660.

3 *Diary*, 10 July 1666.

4 Isabella Beeton, *The Book of Household Management*, London, 1861. For the nostalgic, I will give a shortened version of a menu for November, course by course:
   2 soups
   6 fish dishes
   14 meat, game and fish dishes
   3 more game dishes
   6 sweets
   iced pudding
   dessert and ices

5 *Diary*, 12 May 1667.

6 *Weekly Intelligencer*, 14–21 January 1661.

7 CSPD, 12 August 1663.

8 Hannah Wolley, *The Cook's Guide*, London, 1664.

9 Parkinson, in his *Paradisi in Sole*, London, 1656, gives the following plant list for the kitchen garden:
   artichokes
   melons
   cucumbers
   pompions (a kind of squash)
   a wide range of culinary herbs (in the modern sense)
   asparagus

lettuce, and corn salad for the winter
purslane
coleworts (cabbages)
cauliflower
endive, with directions for blanching
chicory, of which both leaves and flowers were eaten
beetroot
sorrel
chervil
rampion (a kind of shallot)
cress
rocket
tansy
burnet
parsnips

10 CSPD, 25 January 1664.
11 *Diary*, 18 July 1660.
12 *Diary*, 6 January 1660.
13 R. May, *The Compleat Cook* (first published 1655), London, 1984.
14 *Diary*, 6 October 1663.
15 May, op. cit.
16 C. G. A. Clay, *Economic Expansion and Social Change 1500–1700*, vol. II, Cambridge, 1984.
17 Ibid.
18 Archdale Palmer, *Recipe Book 1659–72*, Wymondham, Leicestershire, 1985.
19 May, op. cit.
20 John Murrel, *Two Books of Cookerie and Carving* (5th edition 1638), Ilkley, Yorkshire, 1985.
21 Ibid.
22 Caroline Davidson, *The Ham House Kitchen*, London, 1986.
23 See Chapter 6, p. 92.
24 Palmer, op. cit.

Chapter 10: Sex

1 The inexactitude of date is due solely to a lacuna as to Adam's age when this occurred. We know, from Perkins' *Almanac* for 1664, that Adam was created 5,628 years before that year. Perkins is usually sound on useful dates.
2 Or, as the Book of Common Prayer put it, the sanctification and

joining together in marriage of our first parents by Almighty God.

3 Peter Laslett, *The World We Have Lost – Further Explored*, London, 1983.

4 Ibid. Peter Laslett leaves the matter open:
'Deprivation of marriage did not lead to a greater propensity towards sexual adventures, nor to those which gave rise to pregnancy, whatever happened to sexual activity of other kinds. We can observe strict and efficient control here ... even if it worked in entirely unexpected ways. This should not surprise us if we recognise ... that a force which is capable of keeping people from marrying at all must also be capable of procreating outside marriage.'

5 Jane Sharp, *The Midwive's Book*, London, 1671.

6 *Diary*, 16 January 1664.

7 Robert Burton, *Anatomy of Melancholy*; quoted by E. Shorter, *A History of Women's Bodies*, Harmondsworth, Middlesex, 1983.

8 R. Thompson, *Unfit for Modest Ears*, London, 1979, without which this chapter would be much shorter. Where no other source is given, I have relied gratefully on Thompson.

9 Jane Sharp again, on the clitoris: 'in this lies the chief pleasure of love's delight in copulation, indeed were not the pleasure transcendently ravishing us, a man or woman would hardly ever die for love'.

10 The prohibited marriage periods were from Advent to eight days after Epiphany, Septuagesima to eight days after Easter, and Ascension to Trinity Sunday. For the effectiveness of Lenten abstinence, see Keith Thomas, *Religion and the Decline of Magic*, London, 1971.

11 *Diary*, 1 July 1663.

12 Ibid.

13 B. Danielssen and D. M. Veith (eds), *The Gyldenstope Manuscript*, Uppsala, 1967. Rochester's poems often refer to 'frigging'.

14 In Thomas More's *Utopia*, first published in 1516, the inhabitants of this ideal country divide physical pleasures into two types:
'first there are those which fill the whole organism with a conscious sense of enjoyment. This may be the result of replacing physical substances which have been burnt up by the heat off the body, as when we eat or drink. Or it may be caused by the discharge of some excess, as in excretion, sexual intercourse, or any relief of irritation by rubbing or scratching.'

15 G. Barber, *The Panizzi Lectures*, 1988.

16 *Diary*, 13 January 1668, 8 February 1668 and 9 February 1668.

17 There is a picture of 'Mother Cresswell' (a title implying little respect) in the *Cryes of London*. She looks a decrepit old hag, unlike the next

picture of a 'courtesan' dressed in fine clothes and carrying a fashionable mask.

18 CSPD, 25 March 1668.

19 *Messenger*'s case, quoted in J. Hostettler, *The Politics of Punishment*, Chichester, 1994.

20 Thompson, op. cit.

21 *Diary*, 21 March 1665.

22 Thompson, op. cit.

Chapter 11: The household

1 William Blackstone, *Commentaries on the Laws of England*, London, 1765–9. The position was unchanged in our period: see also note 13.

2 CSPD, 24 March 1662.

3 Sir Thomas Browne, *Religio Medici*, London, 1642. It still, I suggest, expressed the average man's sentiments.

4 For outstanding examples see chapter 9 of Antonia Fraser, *The Weaker Vessel: Women's Lot in Seventeenth-Century England*, London, 1984.

5 Alice Clark, *Working Life of Women in the Seventeenth Century*, London, 1919.

6 *Diary*, 31 December 1662. This condescension may remind readers of Samuel Johnson's dictum a century later: 'a woman's preaching is like a dog's walking on his hinder legs. It is not well done, but you are surprised to find it done at all.'

7 Clark, op. cit.

8 Ibid. Italics added.

9 Ibid.

10 Samuel of all people, money-grubbing as he was, fell head over heels in love with a pennyless half-French girl only just old enough to marry: she was fifteen when he married her, which was about the age of menarche then, but she was very far from emotionally mature. No one knows whether her wishes were consulted.

11 Hannah Wolley, *Guide to the Female Sex*, London, 1682.

12 CSPD, 8 April 1667.

13 Blackstone, op. cit. Writing a century after our period, Blackstone throws an invaluable light on it, since he carefully explains the development of the law up to its then current state, giving authorities. When he describes the apprenticeship system under the Act of Elizabeth, we can apply his description to our period.

14 R. Houlbrooke (ed.), *English Family Life*, Oxford, 1988.

15 Blackstone, op. cit.

16 M. Pelling, 'Child health as a social value', *Journal of the Society for the Social History of Medicine*, vol. I, 1988.

17 F. P. and M. M. Verney (eds), *Verney Memoirs*, London, 1904.

18 CSPD, 27 March 1668.

19 Dorothy Davis, *A History of Shopping*, London, 1966.

20 Magalotti. Italics added.

21 Quoted in Clark, op. cit.

22 Blackstone, op. cit.

23 Ibid.

24 *Diary*, 2 September 1663.

25 *Mercurius Publicus*, 1666.

26 Blackstone, op. cit.

27 *Diary*, 26 October 1663.

28 Blackstone, op. cit.

29 Caroline Davidson, *A Woman's Work is Never Done: A History of Housework in the British Isles 1650–1950*, London, 1982.

30 *Diary*, 17 July 1665.

31 CSPD, 12 September 1667.

32 F. O. Shyllon, *Black Slaves in Britain*, Oxford, 1974, on which, with C. G. A. Clay, *Economic Expansion and Social Change 1500–1700*, Cambridge, 1984, I have drawn for the whole of this section except where otherwise indicated.

33 CSPD, 28 June 1664.

34 Quoted, source unstated, in W. Boyne, *Trade Tokens Issued in the Seventeenth Century*, London, 1889.

35 *Mercurius Publicus*, 30 May 1662. The double branding dates from an Act of Edward VI, that runaway (English) servants should be branded 'on the breast with a V' and bound as slaves to any purchaser, for two years. If they ran away again during those two years, and were caught, they were branded again, on the forehead – where everyone could see it – and adjudged the slaves of their masters for life.

36 *Kingdom's Intelligencer*, 30 December 1661. In theory, the *Intelligencer* and the *Gazette* did not accept small-ads for lost property; but why be a king if one may not even advertise for one's lost dogs?

37 Keith Thomas, *Man and the Natural World*, London, 1983, on which I have drawn extensively in this section.

38 Thomas, op. cit.

39 *London Gazette*, 21 March 1666.

40 Thomas, op. cit.

41 *Diary*, 31 December 1661.

42 Randle Holme, *The Academy of Armoury*, Chester, 1688.

43 Thomas, op. cit.

44 Defoe, *A Journal of the Plague Year*, London, 1722.

45 Thomas, op. cit.

46 *Diary*, 18 January 1661.

47 Thomas, op. cit.

48 *Diary*, 25 August 1661.

49 Henry Peacham wrote an egregiously pompous book called *The Compleat Gentleman* in 1622. It went into countless editions as social climbers tried to worm their way up to the ranks of the nobility, or at least the gentry. The Latin words, which Peacham could so easily have put into English, mean 'things that delight the senses and mind'.

50 *Diary*, 25 January 1661.

51 *Diary*, 22 May 1663.

52 *Diary*, 1 March 1668.

53 *Diary*, 30 June 1660.

54 *Diary*, 2 September 1666. Italics added.

55 Thomas, op. cit.

56 *Diary*, 21 December 1664.

57 Thomas, op. cit.

58 Ibid.

59 Ibid. When I lived in Hackney a magnificent pig lived in the house on the next corner – well, not actually *in* the house perhaps, but it was clear from the size of the plot that man and pig must have lived, so to speak, very cheek by jowl. They used to take occasional strolls round the nearby streets, linked by a piece of string.

Chapter 12: Education, literacy and speech

1 Lawrence Stone, note in *Past and Present*, vol. 24, 1962–3.

2 D. Cressy, *Literacy and the Social Order*, Cambridge, 1980.

3 Ibid.

4 G. Miège, *English Grammar*, London, 1688. M. Miège came to London from Lausanne in 1661, to seek his fortune. His book was written in English, but from the point of view of a Francophone. He lists 'the sounds which seem peculiar to the English [i.e. they exist only in English] and which I am sure are strangers to the French tongue ... But the most peculiar pronunciation, and that which perplexes Foreigners most of all, is the sound of *th* as in ... thanks.' Poor M. Miège. Try any Frenchman on 'Sotheby's'.

5 Not only did secretary hand write several letters in an unrecognisable

way, but it used various abbreviations, the most common being 'ye' for 'the'.

6 Owen Price, *The Vocal Organ*, London, 1665.

7 Hannah Wolley, *Guide to the Female Sex*, London, 1682. 'Every Saturday take an account of every servant's laying out, and once a month an account of all the expenses of the whole house.' This counsel of perfection was too much for poor Elizabeth, who after all was only then learning arithmetic from her omniscient husband. When she got her household accounts in a muddle, on 29 September 1664, Samuel noticed 'things that seemed somewhat doubtful' and she had to confess to creative accounting – 'when she doth miss a sum she doth add something to other things to make it' – whereupon Samuel was 'very angry'. It cannot always have been easy, being married to Samuel.

8 Ibid.

9 I am grateful to the Reverend A. H. Mead, Chaplain Emeritus of St Paul's School, for this information.

10 J. Lawson and H. Silver, *A Social History of Education in England*, London, 1973.

11 N. Penney (ed.), *Journal of George Fox* (Everyman edition), London, 1924.

12 Arthur Bryant, *Samuel Pepys, the Man in the Making*, London, 1933.

13 Mary Evelyn, *Mundus Muliebris*, ed. John Evelyn, London, 1690.

14 *Weekly Intelligencer*, 14–21 January 1661.

15 Quoted in D. Gardiner, *English Girlhood at School*, Oxford, 1929, on which I have drawn for this section.

16 F. P. and M. M. Verney (eds), *Verney Memoirs*, London, 1904.

17 W. Matthews, *English Pronunciation and Shorthand in the Early Modern Period*, Berkeley, California, 1943. Professor Matthews was one of the two principal editors of the *Diary*. For a fascinating and scholarly analysis of Samuel's shorthand by him, readers are referred to the Introduction to the *Diary*, especially pp. xlviii–lxvii.

18 *Diary*, 4 July 1662.

19 Christopher Hill, *Change and Continuity in 17th-Century England*, Bristol, Avon, 1991.

20 *Diary*, 20 June 1662.

21 *Diary*, 9 September 1663.

22 Atlas was the god who held up the world, in Greek mythology.

23 S. Tyacke, *London Map-sellers 1660–1720*, Tring, Herts, 1978.

24 *London Gazette*, June 1661.

25 *Mercurius Publicus*, 30 May 1662. By the Treaty of Breda in 1667 the

Dutch surrendered New Amsterdam to the British, who re-christened it New York; they took Surinam in exchange.

26 Wing's *Almanac*, 1666.

27 Rose's *Almanac*, 1667.

28 Perkins' *Almanac*, 1664.

29 Advertisement in the *Weekly Advertiser*, 1 April 1661. Applicants might also find themselves buying a candle-lighting watch at the same time: the French *emigrés* needed every penny.

30 *Kingdom's Intelligencer*, 2 November 1661.

31 *Mercurius Publicus*, September 1660.

32 *Diary*, 28 March 1660.

33 Gadsbury's *Almanac*, 1666.

34 Thomas Nunnes' *Almanac*, 1666.

35 P. Burke, 'Popular culture in 17th-century London', *London Journal*, vol. 3, 1977–8, gives the price as 2d. B. Capp, *English Almanacs 1500–1800*, Cornell, 1979, gives the normal price as 3d or 4d, the larger ones by Lilly and Wharton selling at 6d or more.

36 Capp, op. cit.

37 Cressy, op. cit.

38 W. Holder, *Elements of Speech*, London, 1669.

39 Lawrence Stone, 'Social mobility in England 1500–1700', *Past and Present*, vol. 33, 1966. Up to the Civil War, 40 per cent of the apprentices recruited by the Carpenters' and the Fishmongers' Companies were from the Highlands of Scotland. By the end of the seventeenth century, the proportion had decreased to 20 per cent.

40 W. Matthews, *Cockney Past and Present*, London, 1938.

41 C. L. Barker, *The Story of Language*, London, 1964.

42 H. W. Wyld, *A Short History of English*, London, 1914.

43 Finkenstaed (ed.), *Chronological English Dictionary*, Heidelberg, 1970.

44 E. Partridge, *A Dictionary of Catch Phrases*, London, 1990.

45 J. McConica, *Erasmus*, Oxford, 1991.

46 R. Hodges, *True-Writing*, London, 1653.

Chapter 13: Hobbies, excursions, family occasions and etiquette

1 Embroiderers may like to know that the embroidery frames were made of two pairs of rollers called 'tents', on which the work was stretched, under tension; hence, tent-stitch.

2 There is a magnificent collection of these embroidered boxes etc. in

the Burrell Collection in Glasgow. Peg Pen's embroidered purse was sold by Christie's South Kensington Ltd in 1987. I have quoted its dimensions from their catalogue.

3 J. Murdoch and others, *The English Miniature*, London, 1981.

4 For an account of Restoration music, the reader should consult Richard Luckett's scholarly and fascinating essay in the Companion Volume to the *Diary*. Seventeenth-century music most likely to be familiar to the average listener would be by Purcell, who was later than our period. He was born in 1658.

5 According to Grove's *New Dictionary of Music and Musicians*, London, 1980, the idea of 'perfect' or 'absolute' pitch did not become current until the nineteenth century. There could be variations of up to six semitones between accepted pitches, the more usual ones being a semitone apart. For someone with as acute an ear as Samuel, this must have produced hideous disharmonies if one neighbour tuned up and the next down.

6 *Diary*, 1 April 1663.

7 *Diary*, 30 June 1661.

8 W. van Lennen (ed.), *The London Stage*, Illinois, 1965.

9 Magalotti.

10 *Diary*, 11 November 1661. Perhaps Samuel's disapproval of this publicity was why Elizabeth and he had private dancing lessons at home.

11 *Diary*, 15 November 1666.

12 Randle Holme, *The Academy of Armory*, Chester, 1688.

13 *Diary*, 17 February 1662.

14 *Diary*, 1 January 1668. Samuel gave a vivid account of playing at dice during the twelve days of Christmas, in Inner and Middle Temple halls.

15 *Diary*, 11 November 1661.

16 Gaming Act 1664.

17 Holme, op. cit.

18 *Diary*, 14 February 1660.

19 B. Reay (ed.), *Popular Culture in Seventeenth-Century England*, London, 1988.

20 *Diary*, Companion Volume.

21 *Diary*, 12 May 1667. The idea of a fixed price was new, and welcome: see *Diary*, 10 May 1663.

22 *Diary*, 21 February 1668.

23 Magalotti.

24 *London Gazette*, June 1661.

25 Magalotti.
26 Tradescant's collection came into the possession of Elias Ashmole in equivocal circumstances. He gave it, with other curiosities he had amassed, including a cloak of deerskin embroidered with shells said to have belonged to the father of Princess Pocahontas, to the University of Oxford, where it may still be seen in the Ashmolean Museum.
27 *Diary*, 21 December 1663.
28 Magalotti.
29 *Diary*, 14 August 1666.
30 Magalotti.
31 CSPD, 10 August 1664.
32 *Diary*, 3 May 1662.
33 *Diary*, 11 January 1660.
34 A. MacGregor (ed.), *The Late King's Goods*, London, 1989.
35 *Diary*, 30 April 1663.
36 *Diary*, 13 October 1660. This may have been the same execution as the sight that greeted George Fox, the founder of the Society of Friends, when he arrived at Charing Cross in 1660 and saw 'multitudes of people ... gathered together to see the burning of the bowels of some of the old King's judges, who had been hanged drawn and quartered'. *Journal of George Fox* (Everyman edition), London, 1924.
37 *Diary*, 20 October 1660.
38 Wharton's *Almanac*, 1666.
39 Magalotti saw them.
40 *Diary*, 14 June 1662.
41 CSPD, 9 May 1668.
42 *Diary*, 21 January 1664.
43 *Diary*, 30 January 1661. George Fox in his *Journal* relates that before the battle of Dunbar (1650) 'O.C. ... had promised to the Lord that if He gave him the victory over his enemies he would take away tithes etc., or else let him be rolled into his grave with infamy.' The Lord kept his side of the bargain, but 'O.C.' did not. 'When the King came in, they took him up and hanged him and buried him under Tyburn, where he was rolled into his grave with infamy. And when I saw him hanging there, I saw his word justly come upon him.' Fox, op. cit.
44 Wharton's *Almanac*, 1665.
45 Ibid.
46 *Weekly Intelligencer*, 25 March 1661: proclamation.

47 P. Burke, 'Popular culture in seventeenth-century London', *London Journal*, vol. 3, 1977–8.
48 *Diary*, 27 November 1662.
49 Magalotti.
50 Ibid.
51 Ibid. His party had left England by then, but he recorded how the Lord Mayor had to be a rich man, since 'every day in the year during his administration the mayor is obliged to keep open table'.
52 Burke, op. cit.
53 *Diary*, 29 October 1663.
54 From time to time the press of our day sees Freemasonry round every corner. I wondered what the Masons were doing in the 1660s. The answer seems to be, building buildings. Their members dealt with a higher class of trade, and stone, than the ordinary 'rough' masons. But their craft guild was ahead of other guilds in opening its ranks to non-craftsmen known as 'accepted' masons, including notable antiquarians and architects such as Elias Ashmole, Randle Holme and Christopher Wren. As the *Oxford English Dictionary* puts it, 'the distinction of being an "accepted mason" became a fashionable object of ambition and before the end of the 17th century the object of societies of freemasons seems to have been chiefly social and convivial'.
55 Magalotti.
56 *Diary*, 22 November 1660 and 30 December 1662.
57 *Diary*, 23 April 1661.
58 *Diary*, 23 April 1665.
59 *Diary*, 15 November 1666.
60 Magalotti.
61 Ibid.
62 Ibid.
63 Van Lennen, op. cit., on which I have drawn for this section, together with the illuminating article on the theatre by Peter Holland in the Companion Volume of the *Diary*.
64 Magalotti.
65 *Diary*, 2 May 1668.
66 *Diary*, 1 January 1668. These undeserving patrons seem to have given themselves a Christmas treat.
67 *Diary*, 27 December 1662.
68 *Diary*, 7 January 1668.
69 Magalotti.
70 CSPD, 27 February 1665.

71 *Diary*, 15 January 1669.

72 *Diary*, 12 June 1663.

73 Hannah Wolley, *Guide to the Female Sex*, London, 1682. Italics added.

74 *Diary*, 11 May 1664. 'What to think of it of a sudden I know not, but I think not to take notice of it to him till I have thought better of it.' And this is the man who was so jealous of the dancing master.

75 White bridal dresses were late Victorian. Religious reasons barred marriages in Lent, but there was another reason for waiting till after Easter rather than rushing the ceremony through before Lent: the new fashions came in at Easter, and who would want to be married in last year's mode?

76 *Diary*, 16 February 1667.

77 S. Porter, 'Death and burial in a London parish', *London Journal*, vol. 8, 1981–2.

78 *Diary*, 12 October 1667.

79 *Diary*, 23 December 1663.

80 *Diary*, 17 March 1664.

81 John Evelyn, *London Revived*, London, 1666.

82 V. Harding, 'Location of burials in early modern London', *London Journal*, vol. 14, 1989–91. The New Churchyard is now itself buried under the Broad Street redevelopment. Of the 194 parishioners of Samuel's parish who died of plague, 146 were buried in the (tiny) churchyard of St Olave's and 48 in the New Churchyard. One wonders whether the painstaking research into parish records under-taken by modern demographers may not sometimes be skewed by this system of out-burials.

83 *Diary*, 6 January 1668.

84 *Diary*, 14 February 1665.

85 Hannah Wolley, *Guide to the Female Sex*, London, 1682. 'Madam' was used to both married and unmarried women.

86 J. Wildeblood, *The Polite World*, Oxford, 1965.

87 Wolley, op. cit.

88 CSPD, February 1669. After all that worry, the two young men met in Charles's closet. Charles 'welcomed His Excellency with a most courteous embrace, a reception reserved only for great and allied princes', as Magalotti recorded. Just as well neither of them was wearing a large, fashionable hat, which makes embracing difficult.

89 *Diary*, 14 August 1666.

90 Wildeblood, op. cit.

91 *Diary*, 22 January 1669.

92 Wolley, op. cit., from which I have taken most of this section.

93 L. Weatherill, *Consumer Behaviour and Material Culture in Britain 1660–1760*, London, 1988. Samuel built up an impressive collection of silver, and was very proud of his 30 silver plates. The *Diary* mentions purchases of six spoons in 1661 and 'spoons forks and a sugar box' in 1664, but those are the only forks that appear. More may have been included in the exchange of some of his plate for 'things more useful' and the £500 worth of plate he was given in 1666. He certainly had plenty of knives: he bought 'a case of very pretty knives with agate hafts' in 1664, and two more cases of knives in 1666 and 1667. His records of acquiring the silver that adorned his rise to prosperity are so detailed that it looks as if forks were not high in his priorities. 'Plate' was, of course, solid silver; Sheffield plate (copper coated with silver) was not invented until 1742).

94 Italics added.

95 J. Murrel, *A New Book of Cookery*, London, 1638.

96 Magalotti.

Chapter 14: Divers events and Acts in the law

1 The title of this chapter was a favourite phrase of conveyancers before 1920, when they were trying to sort out who had done what with a parcel of land over its whole history.

2 Anon., *The Lawe's Resolution of Womens Rights*, London, 1632, referred to in this chapter by its alternative title *Womens Lawe*. Although it was written before the Civil War, and while the ecclesiastical courts were still functioning, it is nevertheless a useful guide to the common law affecting women, when taken with a pinch of salt. Much of it deals with the ownership of land, which was not likely to be as important to the average London woman as property in chattels such as trading stock. It is written in a beguilingly avuncular style, encouraging women to be aware of their legal position even if there was nothing they could do about it.

3 Ibid.

4 William Blackstone, *Commentaries on the Laws of England*, London, 1765–9. The position then was unchanged from the 1660s.

5 Ibid.

6 Ibid.

7 Ibid.

8 Ibid.

9 An Act for the Confirmation of Marriages 1660.

10 *Womens Lawe*.

11 Italics added.

12 Quoted in R. Houlbrooke, *English Family Life 1576–1716*, Oxford, 1988.

13 G. F. Nickalls (ed.), *The Journal of George Fox*, Cambridge, 1952.

14 CSPD, June 1668: 'Note that the man that marries two persons [i.e. performs the ceremony] without licence, and all that are present at the marriage, need a pardon from the King.'

15 Not excluded from the Act of Oblivion (italics added).

16 Lawrence Stone, *The Family, Sex and Marriage 1500–1800* (revised edn), London, 1979.

17 H. Peacham, *The Compleat Gentleman*, London, 1622.

18 *Diary*, 28 February 1668.

19 Lawrence Stone, *Road to Divorce*, Oxford, 1995.

20 K. Hart (ed.), *The Letters of Dorothy Osborne*, London (Folio Society), 1968.

21 CSPD, 30 August 1669.

22 Stone, *The Family*, op. cit.

23 It was excluded from the general pardon in the Act of Oblivion.

24 CSPD, 1 February 1668.

25 *Womens Lawe*.

26 A. Griffiths (ed.), *Chronicles of Newgate*, London, 1987.

27 CSPD, 10 August 1665.

28 Fox, op. cit.

29 Magalotti, who seems to have taken a keen interest in the English legal system. Italics added.

30 Ibid.

31 Tomlin, *Law Dictionary*, London, 1835.

32 Ibid.

33 *Bushell's Case*, 1670, quoted by J. Hostettler, *The Politics of Punishment*, Chichester, 1994. The court seems to have acted in contravention of the Commons' Resolution on the Punishment of Juries passed in 1667, that 'the precedents and practice of fining and imprisoning juries is illegal'. D. C. Douglas (ed.), *English Historical Documents*, vol. 8, London, 1953.

34 *Rex v. Maddey*, 1670, quoted in A. K. R. Kiralfy, *A Source Book of English Law*, London, 1955.

35 S. Milsom, *Historical Foundations of the Common Law*, London, 1981.

36 Hostettler, op. cit.

37 Griffiths, op. cit.

38 Ibid.

39 William Cobbett, *Parliament History*, vol. IV, London, 1808.

40 A sentiment of 1551 equally applicable up to 1670; quoted in A. W.
B. Simpson, *A History of the Common Law and Contract*, Oxford, 1975.
41 CSPD, 21 January 1667.
42 It was extended to women by an Act of James I in 1624.
43 From the 1624 Act.
44 Milsom, op. cit.
45 CSPD, petition 1667; one of many such petitions.
46 CSPD, 23 December 1669.
47 *Mitchel* v. *Alestree*, quoted by Milsom, op. cit. From the Latin they
must have been 'ferocious mares, very little broken to pulling coaches'.
The plaintiff alleged that the defendant was improvident (careless?
dare one use a modern term and translate it as negligent?), incautious
and without due consideration of the unsuitability of that place
(Lincoln's Inn Fields). When I looked up the same case in another
set of law reports, this time in English, the mares and coach had
Cinderella-wise turned into only one horse, which the defendant
'rode into a place called Lincoln's Inn Fields (much frequented by
the King's subjects, and unapt for such purpose) for the breaking and
taming of him, and the horse was so unruly that he broke from the
defendant and ran over the plaintiff and grievously hurt him'. Same
principle, but somehow one expects the facts to be the same in both
accounts of the same case. Such idiosyncrasies are the stuff of
seventeenth-century research.
   Buying horses which were not trained to pull carriages, so that
they had to be trained – somewhere – may have been a common
practice. Samuel's horses had to be trained; he does not say where.
48 Quoted in Ventris, *Notes of Cases Heard in the Reign of Charles II*, London,
1716.
49 Milsom, op. cit.
50 Not until 1730 was an Act passed giving lawyers three years to
change over to English 'written in a common *legible* hand'.
51 *Simmons* v. *Cornelius*, 1663–4, Chancery.
52 *Diary*, 10 December 1660.
53 *Diary*, 5 June 1667.
54 *Diary*, 31 May 1661.
55 At least this was better than the forced loans which Charles's
grandfather, James I, had descended to:
'seeing men have so good experience of our repayment of all those
summes which we have ever required in this kind ... we require
but that of some, which few men would deny a friend ... the sum
we require of you by virtue of these presents is £... which we do

promise to repay to you or your assignee within eighteen months after the payment thereof to the Collector.' (British Library Additional manuscript)

No one who knew Charles's financial habits would have been happy to cough up this 'friendly' help to him.

56 *Diary*, 27 November 1664.

57 Tomlin, op. cit. This lasted till the reign of William and Mary.

58 H. Horwitz, 'Testamentary practice, family strategy and the last phases of the Custom of London 1660–1725', *Law and History Review*, Harvard, 1984.

59 From a copy of a family will in my possession.

60 *Wiseman* v. *Foster*, 1668–9, Chancery.

61 Tomlin, op. cit.

62 Ibid. The whole position of wills was to a great extent sorted out by the Statute of Frauds in 1667.

63 *Womens Lawe*.

64 Ibid.

65 Tomlin, op. cit.

Chapter 15: Money, poverty and class

1 *Dictionary of National Biography*.

2 CSPD, 15 July 1668.

3 Peter Laslett, *The World We Have Lost – Further Explored*, London, 1965, to which I am indebted for much of the material in this chapter, sets out King's analysis in full.

4 In this section I have gratefully drawn on S. M. MacFarlane, 'Poverty and poor relief in London at the end of the seventeenth century', D. Phil. thesis, Oxford, 1982.

5 From Charles's graceful speech to his loyal Commons in August 1660, reported in William Cobbett's *Parliamentary History*, vol. IV, London, 1808:
'for your Poll Bill I do thank you as much as if the money were to come into my own coffers ... I pray very earnestly, as fast as the money comes in, discharge that great burden of the Navy, and disband the Army as fast as you can; and till you can disband the rest, make a provision for their support.'

But as so often, Charles's sensible ideas fell foul of bureaucratic inertia.

6 Cobbett, op. cit., 14 May 1660.

7 *Weekly Intelligencer*, 25 February 1660.

8 *Weekly Intelligencer,* 19 March 1661.
9 CSPD, petition 1666.
10 *Mercurius Publicus,* 18 April 1661.
11 CSPD, petition 1667.
12 *Current Intelligence,* 25 June 1667.
13 CSPD, 12 December 1666.
14 *Diary,* 14 June 1667.
15 CSPD, undated note at the end of the volume: £9,750 for a pair of diamond 'pendants' and £1,200 for a pair of pearl ones.
16 CSPD, 22 September 1669.
17 *Diary,* 19 December 1666.
18 Anonymous letter to the King, quoted in CSPD, 30 June 1660.
19 Italics added.
20 Nowadays, our world being wider, the claimant has to prove habitual residence in the European Union.
21 Preamble to the Poor Law Amendment Act 1662.
22 MacFarlane, op. cit.
23 *Weekly Intelligencer,* 1 April 1661.
24 Italics added.
25 K. Hudson, *Pawnbroking,* London, 1982.
26 *Diary,* 16 September 1664.
27 CSPD, 7 December 1660.
28 It was a very ancient foundation, part of which had been refurbished in 1522 to entertain the Emperor Charles v. John Stow, *The Survey of London,* London, 1598.
29 Ibid.
30 H. Perkins (ed.), *Children in English Society,* London, 1969.
31 CSPD, 11 June 1669.
32 Dudley North, quoted by McFarlane, op. cit.
33 CSPD, 15 July 1668.
34 S. E. Thorne, *Essays in Legal History,* London, 1985.
35 Charles acknowledged about a dozen bastard children:

by Lucy Walter	Duke of Monmouth
by Catherine Pegg	Charles Fitzcharles
by Elizabeth Killigrew	Charlotte Fitzroy
by Barbara Palmer	Duke of Southampton
(Countess of Castlemaine)	Duke of Grafton
	Anne Countess of Sussex
	Charlotte Countess of Lichfield
by Nell Gwyn	Duke of St Albans
by Moll Davis	Lady Mary Tudor

by Louise de Kérouälle   Duke of Richmond
   (Duchess of Portland)

There were others whom he acknowledged, but who died in infancy.

36 William Blackstone, *Commentaries on the Laws of England*, London, 1765–9.

37 *Diary*, 1 and 10 May 1669. Italics added.

Chapter 16: Religion and popular beliefs

1 Matthew, 16:18.

2 CSPD, 22 August 1663.

3 Preamble to the Elizabethan Act of Uniformity. 'Our late sovereign Lady Queen Mary' was Elizabeth's half-sister.

4 Preface to the 1662 version of the Book of Common Prayer.

5 Some editions included the service for Touching for the King's Evil. It was dropped after Queen Anne.

6 Charles I's Prefatory Declaration.

7 'Catholic' to denote one who believes in the doctrines of the Church of which the Pope is the head is, I know, incorrect, since 'catholic' merely means 'universal'. But common parlance almost justifies its use in this sense, while a pedantic insistence on Roman Catholic becomes clumsy. I hope the reader will forgive me this use.

8 Letter, 22 March 1646, British Library Additional Manuscript, Harley 6988.

9 *Diary*, 20 March 1664. For some decades in the 20th century divorcing wives seeking to maximise their alimony threatened to tell the court that their spouses were buggers. More recently, they threaten to disclose their husbands' tax evasion.

10 John L. Nickalls (ed.), *The Journal of George Fox*, Cambridge, 1952.

11 The Friends acquired this nickname from a Derby magistrate whom Fox commanded to 'tremble at the name of the Lord'. Antonia Fraser, *Cromwell: Our Chief of Men*, London, 1973.

12 J. Sharpe, *Early Modern England*, London, 1987.

13 Fox, op. cit.

14 Ibid., quotation from the preface to the first edition, by William Penn.

15 Fraser, op. cit. I am grateful for this vignette of the early Quakers, which does not appear in Fox's own journal. After the first careless rapture, he was anxious to cool his zealous followers down.

16 *Diary*, 14 October 1663.

17 Alan Macfarlane (ed.), *Diary of Ralph Josselin*, Oxford, 1976.

18 R. Houlbrooke (ed.), *English Family Life 1576–1716*, Oxford, 1988. Italics added.

19 Anon., *The Pack of Autolicus 1624–93*, ed. H. R. Rollins, Cambridge, Mass., 1926.

20 *Kingdom's Intelligencer*, 30 December 1661

21 Lilley's *Almanac*, 1669.

22 Vaux's *Almanac*, 1664.

23 All these were believed, or half-believed, by my mother, the daughter and granddaughter of doctors. But she was Scottish.

24 Quoted in Christina Hole, *A Mirror of Witchcraft*, London, 1957. The laws of Tanganyika included a Witchcraft Ordinance, in 1957. Certainly there was, there, a strong belief in occult powers which could be invoked by properly initiated humans.

25 Ibid.

26 Not juggling with three balls, but summoning spirits.

27 Keith Thomas (whose *Religion and the Decline of Magic*, London, 1971, is compulsory reading for anyone interested in the subject, and recommended reading for anyone else) suggests that the normal witch's wardrobe of tall hat and cloak may be remotely derived from the garb of early Quaker women, who were often suspected of being witches because of their tendency to become possessed – they would say, by the Lord, but their enemies blamed the Devil. A witch's normal transport, a broomstick, was disappointingly almost wholly confined to the continent. Nor did British witches go in much for witches' sabbaths, or for giving themselves carnally to the Devil. It was their power to harm, *maleficium*, that worried Britishers.

Chapter 17: The world picture

1 John Blaeu's twelve-volume *Atlas Major* was published in Amsterdam in 1662. Its hundreds of detailed and beautifully coloured maps showed North and South America and Japan and even New Holland, i.e. the north and west coasts of Australia. Few Englishmen, and none of the 'middling sort', might see it; but knowledge seeps out, slowly.

2 That delightful eccentric Sir Kenelm Digby (of the weapon salve) ransomed a few slaves as he was passing, to crew his ship. He asked Charles to repay his expenses later, but there is no record that he recovered anything.

3 Proclamation, 22 March 1662.

INDEX

abortion, 97, 166
accents (spoken), 198–200, 258
accidents, 103
Act of Free and General Pardon (1660),
  162
adolescence, 173
advertising, 140, 176
Albemarle, Anne, Duchess of, 44
Albemarle, Christopher Monck, 2nd Duke
  of, 25, 180
ale, 157
alehouses *see* public-houses
Algeria: 1662 treaty, 275
Alleyn, Sir John, 21–2
almanacs, 193–7
alum, 111, 293n11
animals: domestic, 182; fighting, 210
Anne Boleyn, Queen of Henry VIII, 228
apothecaries, 87
apprentices, 173–5, 198, 230
architecture, 24
Aretino, Pietro: *Postures*, 163
Arlidge, Abraham, 9
Arthur, Prince (Henry VIII's brother),
  227–8
Artificers, Statute of (1583), 173–4, 224
Artillery Grounds, 63
Arundel House, 210
Ascension Day, 213
Ashmole, Elias, 79, 81, 309n26, 310n54
astrology, 196, 271
atlases, 192
Aubrey, John: as source, xv; on maypoles,
  8; on fall of More's head, 23; on Wren
  breaking knitting frame, 122; on hat-
  wearing, 123; witnesses mastiff fight,
  182
Audley, Thomas, 20
Augustus, Roman Emperor, 23
Aylesbury, Robert Bruce, 1st Earl of, 58

babies: birth and care, 94–6
Backwell, Alderman Edward, 27, 31, 246
baldness, 127, 164
Bangor, Bishop of *see* Dolben, David

banking, 5
banqueting houses, 37–8
Barbon, Dr Nicholas, 30
Bartholomew Fair, 213
Batelier, William, 112
Bath: as spa, 104
Bath, John Grenville, Earl of, 58
bathrooms, 40
baths, 128–9
Batten, Elizabeth, Lady, 158, 212
Batten, Sir William, 181, 218
Beale, Mary, 52
bear-baiting, 210
beards, 127–8
Bedlam, 104, 212
beds, 50–1
beer, 157
Beeton, Isabella, 150, 156
beggars, 256–7
Berkeley, George, 1st Earl of: house, 25,
  58
bestiality, 162, 164
bigamy, 227, 232
Biggs, Noah: *The Vanity of the Craft of Physic*,
  104
Billingsgate, 33
Billon la Mare, M. de, 195
birds: domestic and pet, 181–2
Blackcoat school, 186
Blackstone, Sir William, 175
Blackwell, Charles, 57
Blaeu, John: *Atlas Major*, 192, 318n1
Blague, Margaret, 93
Bolsover House, Derbyshire, 283n9
Bonnick, Ralph, 145
Book of Common Prayer (1662), 226, 264–
  5, 268
bookcases and shelving, 52
Bradshaw, John, 139
Brampton, near Huntingdon, 71
bricks, 32, 34–5
Bridewell palace, 23, 256
Bristol: population, 3
Bristol, George Digby, 2nd Earl of, 256
Brooke House, Holborn, 58